PENGUIN BOOKS

THE PENGUIN HISTORY OF CANADA

Kenneth McNaught, Ph.D., D.S.Litt., was born in Toronto in 1918, was educated at Upper Canada College and graduated at the University of Toronto in 1941. He has taught at various universities in Canada, including the history department at the University of Toronto, and as a visitor at universities in Britain, Germany and the United States. He has been editor of *Canadian Studies in Government* (for the Social Research Council of Canada and the University of Toronto Press; 1959–66) and contributing editor of *Saturday Night* (1959–68), to which he contributed about 100 articles. Once on the editorial board of *Christian Outlook* (Montreal; 1961–5) and *Canadian Welfare* (1961–5), he has also been chairman for the C.B.C. Roundtable TV panel (Winnipeg; 1953–7), and chairman for the University League for Social Reform (1964–5). Kenneth McNaught, who has done some public affairs broadcasting on C.B.C. radio and TV, has contributed to various journals and reviews and is the author of the following books: *A Prophet in Politics* (1959), *A Source-Book of Canadian History* (1959; with J. H. S. Reid and H. S. Crowe), *Canada and the United States* (1963; with R. Cook), *The Winnipeg General Strike* (1971) and *Manifest Destiny: A Short History of the United States* (1980).

KENNETH McNAUGHT

The Penguin History of
Canada

PENGUIN BOOKS

PENGUIN BOOKS

Published by the Penguin Group
Penguin Books Ltd, 27 Wrights Lane, London w8 5tz, England
Viking Penguin, a division of Penguin Books USA Inc.
375 Hudson Street, New York, New York 10014, USA
Penguin Books Australia Ltd, Ringwood, Victoria, Australia
Penguin Books Canada Ltd, 2801 John Street, Markham, Ontario, Canada L3R 1B4
Penguin Books (NZ) Ltd, 182–190 Wairau Road, Auckland 10, New Zealand

Penguin Books Ltd, Registered Offices: Harmondsworth, Middlesex, England

First published as *The Pelican History of Canada* 1969
Reprinted with revisions 1971, 1973, 1975
Reprinted with revisions and new concluding chapter 1976
Reprinted with revisions and new Chapter 21 1982
Reprinted with revisions and new Chapters 22 and 23 as
The Penguin History of Canada 1988
5 7 9 10 8 6 4

Printed in England by Clays Ltd, St Ives plc
Set in Linotype Pilgrim

Contents

I

The Land and its Resources

FROM the time of the earliest records Canada has been part of
a frontier, just as in her own growth she has fostered frontiers.
The struggle of men and of metropolitan centres to extend and
control those frontiers, as well as to improve life behind them,
lies at the heart of Canadian history – and geography determined many of the conditions of that struggle.

When the tenth century gave way to the eleventh, on the
almost unrecorded fringes of European society Canada was for
a few brief years a part of the sprawling frontier of the Norse-
men's imperial ventures. At first by maritime accident and then
by daring design a handful of Icelandic warrior-farmers penetrated the fogs of the Labrador Current to live a harried few
years in Markland and Vinland – probably at Anse aux Mea-
dows, Newfoundland. Lacking the numbers with which their
brothers became the creative scourge of Europe, and the firearms with which their successors conquered the New World,
the Vikings withdrew to the island stepping stones of the North
Atlantic. For nearly 500 years this newest European frontier
remained shrouded in the mists of medieval legend. What was
the nature of that new land, and the extent of the multi-tiered
frontier to be revealed by succeeding generations?

Eventually Canada was to comprise some 3,845,000 square
miles, an extent so vast that air-mapping still discovers 'new'
areas of the northern frontier. Reaching from Atlantic to Pacific
and flanked by huge islands on either coast, the half-continent
exhibits sharply etched regions and substantial variations in
climate. The most striking regional boundaries run along north-
south lines, thus conveying the impression that the principal in-
habited regions of the country are northward thrusts of similar
regions in the United States. On the east coast the Atlantic provinces of Newfoundland, Prince Edward Island, Nova Scotia and

7

New Brunswick are part of the rocky uplands of Appalachia whose southern reaches encompass the New England states. The St Lawrence lowlands, which include the most southerly portion of the province of Quebec and the southern part of Ontario which thrusts like a peninsula into what is now the industrial heart of America, are similar in structure to northern New York state, Pennsylvania, Ohio and Michigan. Beyond Lake Superior, and separated from southern Ontario by a thousand miles of rock highlands, stretch the Canadian prairies. Part of the immense interior plain of the continent, reaching from the Gulf of Mexico to the Arctic Ocean at the mouth of the Mackenzie River, the prairies are so integral a section of a north–south region that it is still possible along hundreds of miles of the Canadian–American border to be unsure of one's national location. Again, in the western Cordillera, fruit and timber valleys, mountain ranges and mineral veins run unbroken across the man-made frontier of the forty-ninth parallel.

So evident is this pattern that for years Canadian historians, economists and geographers endorsed the thesis that the 'natural' forces of the continent pointed towards political-economic integration of its parts. The popular, and even academic conclusion was that the Canadian nation had been built in the teeth of incredible geographic obstacles. Occasionally these 'natural' continental forces have been used as a reason for abandoning the effort of nation-building and accepting the fate of annexation to the American republic. In the 1890s such a future was vigorously advocated by Goldwin Smith, an ex-Regius professor of history from Oxford, founder of the history department at Cornell University, and an early example of *homo mid-Atlanticus*. From an editorial chair in Toronto, Smith argued that ultramontanist* reactions in Quebec allied with robber-baron corruption in Ontario made nonsense of the Canadian experiment. In his view English-speaking Canadians should accept the forces of geography and history, scrap the Confederation and lend support to the Anglo-Saxon

---

* The ultramontanist doctrine of papal infallibility was associated with sharp conservative-clerical attacks upon all forms of liberalism.

elements of the United States by becoming the Scotland of a grand North American union. The period was a time of troubles, yet, while the proposal of American union proved seductive, it was rejected, and by the end of the nineties the Canadian experiment seemed to be working very well indeed. Success was the result, at least in part, of geographic-economic forces working counter to the 'natural' north–south pull of the continent. Such east–west forces had, in fact, always existed and have been exploited by generations of men who have found in them support for goals both political and economic.

Historically, the first westward-pulling magnet was the continental shelf reaching out beneath the Atlantic from the Acadian and Newfoundland coasts. The Grand Banks were a treasure house on the extreme edge of the North Atlantic fisheries. John Cabot wrote in 1497 that the cod were so numerous that 'they sometimes stayed his shippes'. Throughout the sixteenth century the teeming waters south of Newfoundland and in the Gulf of St Lawrence sustained a great international fishery and were the principal centre of interest for the peoples of north-western Europe. They have provided an uninterrupted staple of Canadian production to this day, as well as remaining an international ground attracting fleets from lands as distant as the Soviet Union. The Appalachian arc of the Atlantic provinces, while cut off from the continental hinterland, has played an important role in Canada's east–west orientation nevertheless. The region has always cherished its transatlantic connexions and it is no accident that the principal Canadian supporters of closer imperial relations in the nineteenth and twentieth centuries were Maritimers by origin – men like Sir Charles Tupper, Sir Robert Borden and R. B. (Lord) Bennett. Maritime fish found their chief markets in Britain and the British West Indies while Maritime lumbermen and shipbuilders felt their interests to be closely entwined with those of the imperial merchant and naval power. Moreover, because of its long thrust into the Atlantic the Maritime region provided the obvious western base for naval control. Both Halifax and St John's have benefited much from British naval expenditures and establishments.

Although the Atlantic provinces are not well endowed with arable land and never developed sufficient production or population strength to become of crucial economic significance to the French or English colonial empires or, indeed, to the Canadian federal nation, their location has always been considered strategic. Commanding the Gulf approaches to the St Lawrence River, they have been of obvious importance to whatever power desired control of the interior of the continent. Moreover, their resources of fish, timber, coal, iron ore and scattered fertile valleys have sustained a population with strong local and imperial loyalties. It is a region which has accepted and urged subsidization from the day of heavy British naval expenditures and timber preferences to that of federally subsidized railway freight rates and welfare measures. Yet, even taking subsidization into account, the repeated refusal of Maritimers to accept absorption into the United States suggests that the 'natural' pulls of a shared geographic region may easily be exaggerated. The fact that the resources and products of New England are similar to those of the Canadian Maritime region has stimulated a feeling of competition more surely than one of common identity. No one has been more conscious of the need for imperial and national protection services in the fisheries than the trawler captains of Nova Scotia and Newfoundland.

Most striking of the 'determinants' which modify the north–south axes is the spectacular waterway of the St Lawrence River–Great Lakes. Hopefully probed in the early sixteenth century as a route to Cathay, the St Lawrence system became at once the frontier outline of New France and lured generations of French adventurers and priests ever deeper into the continent. Almost as striking, and certainly ambiguous in its historic effect, is the Canadian Shield. This is an immense high plateau of pre-Cambrian granite sweeping in a majestic arc from the archipelago of Arctic islands, south of Hudson Bay and back up to the Atlantic through Labrador. The ice sheet which once covered the Shield smoothed its endless rolling hills, filled its countless lakes and rivers, and gave to it the stark beauty which has attracted many of Canada's most eminent painters. It was the drainage from the ice sheet, also, that created the huge lakes and river systems around the perimeter of the Shield – from the inland seas in the far north such as Great Bear Lake, Great Slave Lake and Lake Athabasca, to Lake Winnipeg, the Lake of the Woods and the St Lawrence system itself.

The Shield, thus, has had a dual impact. Its forbidding stretch of muskeg (sphagnum bog) and rock across the top of Lake Huron, Lake Superior and beyond to the Manitoba plains, was indeed a formidable obstacle to large movements of population from east to west in Canada. This great 'barrier' added much to the cost of building the first transcontinental Canadian railway and provided little by way of a populated traffic area for railways after they were built. Canada has never had a frontier agricultural region corresponding to that of the 'middle west' in the United States. Prior to the middle 1880s the small westward movement of population to the Canadian prairies was compelled to follow American routes south of the Great Lakes and back north through Minnesota to Manitoba. Even after completion of the Canadian Pacific Railway the thousand miles of wilderness north of the lakes remained but thinly populated, the site of trappers, railway workers and scattered mining settlements. Westward from Ontario there was no unbroken advance of a farming frontier such as that which has been celebrated in the United States by Frederick Jackson Turner. One prominent result was an even sharper differentiation between east and west in Canada than in the United States, with a concomitant importance in Canada of metropolitan influence. Lacking a solid intermediate area of farming and industry, the Canadian prairies have not only felt sharply the conflict of regional economic interests but have been inordinately dependent upon eastern-controlled transportation and fiscal policies.

The negative and divisive effects of the Canadian Shield, however, have been less important than its historic and potenially unifying influence. In the colourful days of the fur trade the coniferous forests of the Shield were the haunt of the finest beaver, while interlocking waterways along the edge of the Shield and across its vast northern breadth were ready-made highways for the birchbark canoes of the *coureurs-de-bois*. At a time when the English colonists were still locked in on the Atlantic coastal plain by the Appalachians, the French had penetrated to the heart of the continent across the Shield and by way of the Great Lakes. In more recent times the Shield has yielded a cumulative wealth of natural resources which has fattened provincial treasuries and nourished a national industrial economy. To the rich veins of gold, silver, nickel, cobalt, zinc and copper developed early in this century in northern Ontario and Quebec, have been added towering pulp and paper mills which supply the major paper needs of North America, the staggering iron ore deposits of Ungava which are well on the way to replacing the nearly exhausted Mesabi range of Minnesota as the principal source for North American iron and steel production, the uranium mines of northern Saskatchewan, and a dozen or more major hydroelectric power sites. In the air age the Shield is once more to Canada what it was to New France: a treasure house and a beckoning frontier. As icing on this natural resources cake, the Shield draws hundreds of thousands of well-financed American fishermen and summer campers every year to its pine- and spruce-lined lakes; not less important it provides recreation for the urban populations of Ontario and Quebec who now find its northern wilderness within easy week-end and holiday reach.

Entering the mouth of the St Lawrence, the first Breton explorers saw to the north the great purple capes of the Shield and to the south the distant line of Appalachian mountains. But once they were well into the mighty river itself, the more tempting lowlands spread before them. From the site that was to become Quebec, the valley opens out on each side of the river. The deep, fertile soil of the St Lawrence lowlands covers an area of more than 30,000 square miles, bounded on the north by the Shield and on the south and west by the Appalachian highlands and the Great Lakes. Although the pre-Cambrian rock divides the lowland at Kingston, where it reaches down to the St Lawrence at the river's juncture with Lake Ontario, the whole region constitutes a natural economic unit, if such a thing may ever be said to exist. It is thus one of the ironies of Canadian history that the region should be split not only by the geography of the Shield, which constitutes no serious obstacle at this point, but also by the major ethnic boundary between French and English Canada: a boundary running roughly along the Ottawa River which empties into the St Lawrence just west of Montreal. It is nevertheless the St Lawrence valley, with its long extension through the southern Ontario peninsula, which has been the chief focal point of Canadian history and which contains today the great bulk of Canadian population and industrial production.

Like the Shield, the St Lawrence lowland has played a dual role. Controlling the routes to the continental hinterland (at first by water and later by rail and air), it has always been a metropolitan centre for the west and for the Atlantic provinces. The basic administrative policies and the quasi-imperial ambitions both of New France and of Canada have all been conceived in this pivotal region. The men who have enjoyed control of such a strategic location, from Count Frontenac and his fur-trading associates to the most recent federal cabinet, have inevitably been charged with monopolistic intent. Faced with extremely high overhead costs of transportation, the controllers of successive Canadian economies have steadfastly sought the savings of regulation and limited competition. In so doing they have as consistently stirred envy and political opposition in the far-flung areas of their writ.

Tribute levied on the staple production of outlying regions has not been the only source of central Canadian wealth. Thus the second role of the St Lawrence lowland has been as the principal centre of economic diversity and population. Despite fairly cold winters, its climate is moderate, with an average of 160 frost-free days and summer temperatures averaging over 70° F. The combination of a reasonably temperate climate, fertile soil and the determining northern boundary of the Shield resulted in early concentration of population in this region. As the farming frontier spread down the Ontario peninsula, the extensive forests of hardwood provided a useful income supplement for the pioneers. With population came exportable farm products (particularly wheat), small industry, the accumulation of capital both foreign and domestic, and thus the capacity to exploit the resources of the Shield. The natural highway of the St Lawrence–Great Lakes was improved by canal-building to circumvent the rapids above Montreal and the obstacle of Niagara Falls between Lakes Ontario and Erie. Through successive stages, too, geography stimulated vigorous competition between the merchant capitalists of New York and Montreal. Beginning with a struggle to capture the fur trade, the two powerful centres fought to dominate the export–import route to the interior of the continent. The pull of the Mohawk–Hudson valley route from the top of the Ohio valley to New York has been a constant threat to those who sought to make Montreal the great entrepôt between the continental mid-west and Europe. A struggle that endured through the stages of canoe, canal and railway, it exists still in the phase of motor throughways and airline routes, and has strengthened the economic nationalism of Canada.

The southward thrust of the St Lawrence lowland meant that the Ontario peninsula lay in the path of American westward immigration, a situation which accelerated its population growth, and guaranteed it a central position in North American industrial growth. Sharing with the American mid-west the cheap transportation of the Lakes (both for markets and resources such as iron ore) and a highly concentrated consumer market, southern Ontario and Quebec have emerged as one of the world's most productive industrial regions. A section of large urban centres dominated by Montreal and Toronto (both of which have populations approaching the two million mark) and supported by prosperous, highly protected mixed farming and fruit-growing, it is also the site of the country's political-economic power élite and the focus of its racial tensions.

If climate has been a significant force in central Canada it has been of at least equal importance in the west. Indeed the isothermal lines of the continent have been amongst its chief geographic determinants, substantially modifying the more obvious pattern of geological folds and drainage systems. In particular, the structure of the fur trade tended to follow the

more northerly routes to the west since the cooler temperatures produced the most luxurious pelts; and to no small degree
the pattern of the fur trade created the map of the future
Canada. The case was put in its most decisive terms by the
late H. A. Innis, the principal pioneer of Canadian economic
history:

The northern half of North America remained British because of
the importance of fur as a staple product. The continent of North
America became divided into three areas: (1) to the north in what
is now the Dominion of Canada, producing furs, (2) to the south in
what were during the Civil War the secession states, producing
cotton, and (3) in the centre the widely diversified economic territory including the New England states and the coal and iron areas
of the middle west demanding raw materials and a market. The
staple-producing areas were closely dependent on industrial Europe,
especially Great Britain. The fur-producing area was destined to
remain British. The cotton-producing area was forced after the Civil
War to become subordinate to the central territory just as the
northern fur-producing area, at present [1929] producing the staples,
wheat, pulp and paper, minerals, and lumber tends to be brought
under its influence.

What such an interpretation minimizes, of course, are the
ethnic and cultural passions, the personal ambitions and the
political decisions – the undulating forces of pro- and anti-
slavery sentiment, the French-Canadian and United Empire
Loyalist resistance to cultural-political absorption, and the
newer pride. of the peoples of the Canadian west. Nevertheless,
the cooler temperatures and shorter growing season of Canada
have reinforced the population pattern imposed by the Shield,
with the result that more than 90 per cent of all Canadians live
within 200 miles of the United States border. Long, bitter
winters on the prairies meant, also, that the Canadian west
attracted substantial population only after the most easily available lands to the south of the border had been occupied. Small
pockets of agriculture were first developed on the southern
prairies ancillary to the fur trade, but after the 1880s streams
of eager immigrants from across the Atlantic and from the
northern United States rapidly occupied the immensely fertile
soils of southern and western Manitoba, Saskatchewan and

Alberta. Almost overnight, and despite disastrous lack of planning in the more arid districts of the extreme south-western portions, this region became one of the world's major granaries and a tremendous support for the transportation, industrial and financial interests of central Canada.

Beginning in the 1930s, and accelerated by the industrial demands of the war and post war periods, the development of non-agricultural resources in these three western provinces assumed growing importance. In Manitoba, Winnipeg became the centre of a considerable range of secondary manufacturing, while the province's share of the Shield was developed for hydroelectric power and non-ferrous metals, particularly copper. In Saskatchewan, the most completely agricultural province in the west, there was also a trend to urbanization and an almost feverish exploration of the Shield – which yielded the most important uranium find in North America. Most spectacular, however, has been the development of vast sources of oil and natural gas in Alberta. Bringing very large royalty revenues to the provincial government, these new power sources have also spawned transcontinental pipelines whose financing and construction have been a further stimulus to central Canadian industry.

As one moves westward across Canada one feels increasingly a sense of sectional differentiation. It is, after all, some 1,400 miles from Toronto to Winnipeg, another 800 miles to Calgary in the foothills of the Rockies and another 500 from Calgary through the tortuous barrier of the mountains to Vancouver on the Pacific delta of the Fraser River. While it is perhaps an unflattering exaggeration to call Alberta the Texas of Canada, distance from the centre, together with a plenitude of natural wealth in mines, wells, wheatfields and ranches make the comparison, with its maverick connotations, not entirely inaccurate. In British Columbia the sense of special sectional identity is still more pronounced. The Pacific coast province was incorporated in the Canadian confederation essentially because the westward thrust of the fur trade had established strong British claims to the region. In 1885, after heroic physical and financial efforts, railhead was firmly established on the

Pacific, and determined policies established for integrating British Columbia in the new national state. Thus, despite its marked coastal isolation from the prairies and the east, and its correspondingly easy communications with the states of Washington, Oregon and California, British Columbia has experienced no more than its share of annexation fever. Nevertheless, the people of British Columbia reflect the geographic separateness of their province in their highly developed provincial pride and their alternating indifference and hostility to the east.

Beginning with the magnificent peaks of the Rockies (a mountain range shared by Alberta and British Columbia), the successive ranges of the western Cordillera occupy the entire surface of British Columbia, including the large and heavily timbered islands offshore. Cascading into the Pacific itself, the mountains severely limit the arable area of the province and thus control its population pattern. In the south, wide and fertile valleys between the ranges are centres of fruit-growing while Vancouver became Canada's chief Pacific port. A temperate moist climate produced in British Columbia endless forests on the lower mountain slopes dominated by the stately Douglas fir, while the mountains themselves have yielded up a full range of metals, both precious and industrial, as well as coal. These resources, combined with unlimited hydroelectric power, have led to considerable industrial growth – smelting and pulp and paper in the interior valleys, chemical, plastic and other secondary manufacturing in the Fraser valley. Along the length of the coast the teeming Pacific fisheries feed processing plants which in turn stock the port warehouses of Vancouver. Much of this diversified production moves back through the mountains to the markets of the prairies and central Canada; much also goes to foreign markets by sea across the Pacific and by way of the Panama Canal. The tiny posts established by Montreal and Hudson's Bay Company fur traders, and the straggling communities of the mid nineteenth-century gold rush, have long since been swallowed by the booming economy of the mid twentieth century – an ample justification of the imperial dream of the St Lawrence.

While the immense reaches of rock, frozen tundra and ice

that stretch north past the tree line and across the Arctic archipelago to the pole remain the home of Eskimos, Indian trappers and intrepid, if airborne, prospectors, the far north is an area of growing importance. It is now the scene of weather stations, the radar posts of the Distant Early Warning System and systematic mapping of natural resources. In the air-space age it is already crossed by regular flights between Europe and central North America. Like all frontiers it seems progressively less remote and, since 1945, Canadians have been acutely conscious of the fact that in the Arctic their closest neighbour is the Soviet Union. This geographic circumstance has had a profound effect upon Canadian foreign and defence policies as has the realization of the corollary that the country's postwar position bears some comparison with that of Belgium in 1914.

Reaching, integrating and exploiting the resources of the Canadian half-continent required much in the way of collective as opposed to individual endeavour. The facts of distance, geographic obstacles and population strung in a long, slender line from coast to coast have imposed heavy developmental costs. The felt need of protecting the northern area against both the magnetism and the threats of conquest from south of the border has led government in Canada to take a far from *laisser faire* view of its role. In transportation the credit of private capital was heavily underwritten by government, and in the twentieth century public enterprise spread widely in both rail and air transport. Since the 1850s Canadian manufacturing has been protected by high tariffs and now industry has the assistance of publicly owned hydroelectric power systems in most of the provinces. Recognizing the problem, unique amongst member nations of the Commonwealth, of surviving beside a much more powerful nation, Canadians also endorsed public ownership in broadcasting and film-making as a means of nourishing national sentiment and counteracting to some extent the tidal wave of printed and vocal communication sweeping north from the border.

Of Canada's twenty-four million people, more than half live in cities and towns, while in parts of southern Ontario and Quebec the problem of megalopolis is as real as it is in Chicago, New

York or London. The St Lawrence lowlands contain more than 60 per cent of all Canadians, while few people are ever likely to inhabit the vast northerly reaches of the Shield. Thus while the possibility that Canada might still tempt a conqueror in search of *Lebensraum* is no mere fantasy, it is nevertheless easy to exaggerate and is certainly not to be compared with the earlier temptation offered to an ambitious Henri Quatre or to the 'over-populated' England of Richard Hakluyt's propagandist imagination.

In the sixteenth century some two hundred thousand red Indians and a few thousand Eskimos lived in Canada. Supposedly the original inhabitants of North America, the ancestors of the Indians and of their Eskimo relations are generally thought to have crossed from Siberia to Alaska thousands of years before the Vikings spied out the foggy shores of Vinland. Each of the four major groupings of Indians who were spread more or less evenly across Canada in the sixteenth century lived in one form or another of stone-age culture. Hunting and fishing were the main activities, and although the Iroquois and one or two other groups had developed a quasi-settled life and a primitive agriculture, the nomad was never far beneath the Indian skin.

The Indians were indispensable to the early Europeans in North America, who acquired many pioneer skills from them, but the conflicting 'white' interests of private greed, religious evangelism, imperialism and race were later to corrupt and embitter the Indians, intensifying their indigenous tribal rivalries, and rendering them either uncertain allies or implacable enemies. As yet, however, the riches of the sprawling northern half-continent were unsuspected by the Vikings' west European successors. They had hoped for the easy wealth of Cathay and the Indies, but had to be content for the time being with a more prosaic empire of fish and fur.

2

The Imperial Dream of New France

THE beginnings of North American history are to be found in
the almost frenetic adventuring of renaissance Europe – adventuring which broke through the customary frontiers of politics,
science, religion and economics. But just as the apparently sudden advances of the fifteenth–sixteenth century in Europe had,
in fact, been long in preparation, so too had the discovery of the
New World and the resulting extension of European empire.
The great Italian navigators, Christopher Columbus and John
Cabot were beneficiaries not only of Vasco da Gama and the
graduates of Henry the Navigator's Portuguese school for sea-
men, but also of the travels of Marco Polo, the speculations of
European geographers, the scientific breakthrough of the astro-
labe, the mercantile ambitions of the 'new' bourgeoisie and the
political potential of the nation-state successors to the Holy
Roman Empire. The discovery of America, like that of the Cape
of Good Hope route to India, was part of the unbroken flow of
European history. The nature and exploitation of the discovery
were also governed by the ebb and flow of European ideas and
power.

Columbus, sailing westward for the most powerful of the
European nation-states, sought the riches of the east. John
Cabot, sailing for the more cautious Bristol merchants of Henry
VII's relatively impecunious England, sought a more detailed
knowledge of transatlantic fisheries – fisheries which had already been sporadically tapped by the unrecorded enterprise
of west country mariners. True, the letters patent which Henry
issued to the Venetian Cabot in 1496 reflected renaissance
optimism, empowering him to 'seeke out, discover and finde
whatsoever isles, countrey's, regions or provinces of the
heathen and infidels wheresoever they be, which before this
time have been unknown to all Christians...' Yet Cabot's

Bristol employers knew what they were after and were reasonably content with his exploration of the fishing grounds and the coasts of Newfoundland and Cape Breton. England's claims in North America were asserted, but it was to be another century before serious extension of those claims could be undertaken.

Throughout the sixteenth century Spain and Portugal reaped the reward of their early lead in national unification. Gold and silver from the southern New World, spices and silks from the Orient fed their power in Europe and made good their papally endorsed claim of dividing the overseas world between them. Valois, Tudor and Orange fought back the overreaching Spanish claims in Europe and marauded their mercantilistic lines of empire on the high seas. Faced also with the expensive and divisive struggles of the Reformation, the non-Iberian nations pared to the bone their tentative colonial enterprise. Thus the Newfoundland fisheries remained an international operation. Each year saw hundreds of summer fishing vessels from England, France, Portugal and Spain share the rich harvest of cod, but permanent settlement and deep penetration of the continent were tardy.

On the Newfoundland and Cape Breton Island coasts the French and English established a few fishing stations, while Portuguese, Spanish, French and English all gave fitful attention to more extensive exploration. Of these voyages the most significant were undertaken by a Breton sailor first commissioned by Francis I in 1534. On three voyages Jacques Cartier explored the Gulf, the Bay of Chaleur and the St Lawrence River as far as the Iroquois villages of Stadacona (Quebec) and Hochelaga (Montreal). His high hopes of a water route to the Orient were dashed by the turbulent rapids at Hochelaga which were wistfully named Lachine. In all Cartier made three trips to Canada (an Indian word whose meaning is obscure) but apart from discovering the St Lawrence route and disproving a number of imaginative Indian tales of glamorous kingdoms on the Saguenay, these voyages were succeeded by no permanent plantation.

Not until the long years of religious warfare came to an end in the strong new monarchy of Henry IV did French royal authority again interest itself in the potential of North America. By then, however, the men who had continued the annual fishing voyages had begun to develop a new staple of trade – one which caught the imagination of the merchants of Rouen as well as of the monarch. Impressed by the readiness of the Indians to bring furs to the fishing stations to be traded for trinkets and relatively cheap manufactured goods, the crown and the merchants entered a typically mercantilist alliance to exploit the new Canadian staple. In 1602 Henry granted the first of a series of fur-trade monopoly charters to a group of Rouen capitalists and thus founded the industry which was to be the dominant force throughout the entire history of New France.

But if hope of immediate profits informed the minds of the Rouen businessmen, many other ambitions, equally typical of the age, also characterized the French return to the St Lawrence. Personifying all of these was Samuel de Champlain, the company's chief agent and the real founder of New France. Champlain was ardently religious and, like Henry himself, a Catholic with a Protestant background. He was born and raised near La Rochelle in a bourgeois, sea-going family, served with the Catholic forces in the French religious wars, and in 1599 sailed for a season with the Spanish fleet to New Spain. His renaissance curiosity, fired by the experience, impelled him to draw up a report of his trip which earned him a pension and the position of royal geographer. A skilled observer, cartographer and ship's captain, Champlain was also patriotically ambitious for France to match the feats of Spain in the New World. Since Henry, unlike the sceptical Duc de Sully, believed that European power would in the future depend upon overseas possessions, Champlain was a fitting favourite, the more so since, in addition to his other attributes, Champlain possessed a genuine zeal for the conversion of the heathen. This lean ascetic who was to brave the outrageous rigours of the trackless forest and the bloody terror of Indian warfare was finally to conceive a new patriotism for his empire of the St Lawrence which would make him the natural hero of the French Canadian nation.

In 1605 the French founded a colony at Port Royal in the Annapolis Valley of Acadia, but while it was to survive and become significant in the later imperial strategy of North America, Champlain concluded that neither there nor on the rugged Appalachian coasts to the south would he find the sources of wealth and power which he sought. Thus in 1608 he followed Cartier's path and with the combined instincts of a soldier-geographer established his main post at Quebec where the narrowing river is guarded by the great bulk of Cape Diamond. Here he built a rude wooden fort, made friends of the local Algonquin Indians and in 1609 began a series of intrepid explorations covering the Ottawa River, Georgian Bay, Lake Ontario and even Lake Champlain to the south of the St Lawrence. In addition to producing a sudden expansion of geographical knowledge, these astonishing canoe journeys also plunged the French empire-builder into the midst of a bitter internecine Indian war. Having laid the basis of the fur trade by friendship with Algonquin and Huron Indians who commanded the Ottawa River and upper Great Lakes routes to the interior, Champlain felt compelled to support them in raids against the Five Nations Iroquois tribes who had lately been evicted from the St Lawrence valley and forced south. Scattered by fire from French musketry, the miserable Iroquois retired in dismay – but only to plan a savage revenge. Before long they too obtained firearms as the fur-trading allies first of the Dutch and later of the English working out of the Hudson River valley. The Iroquois became the scourge of New France in response to the thoroughly European mixture of motives that had prompted Champlain's first alliance.

Champlain's exploration of the waterways south of the Shield was quickly extended by several young lieutenants whose success in pushing the fur trade into the centre of the continent served both as a stimulus and a threat to the infant French colony on the St Lawrence. The work of the early *coureurs-de-bois*, such as Étienne Brulé and Jean Nicolet tempted the directors of successive charter companies to concentrate on the trade at the expense of a solid population base in the St Lawrence valley. The resulting imbalance, which was to characterize the whole subsequent history of New France, was further aggravated as generations of vigorous young farmer-colonists also succumbed to the lure of the *pays d'en haut* and themselves became hard-living associates of the Indian middlemen. After ten years, and despite Champlain's encouragement of agriculture around Quebec there were only sixty-five permanent settlers. Thus when as a by-product of European warfare Quebec was attacked by English buccaneers in 1629, the ageing Champlain had no alternative but to surrender. As a further consequence of European diplomacy Quebec was returned to France in 1632, and Champlain came back to the St Lawrence where he died in 1635, still full of hope for the fulfilment of his magnificent dream.

Behind the later work of Champlain and his handful of adventurers in Canada lay the tangled intrigues of Cardinal Richelieu's France. The Prince of Condé and a host of other courtiers competed as influence-peddlers for the businessmen who were prepared to invest in the fur trade, and as a result the monopoly charter passed through many hands. Yet despite Richelieu's own interest in the colony the demands of the Thirty Years War left little opportunity for serious state support, and meagre profits deterred investors. As a result real control of the trade passed to a group of merchants living in Canada who, in return for a small annual rent to the monopoly-holders, creamed off whatever profit the fur trade could produce.

The tribulations of investors and consequent vacillation in colonial government left wide the door to those whose interest in New France was more than merely economic. The missionary zeal of the counter-reformation led to the early establishment of French Canada's most enduring purpose: the preservation and extension of a specifically Catholic French civilization in North America. Champlain himself had brought to Canada several members of the Récollet order but it was natural that the immensely successful and powerful Society of Jesus should assume direction of French frontier spiritual activity. The first Jesuits, in fact, landed at Quebec in 1625. They were followed by a steady stream of missionary and parish priests, including some of the most dedicated and courageous as well as some of the most hard-headed men in Canadian history. The annual reports on the affairs of New France, known as the Jesuit *Relations*, stimulated others in France, both lay and clerical, men and women, to seek in Canada fulfilment of their religious vocations. Jesuit influence in Rome and in France also secured the appointment of Francois de Montmorency-Laval as head of the church in New France in 1659. Laval was created Bishop of New France in 1674, by which time he had established an ultra-montanist tradition guaranteeing that while the colony would remain French politically it would nourish an almost equal allegiance to the See of Rome. Until very recently the papal ensign was as common a sight in Quebec as the fleur-de-lis.

Equally important in the seventeenth century was the entire agreement amongst Laval, Richelieu and his successors, and the Jesuits, that New France should be a province of the counter-reformation as far as immigration was concerned. Thus, while Huguenots played a considerable role in the early fur-trade groupings, Protestants were sharply discouraged from settlement in the colony. Even after the revocation of the Edict of Nantes in 1685 Huguenots continued to emigrate to the English American colonies and to South Africa, while few came to New France. While this policy undoubtedly nourished a fierce spirit of *survivance* amongst French Canadians it also left them far behind in the comparative growth of North American population and in the evolution of native commerce and industry. The failure-success of immigration policy was to be a partial explanation of the English conquest of 1759 as well as of the growth of French-Canadian nationalism in the years following the conquest.

Missionary work in New France, despite the most vigorous precautions, became inextricably involved with the fur trade, which remained the colony's principal, if inadequate, means of support. Travelling widely with the *coureurs-de-bois* the Jesuit black-robes made contact with many tribes, and to the north of Lake Ontario they gradually won the confidence of the Huron Indians who permitted the establishment of a mission named Ste Marie on the shores of Georgian Bay. Since the Hurons were the chief middlemen bringing furs from the north and west, the mission was viewed with favour by the traders, and the Jesuit fathers sensed success as neighbouring villages accepted off-shoots from the central mission. By 1640, however, the Iroquois were preparing to eliminate the Hurons and thus divert the luxurious flow of northern furs to their Dutch sponsors in Fort Orange (Albany). The Huronia mission found itself caught in a murderous web of conflict between the Hudson valley and the St Lawrence valley trading interests, the Iroquois and the Hurons, the Dutch and the French, the Protestants and the Catholics. In 1648 a large Iroquois war party moved across the Ontario peninsula decimating the Huron villages in their path and finally wiped out Ste Marie. Father Jean Brébeuf and his courageous colleagues died at the stake, martyrs to the cause of Christianity and the French empire.

The Iroquois at once laid siege to the French centres on the St Lawrence. Both Quebec and Three Rivers were raided and the precarious outpost of Montreal was in constant peril throughout the 1650s. Founded in 1642 by the Sieur de Maisonneuve, a soldier with the religious proclivities of a Loyola, and by Jeanne Mance, an equally devout *religieuse*, Montreal had quickly become more than a mission to the Indians. Situated on an island in the St Lawrence close to the junctions of that river with the Ottawa and the Richelieu, Montreal was the natural St Lawrence control point for the fur trade. A decade of Iroquois harassment of Montreal culminated in 1660 with a massive assault that was, traditionally, only beaten off by an heroic fight to the death led by Adam Dollard and a tiny band of followers at the Long Sault rapids on the Ottawa River. Dollard, with the Jesuit martyrs, ranks high in Canadian legend. The colonial plight which such sacrifices revealed coincided with basic changes in France and led at last to a systematic reappraisal of the French position in America.

In 1661 Louis XIV assumed power in his own right. Spain had been humbled by the struggle which led to the Treaty of the Pyrenees in 1659, French royal power had been centralized and consolidated by the work of Richelieu and Mazarin, England under Charles II was no problem, and the Dutch were shortly (1664) to be evicted from the Hudson valley by the Duke of

York. Moreover, the ambitious Sun King was encouraged by his chief minister, Jean-Baptiste Colbert, to look favourably upon mercantilistic imperial projects. The result, for New France, was revolutionary.

The price of revived royal interest was the ending of the private fur-trade monopoly. In 1663 New France, with a population of roughly 3,000, became a royal province complete with a replica of French provincial government and law. A superior council was established to administer local affairs and to carry out the edicts of the king's council in France. The elements of representative government which had been emerging within New France during the final years of company rule were snuffed out and all public officers were henceforth appointed directly by the crown. Within the superior council of Quebec three figures of power dominated the proceedings and not infrequently frustrated each other's dearest purposes: the governor, with primary responsibility for defence and external relations; the intendant, like his counterpart in old France, with special concern for the maintenance of royal power and the administration of justice and economic growth; and the bishop, who wielded considerable authority due to the early groundwork of religious influence laid by the Jesuits. In its early years, and despite frequent bitter in-fighting, the conciliar government worked reasonably well. Yet, while it provided scope for men of outstanding capacity and determination, it failed to develop a body of political representatives with a growing sense of community, such as appeared in each of the English colonies to the south. Whether one sees in English colonial representative government the beginnings of democracy or simply the advent of Whiggish mixed government,* the contrast with New France is none the less striking. The tendency of local interests to look to particular men of influence in the government and to think of them as *chefs* with a natural right to patronage was one which grew steadily in New France. It was an attitude which carried over into the post-conquest period and has by no

---

* That is to say, of government reflecting established interests in balance against each other.

means disappeared in the democracy of present-day French Canada. One result of the authoritarian nature of New France is that its history, perhaps more than most, is that of bio-graphies: even the limits imposed upon authority by the cir-cumstances of frontier existence are revealed in the activities of adventurous individuals more than in the evolution of classes.

In 1665 a veteran French regiment, the Carignan-Salières, was sent to Canada. With a strength above a thousand these veterans of the Turkish wars wrought havoc amongst the Iroquois vil-lages, secured the approaches to the St Lawrence and, like Roman legionaries, were settled on strategic lands. The way was now open for Jean Talon, first and one of the greatest of the intendants, to impose orderly growth upon the lusty but strag-gling colony. Accustomed to overcoming opposition during ten years as intendant of Hainault, Talon was not only an excellent administrator. His imagination was caught by the economic possibilities of New France and in his brief seven-year term he showed (in the words of the Jesuit *Relation* for 1665) 'tireless activity to seek out the means for rendering this country pros-perous'. It was partly Talon's urging that led to retention of the Carignan-Salières regiment as a fillip to settlement in the colony and by 1762 the *habitant* population had grown to more than 6,000 – including several hundred young women from the Normandy countryside brought as wives for the soldiers and other bachelors of the colony. Although Louis XIV's wars of aggrandizement led to cessation of state-supported emigra-tion after 1672, the French-Canadian population showed re-markable natural growth – partly stimulated by a system of rewards for large families. Indeed it was not until the middle of the twentieth century that the French-Canadian birth-rate was surpassed by that of any other part of Canada, thus ending *nationaliste* talk of a 'victory of the cradle'.

Talon did all in his power, by edict and bounty, to encourage the growth of stable farming communities and to diversify the nascent economy. He gave strong support to a tiny shipbuilding industry, to the expansion of lumbering and its by-products such as tar and potash, to a brewery and to the manufacture of clothing from hides and wool. But these, as well as plans for trade in fish and lumber with the French West Indies, were all hampered by shortages both of labour and capital. A native mercantilism was difficult when it had to compete for capital with its imperial parent. And in several important respects geography imposed sharp restrictions.

The goal of communal farm villages on the French pattern was frustrated by the fact that the colony's only roads were the rivers and thus that farms had to be granted in long strips, each with its river front. Moreover the seignorial structure of landholdings, which had also been designed to provide a disciplined social system, was deeply affected by frontier circumstances. In a society where wealth was scarce, differences in landed rank with few exceptions meant little and the modified feudal dues were never a serious burden upon the *habitant*. Much of the intendant's time, indeed, was spent in compelling the seigniors to fulfil *their* obligations – such as providing flour mills and granting deeds consonant with the ever more detailed regulations issued by the council. Yet, despite the limitations of the time, Talon's success in immigration and in regularizing many aspects of land and legal administration was considerable, and undoubtedly helped New France survive the succeeding years of heavy French involvement elsewhere.

Within New France the work of the church was in many ways as important as that of the intendant; and in the church Bishop Laval exercised the most lasting influence. Chief prelate from 1659 to 1685, Laval, through his control of parish clergy, his close understanding with the Jesuits and his position in the Council, exercised considerable power. Unbendingly ultramontanist, he incurred the almost constant hostility of the strongly Gallican Talon as well as opposition from Governors such as d'Argenson and the irritable, precedence-conscious Frontenac. In matters of morals Laval was virtually Jansenist and much of his influence flowed from his own ascetic way of life. Although his imperious insistence upon the right of the clergy to a detailed regulation of colonial morals incensed many merchants and some of the merrier characters of the woods and parishes, the clerical claims were accepted by most of the *habitants*. The church remained central to the ordinary life of New France and the modified theocracy that resulted left an indelible imprint upon the minds of French Canada. Laval guaranteed the development of this theocratic trend by securing large seignorial land grants for the church, and by supporting the substantial land endowments of the Jesuit order. In establishing a seminary at Quebec (forerunner of Laval University) for the training of a Canadian priesthood, he provided an intellectual centre for the colony, and from it gained support for central as opposed to seignorial control of parish appointments. All education in the colony remained in the hands of the church and heresy was a problem virtually unknown in New France.

Despite the sleepless moral vigilance of Laval and his thundering *mandements* penned in a cheerless, unheated cell-office in Quebec, a modified replica of French provincial life emerged slowly on the banks of the St Lawrence. In the tiny towns of Three Rivers, Montreal and Quebec the upper class of officials and merchants was joined frequently by the more prominent seignorial couples in grand, if slightly *démodé*, festivities in the governor's Château St Louis or one or another of the principal houses. Craftsmen began to produce furniture and architectural decoration based upon French designs but so qualified by materials and local circumstances as to constitute a distinctive French-Canadian style – now as much treasured and copied in Quebec as the French originals themselves. Paris clothing was supplemented by colourful homespun, and unique patterns were evolved for such ordinary articles as sleighs which were the ubiquitous form of travel during the long river-frozen months of the year. In short a sense of style and of hierarchy developed early. Much of this was astutely observed by one of the intendants, Gilles Hocquart, who reported of the French Canadians in 1737:

They love distinctions and attentions, pride themselves on their bravery, and are extremely sensitive to slights or to punishments: they make great use of spirits, so much that it is hardly credible. ... All are attached to their religion. One sees few criminals. They are fickle, have too good an opinion of themselves, which prevents them from succeeding as they should in the trades, in agriculture and in commerce. We should add to this the idleness which is forced upon them by the length and the severity of the winter. They love hunting and exploring and have not the rustic manners of the French peasants. They are commonly quiet enough when governed justly, but they are by nature hard to govern.

The love of hunting and exploring was well noted by Hocquart. The fur trade, which flourished as a result of these affinities, remained the principal limitation upon the purposes of a Laval or of the intendant-planners. In vain did the bishops prohibit the use of brandy as an incentive for the Indians to trade only with the French, and every year found new voices amongst the colonial merchants supporting the lucrative use of such corrupting spirits. Of no avail were the endless exhortations by the intendants to the young men of the colony to stay on their seignorial subdivisions and raise large farm families. The fur trade was a continual drain on settlement as well as an encouragement to incautious extension of continental claims. Moreover, since the fur trade continued to provide the only relatively sure source of revenue and fortune for the colony, the sporadic endeavours of the French Ministry of Marine and the intendants to establish a trading system to include the languishing outpost of Acadia and the sugar islands of the French West Indies came to naught. New France thus failed to duplicate the spectacular triangular trading system of New England and was to pay heavily for her almost exclusive concentration on the interior of the continent. While it is true that the long winter freeze-up of the St Lawrence was an inhibiting factor, it was not a prohibitive one. More important was the continued domination of the French Atlantic fisheries by the merchants of the mother country and the French refusal to subsidize the Acadian base even to the limited extent that the St Lawrence community was assisted. Thus while Acadia and French Newfoundland remained almost integral parts of the French metropolitan economy, the St Lawrence settlements were striking out in the opposite direction and no economic integration of the French New World evolved.

Indian affairs by the mid 1660s created an irresistible lure to profit and adventure. The Iroquois assault of the preceding decade had removed the strategically located Huron tribes who had acted as middlemen between western Indians and the French fur traders. Then the reinforcement of New France by royal intervention had frightened off the Iroquois and a vacuum was created in the area stretching from the lower Ottawa River to Lake Huron. Beyond this were Indians rich in furs and anxious to re-establish their sources of manufactured goods. Into this vacuum poured hundreds of French-Canadian *coureurs-de-bois*, explorers and priests each imbued with his own version of French imperial interest, and not a few inspired by indigenous Laurentide pride and ambition. Once again beaver pelts began to flow into the storehouses of Three Rivers and Montreal. Missions and fur-trading posts were established on the shores of Lake Michigan, Lake Huron, and as far west as the Lake of the Woods. Each garnering canoe voyage pushed further the French frontier. In 1673 the Jesuit Father Marquette teamed with the trader Louis Jolliet, journeyed from Green Bay on Lake Michigan to the upper waters of the Mississippi, and from there paddled down the great river as far as its junction with the Arkansas. Nine years later the Sieur de la Salle, one of the most acquisitive of the traders and a man who profited greatly from a mutually rewarding intimacy with Governor Frontenac, reached the mouth of the Mississippi. Although he was murdered there by suspicious companions, a French colony was founded on the Gulf at Biloxi in 1699 by Pierre le Moyne, Sieur d'Iberville – an intrepid Canadian who was also to travel north across the Shield to lay French claim to Hudson Bay.

By 1700 the *voyageurs* of New France had established a vast interior network of mission-trading posts covering the whole region of the Great Lakes and the Mississippi valley, and with tentacles reaching into the Ohio valley, westward to the edge of the plains and northward to the Bay. This system, slightly secured though it was, was bound to bring conflict with the slowly but solidly expanding English interests in North America.

Already, as a result of the defection of two French-Canadian traders who had resisted the demands of the governor for a heavy share in their profits, the English had learned of the wealth in furs to be had by penetration of Hudson Bay. In 1670 Charles II granted a monopoly charter to a company headed by Prince Rupert and subscribed by court favourites. The Hudson's Bay Company was given not only a trade monopoly but also the right to govern all the land draining into the great Bay and it at once established posts to compete with the French for the western trade. Supplied by sea, the English posts were economical and located within reach of the finest fur territory. To the south of the St Lawrence, the English successors to the Dutch in the Hudson valley had taken over their predecessors' alliance with the Iroquois and were pressing hard for control of the Ohio valley fur trade and even threatening the French-Indian system to the west and north of the Ohio country. It was into this pulsing mixture of imperial and local competition that Louis de Buade, Comte de Frontenac, stepped in 1672 to become one of the more controversial figures in Canadian history.

Appointed by the crown apparently to provide an opportunity whereby he might recoup private fortunes which he had totally mismanaged, Frontenac had enjoyed a rather chequered military career and he possessed practically no administrative experience. His mercurial personality and his insistence on pomp and precedence led him into chronic conflict with intendant and bishop. While he did something to regulate the fur trade by a licensing system, he also struck bargains with leading traders like La Salle whereby he lined his own pockets and incurred the bitter hostility of other traders. Renowned in myth and legend as the Fighting Governor, Frontenac actually pursued a course of military diplomacy which was colourful, dangerous and occasionally weakened by his own lack of integrity and courage. It was not enough to dance around Indian ᵤres brandishing high the warlike tomahawk if in succeeding months promises of support against the Iroquois went unfulfilled. Gradually Frontenac's bravado was recognized by the Iroquois as a mask for insincerity and weakness and by the end of his first term of office New France was in a parlous condition. He was recalled to France in 1682 largely because of his interminable quarrels with practically every official in the colony – the record of which fills a large space in the French archives. Indeed Frontenac wrote so voluminously to the home government (his reports being appreciative of his own role and derogatory of the activities of everyone else) that for long historians tended to accept the Frontenac version of this period. In fact he left the colony virtually defenceless. Once more the Iroquois wrought havoc amongst the French Indian allies and in 1689 massacred the inhabitants of Lachine, hard by Montreal. However, the difficulties faced by Frontenac's successors, La Barre and Denonville, were used by Frontenac at the French court as evidence of their own incapacity and in consequence he was reappointed as governor in 1689.

The reappointment of Frontenac reflected also the outbreak of the War of the League of Augsburg, commencement of the long-brewing struggle between France and England. The tattered and belligerent old aristocrat was to be given a chance to strike openly and unreservedly at the tormenting English in New York and New England, and he seized it. In the winter of 1689, after the failure of plans for a combined naval–military assault on New York, he sent out raiding parties composed of *coureurs-de-bois*, soldiers and Indians to strike terror along the English frontier. The French fell with musket, tomahawk and fire upon the villages of western New England and New York. Religious distrust of colonial protestantism, the political-economic fear of English expansion, frustration flowing from the failure of naval support from the mother country, and the long-standing goal of extinguishing the Iroquois threat all combined to scar these raids with scalping, torture and massacre.

Yet the disruption of the English colonial frontier was inconclusive. While the Iroquois were impressed and, after an agreement in 1701, ceased to be a serious threat to New France, the English colonists were deeply embittered and renewed their pressure on New France. In the autumn of 1690 assaults on Montreal and Quebec by land and sea were defeated. During the continuing warfare the French fur trade reached its peak of expansion, yet the threat to New France deepened as a New England force attacked Port Royal and menaced the whole of

Acadia. Again, while the heroic exploits of d'Iberville, who raided the coast of Maine, pillaged English fishing posts on Newfoundland and captured all but one of the Hudson's Bay Company posts in the north, may have restored the balance, the issues at stake were by no means decided.

All of this was reflected in the Treaty of Ryswick in 1697 whose colonial clauses left Acadia with France and generally recognized the *status quo*. And, just as in Europe where the treaty provided only a breathing spell in the 'second hundred years war', so in America the imperial probing continued apace. In 1698 the fiery, if rascally, old Frontenac died at Quebec. It was becoming clear that the outcome of the imperial conflict would be decided, fundamentally, not by the intensely concerned indigenous interests of 'North Americans', but by the course of war in Europe.

3

The Struggle for the Continent

BY the opening of the eighteenth century the lines of battle
had been clearly drawn. If the European mother countries were
to waver in their assessment of the relative mercantilistic importance of Madras and Cape Breton Island, Guadeloupe and
Canada, the local custodians of their North American colonies
were never in doubt. In the English Atlantic seaboard colonies,
population was growing rapidly and the interests of the
colonists were clearly expressed both in elective legislatures
and governors' councils. Already the merchant-capitalists of
New England were subsidizing combined operations to remove
the French from the St Lawrence valley and the Gulf, while New
England's trade with both the French and British West Indies
grew rapidly. In Albany, Williamsburg and other English
colonial towns, businessmen who controlled the trans-Appala-
chian trade in buckskins and furs were learning about the interior, and what they discovered led them to dream of profits
to be made from future land speculation and development. The
beginnings of a driving English–American 'manifest destiny'
were stirring in the breasts of farmer-pioneers as well as in
the counting-rooms of the sea-coast towns – a protestant ethic
at least as dynamic as the Gallic-Christian thrust from New
France. The North American warfare of the eighteenth century, while nearly always related to European conflicts, showed
an increasingly indigenous character.

During the War of the Spanish Succession (1702–13) the French
renewed their border raids but the shape of the future was foretold when in 1710 the British government sent six men-of-war
and a regiment of marines to Boston. Supplemented by militia
raised in New England this force captured Port Royal in Acadia.
Although another ambitious campaign to capture Quebec collapsed, the seizure of Acadia, together with the difficulties of

Louis XIV's European armies, produced significant strategic changes in North America. By the Treaty of Utrecht the French recognized English possession of Hudson Bay, Newfoundland and Acadia (henceforth known as Nova Scotia, from an earlier optimistic charter granted to Sir William Alexander in 1621).

The French were spurred to fresh efforts by the definite loss of Hudson Bay and by the threat to their control of the Gulf. In the latter region they had retained Isle Royale (Cape Breton Island) and Isle St John (Prince Edward Island). At Isle Royale, France decided to make its grandest imperial effort. Here, according to plans drawn up by the great military engineer, Vauban, they built the massive fortress of Louisbourg complete with four-storeyed governor's residence, workshops and a garrison of 1,400 regular soldiers. Louisbourg was an immensely costly effort which, with its facilities for naval ships, its exotic show of pomp and pageantry, and its menace not only to the fisheries but also to Nova Scotia, in turn spurred the English to countervailing action. On the south shore of Lake Ontario they built Fort Oswego close to the beginning of the St Lawrence. Oswego was an obvious threat to the French fur trade and furthermore it was on soil previously considered French. Conversely, the French built forts south of the St Lawrence at Crown Point and Ticonderoga to block any further attempts at an overland invasion of New France by way of Lake Champlain and the Richelieu River. In the west beyond the Great Lakes the English working out of Hudson Bay and the French moving on from their prairie post at Lake Winnipeg parried each other's thrusts for control of the far western fur trade. In the 1730s La Vérendrye, leaving behind him a trail of fortified posts, reached the Saskatchewan River, and twenty years later Antony Henday, from the English company's post on the Bay, beat his way right to the foothills of the Rockies.

When the War of the Austrian Succession broke out in Europe in 1740 the challenge was all too readily accepted in North America. While there was fighting all along the extended lines of contact, the centre of the crisis was on the north-east Atlantic seaboard. There, Governor William Shirley of Massachusetts had imbibed the economic-political draughts of ambition proffered by the Calvinist merchants who surrounded him. Planning the final eviction of the French from the Gulf area and a later extension of English settlement up the St Lawrence, Shirley authorized an expedition against Louisbourg. In the absence of French support the fortress fell and it was successfully held by a combination of New England militiamen and English seapower against a French attempt to recapture it in the following year. In Europe, however, French arms fared better and thus the Peace of Aix-la-Chapelle (1748) returned Louisbourg to France. It was a hollow diplomatic victory which simply intensified English-American determination to be rid of the encircling line of French Catholic power.

In the year after Aix-la-Chapelle the British government, urged on by Shirley of Massachusetts, decided to check decisively the threat of Louisbourg and at the same time establish a permanent North Atlantic base in Nova Scotia for its increasingly important sea power. Thus on the hill of Halifax, overlooking the fine harbour of Chebucto, a fortress was constructed and 2,500 settlers dispatched to found the new capital. One Nova Scotian weakness, however, had still to be remedied. Across the peninsula in the Annapolis Valley the 10,000 French Acadians followed resolutely the advice of their priests not to take the oath of allegiance to the British crown, asserting their desire to be neutral. At the same time Frenchmen from the St Lawrence had built a fort on the isthmus separating Nova Scotia from mainland Acadia, which they claimed had not been included in the 1713 treaty cession, and persuaded some Acadians to join them. This problem was 'solved' in 1755 after the outbreak of war by the simple and ruthless device of expelling the Acadians from Nova Scotia. Uprooted from their dyked farmlands and hillside orchards on the Bay of Fundy, thousands of Acadians were shipped off to be scattered through the English colonies to the south. Eventually some of them found their way back to the Annapolis Valley to become a permanent French-speaking enclave in Nova Scotia – and to lend their name to the thousands of Quebeckers who were to spill over into New Brunswick in the late nineteenth and twentieth centuries. Today the combined Acadian populations of Nova

Scotia and New Brunswick retain a kind of ancient neutrality in the cyclical tensions between English- and French-speaking Canadians and are one of the principal supports of a movement to unite the Canadian Atlantic provinces politically. The expulsion of the Acadians, however, was a measure of the deepening intensity of English colonial purpose in the mid eighteenth century and this expansionist drive had still more bitter reflections elsewhere.

Just as the central problem of New France itself, prior to 1700, was the conflict of interest between the far-reaching empire of the fur trade and the settlement needs of the St Lawrence valley communities, so the whole Anglo-French conflict was a struggle between the long-drawn fur-trade line of the French reaching from the St Lawrence across the Lakes, down through the Ohio and Mississippi valleys to the Gulf of Mexico, and the rapidly growing land settlement base of the thirteen English colonies on the seaboard. By 1754, when war broke out in North America (two years before the opening of the European Seven Years War), the population of the English colonies was roughly two million, while in all of North America there were no more than 80,000 Frenchmen. Even without English superiority on the high seas the struggle would have called for an extraordinary degree of French coordination and valour. Of valour there was little lack, but coordination was notably deficient, especially as France became more deeply enmeshed in the European war.

The first four years of the French and Indian War went extremely well for the French and were, in fact, mainly a continuation of the struggle for the Ohio country. This struggle was sharpened as the English developed their Indian trade, but it came to a head as colonial investors in Virginia mobilized for the great population leap across the Appalachians. In 1749 a group of Virginian businessmen who had the ear of Governor Dinwiddie and the support of several English capitalists secured a grant of 500,000 acres of Ohio valley land for settlement purposes. The Ohio Company was unimpressed by the work of Joseph Céleron, Sieur de Bienville, who in the same year had buried a series of leaden plaques throughout the region, claiming it for France, and cemented the Franco-Indian alliance system. In 1753 the Virginians sent a small force under George Washington, a planter-investor and major in the colonial militia, to inform the French that they must leave. The French declined and in the following year made good their position by defeating a second, larger expedition under Washington, and building Fort Duquesne at the juncture of the Allegheny and Monongahela Rivers (Pittsburgh). While this was an impressive rebuff, and the French-Indian forces repeatedly revealed their mastery of forest warfare, the confrontation also meant that the power élite of Virginia was conceiving an anti-French drive which would eventually thrust deep into the French-controlled trans-Allegheny west. Clearly the best French hope lay in tactics which would prevent these English forces from pursuing their purpose in one concentrated sector of the struggle.

In 1755, of four major attacks upon New France, only one succeeded – the capture of the French positions in mainland Acadia. In 1756, the first year of the war in Europe, France sent substantial reinforcements to the St Lawrence under a brilliant general, the Marquis de Montcalm. It was unhappily fitting that, like James Wolfe, Montcalm was an avid reader – an aristocratic devotee of the *philosophes* – and that in the final clash each empire should thus sacrifice both brilliance and sensitivity on the altar of Quebec.

At first Montcalm overcame his heavy numerical disadvantage by a series of brilliant strikes which boldly employed the combined skills of his 10,000 French regular troops with those of the Canadian militia and fur traders. Assisted by the disunity of the English colonies, and by British generalship which was inexperienced in the ways of wilderness warfare, he captured Fort Oswego, destroyed the English outposts in northern New York, and kept the British colonial forces off balance along the entire frontier. Three principal elements beyond his control were, however, to lead Montcalm into the vortex of the mounting tragedy of New France.

One such determinant was the corruption and petty intrigue which riddled Quebec society. From the outset of his command Montcalm held suspect his colleagues in the government of

Quebec and they repaid his lack of respect with envious hostility. The Governor, the Marquis de Vaudreuil, had been born in the colony, son of an earlier Governor, and symbolized the rapidly growing feeling of Laurentide nationality which increasingly resented both overseas control and inadequate French support of the colony. Unfortunately Vaudreuil and Montcalm could not resolve their differences and this resulted in a disastrous conflict both of purposes and strategies. In addition merchant avarice let loose by the mounting demands of war was fanned rather than smothered by the very official who should have checked it – the intendant, François Bigot. A libertine intent upon making a private fortune while the colony floundered in a wave of inflation, corrupt influences and fraud, Bigot compounded Vaudreuil's more positive undermining of Montcalm's ceaseless efforts.

A second source of disadvantage for Montcalm was the swelling determination of the English colonies to clear the French from their path of expansion. This determination, based upon growing economic self-sufficiency and immense numerical superiority was, moreover, harnessed ever more closely to a third ingredient: the intensified sense of purpose of the reconstructed British government under William Pitt.

In 1758 Pitt dispatched to America the fresh sea and land forces that were to bring to a close the first phase of Canadian history. At once a huge pincer movement was begun. Despite Quebec's noblest efforts, numbers began to tell. Fort Frontenac, guardian of the Lake Ontario approaches to the St Lawrence valley, fell in the summer of 1758, while at the same time a combined force under Generals Wolfe and Amherst smashed its way into the great fortress of Louisbourg, thus securing the sea approaches to the St Lawrence. In June of 1759 an even larger assault force sailed up the great river and came to rest just below Quebec. On land Montcalm's army was slightly larger than that of Wolfe, but it was torn by rivalry between French regulars and the *Canadiens*. Even so he beat off the first attacks on his well-constructed defences along the low-lying land stretching to the Montmorency River. This was at the end of July, and from then until early September the British forces played cat and mouse with Quebec, making feints both above and below the citadel. As autumn approached both Montcalm and Vaudreuil became convinced that Wolfe planned a direct assault on the citadel – for the British obviously could not risk a lengthy land campaign which could see them trapped by the winter ice of the river. This opinion was confirmed when lookouts observed a small British detachment making a detailed survey of the great rock from across the river. At once the defences were strengthened on the heights above Anse au Foulon, a cove which provided the only feasible approach to the Plains of Abraham. Unwisely, however, Montcalm withdrew the regiment stationed there and the following night, after duping a single sentry, the British performed the feat, which even Wolfe had considered improbable, of scaling the rock.

In the morning Montcalm awoke to find the British drawn up in the classic battle order of two long lines, not a mile from the main town gate. The French battalions were hastily assembled and, flanked by native forest warriors, rushed upon the British at Montcalm's signal. For once in the long French and Indian War the conditions were auspicious for successful application of European rules of war. The British held their fire unnervingly until the attackers, already wavering, were within forty paces. The ensuing volleys shattered the French assault completely and mortally wounded Montcalm himself. As Wolfe, too, lay dying on the bloody plain, Vaudreuil escaped with the remnants of the French army, to make his way to Montreal; Quebec surrendered four days later.

The agony of defeat dragged on for another year. While General James Murray, in charge of the British garrison at Quebec, watched his forces wither from disease and lack of supplies, the French at Montreal were preparing for re-conquest of their cherished capital. In the spring of 1760 they very nearly succeeded but once again were frustrated by British sea power. The first ships to chase the ice up the St Lawrence that spring were British, not French, and they were loaded with men and supplies. Driven back again upon Montreal, the French capitulated under a three-pronged assault – from Quebec, from Lake Champlain and from Fort Frontenac. On 8 September Vaudreuil signed the Articles spelling out the terms of surrender. Yet no more than the conquest of Quebec city, no more than the expulsion of the Acadians, was this to mean the end of the 'French fact' in America. Through the operation of British imperial interest and political experience, as well as the firmly based French-Canadian sense of identity and purpose, the Laurentide homeland was to remain both unassimilated and uniquely influential. No Louisiana fate lay in store for the descendants of the fur traders and *habitants*. Nevertheless, the rankling presence of the Conquest in the imaginative and retentive mind of Quebec was itself to explain much of the vitality of latter-day French-Canadian nationalism.

The future was by no means clear in 1760. Indeed, everything was done, as far as London was concerned, to ensure a standard assimilative pattern across the whole of British North America. Faced with a huge accretion to her New World holdings, Britain sought to replace her earlier 'salutary neglect' with a systematic imperial policy. The problem was sufficiently complex. By the Treaty of Paris which brought the Seven Years War to an end in 1763 the British fell heir to the Franco-American empire, with the exceptions only of Louisiana west of the Mississippi (which went to Spain) and the tiny islands of St Pierre and Miquelon in the middle of the Gulf fisheries. At once the British government issued a Royal Proclamation intended to foster orderly, planned growth of her colonial domain from the Floridas to Quebec and from the seaboard to the Mississippi. Already the older English colonies (including Nova Scotia) possessed a fairly standard pattern of government: appointed governor and council, and elective legislative assembly, together with English common law supplemented by local legislative acts. These constitutional forms were now applied to the 'new' provinces of East and West Florida and Quebec on the assumption that such arrangements would encourage a flow of English-speaking population into the areas. Further to induce a controlled population movement the Proclamation included a firm (although avowedly temporary) prohibition of settlement west of a line drawn along the crest of the Allegheny mountains. The policy seemed especially justified by the outbreak early in 1763 of a major Indian rising under Pontiac and the continued disruption of the frontier. Thus the west, from the Great Lakes to the Floridas and from the Alleghenies to the Mississippi was put under the administration of Superintendents of Indian Affairs appointed by London. It was the job of the Superintendents to arrange Indian treaties which would stabilize the west both for the continuing fur trade and for eventual settlement. To back up the western policy a permanent army of 10,000 regulars was authorized, to be financed by new revenue measures applicable in all the colonies.

It was an orderly and even brilliant conception, but it failed to take adequate diplomatic account of several crucially important North American facts. One of the principal origins of the French and Indian War had been the English-American goal of throwing the Ohio country open to land speculation and settlement and thus making good the various western territorial claims of the seaboard colonies. Now that the ancient French threat had been removed by war the Atlantic colonists experienced a sharp increase both in their sense of security and in their expansionist ambitions. They were extremely irritated to find, in the moment of triumph, that they were to be blocked once again. They were no less irritated by revenue measures imposed by the imperial government since these seemed an almost equally obnoxious limitation of their increasing self-sufficiency. Such fears were not diminished by apprehension that the old empire based upon the St Lawrence had not really disappeared at all.

The population controls of the new imperial policy were both a success and a failure. As part of the political rearrangements the province of Quebec found itself cut off administratively from its old Ohio–Mississippi and Atlantic extensions. The boundaries were tightly drawn: in the east the vague coastal area of Labrador was included within the province of Newfoundland and mainland Acadia was definitively annexed to Nova Scotia; the northern boundary ran through Lake St John to Lake Nipissing; on the south the boundary ran from

Lake Nipissing to the St Lawrence just above Montreal and thence along the forty-fifth parallel of latitude and the height of land north of New England and Nova Scotia. Such a boundary removed nearly the whole fur-trade area from the jurisdiction of the new province. Yet in fact Montreal continued to dominate not only the north-western trade but also that of the Ohio country, and the Atlantic colonists suspected that the Proclamation policies were a device for frustrating their dearest purposes. What population movement that did occur simply confirmed their worst fears.

The results of 1763, therefore, were extremely complicated. In one sense they represented an unqualified British victory. But in another, they established the most perilous conditions imaginable for British control of North America. Removal of French imperial power laid bare the great mercantilist problem of frontier growth and consequent demands for expanding autonomy. It also called into question the role of a self-conscious and substantial minority nation within an empire whose members were to reveal deeply conflicting purposes. The 'solution' of these problems created the framework for the second stage of Canadian history.

4

Default or Decision?

THE twenty years following 1763 form perhaps the most ambiguous period of Canadian history. They are the years in which the first British Empire reached its shattering tragedy in the great civil war of the American Revolution, with the resulting permanent division of the English-speaking peoples. They are also the years in which modern Canada was founded. The differentness of the Acadian and the St Lawrence regions – a differentness compounded of geography, historical experience, economic interest and population diversity – decreed that the leaders of the Thirteen Colonies would be denied their goal of continental union. Indeed only by political accident was much of the Ohio country, the 'natural adjunct' of New France, excluded from the control of the St Lawrence legatees. Despite the fact that the failure of the northern areas to join the rebel Thirteen was heavily influenced by neutralism and simple disinterest, much of what happened was the result also of positive decision – the first of a long line of Canadian decisions to resist continentalism. Thus achievement of American independence meant also the liberation of the northern half of the continent from the gigantic assimilative process of American republican democracy.

Rejection of assimilation lay at the heart of the matter. Yet in Quebec the first approach to the question after 1760 was definitely assimilative. The 1763 Proclamation provided for the summoning of an elective legislative assembly 'in such manner and form as is used and directed in those colonies and provinces in America which are under our immediate government' and also announced that 'all persons inhabiting in or resorting to our said colonies may confide in our royal protection for the enjoyment of the laws of our realm of England'. Even the practice of the Roman Catholic religion was to be 'insofar as the laws of

46

England permit'. Instructions to the first governor of Quebec, James Murray, made it quite clear that while the Romish Church might survive in the province every step was to be taken to establish the Church of England. In short, it was hoped that a French population, diminished in importance by emigration, would quickly be swallowed up by a northward-moving wave of Protestantism. Such was not to be the case, and assimilation was soon replaced by a quite exceptional tolerance as the basis of policy.

There was no mass exodus from Quebec nor, for twenty years, was there large-scale immigration. Most of the regular French officers and government officials, and a few of the wealthier Canadian merchants, returned to France after the 1760 capitulation of Montreal. But, more important by far, the great bulk of the French Canadians remained. Their clergy also remained, and since the church was the only institution not immediately taken over by the English, it assumed an importance in the life of the province much greater than had previously been the case. The English who did come to Quebec were mostly merchants from England, Scotland and Albany – army contractors and fur-traders eager to fatten on the promises of the new imperial policy. About 200 families of them arrived in the first few years after the conquest and they quickly took over the economic life of Quebec, from the fur-trade to importing and exporting. As Murray watched the predictable tensions mount he refused more and more decisively to implement his very precise instructions to anglicize Quebec. Irritated by the insatiable demands of the English-speaking merchants, he grew increasingly sympathetic to the seignorial-pastoral life of the *habitants* and their comparatively cultured clerical and professional spokesmen. In 1764 the Governor summed up his views thus:

Little, very little, will content the new subjects [the French-Canadians] but nothing will satisfy the licentious fanatics trading here but the expulsion of the Canadians who are perhaps the bravest and the best race upon the globe, a race who, could they be indulged with a few privileges which the laws of England deny to Roman Catholics at home, would soon get the better of every national antipathy to their conquerors and become the most faithful and most useful set of men in this American empire ...

Yet what the merchants wanted – a council and legislative assembly which would religiously exclude the French Canadians and the establishment of English common law – was what Britain had promised them. Thus, upon their petitioning London, Murray was recalled in 1765 and Sir Guy Carleton sent out to replace him. Carleton, however, was an even greater disappointment to the merchants than Murray. An Anglo-Irish aristocrat as well as a professional soldier, he had a deep-grained respect for order and authority. Thus, like Murray, he refused point blank to shake the French-Canadian establishment by calling an assembly and he endorsed Murray's roundabout device whereby episcopal succession in the Canadian church was secured – despite the laws of England. Moreover, he also condoned continuance of land granting *en fief et seigneurie* and the decision of commercial cases by the courts on the basis of the Custom of Paris. Whatever the motives of these governors, and they were certainly mixed, the men themselves did not appear to their French-Canadian contemporaries as *conquistadores*.

Progressively persuaded that Canada was destined to remain French 'to the end of time', Carleton soon found reasons, beyond dislike of the local English-speaking businessmen, for conciliating the French Canadians. In the authoritarian structure of Quebec society he thought that he discerned a sheet anchor for British power in North America. Such a firm stay appeared to his military mind to be very necessary indeed as other presumptuous merchants to the south began their long clamour for autonomy. From 1765 to 1770 the uncertain challenge and response of colonial businessmen and imperial mercantilists brought recurring crises. One thing seemed increasingly clear to Carleton: the attempt by London to tighten the laws of trade and navigation and to raise a revenue within the Thirteen Colonies was very likely to end in the maintenance of imperial authority by force. It thus became his fixed purpose to improve the defences and increase the military strength of Quebec. Realizing that, if loyal, the French Canadians could muster about 18,000 men, Carleton sought ways to ensure their loyalty.

The Carleton plan was simple and based upon an aristocrat's analysis of society. Since the 1763 hope of swamping the French by heavy English-speaking immigration had aborted, it was necessary to accept the full implications of a continuing French-oriented community. To Carleton this meant unstinting support for the leaders of that community – the clergy and the seigniors. He sold his scheme to the British government. Following lengthy hearings before the House of Commons, in which representatives of the merchants bitterly opposed Carleton's arguments and offered many alternative concessions designed to conciliate French-Canadian sentiment, the entire Carleton plan was given legislative form and passed in 1774 as the Quebec Act.

Passage of the Quebec Act was made easier by the fact that in 1774 the Thirteen Colonies were rapidly approaching their point of no return. Thus both the government and the Commons of England were moved to reject once again the Burke-Fox arguments in favour of conciliating America and to choose instead the stern authoritarianism of Carleton and the king's friends. That the fierce 'coercive Acts' of 1774 levelled against Massachusetts were unwise there can be little question. About the wisdom of the Quebec Act there is more debate. The Act set aside definitively the 1763 policy of uniform colonial constitutional growth and placed full authority in Quebec in the hands of the governor and an appointed council. Furthermore it poured a cornucopia of benefits upon the French-Canadian upper class: the provision for an assembly was withdrawn, Roman Catholics, by means of a special oath, were permitted to hold civil office, the seignorial land-holding system was confirmed as was also the French civil law, and the Roman Catholic Church was established by giving it the power to collect tithes. Partly as a function of the Carleton military approach towards containing the aspirations of unruly colonists to the south, and partly to appease the English-speaking merchants of Quebec, the province's boundaries were extended to include much of the old French empire – the spacious region between the Ohio and the Mississippi in which the Montreal fur traders were still the dominant economic force.

The Quebec Act, despite it obvious motives, has been seen by some historians as a wise and generous recognition of the rights of French Canadians; and it is, of course, frequently referred to by French Canadians as a fundamental part of their 'guaranteed' special position within the British and later Canadian constitutional framework. By others it is regarded as worse than foolish, inasmuch as it seemed to base policy on a reactionary endeavour to woo the French by means of seducing their leaders with special favours while ignoring the mass of the people and leaving them with a 'feudal' land system and enforced tithes (despite little evidence of opposition). Critics of the Act emphasize its disavowal of the promises made in 1763 to English-speaking immigrants and argue that the granting of an assembly (as opposed to the conciliar government of the Act) would have shown better faith and would have been more conducive to a 'progressive', democratic evolution of Quebec.

Whatever the merits of the Act with respect to Canada, it had none with respect to the rebellion brewing to the south. To Sam Adams and his colleagues in the Continental Congress which they had summoned to deal with the threat of repression, the Act appeared much as it did to Charles James Fox when it was debated in the British Commons: '. . . but to go at once and establish a perfectly despotic government, contrary to the genius and spirit of the British constitution, carries with it the appearance of a love of despotism, and a settled design to enslave the people of America, very unbecoming this country.' The 'Americans' were, of course, especially enraged by the geographical extension of Quebec. The Act confirmed their worst predictions about the purposes of the Indian Line of 1763, namely, that the Ohio country was to be permanently sealed off against their control and expansion. Moreover, the fact that the punitive measures against Massachusetts which resulted from the Boston Tea Party, as well as the Quebec Act, constituted a British declaration that henceforth colonial constitutions were at the mercy of Parliament, sent a chill of apprehension up and down the seaboard colonies. At the very point when colonial lawyers were arguing that the empire had become federal and that Parliament had no jurisdiction within the colonies, the theory was struck to the ground. While it was to take two full years before the radicals in America could muster sufficient support to declare independence of the Crown, the Quebec Act did much for their cause.

After the British rejection of petitions from the first Continental Congress, after Lexington and Concord, the Atlantic seaboard leaders planned military resistance and of necessity took Quebec into full account. Aware of Carleton's long-term plan to use Quebec as a base from which to reduce rebellion, they sought at first to undermine his position by appealing to the general populace against the 'despotism' of the Quebec Act. In a manifesto to the people of the province the Congress noted that

The power of making laws for you is lodged in the governor and council, all of them dependent upon and removable at the *pleasure* of a minister. ... Have not Canadians sense enough to attend to any public affairs, than gathering stones from one place and piling them in another? Unhappy people! who are not only injured but insulted. Nay more! – With such a superlative contempt for your understanding and spirit has an insolent ministry presumed to think of you, our respectable fellow-subjects, [that they expect you] to take up arms, and render you the ridicule and detestation of the world, by becoming tools in their hands to assist them in taking that freedom from us, which they have treacherously denied to *you*. ... We do not ask you, by this address, to commence hostilities against the government of our common sovereign. We only invite you to consult your own glory and welfare ... and elect deputies who after meeting in a provincial congress, may choose delegates to represent your province in the continental congress to be held at Philadelphia on the tenth of May, 1775.

This first appeal to continental union failed. The English-speaking populace, with few exceptions, were openly hostile to it. The *habitants* wavered, but were influenced towards neutrality in the coming struggle by two principal considerations: the heavily worded *mandements* of their grateful clergy, and the fear, partly inherited and partly reasoned from the existing circumstances, of being overwhelmed in an English-speaking continent. The agent sent north by the Congress in

1775 reported bluntly, 'There is no prospect of Canada sending Delegates to the Continental Congress.'

A similar sort of mass neutrality prevented Nova Scotia from throwing in its lot with the American rebels. As with Quebec, Nova Scotia had more to lose than to gain, economically, from overthrowing the imperial trading system. Just as the finances and markets of the Montreal fur trade depended upon London, so the prosperity of the Halifax mercantile class derived much more from its overseas connexions than from its own maritime endeavours or from any local markets. Unlike New England, neither Quebec nor Nova Scotia had developed substantial economic interests hostile to the navigation laws. Nova Scotia felt no resentment about the closing off of the west since her own frontiers were still largely open, and because her geographical position inclined her away from serious concern with the continental hinterland. Although a majority of Nova Scotia's population of 17,000 in 1775 had come from New England, it was not a concentrated community. Sprinkled thinly around the coastal coves of the peninsula, these 'pre-loyalist' Nova Scotians showed little interest in springing to the aid of their New England cousins and even had they thought of doing so their situation would scarcely have permitted effective action. The Council and Assembly at Halifax were both dominated by a merchant oligarchy with close connexions, through one Joshua Mauger, in the City of London. Between them they controlled the province and throve on military-naval subsidies which, according to the disgusted Edmund Burke, had already cost the British treasury 'not less than seven hundred thousand pounds'. It was a very rich bounty and the Haligonian businessmen saw to it that the occasional radical assemblymen from the outports gained no significant influence over policy or opinion in the province. Favoured by corrupt customs officials and swelling war contracts, the 'Mauger Group' ensured Nova Scotian loyalty throughout the American war while continuing a lucrative trade with the 'enemy'. Noting the almost cynical attitude of Nova Scotia to the continental cause, and estimating the fortified strength of Halifax, George Washington decided to leave the province strictly alone.

Default or Decision?

Whether one thought of suppressing the rebellion or simply of retaining British control of the northern half of the continent, Quebec remained the key. In the 'great war for the Empire', as was also to be the case in the curious struggle of 1812–14, the 'Americans' moved first. Accepting George III's ill-considered decision that 'blows must now decide whether [the colonies] are to be subject to This Country or Independent', the Congress dispatched two hastily organized armies to capture Montreal and Quebec in the hope of eliminating the threat posed by Governor Carleton's known plans. In November 1775 the poorly defended Montreal fell to General Montgomery's assault and towards the end of December, Montgomery joined forces before the citadel of Quebec with General Benedict Arnold. Neither of the tattered American groups was in shape to launch an effective attack upon Quebec – especially Arnold's, which had just completed a harrowing autumnal march up the Kennebec valley, across the Appalachian height of land and down the Chaudière to the St Lawrence. Nevertheless, partly because some of the colonial militiamen's terms of service ran out at the end of 1775, and partly in the hope of surprising Carleton, Arnold and Montgomery attacked the great rock in a howling snowstorm on the night of 31 December. With only a few hundred soldiers Carleton beat off the attack which resulted in the death of Montgomery and the capture of nearly four hundred of the attackers.

Despite this initial success Carleton was embittered and the British government less than totally gratified. While the small English-speaking population of Quebec province had responded handsomely to the call to arms, the *habitants* greeted it with studied indifference. Only a few hundred of the 18,000 which had been estimated by Carleton actually presented themselves for service, and many of these were undoubtedly influenced by Bishop Briand's threat to refuse the sacraments to laggards. Carleton's opinion of the French Canadians underwent a remarkable revision and henceforth he placed almost exclusive reliance on reinforcements from overseas. These came abundantly in the spring of 1776 and, despite Carleton's disillusioned flirtation with a soft American policy, a great two-pronged military strategy was planned for 1777. Originally General Howe was to march a British army north from New York towards Lake Champlain, and General Burgoyne was to lead another British army of 7,000 regulars south from the St Lawrence and effect a juncture with Howe's force. If successful, this manoeuvre would have cut New England's communications with New York and sealed off the very heart of the rebellion. Carleton's temporary hope of conciliating the Americans had induced him to allow their retreating forces to escape from a trap he could easily have sprung. Moreover, 'Gentleman Johnny' Burgoyne was not cut out for backwoods warfare. When he did move south he permitted a large and debilitating gaggle of female camp-followers to slacken his progress, and failed to take the careful scouting precautions required by the heavily forested and mountainous terrain. As a result, a re-grouped American militia force surprised him at Saratoga and he was forced to surrender his entire army.

Saratoga was crucial. Although Quebec itself was safe for the remainder of the revolutionary war, the American success in 1777 put the cap on that essentially diplomatic document, the Declaration of Independence. In July of 1776 the authors of the Declaration had noted that it was issued out of a proper respect for the opinion of mankind. But the particular portion of mankind they had in mind was that which lived in France. The Declaration proved the congressional intention of breaking rather than reforming the empire; Saratoga suggested that Congress, with French help, might realize its intention. Thus in 1778 Louis XVI signed the Franco-American treaty of mutual 'defence' against England and made of the imperial civil war a world war. By 1781, when Lord Cornwallis found himself hemmed in at Yorktown, well over half his assailants by land and sea were French. Foreign intervention and the recurring Gallic (one might almost say Gaullist) dream of recovering New World prestige had made good the American 'right' to sunder the first British Empire. The triumph of Adam Smith, in certain Whig circles, was to endorse the most extravagant hopes of the Americans.

British conduct of the war had been abysmally inept and Lord

North's government fell as the direct result of the disgusted clamour for peace. For a crucial few months in the summer of 1782 the Shelburne Whigs came to power and at once began negotiations for peace. In addition to their over-pessimistic assessment of the world-wide military situation, they were dominated by Adam Smith's anti-mercantilist notions. The combination led to two related, if curious conclusions: that peace with America was necessary on almost any terms, and that the parting of the ways should be as amicable as possible, in the interest of future freedom of trade between Britain and America. With such principles firmly fixed, the British did not exploit the situation in America as it existed in 1782, or even as it developed during the negotiations which stretched out for more than a year. In America the whole of the trans-Allegheny west was held by a combination of British regulars, American loyalist militia and Canadian fur traders. Newfoundland, Nova Scotia and Rupert's Land (the Hudson's Bay Company domains) had not been touched, and the French fleet which had successfully blockaded Yorktown was smashed in the West Indies by Rodney during the negotiations. Despite all this Richard Oswald, the British negotiator, began by considering the desirability of offering all of Canada as a means of sweetening the departure of America from the empire. Gradually the British attitude stiffened, but not enough to accept the French bait which would have meant excluding the United States altogether from the west as a means of keeping the new nation dependent upon French help. The upshot was that the entire Ohio country, sometimes considered a dependency of Canada and the St Lawrence system, went to the United States, with but minimal trading concessions from the Americans.

Undoubtedly the temporary influence of the doctrines of free trade and peaceful parting explain much of the astonishing give-away of 1783. But other considerations entered the picture also. At the very outset of the negotiations British war-weariness weakened the British position, especially since that weariness was recorded in a Commons resolution which branded as enemies of their nation any who advised further prosecution of the war in America. Moreover, the desire to placate the United

States was heavily reinforced by the hope of weaning her from French influence. Yet, however sophisticated the British reasoning may have been, it vastly underestimated the expansionist psychology of the new nation. The British also showed little concern for the interests of the Montreal merchants or their London backers, all of whom bombarded the government with demands that the new boundary should recognize both the historic and existing circumstances. The future of Canada was thus deeply influenced by the convolutions of imperial politics under George III and by a misreading of American destiny. Had most Englishmen not believed that the new nation was unlikely to survive, it is improbable that they would have tolerated the misinterpretation of imperial interest that occurred in 1783. It is also likely that, had the French Revolution occurred seven years earlier than it did, the republican demands of 1782–3 would have met with a less benign reception.

Apart from the cession of the Ohio valley, the 1783 treaty showed a mixture of conciliation and stiffness governed by conflicting concerns to wean the United States from the Franco-American alliance and to play fair with the Loyalists who had been despoiled by the Americans. Thus Americans were granted entry to the inshore fisheries of Nova Scotia and Newfoundland, and the right to land in unsettled areas. The boundary was also a generous compromise, following the line of the St Lawrence (where the river intersects the forty-fifth parallel) through the Great Lakes to the Lake of the Woods and thence straight west to the Mississippi. The eastern part of this boundary began at the St Croix River and followed the height of land along the northern Appalachians to the forty-fifth parallel. Indefinition and friction were inherent in all these aspects of the treaty: the Mississippi rises to the south of the imaginary intersection in the west, the eastern part of the boundary was imprecise and, because of its extreme northward thrust, was to be a major obstacle to British North American communications, and the fisheries question was to exacerbate Canadian–American relations throughout the nineteenth century. In return for British generosity the American negotiators promised that the American Congress would 'earnestly recommend' to the state governments action to obtain either return of Loyalist property or compensation for those who had been plundered. The Loyalist clause in the treaty was a face-saver in most respects. Only South Carolina made any serious effort to honour it while in the other states persecution of Loyalists who returned to seek redress was as fierce as had been the original pillaging. The principal results of this aspect of the peace settlement were that the British government undertook to subsidize the resettlement of many thousands of Loyalists and at the same time felt justified in retaining a strong line of posts on territory granted by the treaty to the United States. These posts controlled most of the American north and west and included such key points in the fur trade as Oswego, Niagara, Detroit and Michilimackinac. Plainly such policies represented unfinished business in Anglo-American relations. British retention of the western posts reflected second thoughts in London (and certainly in Montreal) about both the wisdom and the finality of the 1783 treaty. Such ruminations led to Canadian revisionist ambitions which, given the terms of the treaty, were bound to be frustrated by the westward thrust of American settlement. Such settlement was also to frustrate the other British purpose in retaining the posts: that of honouring treaty rights bestowed upon the Indian tribes as part of the 1763 policy of pacifying the frontier.

If the circumstances of 1783 were not completely felicitous from the point of view of the future Canada, at least the area had been blocked off from the continental unionism of the American republic. And with the division of the continent there came to British North America a critically important addition to the population. About 40,000 Loyalists found their way to Nova Scotia and Quebec bringing with them one of the strongest determinants in Canadian history – an abiding distaste for the American version of republican democracy. The almost legendary role of the Loyalists is today frequently held up to ridicule, partly because some of their descendants claim a special, almost aristocratic social precedence (not unlike the Daughters of the American Revolution south of the border), and partly because some of the more prominent Loyalists formed the core of powerful colonial oligarchies (the family compacts) after their arrival. Yet while many of them exploited their favoured positions of influence and contributed markedly to a conservative, time-serving element in early nineteenth-century Canada, the majority felt themselves to be expressing firm political conviction and certainly they suffered much for their decision. Moreover, if they strengthened conservative tendencies in the nascent Canada they also demanded and obtained the extension of representative assemblies, and contributed their share of political reformers throughout the succeeding years.

Of the 40,000 Loyalists who moved north during and at the end of the Revolution, 32,000 went to Nova Scotia, most of them in the fleets of ships organized at New York by Sir Guy Carleton. They had come mostly from the eastern seaboard and many of them were cultured townsmen. A few brought considerable quantities of their hastily assembled possessions, but the great majority came with virtually nothing. Small groups found their way to Prince Edward Island, some went to Cape Breton Island; larger numbers settled on the 'South Shore' of Nova Scotia in such enduringly Loyalist towns as Shelburne; but the bulk went to the St John River valley and the shores of the Bay of Fundy. A setting of majestic beauty met them, but it was a virgin land also. Aided substantially by government rations, tools and land grants, they carved homes out of the forests and began the long, tough job of pioneer settlement.

The Maritimes influx trebled the existing population of Nova Scotia and thus heavily outnumbered the 'Neutral Yankees' who had moved north prior to the Revolution. In the Fundy–St John region they at once demanded their own government complete with elective assembly, largely on the ground that they did not wish to be governed from remote Halifax, or to be under the influence of the pre-Loyalist population. The British government, drawing the conclusion that the American Revolution had been the result of too much, rather than too little liberty fell in quickly with the request and broke up the old province of Nova Scotia in 1784, hoping by division to rule more easily. Cape Breton Island was made a separate province (to be re-united with Nova Scotia in 1820) and New Brunswick was created at the same time, incorporating most of the mainland of the old Nova Scotia and with an elective legislative assembly. While New Brunswick thus became the Loyalist province *par excellence* (the 'most gentlemanlike on earth' as one inhabitant put it) the Loyalist impact throughout the Maritimes was also definitive. From the proud and proven Maritime stock were to come a disproportionate share of Canada's leaders in politics, business and the professions – men, in fact, who were the most significant exports of a region whose own economic development was to be erratic in the extreme.

Of the 8,000 Loyalists who filtered into Quebec most came up the Lake Champlain–Richelieu River route – the classic military passage between the St Lawrence and the Hudson – while smaller streams moved across the wilderness of northern New York to emerge at Kingston where Lake Ontario empties into the St Lawrence, or at Niagara at the western end of the lake. Many of these had served in the Loyalist regiments during the war, many others came ·because they lived in communities which were predominantly Loyalist and thus had little choice. Few had the quasi-urban background of the eastern Loyalist migrants, but, by the same token, they were better fitted to the frontier struggle which faced them. They, too, were heavily subsidized with equipment and free land grants. Moving through the upper St Lawrence valley, along the north shore of Lake Ontario, and sending offshoot settlements into the Ottawa valley, these people formed the nucleus of what was to become the province of Ontario.

The comparatively large-scale migration of the Loyalists thus tipped the 'Canadian' scales decisively beyond the mere point of neutrality on the central question of continental union. With the French Canadians, the Loyalists form indisputably the most basic historical ingredient of Canadian nationhood. Their arrival, however, also intensified and extended the already perilous tension between French and English in the old province of Quebec. There, in contrast to the Maritimes, the deepening racial question was to complicate vastly the problem of constitutional evolution, both for the immediate and the long-term future.

5

The Age of the French Revolution

POPULAR opinion has long adhered to the notion, popularized by Frederick Jackson Turner and his followers, that the creative, determining forces in America have been generated on the frontier. For the period from the Revolution to the American War of 1812–14 the frontier thesis is used to explain American neutrality in the long wars of the French Revolution and Napoleon. Americans, it is said, were too absorbed in the business of consolidating their new nation and in extending its frontiers to risk involvement in the affairs of Europe. Yet, while there was immense activity on the American frontiers in these years, most of it was deeply conditioned by what was happening overseas. American political parties found their first battleground over the question of the French Revolution and it was the vicissitudes of Napoleon Bonaparte that gave Thomas Jefferson the opportunity of acquiring the sprawling empire of Louisiana in 1803. Recent scholarship, moreover, is agreed that when the United States declared war against Great Britain in 1812 the ambitions of the frontier were only one (and not the most important) of many causes. Involvement with British power on the high seas was of at least equal significance.

In the case of Canada the impact of the French revolutionary period was no less formative. Rejection of the rationalist revolution by the majority of French Canadians meant that no fresh foothold on the St Lawrence could be found by France – especially by such flamboyant agents as Citizen Genêt, the incautious and ineffectual ambassador sent to the United States in 1793 to raise trouble for Britain in America. An even more direct result of the French Revolution was the stiffening of British views on the subject of democracy. In England the spread of lower-class radicalism, the catastrophe of the American Revolution and the partially related explosion in France against the *ancien régime* led most members of the unreformed regime in Britain to support stern counter-revolutionary measures wherever they might be effective. When Edmund Burke founded the modern Tory party on the firm foundations of his *Reflections on the Revolution in France* (1790) it was clear that colonial policy would not go unaffected. Indeed the brief parliamentary debate on Quebec in 1791 anticipated the ideological restructuring of the British party system.

The Canada Act of 1791, providing for division of Quebec into two separate provinces, sprang from the demands of the Loyalists for a legislative assembly, but the Act and the spirit in which it was passed and implemented were also expressions of the new anti-French conservatism. In 1786 Guy Carleton, now Lord Dorchester, had been sent back to Quebec to govern and to advise London on policy for the rapidly changing colony. Dorchester, somewhat abashed by the conspicuous lack of success of the Quebec Act, procrastinated while the British government was bombarded by petitions · for change. The English-speaking merchants of Montreal hammered away at their long-standing demand for a legislative assembly and English common law, hoping thus to control the huge province and make the St Lawrence the chief entrepôt for the trade of the whole British-American interior. The new Loyalists of the western or 'upper' part of the province also wanted representative government which they had been accustomed to in their former colonial homes, and English law which would bring with it freehold tenure to replace the seigniorial tenure obligatory under the Quebec Act. In 1791 the British government decided to impose a solution without further delay.

The Canada Act accepted the general ethnic line of division and provided for a government in Upper Canada, west of the Ottawa River, separate from the government of Lower Canada. But the laws of Lower Canada (based upon the Custom of Paris) remained in force and so did the establishment of the Roman Church. Both the division of the province and the retention of French civil law infuriated the English-speaking merchants who saw their economic empire again subdivided politically as it had already been halved by the treaty of 1783.

And at the very time when the Loyalist influx (which was continuing unabated as 'late Loyalists' streamed into Upper Canada) gave hope of balancing the French-speaking population, the merchants of Montreal found themselves left as a tiny island in a French-Canadian province.

In Upper Canada, English common law and freehold land tenure were established but the political-social structure envisioned by the Act in both provinces was unabashedly reactionary. The Westminster debate on the Bill had more to say about the perils of French democracy and American republicanism than about the actual condition of the Canadas. The government left no doubt about its intentions: the Canadas were to become a North American bulwark against the presumptuous levelling tendencies of the age. They were to have an establishment which would be the 'very image and transcript' of British eighteenth-century society and government. Despite the bitter scorn heaped upon the Bill by Foxite Whigs its clauses permitting the granting of hereditary aristocratic titles in the Canadas were left untouched. A huge reserve of public land was set aside for the establishment in each province of a 'Protestant clergy' and a second large land reserve was provided for the Crown, to render the executive independent of legislative money grants. In each province an elective legislative assembly was provided, but in each the legislative power was shared with an appointive upper house, the legislative council, on the fatuous assumption that such a body in a frontier society could emulate the role of the Lords in Britain. While French-Canadian Catholics were permitted to become, and to vote for, assembly members, two unwarranted assumptions were made: that they would soon so admire British law and institutions that they would rapidly be assimilated and that, being unaccustomed to the system of election, they would probably not exercise much influence in the assembly. Neither of these contradictory assumptions was correct. French-Canadian nationalism was to find its chief focus in the Lower Canadian assembly and to produce remarkably skilful democratic politicians.

By 1791, then, British North America was a strange constitutional *mélange*: Newfoundland, a crown colony in the Gulf; Prince Edward Island, Nova Scotia and New Brunswick, royal provinces with single elective assemblies; Cape Breton Island with conciliar appointive government; Upper and Lower Canada as established by the Canada Act; Rupert's Land under a charter company and comprising the western country drained by rivers emptying into Hudson Bay; and the far northwest to the Pacific and Arctic oceans claimed by Britain but without any local constitution or any defined southern boundary. In formulating the future, economic growth, geography, American expansion and British imperial policy were to vie as determining factors.

In the Maritimes, population growth was slow and by 1812 the total figure was still under 100,000. The fisheries encouraged the building of ships, and the expansive forests of Nova Scotia and New Brunswick provided the materials. Fully-rigged ships, especially the swift Bluenose schooners, plied the North Atlantic and the Caribbean carrying out fish, timber and to a lesser extent foodstuffs. Yet despite the advantage of protected markets offered by the continuing imperial Navigation Laws, the Maritimers failed to replace New England in the long-established triangular trade routes touching North America, the West Indies, West Africa and England. They lacked the population and capital-forming base and also their surplus agricultural production was not adequate to this task. Nevertheless they prospered in these years, especially when Britain was compelled to seek more of their timber and foodstuffs during the Napoleonic wars; and the West Indian trade which exchanged codfish for rum, sugar and molasses was substantial.

In the Canadas expansion was both more marked and more varied. Largely because of an extraordinary birth-rate, Lower Canadian population trebled between 1783 and 1812 to reach 330,000. *Habitant* farm production mounted rapidly, but was largely for the home market. The most vital economic centre was Montreal with a population in 1812 of 30,000. The English-speaking businessmen of the ancient fur-trade capital controlled the commerce of both Lower and Upper Canada since the upper province was dependent upon the St Lawrence for imports and exports. In addition to their management of the forwarding trade to Upper Canada and the slowly growing export trade in foodstuffs, potash and timber, the Montrealers remained lords of the western lakes and forests. It was in this role that they challenged once again the twin threats from north and south: the Americans and the Hudson's Bay Company.

In the Northwest the Montrealers organized the largest commercial operation of its day in North America. Grouped in a series of trading partnerships under the general name of the North-West Company, the Montreal traders organized the system in three stages: the Montreal financing and forwarding base, with British commercial connexions and symbolized by the exclusive Beaver Club which was the centre of the real power élite of the Canadas; Fort William at the head of the Great Lakes, where the emissaries from Montreal met the 'winter partners' who brought to the post the furs from their winter's trading and decided policy for the following year; and, of course, the winter partners themselves who were responsible for organizing the trade in the west and the employment of Indian and French-Canadian canoe-men – descendants of the old western empire of La Vérendrye.

Despite the crushing overhead costs of this transcontinental trading system the Nor'westers flourished. Under the leadership of romantic yet hard-faced men such as Simon McTavish and Joseph Frobisher, the Company partners fought their competitors from the Bay every inch of the way across the prairies. Although the lower costs of the Hudson's Bay Company with its sea route almost into the heart of the northern fur country, together with other unfavourable factors, were to overwhelm the Nor'westers by 1821, the Montrealers accomplished almost superhuman feats of organization and exploration. From the far northern post on Lake Athabasca, Alexander Mackenzie, with a tiny party of French Canadians and Indians, found the great river which bears his name and took his tough birchbark canoes down its length to the Arctic Ocean. In 1793 he followed the turbulent Peace River from Lake Athabasca westward to the Rockies and then overland through the mountain barrier to the Pacific 'coast. Such adventures, and the trade that resulted from them, strengthened the British claim to the northwestern part of the continent – a claim already laid by the Pacific voyages of Captains Cook and Vancouver. As in earlier years the fur trade had, by following 'natural' geographic lines and giving opportunity to the instincts of acquisitiveness and adventure, roughly marked out the boundaries of the future Canada.

In the newest province of Upper Canada these years were a time of rapid growth and cautious ambition. Presided over by its first governor, John Graves Simcoe, the province grew in population from 14,000 in 1791 to 90,000 in 1812. Most of the new settlers were from the United States, a part of the westward-moving American frontier which simply found Upper Canada lying in its path. Simcoe, despite his deep aversion to American republicanism, welcomed these new Canadians in the knowledge that population growth was the only sure means of keeping Upper Canada out of the American union. A soldier with an unusually deep sense of loyalty, Simcoe was almost unbelievably conservative. He was also imaginative and possessed high organizing ability. Once the new settlers had taken the oath of loyalty he agreed to their receiving free land grants similar to those provided for the earliest Loyalists. He also initiated, by the use of military labour, a substantial road-building programme and inspired the councils and assembly to encourage a number of industrial and commercial ventures. The use of the one great source of social capital – land – was the key to his developmental ideas. Thus free grants were used to establish settlers who could then develop the first surplus exportable commodities of grain, lumber and potash, and on this basis settlement spread slowly north from Lake Ontario and down through the province's south-western peninsula.

Unhappily, Simcoe accepted unquestioningly the Canada Act's purpose of establishing a backwoods version of eighteenth-century England. Sensing a British reluctance on the subject he sent plaintive appeals to London:

... since all my statements previously to my leaving England, and during my administration of this government, have been formed on the propriety of supporting that just aristocracy which the Canada Bill has provided for; and since I have always estimated this power, as barring the avenues to disaffection and sedition, by making a constitutional provision against those turbulent talents which may otherwise with great facility gain a more than aristocratic ascendancy over a people ... and since I have always contemplated this aristocratic power as being the truest safeguard of the Sovereignty against such machinations ... so I beg leave with all due deference to Your Grace, from these opinions to deduce the observation that I should be very happy was their sufficient property and other qualifications in any members of the Legislative Council to see the provision of the Canada Act, in this respect, immediately completed by an hereditary seat derived from a title of honour being vested in their families.

Simcoe was the very model of an early nineteenth-century British colonial governor (indeed, prototype, since he was a cut better than many) and the Colonial Office and Canadian archives are mercilessly crammed with such pompous, wrongheaded assessments of colonial prospects. Although London did not act on Simcoe's advice in this matter, as in many others, Simcoe proceeded to endow in as many ways as were open to him the 'well-affected and respectable classes' of the province. This meant extreme favouritism in land-granting which threw wide the door to vicious speculation. By 1806 over 4½ million acres of land had been granted to individuals or groups. While ordinary Loyalists received 200 acres each, ex-officers could claim up to 5,000 acres. Legislative Councillors got 6,000 acres apiece and entire townships were granted to 'entrepreneurs' for speculative development. It was to be years before most of these lands could be cleared and actually settled. In the meantime together with the two-sevenths of all public land tied up in Crown and Clergy Reserves, they remained as undigested obstacles in the path of contiguous community growth.

The governor's friends in the councils and their hangers-on across the province formed the basis of an early power élite, to which the name Family Compact came to be applied by critics of the system. At a time when practically all the Upper Canadians were struggling to clear the land, establish the tiny capital at York (Toronto) and simply to survive, the structure of privilege could survive in comparative security. When the future of the society came to be considered more seriously by the non-élite after 1815 the built-in tensions developed rapidly.

So, too, in Lower Canada, the 1812–14 war was to serve as a catalyst strengthening both the fears and ambitions of the majority. In the lower province the basis of social conflict was, of course, more complex and of earlier origin. The powerful minority in control of economic life was English-speaking. It had the ear of the governor and, together with the senior clergy and wealthier seigniors formed a Château Clique able to use the carefully buttressed executive power in its own interests. However, the long-established farming community of French Canada seized quickly the opportunity offered by an elective assembly to organize an essentially nationalist opposition to the Château Clique. Under the leadership of young lawyers and small merchants, supported by most of the parish clergy, the commonalty of Lower Canada controlled the assembly. They successfully opposed executive attempts to shift the basis of revenue from commercial duties to land taxation, resisted pressure to replace the Custom of Paris with English mercantile law, and formulated the philosophy of *la survivance française*. Furious at the settlement of some 9,000 English-speaking farmers who moved in from Vermont and took up land in the Eastern Townships (east of Montreal) under the freehold option provided by the 1791 Act, the emergent French-Canadian radical party established the newspaper *Le Canadien* as a vehicle for the spreading of nationalist convictions. With its motto 'Our language, our institutions, our laws', *Le Canadien* was the founding organ of Quebec nationalism. That nationalism was a complex, if vital amalgam of ideas, sentiment and ambition. It combined agricultural clericalism of the most conservative variety with racial self-consciousness and the status-seeking opportunism of a legal-professional clan which was very aware of 'foreign' control of economic power. As with most nationalism which finds itself in a colonial or quasi-colonial situation its real goals were, and remain, impossible of precise definition. Despite its strong religious backing, its first great leader in the assembly, Louis-Joseph Papineau, was an able disciple of the *philosophes* and while its voting strength was agrarian its leaders were mostly professional men.

The first peak of friction was reached under Sir James Craig, governor of Lower Canada from 1807 to 1811, who gave fulsome support to the policy of anglicization – a policy endorsed with equal enthusiasm by London and by the Montreal merchant class. Craig gave in to demands that the French party be curbed by dissolving the assembly, cashiering many French-Canadian militia officers, suppressing *Le Canadien* and jailing its owners. In the riotous elections that followed these ill-considered actions, the number of radical French deputies was increased and London decided to temporize. Craig was recalled and replaced by a talented French-speaking conciliator, the Swiss-descended ex-New Yorker, General Sir George Prevost. Prevost called off the anglicization campaign, appointed French Canadians to the bench and the militia, and within a year of his appointment had taken much of the radical tone out of the nationalist demands; enough, at any rate, to ensure the loyalty of Lower Canada in the war of 1812. Indeed, Prevost's appointment was the result not only of the domestic crisis in Lower Canada but also of a disastrous deterioration in Anglo-American relations.

The international tension had many causes of which inflammation of the Indian frontier was but one. So prominently did the alleged British-Canadian support of the 'Indian menace' figure in the speeches of American war hawks, however, that this cause has long been vastly overrated. The western background of the war can be briefly related.

London and Montreal had two continuing interests in the Ohio country after 1783: the British treaty guarantees of tribal land rights to the Indians, stemming from the pre-revolutionary work of the Superintendents of Indian Affairs, and the extensive fur trade which remained very largely in the hands of Montrealers. The treaty settlement had guaranteed free entry of Canadians for commercial purposes, and also an attempt to obtain satisfaction for Loyalist debts. Both were in jeopardy and as a result the British retained possession of fortified trading posts south of the Great Lakes. In 1794 the British agreed, in Jay's Treaty, to withdraw from the posts by 1796; the Americans agreed to guarantee free commercial entry and to act more effectively on the Loyalist claims. The British abandoned the posts on schedule but the Loyalist question was never settled, while the Canadian traders were progressively impeded by American fiscal action. At the same time, the Indians grew restive as the frontier of settlement moved even further into their hunting grounds. They continued to trade with the Canadians, usually crossing the border to do so, and receiving supplies (including firearms and ammunition) with which to carry on their fur-gathering. Several sharp battles between the Indians and American advance guards culminated in a particularly bloody affray at Tippecanoe in which General W. H. Harrison dispersed the followers of the Shawnee chief Tecumseh and his brother 'the Prophet' in 1811. Although Governor Simcoe of Upper Canada and, for a while, Lord Dorchester and the Montreal traders, dreamed of establishing a neutral Indian state in the Ohio country, and perhaps eventually undoing the crippling boundary settlement of 1783, actual British policy was quite the reverse – to the lingering regret of the Montrealers. Even Sir James Craig, before wearily giving up his beleaguered position as governor of Lower Canada, took time to advise the British chargé in Washington to warn the American government of the warlike intentions of the Indians in their western territory. Britain, in fact, and her Canadian representatives, did all in their power to pacify the frontier. But this was never believed by the Americans. And to suspicions about intrigues in the west were added the irritations of frustrated commerce on the Atlantic.

American response to the respective efforts of France and Britain to supervise neutral shipping was both erratic and ineffectual, from an American point of view. Impressment, seizure and blockade did not pause before the American Embargo and Non-Intercourse Acts. On the other hand, British North America benefited greatly from the exigencies of the Napoleonic Wars. Excluded from Baltic timber markets, Britain increased sharply the tariff preferences on timber from her North American colonies. Soon the ports of Quebec and Saint

John were jammed with timber shipping, while these and other ports of the St Lawrence and Maritimes served also as back-door entrances to the British market for merchants of the north-eastern States. Yet while many New Englanders evaded the federal trade restrictions and held pro-British sympathies, a national American sentiment for war mounted steadily. The time came when farmers, planters and many merchants felt that the control of the seas must be challenged. To their economic concern there was added national resentment at 'insults to the flag' on the high seas and a feeling that the need (and right) of American continental expansion coincided with the need to capture Canada as the only facet of British power vulnerable to American assault. It was also convenient that the process of acquiring Florida, which had already been commenced, could be speeded up by a war which would automatically involve Britain's ally, Spain.

In June of 1812 the Congress, despite opposition which was centred in New England, responded to Madison's war message. At that time the population of British North America was under 500,000, while the American figure was about 7½ million. Britain was at the height of her struggle on the continent of Europe, and there were no more than 5,000 British regular troops in America – with little prospect of reinforcement. Knowing these facts, Henry Clay spoke for the war party in Congress when he said, 'I verily believe that the militia of Kentucky are alone competent to place Montreal and Upper Canada at your feet.' Enthusiasm for the actual conduct of war, however, evaporated almost entirely upon its declaration. The Madison government fumbled every aspect of military administration; most state militiamen refused to go outside the borders of their states; and New England withdrew completely, refusing to commit her militia, trading regularly with the enemy and finally moving close to secession. As Daniel Webster put it during the course of the struggle:

... a large portion of the people believe that a desire for the conquest and final retention of Canada is the mainspring of public measures. ... You are, you say, at war for maritime rights, and free trade. But they see you lock up your commerce and abandon the ocean. They see you invade an interior province of the enemy. They see you involve yourselves in a bloody war with the native savages; and they ask you if you have, in truth, a maritime controversy with the Western Indians, and are really contending for sailors' rights with the tribes of the Prophet.

While for England the war was an incident in the long struggle against Napoleon, and for the United States it was (however inaccurately construed) a 'second war of independence', for Canada it was clearly a struggle for survival against a second military assertion of continentalism. As such it was conducted in two distinct areas: the Atlantic seaboard and coastal waters, and the St Lawrence–Great Lakes basin. In the Atlantic region the Americans lacked any significant naval strength and their exploits were confined to commerce raiding in which they showed remarkable zeal. New England remained open to British and Maritimes commerce throughout, and the Maritimers profited not only from swollen military contracts but also from illicit trade with New England and their own commerce raiding which garnered some 200 American ships. By the concluding months of the war the Royal Navy had virtually sealed off the American coast and swept most American raiders from the sea.

On land it was the British and Canadians who were on the defensive and the Canadas were saved by three decisive factors: the loyalty of French Canadians and 'late Loyalists'; the superior training and tactics of the small British regular force; and the almost total incompetence of the American generals. The last of these factors was probably the most important. Had the Americans decided to concentrate their initial effort in one grand assault upon Montreal, the city would almost certainly have fallen to immensely superior numbers. This would have cut off the whole of Upper Canada from its one supply route of the St Lawrence. Instead, the Americans dispersed their forces in three poorly organized attacks at widely separated points: the Richelieu River approaches to Montreal; Niagara; and Detroit. All three failed. In Lower Canada the conciliatory policies of Prevost, together with mounting alienation from atheistic France and recognition that the province's special rights of religion, language and laws would be obliterated in an American union, ensured majority loyalty. At Lacolle and Chateaugay the invasion was repulsed by militia units composed mainly of French Canadians.

In the invasions of Upper Canada the Americans counted heavily upon disaffection among the large numbers of farmers who had been streaming into the province from the United States ever since the first Loyalist influx. The governor, General Sir Isaac Brock, was well aware of the dangers of this potential fifth column and of the propaganda distributed by the Americans throughout the province. General Hull's Appeal to the Inhabitants of Canada, issued from Detroit, left no doubt about American hopes:

The army under my command has now invaded your country. .... Separated by an immense ocean and an extensive wilderness from Great Britain, you have no participation in her councils, nor interest in her conduct. You have felt her tyranny; you have seen her injustice. .... Many of your fathers fought for the freedom and independence we now enjoy. Being children, therefore, of the same family with us, and heirs of the same heritage, the arrival of an army of friends must be hailed by you with a cordial welcome. .... If the barbarous and savage policy of Great Britain be pursued, and the savages are let loose to murder our citizens, and butcher our women and children, this war will be a war of extermination. The first stroke of the tomahawk, the first attempt with the scalping knife, will be the signal of one indiscriminate scene of desolation. No white man found fighting by the side of an Indian will be taken prisoner – instant death will be his lot.

But Hull's exhortations also reflected his fears. Brock had moved quickly and with skill to undermine the impending invasions. Striking at Michilimackinac at the top of Lake Michigan, he captured it with a small force of British regulars, Indians and fur traders. For the duration of the war the western fur country was in the hands of the Montrealers, and the Indians moved definitively to the British side. After Michilimackinac, Brock attacked Detroit. Although General Hull's defending force was much larger, it was undisciplined and in mortal fear of Brock's Indian allies, whose actual number was exaggerated by report. Hull abjectly surrendered the post and was later court-martialled for cowardice. These early successes threw the Americans off balance and confirmed the loyalty of Upper Canada by extinguishing the annexationist hopes of some of the recent immigrants and strengthening the determination of the Loyalists who formed the core of the militia. Brock himself was killed later in 1812 during a dashing, if foolhardy, attempt to dislodge American forces who had taken the heights at Queenston on the Canadian side of the Niagara River. The Niagara invasion was repelled, however, and by the end of 1812 American hope of an easy victory was gone forever. If English-speaking Canada has a national hero (and it is not a people to recognize such things readily) he is Sir Isaac Brock. Certainly it is difficult to imagine that Upper Canada could have survived without Brock's combination of sound strategy and courageous tactics.

Two more years of war were not to alter the main positions established in 1812. The Americans gained virtual control of the Lakes, sacked and burned the capital at York and conducted several further invasion attempts but were unable to hold any territory. On the other hand British-Canadian forces continued to hold the western fur country and to seize and hold the coast of Maine, while the tightening British control of the Atlantic permitted a successful raid on Washington and the burning of the Capitol in retaliation for the devastation of York.

Yet the peace settlement reflected not the balance of war in America but the threatening resurgence of Napoleonic strength in France. The British felt unable to mount any large effort overseas as 1814 moved towards its close, while the Americans at the negotiations in Ghent refused to concede the areas whose control they had lost. As a result the Treaty of Ghent said little more than that the war was closed. Inept British negotiators failed to make more than a half-hearted endeavour to secure boundary revisions with the result that the irritating boundaries of 1783 were confirmed – despite vigorous protests from the Montrealers. The real settlement was left to international commissions and this precedent was an augury of less bellicose, if no less controversial, Canadian–American relations in the future. The resulting Conventions of 1817 and 1818 provided that no major warships would be permitted on the Great Lakes; that the western boundary should go straight along the forty-ninth parallel from the Lake of the Woods to the Rockies where it ended indefinitely at the Oregon country which was left to the joint control of Britain and the United States; and that American fishermen, while still permitted to land for repairs and provisions in the Maritimes, were denied the privilege of the inshore fisheries. The right of free Canadian entry to the southern section of the western fur country was finally ended and this speeded the collapse of the North-West Company. After a last bitter and bloody struggle against the Bay, the Montreal interests were bought out by the Hudson's Bay Company in 1821. The whole 'Canadian' west remained under the control of the factors from London until it was again claimed for Canada in the 1860s. In the meantime Montreal was to try rehabilitating its St Lawrence commercial empire on the basis of the valley's staple trade in timber, grain, potash and the settlement needs of manufactured goods from England.

It had been a small war by European standards; but in North America it was none the less definite in confirming the results of 1783. All sections of British North America found their interest in the empire confirmed by wartime opportunities and prosperity as well as by intensified anti-Americanism. French-Canadian pride in their militia defence was matched by Upper Canadian Loyalist enthusiasm for the work of Brock and their own volunteer regiments. For many years memorial services revealed the emotional content of the tradition in English-speaking Canada. In 1875 a speaker at one such occasion reminded his audience that

... when the war was declared, our fathers knew their duty, and knew the worthlessness of the pompous proclamations and promises of President Madison's generals and agents. The blood of our United Empire Loyalist forefathers warmed again in their own bossoms, and pulsated in the hearts of their sons and grandsons, and in the hearts of hundreds of others who had adopted Canada, under the flag of British law and liberty as their home. ...

If French- and English-speaking nationalism in the Canadas and pro-British and regional loyalties in the Maritimes had differing aspects, they had also one thing in common: appreciation of the benefits and security of British power and institutions and deep distrust of American republicanism. That these sources of strength were imperilled by the unimaginative conservatism of the second British Empire between 1815 and 1837 is one of the tragedies of Canadian history.

6

Oligarchs and Democrats

BRITISH North America had survived the 1812 war almost in spite of the system of government which she 'enjoyed'. It remained to be seen whether that system, in its domestic and imperial forms, would be sufficiently flexible to accommodate rapidly growing communities in time of peace. The events of the years from 1815 to 1837 were to prove that, while the old colonial economic system of the preferential navigation acts was still useful to the North American colonies, the extension of a system of preference into their social and political life was not tolerable. The aspirations of widely scattered pioneer farmers as well as the intense national consciousness of French Canadians strained steadily against the restrictions of a pseudo-aristocratic form of representative government. Restive spokesmen of 'the people' were further stimulated by a new flow of immigration as well as by the heady experience of living cheek by jowl with Andrew Jackson's United States. The result was armed rebellion and the launching of the third British Empire.

If the twenty-five years following 1812 were to culminate in frustration and rebellion, they were nevertheless years of steady growth. They were years, too, in which a sense of identity deepened in each of the three main settlement regions. In the English-speaking areas changes in the population balance strengthened such a sense, while in Lower Canada resistance to pressures for anglicization had much the same effect.

Two external factors, and a third domestic one, determined the nature and extent of immigration to British North America in these years. In the United States the gigantic westward migration had already rolled beyond the Ontario peninsula into the midwest and was preparing for its great leap to the Pacific. Moreover in Upper Canada postwar bitterness brought an end to the earlier tolerance of American immigration. Restrictive laws now required seven years residence as a condition of land-holding for Americans. This brought to an end significant movement of Americans into British North America until the prairie west began to béckon in the late nineteenth century.

The second external factor was the post-Napoleonic combination of distress and unrest in the British Isles. Between 1815 and 1850 a massive human wave moved across the Atlantic, often in desperation, frequently in hope, and usually to a new success. While the larger portion of this startling population movement found its way to the United States to be homogenized in the absorptive culture of Manifest Destiny, some 800,000 came to British North America. In the smaller communities to the north of the United States such an influx was bound to exercise a decisive influence. In the case of the more than 100,000 who went to the Atlantic colonies, the British character of the region was heavily reinforced and its marked imperial loyalism firmly founded.

Up the valley of the St Lawrence flowed a much larger stream, almost, as it seemed to good Tories, by design to offset the diminished and more dangerous seepage to the south. Some of these, particularly the Irish, remained in Montreal or took up land in the Eastern Townships of Lower Canada, but the great bulk moved on to an Upper Canadian life of pioneer forest-clearing. In the single year of 1832 some 66,000 arrived in the upper province and, while the movement was abated in the later thirties, it was renewed in full vigour in the forties, impelled by such untoward events overseas as the Irish potato famine and the high price of corn in England. By 1850 the population of Upper Canada had reached nearly a million.

Those who sought refuge from the economic storms of the United Kingdom were not often affluent. Most came to North America in the holds of ships which were designed basically for transporting lumber to Britain. Multi-tiered bunks, inadequate sanitation and food, and general filth wreaked havoc on the long north Atlantic crossings. Hundreds died en route and many more died in the quarantine hospitals and immigration sheds of Montreal and Quebec. At one point irate Montrealers were almost persuaded that it was the settled design of the British government to dump the destitute and the diseased upon the struggling colonies. And to some extent this was true since many of the emigrants received either state or charitable assistance for their passages. It was perhaps one way of mitigating the rigours of the New Poor Law. Only a tiny fraction brought with them a competence with which to begin life anew. Those who did so, travelled comfortably in deck cabins of packet ships and later introduced an odd note of querulous sophistication to the backwoods of Upper Canada. Memoirs such as Susanna Moodie's *Roughing It In The Bush* contain fascinating accounts of the rude democracy of Upper Canada as it appeared to English gentlewomen of the day. Such ladies and their half-pay husbands usually left the back clearings in favour of lake-front towns and small preferments such as county sheriff's offices. They also contributed to the establishment of a rather hot-house tradition of polite letters by their pieces in such journals as the Montreal *Literary Garland*. In society and politics the 'more substantial' immigrants strengthened both the habit and acceptance of authority which were already features distinguishing life in the northern part of the continent.

The habit and benefits of authority, however, remained for long in the chief possession of the early-established. Poorer settlers were frequently fouled in the maze of land-granting regulations which were conversely of immense advantage to the Family Compact and their friends who controlled all seats in the two councils and many also in the elective assembly. Immense land-grants were received by favoured individuals and companies who then developed them or held them for speculative purposes according to their whims and resources. Colonel Thomas Talbot was a prototype in this process. An eccentric alcoholic bachelor and veteran of the French revolutionary wars, Talbot was private secretary to Governor Simcoe and later a member of the Legislative Council (that body which Pitt's ministers so fondly hoped in 1791 would duplicate the House of Lords). In 1801 Talbot was given 5,000 acres on the shore of Lake Erie, and set about peopling his almost feudal domain with English immigrants. Immensely wealthy and arbitrary, he nevertheless gave encouragement and some assistance to the growth of community institutions throughout the 'Talbot Tract', which by the time of his death in 1853 was almost entirely alienated by freehold tenures.

More clearly mercantile undertakings were also numerous. In 1823 the Canada Land Company purchased a million acres of land, bordering Lake Huron, at a knock-down price. Within ten years the company had sold half its property and there were more than 2,500 people living in the region. A counterpart activity in Lower Canada illustrated the growing difference between the two provinces. In 1833 the British American Land Company received, through influence with the Château Clique and in London, some 800,000 acres in the Eastern Townships (south of Montreal). Because most English-speaking immigrants moved on to Upper Canada, the British American Company sold most of its land to French Canadians. Yet many English-speaking families were already established in the region and controlled most of its commercial enterprises. The British American Company, therefore, devoted its attention increasingly to business enterprise. Profits derived from land sales were put into railway projects and other businesses and became one of the sources of social capital. The Company's chief Canadian agent, Alexander Tilloch Galt, expressed well its identification with the point of view of the English-speaking commercial élite of the lower province when he wrote: 'I consider the interests of the Company and of the country to be identical ... my views are all for objects of material advantage.'

Despite the influx of some British capital, largely through merchant houses and the land companies, capital accumulation was slow and economic growth in the Maritime provinces and the Canadas lagged noticeably behind the headlong rush of the United States. Yet the picture was cloudy only by comparison. Canadian lumber continued to receive preference in the British market as did the steadily increasing production of grain and flour – despite the vagaries of British trade and navigation laws under Huskisson's approach towards free trade. In the Maritimes, businessmen and fishermen took full advantage of the last golden glow of the protective imperial trading system. Sawmills and shipyards turned out lumber and ships for the trade of the North Atlantic while the fisheries dispatched their catches to markets bordering the Atlantic basin. And while Nova Scotia's Bluenose schooners were a familiar sight in the world's ports, shipbuilders were active also in the St Lawrence–Great Lakes region. In 1833 a Quebec company, of which Samuel Cunard of Halifax was a shareholder, launched the *Royal William* which became in that year the first vessel to cross the Atlantic entirely under steam. But the farther one moved up the St Lawrence system the more difficult one found the economic circumstances.

Deprived of the far-western hinterland of the fur trade, Montreal businessmen turned their attention in the 1820s to exploitation of their nearer hinterland in Upper Canada. Here again the essential problems of Canadian economic growth confronted them: the scarcity and caution of domestic capital; high transportation costs over great and thinly populated distances; divided political jurisdictions which were complicated by the differing social goals of region and 'race'; and the ever threatening competition offered by the higher prosperity and tempting transportation routes of the United States. The population–distance ratio dictated then, as it has continued to do down to the present, a more active use of government planning and financing of basic economic facilities than was the case in the United States. In particular, if the 'natural' east–west St Lawrence route were to bear the potential traffic in the new staple products of Upper Canada through the warehouses of Montreal, rather than the great western canal projected in New York to connect Lake Erie with the Hudson River and thus with the port of New York, canals must be built to circumvent the various rapids which blocked the St Lawrence. In 1821, after private capital through the Lachine Canal Company had failed to solve the problem, the Lower Canadian legislature voted to have the government undertake the work. The government did in fact complete the work at Lachine but only to reveal the basic political problems which threatened to cripple this promising start. And for the Montrealers the matter became rapidly more urgent.

The great Erie Canal, which was completed in 1825, was inch-

ing along through the Mohawk valley towards Buffalo, while
in Upper Canada an enterprising promoter, William Hamilton
Merritt, had incorporated a company to build a canal at Welland
to by-pass the Niagara cataract between Lakes Ontario and Erie.
Potentially, the St Lawrence system, with its Welland extension
to Lake Erie, could become the major transportation route by
which the primary produce of the American–Canadian interior
found its way to overseas markets, and by which British manufactured goods could move to the towns and farms of the
advancing frontier. Thus Montreal businessmen invested some
of the stored-up profits of the old fur trade in the Welland
Company and the canal was completed in 1829. But completion
of other essential canals and improvements on the upper St
Lawrence (much of which lay within Upper Canada) was delayed until 1848, by which time American railways posed an
added threat – or advantage, depending on one's location and
occupation. Upper Canadian farmers were anxious to secure
cheap transportation to markets, nor did they much care
whether their imports were of American or British make. Thus,
while they generally supported their legislature's subsidization
of canals (both at Welland and on the St Lawrence) they also
made use of the Erie, as did the local importers from Port
Hope and Toronto to Sarnia at the western tip of the peninsula.

If many Upper Canadians were somewhat ambivalent about
contributing to a Montreal monopoly of their trade, they also
had financial-political reasons for dragging their feet. As entrepôt for the upper province, Montreal was in a separate
political jurisdiction and simply added to imported items the
cost of the customs duties levied by the Lower Canadian legislature. Moreover, discussions between the two provinces had
produced, by 1822, an agreement on division of the customs
revenue that was highly unsatisfactory to most Upper
Canadians. Despite heavy reliance on imports the upper province was given only one-fifth of the customs revenue. As a
result, government expenditures on 'internal improvements'
rapidly ran up a large provincial debt. One solution to these
questions of transportation, finance and political friction would
have been to unite the two provinces but proposals in 1822 to

do just this foundered on the solid shoal of mutual racial mistrust.

Few French Canadians had any direct involvement in the larger commercial enterprises of the period and through their deputies in the legislature they had regularly negatived bills for navigation improvement. It took them no time at all to discover in the proposed Union Bill its real purpose: to achieve the public expenditures required by the English-speaking business community of Montreal and at the same time to provide for the gradual elimination of the French culture in Canada. In a common legislature the population of Upper Canada, added to the minority English-speaking population of the lower province, would fairly soon give an overall English-speaking majority. The Bill also provided thoughtfully that legislative records would be kept in English and that after fifteen years members would be able to debate only in English. The imperial government shelved the Bill hastily when it measured the extent of French-Canadian resentment and when it discerned that in Upper Canada only the Family Compact was genuinely in favour of union. Most of the farmers and many small businessmen of the upper province suspected the Bill was designed to advance the already privileged interests of the entrepreneurial oligarchs of Montreal and Toronto. The abortive 1822 union proposals thus occupy a justly prominent place in the lexicon of French-Canadian historical grievances – although it might well be argued that their defeat deserves equal recognition. At the time, conflict over the proposals reflected mounting discontent with the colony's constitution and social structure.

Indeed in all the British North American colonies the 1820s and 30s were a time of growing unrest. And at the root of the unrest lay a tangle of inconsistency, misunderstanding and faulty information. In London the directors of imperial destiny were moving erratically, but with increasing conviction, towards a dismantling of that mercantilist 'system' which had been cumulatively embodied in the Acts of Trade and Navigation. As the glow of a free-trading future suffused the spirits of Whitehall, many of the more advanced minds concluded that maintenance of a politically dependent empire had little to recommend it as a continuing policy. The costs associated with the defence and governance of such an empire were scarcely justifiable when one was prepared to forgo whatever benefits had derived from a protective economic system. This 'separatist' view of empire, which anticipated that colonial settlements would, like ripe fruit, fall from the mother tree into a condition of independence, grew slowly. By the 1860s it became a principal reason for the easy passage of the British North America Act, which was seen by many as a definite step towards Canadian independence. In the 1830s, however, in its nascent form, separatist feeling induced a casual indifference to colonial problems. It was thus that while the first steps towards free trade were being taken, with resulting uneasiness amongst colonial producers and businessmen, no concomitant change in constitutional structure was envisaged save by a few radical 'colonial reformers'. In the Colonial Office 'Mr Mother Country' continued to heed the views forwarded so diligently by governors and the appointed councillors upon whom successive governors in each colony relied almost exclusively in policy-making.

While no peerages were bestowed upon even the most affluent of the colonists, the close little cliques of councillors and other office-holders did in fact view themselves as local aristocrats. Certainly they laid claim to every conceivable privilege and exercised complete control of policy. Some of them such as Sir John Beverley Robinson of Upper Canada, possessed genuine distinction of mind and evolved a sophisticated defence of the existing system, occasionally seeking 'moderate' changes such as that proposed in 1822 and always showing distaste for the noisy republican society to the south. Most, however, exploited outright and without compunction their connexion with the ruling families, sharing in the land-grabbing, the bank and canal charters, and in the patronage plums of inspectorships and lesser offices. The majority of Compact members belonged to the semi-established Anglican Church and agreed that the Clergy Reserves (that one-seventh of the public land set aside in 1791 for the establishment of 'a Protestant clergy') should belong to their communion. Reluctant to vote much money for the tentative beginnings of public education, they strongly supported the founding of private schools such as Upper Canada College and the establishment of church-controlled universities such as the King's Colleges in Halifax and Toronto. Such a monopoly of power and prestige could not long endure unchallenged in the circumstances of the 1830s.

Protest was scattered and ineffectual at first, but by the 1830s several factors imparted a growing vitality to reform demands. In two of the provinces resistance to such demands sparked armed rebellion. In Upper Canada reformers contrasted their land grievances, lack of influence upon government, and generally slow economic growth unfavourably with the robust iconoclastic democracy presided over by Andrew Jackson. Some of them borrowed directly the ideas of Jacksonian democracy, and certainly William Lyon Mackenzie's condemnation of the Bank of Upper Canada's monopoly owed much to Jackson's attack on 'the Monster' Bank of the United States. Yet, amongst the flood of British immigrants, were not a few who had experience of the reform ideas which gave rise to chartism, utilitarianism and radicalism; and in the welter of ideas in this turbulent period a striking feature is the continuing preference, even amongst most of those whom the Compacts called 'disaffected', for British political-constitutional traditions.

In addition to voicing land grievances the reformers reflected social change in the growing province. In religion, for example, Upper Canadian Methodism appealed more strongly to frontier communities than did Anglicanism, and by 1830 Methodists outnumbered Anglicans by a considerable margin. Led by the stern and intelligent Egerton Ryerson, editor of the widely read *Christian Guardian*, Methodists laid siege to the bastions of Tory-Anglican privilege. They criticized the political role of the chief Anglican, Archdeacon John Strachan, demanded that the Clergy Reserves be 'secularized' and the proceeds of their sale be used to support public schools, and that church and state be kept strictly separate. In these demands the Methodists were supported not only by minority Protestant groups but by proponents of reform who went well beyond the relatively mild claims of Ryerson. These latter were not Owenite or Fourierite, but simply 'democratic'. And while their democracy usually eschewed republicanism, its aims were similar to those of the Jackson democrats: the elimination of privilege based upon economic position, control of the executive power by a broad electorate, and expansion of credit facilities for small business-men. While their growing influence was based electorally upon the farming frontier, the reform leaders themselves were al-most invariably townsmen, as was the case also with the Jack-sonians.

The usual Compact response in the 1820s to reform agitation was to expel the leaders, either from the country or from the legislature. The response in London was to ignore the reformers' petitions, especially as they were usually supported by radicals such as Hume and Roebuck. These tactics led to a steady deepen-ing of popular resentment and to the emergence of much more determined leaders. Most notable amongst these was William Lyon Mackenzie, a fiery, vociferous little Scot who had read widely in the various tracts on British and American liberty. As editor of the *Colonial Advocate* Mackenzie became the scourge of the Compact. In the legislature he obtained com-mittees to investigate the government's relations with the Wel-land Canal Company and to air the full range of the province's grievances. For his trouble, young scions of the Compact families hurled his presses into the harbour at Toronto, and a tame Tory majority expelled him four times from the Assembly. Castigating the Assembly for degenerating into a sycophantic office for registering the decrees for as mean and mercenary an executive as was ever given as a punishment for the sins of any part of North America in the nineteenth cen-tury', Mackenzie was elected first mayor of Toronto in 1835 and was steadily returned to the Assembly.

By 1835 it was already clear that Mackenzie and his sup-porters were moving towards open rebellion. Unable to in-fluence the executive, unheeded by the Colonial Office, Mackenzie wrote with increasing frequency of the virtues of the American elective system as applied to executive officers. There is no doubt that he was driven to this extreme, with its in-

evitable connotation of independence, by the intransigent defence of privilege in Toronto and London. Joseph Hume was
probably right when he wrote to Mackenzie, after the rebellion:

> The influence you possessed in the House of Assembly, and the
> industry which you bestowed on explaining fully the grievances of
> the Canadians, entitled you to more attention from the Colonial
> Minister than you received; and I can fearlessly state that if the
> representations you then made of the general discontent of the
> Canadians ... had been listened to, the misfortunes and rebellion in
> Canada would have been avoided and prevented.

But even if Hume's assessment was correct, the Canadas were
not the United States, and as the Mackenzieites began to advocate
increasingly American solutions, Ryerson and the bulk of the
Methodist (and other) reformers drew back. Ultimately the
majority in Upper Canada would refuse, once again, the North
American republican destiny.

Meanwhile in Lower Canada, an equally stormy path was
being followed – a path made more tortuous by differences of
language and culture. Louis-Joseph Papineau, the principal
spokesman of reform in the lower province, was, like Mackenzie, an outspoken admirer of British institutions. As perennial
Speaker of the Assembly, Papineau symbolized the manner in
which French Canadians had mastered the politics of representative government – an achievement totally unanticipated
by Pitt's ministers when they framed the Act of 1791. Papineau,
like the reform leaders in Upper Canada, spoke for the farmers
and small professional and business people of his province (and
of his race), but he himself was a seignior and possessed basically conservative instincts. He had some acquaintance with the
ideas of the French Revolution, and some, too, with those of
the swiftly moving American democracy. As he discovered the
extent to which the senior Roman clergy and French-Canadian
official class were prepared to cooperate with the English-
speaking Château Clique in the maintenance of favouritism and
the mercantile interests of the Montreal businessmen, Papineau
moved in an ever more radical direction. In 1831 the Assembly
gained control of the revenue, but no recognition of ministerial

'responsibility' to the majority in the House. By 1834 Papineau made it clear that some democracy was needed both in church and state. In his famous Ninety-Two Resolutions he listed the province's political grievances and in other statements called for election of parish priests. The hierarchy stiffened its back, and Lord Russell, for the British government, made it perfectly clear that the kind of colonial autonomy demanded by the reformers would not be conceded. By May of 1837 Papineau was on the brink of rebellion when he said: 'The democratic flood has poured irresistibly down the slope of time and, growing faster and faster, will topple the unavailing barriers which may be erected against it ... to march in the footsteps of the Patriots of '74 would be to align ourselves, so to speak, with the greatest and most unsullied names of modern times.'

Yet, in appealing to the American example by calling for direct election of the executive officers of church and government, Papineau went well beyond what he really wanted. He, like the bishops who issued against him their thundering *mandements*, knew well that the French-Canadian nationality for which he spoke would not survive a decade within the compelling American democracy. In the last analysis, many of Papineau's followers found themselves in arms despite themselves, while the majority (as in Upper Canada) heeded the warnings of officialdom. The habit of authority was deeply ingrained in the people of both provinces, and asserted itself especially in response to clever arguments which used democracy against itself – as in a joint statement issued by the bishops of Montreal and Quebec:

The too famous National Convention of France, though obliged to admit the principle of the sovereignty of the people ... took good care to condemn popular insurrections, by inserting in the Declaration of Rights ... that the sovereignty resides not in a part, nor even a majority of the people, but in the entire body of the citizens. Now who will dare to say that, in this country, the totality of our citizens desire the overthrow of the government?

The number of citizens who did desire just such an event was increased by the onset of a savage economic depression in the summer of 1837. Reflecting a financial collapse in the United

States and a curtailment of trade in England, and intensified by crop failures, the Canadian depression sent hundreds of farmers, working-men and merchants to the brink of ruin. Revolutionary talk at this stage was bound to spark action. In Montreal spontaneous rioting followed a mass meeting called by *les Patriotes*, leaders of Lower Canadian reform, in November of 1837. Papineau, still curiously ambivalent, retired from the town, believing that his presence might lead to further violence. A vigilant government mistook his move as a sortie to the countryside to rouse armed support. Military detachments were at once sent to the chief centres of *Patriote* feeling and attempts to arrest reform leaders brought about a series of bitter clashes. A member of Sir John Colborne's staff reported on the engagement at St Eustache:

Our Artillery immediately opened fire upon [the rebels], and when no longer within range turned upon the village and bombarded the church, the fortress of the rebels. Congreve rockets were at first fired, but laid aside, for one in its progress struck a rail, reverted upon the troops and exploded within a few feet of the General, fortunately without doing any injury ... One hundred and twenty were made prisoners, but the estimated loss in killed and wounded was great.

The rebellion, so ineffectually planned and almost accidentally begun, was quickly snuffed out, while Papineau and several lieutenants fled to the United States.

No better planning was afoot amongst the followers of Mackenzie in Upper Canada. Yet Mackenzie's determination was perhaps stronger than that of Papineau and was certainly less clouded by the afterthoughts of a quasi-aristocrat. With the first news of the bloody events in the lower province Mackenzie issued a broadsheet containing a stirring call to action (although there had been no coordination with the *Patriotes*):

Canadians! The struggle will be of short duration in Lower Canada, for the people are united as one man ... if we rise with one consent to overthrow despotism, we will make quick work of it. ... It is the design of the friends of liberty to give several hundred acres to every volunteer, to root up the unlawful Canada Company, and give free deeds to all settlers who live on their lands; to give free gifts of the Clergy Reserve lots to good citizens who have settled on them. ... With governors from England, we will have bribery at elections, corruption, villainy, and perpetual discord in every township, but independence would give us the means of enjoying many blessings.

Mackenzie followed this promising document by assembling an enthusiastic but small and untrained group of farmers and 'mechanics' at a tavern north of Toronto. His inability as a general was matched by that of the almost incredibly arrogant and volatile governor, Sir Francis Bond Head. In the one major 'engagement' fought across the stump fences north of the capital, the rebels were dispersed – largely because of a heavy turnout of volunteers who feared the extremism of the course chosen by the rebellious little Scot. Mackenzie himself made his way, farm by farm and with a heavy price on his head, to the United States – a dangerous trip which suggests a degree of general support for him not reflected in the actual skirmish at Montgomery's Tavern. Nor were Mackenzie and Papineau able to secure official American help to recoup their lost cause in the months which followed. The sporadic border raids which were organized by private American sources merely underlined the unwillingness of Washington to imperil Anglo-American relations unnecessarily. They also tended to intensify appeals to Canadian loyalty.

Yet, disheartening as was the story of the rebellions, they none the less made their point. It was no longer possible for the British government to believe that reports from imperial appointees sent out as governors and from the little colonial oligarchies reflected the true condition and needs of the Canadas. The full-scale investigation that was to follow, together with the wide-ranging results of that investigation, were the true measure of the efforts of Mackenzie and Papineau.

7

Aristocrats of Reform

WHILE the almost querulous appeal to arms was vastly magnified in most of the accounts of the day, and while the rebellions were utterly crushed, the immediate British response was not punitive. Some leaders of opinion may have read with satisfaction Alexis de Tocqueville's perceptive remarks about the tyrannical potential of American democracy but they did not miss the French aristocrat's main point. Democracy was the wave of the future. America had simply gone further than any other nation into the nineteenth century. If some English Whigs took more comfort than they should have from the cautious advance of 1832, others on the radical edge of the party sensed clearly enough the need for greater constitutional resiliency – both at home and in the colonies. Moreover, several significant facts about British North America did not go unremarked in London despite serious distortions in colonial reports.

In the Maritime provinces there had been no rebellion. Despite similar political-social grievances the Atlantic colonies were prospering and reformers there, such as the influential Nova Scotian editor, Joseph Howe, steadily counselled moderation. Seaboard representatives in London received attention of a sort not frequently accorded those from the more raucous colonies of the St Lawrence. The Melbourne government, with its broad resources of talent, decided to look closely into the problem of the Canadas and to seek a solution which would provide avenues of self-reliant development for all the British North American colonies – and one which would, in particular, minimize unfavourable comparisons with American development.

Lord Melbourne commissioned John Lambton, first Earl of Durham, to conduct a thorough investigation of the British North American colonies. Durham's qualifications for the job were superb. He had played a significant part in the passage of the 1832 Reform Bill and as an advanced liberal had earned the nickname 'Radical Jack'. He was, moreover, the darling of the Colonial Reformers – those Whigs who disagreed with the dark prophecies of imperial disintegration put forward by radical separatists. Durham believed that a liberal empire could evolve which would gain in real strength by an intelligent devolution of power without actually relinquishing imperial direction of trade, foreign policy and defence. He was well connected with the leading Whigs, both politically and by marriage, and was widely trusted by the new men of business as one who understood the relationship between coal and industry. And from the point of view of impressing colonists Durham was amply endowed. A glittering aristocrat, he arrived in Quebec with the full panoply of vice-regal glory. The High Commissioner and Governor-General of British North America disembarked below the Citadel towards the end of May 1838. Mounted on a spirited white horse, Durham sported his most elaborate uniform for an ostentatious progress through the streets of the Lower Canadian capital. At the docks his luggage, with its stock of plate, crystal, wine and finery was unloaded in preparation for a truly imperial tour.

Durham brought with him to America not only the trappings of power but also the ideas and leaders of the colonial reform movement. Charles Buller contributed secretarial skills as well as firm ideas about 'responsible government' – that is, the application to the colonies of the recently evolved British cabinet system. Buller and his colleagues were convinced that if the executive council in a colony were transformed into a ministry, or cabinet, which would hold office only as long as it retained the support of a majority in the legislative assembly, the principal source of trouble would be removed. By making the ministers of the Crown responsible to the assembly, rather than to the governor and his self-perpetuating group of advisers, the 'compacts' could be dissolved. This method of reform required no legal change, but only a new slant in instructions to the governor who would become, in effect, a constitutional monarch. It would have, according to the colonial reformers, the great advantage of ensuring majority loyalty and thus solving the local autonomy problem which had defeated George III and his advisers. And perhaps its greatest virtue was that it was the very solution already propounded by leading advocates of constitutional reform in the provinces – men like Robert Baldwin of Upper Canada and Joseph Howe of Nova Scotia.

Like most brilliant concepts, responsible government was deceptive in its simplicity. The hidden complication was, of course, that it would be extremely difficult for a governor appointed in London to be responsible both to his colonial legislature and to the imperial authority. The working out of this problem was to absorb much political attention right down to 1931 – and beyond. And certainly Durham and his entourage had no intention of stripping London of its essential imperial powers. The point was continually stressed by Edward Gibbon Wakefield who was Durham's most colourful associate. Author of the influential *Letter from Sydney*, Wakefield had written his imaginative discussion of the Australian colony's affairs while languishing in prison after a conviction for abducting a young heiress. His main contribution to the Commission's thought was the package proposal for large-scale subsidized emigration from Britain to the settlement colonies and tight control of land distribution within the colonies. Clearly, imperial supervision of land-disposal within a colony would severely infringe the colonial autonomy implicit in the idea of responsible government, as would London's continuing control of trade, foreign affairs and the form of the constitution. However, despite long-range complications, the liberalizing spirit of the Durham mission was sufficiently evident to frighten many established interests in the Canadas, and the new governor-general set about his job with dispatch.

In Lower Canada the constitution had been suspended and Durham exercised his authority through a special council. Recognizing the peril of French-Canadian resentment at being temporarily deprived of majority influence in the legislature, Durham acted quickly to dispel suspicions that he was merely a cover for re-establishment of the Château Clique. He ordered withdrawal of charges against participants in the 1837 rebellion, except Mackenzie and Papineau, and decreed exile to Bermuda for eight rebels who had already been convicted. Ironically, this latter act of generosity opened Durham to sharp attack from political enemies in England, led by Lord Brougham, who seized upon the technicality of his stepping beyond his jurisdiction. Melbourne, surprisingly, failed to stand behind Durham, although he had assured the High Commissioner at the time of his appointment of total support. As a result Durham was to resign his position in disgust – although he was left enough time before this crisis to complete his survey of British America and write his great Report.

In addition to calming the most immediate fears of French Canada, Durham dealt successfully with the other critical danger of the moment. Brigand border raids conducted by shiftless Irish-American groups were troubling the military commanders who feared that Canadian exiles might persuade the American government to lend support to such raids or even launch an invasion. Travelling to Niagara, Durham conducted a ceremonial review of British regulars and Canadian militia. Then, at a series of formal entertainments on the American side of the frontier, Durham succeeded in impressing his hosts with the liberal purposes of his mission. His aristocratic graces worked somewhat incongruously with the shirtsleeves diplomacy of Jackson's government, which was intent upon gaining re-entry to the British West Indian markets for American shippers. But the result was a distinct improvement along the border which, despite several further incursions by secret 'Hunters' Lodges', was to lead to two significant boundary treaties in the 1840s.

Meanwhile the Durham staff was busily gathering material for its report on British-American affairs. In Lower Canada the commission's chief sources of information and opinion were in the English-speaking business community. This was a natural, if regrettable, outcome of the Durham group's own predilections. Believing in the business virtues, these men easily accepted the Montrealers' view that French-Canadian society was priest-ridden and unprogressive. Accepting the notion that Lower

Canadian troubles all stemmed from an obscurantist refusal by the French-Canadian majority to vote taxes for internal improvements, municipal services and education, the mission arrived readily enough at its principal conclusion. The deplorable determination of the French to retain their culture was the core of the Canadian problem, and Durham wrote in his Report: 'I expected to find a contest between a government and a people; I found two nations warring in the bosom of a single state: I found a struggle not of principles but of races.'

In the Report Durham concluded that the 'loyalists' of the English-speaking minority in Lower Canada rightly held the imperial government guilty of too greatly appeasing the French Canadians and that if prompt remedial action were not taken the English-speaking business leaders would seek admission to the American union – where the French would meet the fate of their brethren in Louisiana. Writing with the classical assumptions of nineteenth-century liberalism, Durham observed that

... It will be acknowledged by everyone who has observed the progress of Anglo-Saxon colonization in America, that sooner or later the English race was sure to predominate even numerically in Lower Canada, as they predominate already by their superior knowledge, energy, enterprise, and wealth. The error, therefore, to which the present contest must be attributed, is the vain endeavour to preserve a French-Canadian nationality in the midst of Anglo-American colonies and states.

With such opinions at its core the Durham Report became the object of intense hatred amongst the French Canadians and, indeed, the launching point of a deepening sense of French-Canadian identity. Its basic constitutional liberalism, which was to pave the way for the long-term survival of a French-Canadian nation and for the development of a multi-racial and freely associated Commonwealth of Nations, thus stands in ironic relationship to its Anglo-Saxon racism. Nor did Durham fail to spell out the political conclusions of his racism. Judging that responsible government could not be entrusted to the backward French, he called for a union of Upper and Lower Canada declaring that 'it must henceforth be the first and steady purpose of the British government to establish an English population, with English laws and language ... and to trust to none but a decidedly English legislature'. That is, he recommended the long-standing purpose of the Montreal English to give political unity to the St Lawrence economy and to anglicize the French.

Within the proposed anglicizing union, however, responsible cabinet government should be established. If the French-Canadians were 'an utterly uneducated and singularly inert population ... destitute of all that can invigorate and elevate a people', the English-speaking Canadians, particularly the political reformers and substantial businessmen, were to be trusted with virtually autonomous government. And in this area of revision Robert Baldwin was a better guide than the Montreal merchants. The latter wanted a union in which they would be able to manipulate government by means of Compact-like influence upon the governor without resort to legislative majorities. Baldwin, however, insisted that no political re-arrangement could hope for success unless it were based upon responsible government. Indeed the phraseology of the Durham Report on this subject is remarkably similar to that employed by Robert Baldwin in a memorandum which he had submitted to the Colonial Office in 1836. Although he had been cold-shouldered by the colonial secretary, Lord Glenelg, Baldwin had sent a copy of his detailed proposals to Durham, and there is thus good reason to argue that the credit for originating the principle on which the Commonwealth was to be based belongs jointly to Canadian and British reformers. Perhaps, since the success of responsible government in Canada depended upon racial tolerance, and since the Baldwin reformers did not share Durham's anglicizing views, the Anglican lawyer from Toronto deserves a slight edge in the matter of credit. But then, without the Mackenzie–Papineau rebellion, it is unlikely that Baldwin would have been listened to in London with any greater interest than that shown by Glenelg in 1836.

The Report itself covered a vast range of British–American problems, from local government and land policy to immigration, finance and the constitution. But its reception was governed by its three central proposals: the conceding of responsible government, the union of Upper and Lower Canada and the separation of local from imperial jurisdictions. In Upper Canada, Tories bitterly attacked Durham for recommending a democracy as reward for rebellion while the reformers were wildly enthusiastic. In Lower Canada, with few exceptions, French Canadians were deeply hostile and personally wounded, while the English-speaking minority was somewhat baffled, applauding union and suspicious of responsible government. In London, in the midst of political criticism and within months of Durham's premature death, the government chose to accept the recommendation of union but not that of responsible government. The 1840 Act of Union created a single province in the St Lawrence–Great Lakes area with a legislature in which Canada East and Canada West enjoyed equal representation. This curious provision of equal representation for the two old provinces within the new union was made on the assumption that since the English-speaking population was slightly in the minority any other arrangement would risk French-Canadian domination of the assembly. It was a grave error, since immigration was quickly to reverse the minority–majority relationship and create a new and deepening sense of grievance on the part of English-speaking Canada West.

Even more immediate in its consequences was the withholding of responsible government. Lord John Russell, the colonial secretary, put the case with impeccable logic:

It may happen ... that the Governor receives at one and the same time instructions from the Queen and advice from his Executive Council, totally at variance with each other. If he is to obey his instructions from England, the parallel of constitutional responsibility entirely fails: if, on the other hand, he is to follow the advice of his Council, he is no longer a subordinate officer, but an independent sovereign.

What, in fact, Russell determined upon was a kind of half-way house to responsible government, and he instructed the first governor of the Union to choose his advisers from those whose 'principles and feelings were in accordance with the majority' in the assembly. Russell remained clear, however, on the point that there might well be cases in which the governor might not be able to secure policy support from a majority, in which case his authority from the Crown must be exercised. The years from 1841 to 1846 were to prove that strict logic is not a particularly good guide in political matters; that having abandoned the principle of oligarchy, a truly representative system was bound to move flexibly from one area of authority to another.

Charles Poulett Thompson, Lord Sydenham, who inaugurated the Union government, was extremely able. A wealthy businessman who represented Manchester in the British Commons, he was noted as a liberal and one who enjoyed departmental work rather than active politics. In Canada he became, in effect, his own prime minister and succeeded in presenting a series of measures which commanded shifting majorities in the legislature. In thus avoiding a direct test of 'responsibility' Sydenham was greatly assisted by a large imperial loan which permitted him to sponsor a fresh round of public works and to alleviate the debts accumulated by the old Upper Canada.

Already, however, a powerful reform coalition was forming which shortly would render the Sydenham system inoperable. This coalition was composed of moderate French-Canadian reformers from Canada East led by the brilliant lawyer Louis H. Lafontaine; and the Canada West reformers led by Baldwin and Francis Hincks, the latter a very able editor and financier. This nascent Reform Party, forerunner of the Canadian Liberal Party, set a pattern of political action which showed both the weaknesses and strengths of racial cooperation. Lafontaine, while unhappy with the Union arrangement, recognized that French-Canadian cultural survival could only be secured if the French Canadians remained politically vigilant and pressed hard for the completion of responsible government. Strangely, the device of equal sectional representation in the legislature and elimination of French in debates, by which the British government thought to achieve assimilation, strengthened the French-Canadian sense of identity. Within the legislature the French operated en bloc more readily than did the English-speaking members, and soon obtained recognition for the French language in the legislature.

The English-speaking side of the reform coalition, while it placed high value on the constitutional goal sought by reformers and the healthy increase of colonial self-reliance which it implied, had somewhat wider goals as well. These goals included the smashing of Compact favouritism in economic affairs and the widening of entrepreneurial opportunity. Because of this it proved possible for a skilful governor like Sydenham to eat into potential reform voting strength to get support for particular measures of economic policy (such as canal-building) in his programme. However, by the time of Sydenham's tragic death in a riding accident in the autumn of 1841, his habit of ensuring that those whom he appointed to the executive council should be members of, and retain majority support in, the assembly, had created a constitutional situation from which it would be difficult to retreat. And the reformers were quick to exploit it under Sydenham's successor, Sir Charles Bagot.

Bagot was a singularly attractive member of the aristocratic reform group that played such a significant role in the decisive, if tortuous, evolution of Canadian self-government. A distinguished diplomatic career lay behind his 1841 appointment as governor-general of British North America, a career which gave him a humane and sophisticated appreciation of the race relations and politico-economic ambitions he encountered in his new jurisdiction. Bagot had been ambassador to Russia, the United States, France and Holland and in 1817 had negotiated with the American, Richard Rush, the useful convention which strictly limited naval armament on the Great Lakes. Bagot's real stature is best measured by reference to the fact that he set aside completely the instructions given him by Lord Stanley, the colonial secretary of Sir Robert Peel's Conservative government which had come to office in England in 1841. Stanley instructed Bagot to follow Sydenham's methods, but Bagot saw that it was already too late to forestall the full working out of responsible government. When the ministry left over from the Sydenham régime was defeated in the House, Bagot accepted a ministry led by Baldwin and Lafontaine, for the reform alliance possessed a clear majority. It was still not the full principle contended for by the reformers, because the cabinet contained several conservatives. Yet Bagot was right when he reported to his horrified superior in London that 'whether the doctrine of responsible government is openly acknowledged, or is only tacitly acquiesced in, virtually it exists'.

Formation of ever clearer party lines, evolution of a disciplined French-Canadian group, the willingness of that group to work closely with the Baldwin reformers, and the diplomatic realism of Bagot pushed the 'system' past a point of no return. The Baldwin-Lafontaine alliance established the real basis of the Canadian experiment in bi-cultural cooperation. Unlike the tentative relationship between Mackenzie and Papineau, that between the Baldwin and Lafontaine wings of the emergent Reform Party was based upon a clear understanding of goals, strategy and tactics. It established the point which Bagot reported to his superiors and which remained central to effective government thereafter: Canada could not be governed without the French. But even more important, it showed that Canada could be governed with the French. It was a point that would be challenged many times in the future, but with each challenge its validity became clearer. Without perceiving it precisely, the Canadians were launching a system of tolerance within a legislative union that would force them inexorably towards the practical modifications of federalism. In once more rejecting the American organic union they were anticipating the argument of Lord Acton: 'A great democracy must either sacrifice self-government to unity, or preserve it by federalism. ... The coexistence of several nations under the same state is the test, as well as the best security of its freedom.'

Yet the evolution continued to be marked by successive crises and personal tragedies. A fatal illness forced Bagot to resign in 1843 before he conceded control of patronage to his ministry – an inevitable corollary of responsible government, and a prime goal of the reformers. The irate British government sent out as replacement an able but inflexible Tory to recoup the ground surrendered by Bagot. Sir Charles Metcalfe, whose administrative experience had been gained in the Indian civil service and as governor of Jamaica, accepted with pleasure the resignation of Baldwin and Lafontaine when they objected to his refusal to take their advice on appointments. After a lengthy struggle with the assembly, Metcalfe called an election which, by appeals to loyalty, rendered a slim conservative majority to support his clock-stopping operation. Castigated as 'Charles the Simple' by the reformers, Metcalfe, despite this temporary victory, demonstrated the practical impossibility of the Tory position. In 1845, overtaken by malignant disease, he went home to die and the issue in Canada was brought to a head by events in England.

The year 1846 saw the culmination of two long-maturing trends in British imperial-economic thought. The ending of the Corn Laws spelled the doom of mercantilist control of imperial trade, and the argument for refusing colonial self-government was fatally weakened by removal of the principal reason for retaining colonial dependency. But whether the 'final' granting of responsible government is to be seen simply as a corollary of the British shift to free trade remains debatable. Much political experience and the growth of very strong colonial opinion lay behind the final concession, and certainly the liberal section of the British Whigs had moved decisively in *their* opinions as they contemplated events following the union of the Canadas. When the Whigs returned to office in 1846 it was Durham's brother-in-law, Lord Grey, who became colonial secretary, and it was Durham's son-in-law, Lord Elgin, who was appointed governor-general of British North America. At the outset Grey made it perfectly clear that he would grant full responsible government, while Elgin wrote to his wife shortly after arriving in Canada that achievement of responsible government would be 'the real and effectual vindication' of her father's memory. No doubt these men were influenced by the course of economic policy, but equally they were led by genuine liberal political convictions.

The first formal recognition of responsible government came in Nova Scotia, partly because the situation there was less complicated at the time of the change of government in England and partly because Joseph Howe had sharpened the confrontation of principles both by his astute leadership in the assembly and by a series of brilliant open letters to Lord John Russell.

In the letters Howe emphasized that the 'French problem' which had worried Durham did not exist in the Maritimes. 'If the Frenchmen in one province', wrote Howe, 'do not understand, or cannot be entrusted with this valuable privilege, why should we, who are all British or of British descent, be deprived of what we do understand and feel that we can never be prosperous and happy without?' Yet, while the Nova Scotian reformer betrayed a strong sense of 'Anglo-Saxon' racial superiority which was long to remain a force in Maritimes culture, he also put the general case for reform irrefutably. And in doing so revealed the deep concern in the Maritimes for the imperial connexion:

It is indispensable, then, to the dignity, to the independence, to the usefulness of the Governor himself, that he should have the power to shake off this thraldom [to the irresponsible Council members], as the Sovereign does if unfairly hampered by faction; and by an appeal to the people, adjust the balance of power. Give us this truly British privilege, and colonial grievances will soon become a scarce article in the English market.

Following this reasoning, as well as that of the Baldwin-Lafontaine party in the Canadas, Lord Grey instructed the Nova Scotian governor to implement responsible government in 1846. Grey's letter to Sir John Harvey in Nova Scotia noted that the concession must be made 'since it cannot be too distinctly acknowledged that it is neither possible nor desirable to carry on the government of any of the British provinces in North America in opposition to the opinion of the inhabitants'. In future the governor would accept as his adviser the leader of whatever party commanded a majority in the assembly, and allow that leader to choose (with the authority of the Crown) a cabinet. To the governor would be reserved only that power which an 'honourable influence' might give him in moderating corruption or in defending the reserved imperial jurisdiction in foreign and defence policy, trade and the form of the constitution.

After Lord Elgin arrived in Canada in January of 1847 his correspondence with Grey at the Colonial Office reads like a primer on the principles of responsible government. Within a year an election had produced a Reform majority and without hesitation Elgin called upon Baldwin and Lafontaine to form a distinctly party government. That the governor entrusted the task, in effect, to two men, rather than one was eloquent testimony to the incipient federalism of the United Province of Canada. But for the moment this was less important than the political test which soon followed Elgin's action. Party lines hardened rapidly, and in 1849 the Baldwin-Lafontaine government obtained passage of a bill to compensate those who had suffered loss during the Lower Canadian rebellion. A similar Act signed by Metcalfe had already compensated Upper Canadian losses, but the new bill was much more sweeping and included a number of people who had clearly been on the rebel side. Tories, who liked to call themselves the loyalist party, demanded that Elgin refuse his assent to legislation which would 'reward rebellion'. Enraged by their loss of control over the governor and frantic at the loss of preference in the British market as London completed dismantling the Navigation Acts in 1849, the Tory business community of Montreal burst into violence far more destructive than that of 1837.

When Elgin, despite his disapproval of some parts of the legislation, signed the Rebellion Losses Bill, he gave clear and final expression to the achievement of responsible government His own account of the immediate Tory reaction is most succint:

When I left the House of Parliament after giving Royal Assent to several Bills ... I was received by mingled cheers and hootings by a crowd by no means numerous which surrounded the entrance to the building. A small knot of individuals consisting, it has since been ascertained, of persons of a respectable class in society pelted the carriage with missiles brought with them for the purpose. Within an hour after this occurrence, a notice, of which I enclose a copy, issued from one of the newspaper offices, calling a meeting in the open air. At the meeting inflammatory speeches were made. On a sudden, whether under the effect of a momentary excitement, or in pursuance of a plan arranged beforehand, the mob proceeded to the House of Parliament where the members were still sitting, and breaking the windows, set fire to the building and burned it to the ground. By this wanton act public property of considerable value, including two excellent libraries, has been utterly destroyed. Having achieved their object the crowd dispersed, apparently satisfied with what they had done.

Not quite satisfied. Six months later many of the same men, leaders of that Montreal business world which had hoped to make the St Lawrence route, with the aid of the old preferential tariff system, beat out the Americans in competition for the trade of the continental interior, gave vent to even more dangerous purposes. In October 1849 the Montreal *Gazette* published an Annexation Manifesto, signed by more than 300 English-speaking Montrealers, including the most prominent men, and calling for 'a friendly and peaceful separation from [the] British connexion and a union upon equitable terms with the great North American Confederacy of Sovereign States'. While this was not to be the last time that English-speaking Canadian merchants would be tempted by 'continentalism' it was certainly one of the most critical of such occasions. From the point of view of successful translation of the old empire into a federal imperial organization, 1849 was crucial. And it was the more so since prominent English Whigs like Lord John Russell had come to accept the 'logic' of the imperial separatists and now believed responsible government to be an acceptable step towards early and inevitable colonial independence. Elgin, closer to the scene, recognized that 'no one advocates independence in these colonies except as a means to the end, annexation'. The overwhelming majority clearly wished a growing autonomy based upon a British connexion which would protect them against absorption in the expansive American republic. When Elgin detected signs even in Lord Grey of giving in to the separatist position he wrote to Grey, 'If you say that your great lubberly boy is too big for the nursery, and that you have no other room for him in your house, how can you decline to allow him to lodge with his elder brethren over the way, when the attempt to keep up an establishment for himself would seriously embarrass him?'

Elgin recognized, and persuaded London, that a more creative and natural relationship could be sustained by using the diplomatic influence and talents of Britain to secure alternative economic benefits to those lost by the Canadians through removal of preferential imperial trade controls. Such British action was to come none too soon, for in addition to the Montrealers' grievances two passages in British diplomacy in the 1840s had deeply disturbed the more perceptive colonial leaders.

By 1842 sporadic 'warfare' between competing lumbermen of Maine and New Brunswick necessitated more precise definition of the eastern boundary with the United States. Negotiations to this end were conducted by Lord Ashburton for Britain and Daniel Webster for the United States. Each man had close connexions with the financing of American development, Ashburton as a member of the great British financial family of Baring, Webster as a leading American Whig whose party depended upon the support of the controllers of investment in the United States. Neither negotiator wished to imperil the profitable transatlantic lending-borrowing arrangements by permitting the war scare to deepen. In the outcome, however, it was clear that the New England states could bring pressure for an advantageous territorial settlement more effectively upon Webster than New Brunswick could influence Lord Ashburton. The resulting Webster-Ashburton Treaty conceded, without significant resistance, a northward thrust to Maine that placed a grave impediment in the path of proposed railway connexions between Quebec and New Brunswick – a concession which left a legacy of serious railway difficulties for British North America. The negotiators, while they also agreed to transfer to the United States a considerable portion of land west of Lake Superior, failed to settle the long-pending Oregon question in the far west.

In 1818 the forty-ninth parallel had been accepted as the boundary across the prairie west to the Rockies. Beyond that the Oregon territory, reaching from California to Russian Alaska, was to be jointly controlled for ten years by Britain and the United States. This agreement was extended indefinitely in 1827, but by the mid forties was no longer acceptable to the Americans. Settlers from the Mississippi Valley were pouring across the Oregon Trail to the Pacific coast and in 1844 James

K. Polk won the American presidency with the cry 'Fifty-four Forty or Fight'. The demand was for the entire Pacific coast, but in practice the Americans were prepared to accept an extension of the forty-ninth parallel to the coast. Such an extension was in fact agreed to by both countries in 1846. Britain, in the interest of good relations with the newly intensified Manifest Destiny of the United States, made no serious effort to save the rich Columbia valley to which she had strong claim by virtue of prior discovery and use. Once again, threats of war (which would have put central Canada in jeopardy) together with the interest of British investment houses had produced a major limitation on Canada's future growth. While the settlement was entirely understandable in terms of immediate British imperial interest, it gave Canadian political leaders much to think about. In particular it underlined the dangers of permitting American migration to move uncontrolled into any potentially 'Canadian' western area, and it strongly suggested that the retention of control over foreign policy in imperial hands might not be compatible, after all, with responsible government.

These problems, together with the well-being of the Province of Canada and the Maritimes, were of intense concern both to Lord Elgin and to the colonial businessmen-politicians at the end of the 1840s.

8

Problems of Destiny

BUFFETED by Anglo-American forces well beyond their un-aided control, subject to mounting regional concern for survival, and conscious of beckoning possibilities stretching away to the Pacific, British North Americans moved through the 1850s and early sixties towards a modestly spectacular resolution of their various ambitions and problems.

Central to the success of the combined experiments of responsible government and Canadian union was the growth of the economy – and such growth could not be unrelated to basic political decisions, to the willingness of English capitalists to invest in British America and of the British government to lend diplomatic support to the colonies strung so precariously along the northern borders of the American republic. Given the dramatic warning of the Annexation Manifesto, and despite the refusal of the majority of Canadians to support that proposal, Lord Elgin saw most clearly what was required. Appealing directly to the Colonial Office to take the initiative, he wrote to Grey:

> You have a great opportunity before you – obtain reciprocity for us [i.e. reciprocal lowering of American-Canadian tariffs] and I venture to predict that you will be able shortly to point to this hitherto turbulent colony with satisfaction in illustration of the tendency of self-government and freedom of trade to beget contentment and material progress. Canada will remain attached to England though tied to her neither by the golden links of protection, nor by the meshes of old-fashioned colonial office jobbing and chicane.

Fortunately Elgin's assessment of the situation was endorsed both by the Colonial Office and by most British Americans. In the Province of Canada and in the Maritimes businessmen began pressing governments for action to gain access to the rapidly growing American market for fish, lumber, coal and even farm products. In Canada this movement was given full support by the Reform administration. From 1851 to 1854 the prime minister was Francis Hincks who, as a financier with banking and railway connexions, did much to promote preliminary negotiations for reciprocal tariff reduction. Moreover, a complex triangular interplay of interests offered an exciting opening to nascent Canadian diplomacy. The focal point was the problem of the inshore Atlantic fisheries, for these represented a potential bargaining counter and a dangerous area of Anglo-American friction.

By the convention of 1818 American fishermen had been given some privileges on the Newfoundland and Labrador coasts, but were excluded from the rest of the inshore fisheries. As a result of conflict over definition of the limits, both Britain and the United States had naval vessels patrolling the region by 1852. The costly and dangerous situation clearly required early settlement and those who had been pressing for a tariff agreement saw the opportunity to combine the two questions. Despite some reluctance on the part of Nova Scotia, formal negotiations were begun in 1852 and by 1854 the time appeared ripe to bring these to a conclusion. In May, Elgin was given a special British commission to Washington for this purpose and set off, supported by Canadian advisers headed by Francis Hincks, to take Washington by storm.

Elgin proved to be even more popular with the Americans than had Durham. Moreover, he and his advisers recognized accurately that their major job would be to soothe the fears of the Democratic majority in the Senate on the subject of future relations between Canada and the northern states. Many southerners, in the midst of the mounting slavery controversy, and in the year of the Kansas-Nebraska Act, suspected that reciprocity would be merely a step towards political absorption and felt no strong desire to add so much 'free-soil' territory to the north. Consequently, in the midst of lavish entertainments, the Elgin group worked assiduously to convince southerners – by the same reasoning that had been successful with London – that reciprocity, by satisfying Canadian economic needs, would actually rob the annexationists of their principal appeal. As Elgin's secretary observed in his memoirs, he could not quite see the purpose of all the 'feasting and gaiety' into which his chief had plunged, but, 'at last, after several days of uninterrupted festivity, I began to perceive what we were driving at. To make quite sure, I said one day to my chief, "I find all my most intimate friends are Democratic senators". "So do I," he replied dryly.'

Traditionally the resulting Reciprocity Treaty was floated through on a sea of champagne. But whatever the means, it was secured; and it gave a strong boost to the Canadian economy. The treaty, which had a renewable ten-year term, removed tariffs on the flow of natural products between the British colonies and the United States. It also authorized reciprocal use of the Atlantic fisheries and the St Lawrence–Great Lakes waterways. The latter provision did encourage some American produce to go by way of the St Lawrence canals to Europe, but already railways in the United States had introduced a new element of competition between the St Lawrence system and that of the Mohawk–Hudson route. While the major colonial markets remained in Britain, grain, fish, timber and some coal found substantial new outlets to the south. Railway-building, canal and harbour improvements, shipping and many other areas of investment felt immediately the stimulus of expanding trade. And in a psychological sense the treaty's ramifications were perhaps no less important. While constitutionally subordinate to the British government, Canadian participation in the diplomatic action had been significant, which sharpened awareness, particularly in Canada proper, of the possibilities of increasingly independent initiatives within the realm of Anglo-American power. The immediate effect of this appetizing taste of influence was Canadian assertion of a sharp extension of responsible government.

Of the original fields of jurisdiction reserved to the imperial government, that of land policy had never been exploited, for the good reason that it would have impinged upon nearly every field of domestic administration. Imperial control of trade, just as clearly, had a bearing upon the raising of revenues for internal purposes and this jurisdiction was challenged quickly and effectively by the Canadians. In 1859 the Canadian government decided to enhance what it thought were the benefits of the Reciprocity Treaty, namely a stimulus to nascent Canadian manufacturing and a shift of the colonial trade patterns towards the North American market. The device it chose for the purpose was a mildly protective tariff.

In 1846 imperial legislation in support of the new British policy of free trade permitted colonial governments to remove duties which discriminated against particular foreign imports. The opportunity to juggle tariff rates was, however, seized upon by Canada as a necessary solution to the chronic shortage of revenue needed for developmental purposes. Instead of lowering the rates Canada raised them. From a general level of 10 per cent in 1847 they moved to 15 per cent by 1856, and in 1859 became clearly protective with a general rate of 20 per cent and special rates of 25 per cent. British manufacturers at once raised a howl of protest. 'The Merchants and Manufacturers of Sheffield' wrote belligerently to the Duke of Newcastle at the Colonial Office:

... the policy of protection to native manufacturers in Canada should be distinctly discountenanced by Her Majesty's Government as a system condemned by reason and experience, directly contrary to the policy solemnly adopted by the Mother Country, and calculated to breed disunion and distrust between Great Britain and her colonies.

The Duke was perfectly sympathetic and passed on the Sheffield protest to A. T. Galt, the Canadian finance minister and author of the offending tariff legislation. While Galt was told by Newcastle that the legislation would probably not be disallowed by London, he also was urged to consider the Sheffield argument. The Colonial Office regretted 'that the experience of England, which has fully proved the injurious effect of the protective system ... should be lost sight of'. These liberal views, however, made no impression at all on the conservative administration of which Galt was a member. Galt himself was particularly immune to them, having entered politics because he believed such action was necessary to the advancement of his business interests. A leading spokesman for the English-speaking business community of Canada East, he had signed the

Annexation Manifesto of 1849 believing with his friends in Montreal that all was lost with the simultaneous terminating of the mercantile system and granting of responsible government. When, instead of collapse, there came a revival of trade, the Reciprocity Treaty, and a minor boom in railways, Galt and his friends saw new hope. Like Papineau and Lafontaine, the businessmen turned politicians and pressed for still further extension rather than diminution of self-government. The combination of free trade in natural products and protection in industry suited them perfectly, and even made nationalists of them. Almost overnight the old dream of an empire of the St Lawrence revived – an empire no longer based upon the fur trade, but upon the transportation, financing and servicing of a varied economic growth westward across the continent. Without a moment's hesitation Galt penned a courteous but firm repudiation of the Sheffield arguments, using precisely the same guile with which Boston merchants had earlier claimed that trade-controlling tariffs were really taxation:

Self-government would be utterly annihilated if the views of the Imperial government were to be preferred to those of the people of Canada. It is therefore the duty of the present government distinctly to affirm the right of the Canadian legislature to adjust the taxation of the people in the way they deem best, even if it should happen to meet the disapproval of the Imperial ministry.

Making certain that there was no misunderstanding about his declaration of economic independence, Galt added his appreciation of Newcastle's reluctance to advise disallowance, noting that 'as serious evil would have resulted had His Grace taken a different course, it is wiser to prevent future complication by distinctly stating the position that must be maintained by every Canadian administration'.

Behind this substantial move towards full autonomy lay not only a business dream. Colonial growth was steady, boosted by heavy immigration, and the sprawling communities of British America were beginning to mature, to take on a sense of identity which was both regional and, in the minds of some, intercolonial also. In the Maritimes, while growth had begun to level off, by 1861 the total population was above 650,000. In the late fifties and sixties the region enjoyed a rounded prosperity which was later dubbed its 'golden age of wood, wind and water'. Based upon production and export of the staple products of forest and sea, Maritimes economic life was reaching a balance in which the carrying trade and farming also played a healthy rôle. Lumber barons of the St John and other river valleys, already possessed of considerable capital, moved from the trade in squared timber to that in sawn lumber and found expanding markets both in the United States and Britain. Shipyards around the many-harboured coasts turned out not only cumbersome cargo vessels for the timber trade (and return immigrant-carrying voyages) but also some of the finest clipper ships in the world. Maritimes merchants and captains competed effectively in the world's sea-going trade, not only with their native products of wood and codfish, but also with the commodities of the ports to which they sailed. For a brief period in the mid nineteenth century the Maritimes had achieved to the full what New France, and they themselves earlier, had failed to achieve – successful exploitation of the great triangular trade routes of the Atlantic.

Many Maritimers were content to enjoy the fruits of this new prosperity, to build more comfortable and even elegant houses, to travel in Britain and Europe, and to affect some disdain for the Canadians – the unreliable French of Canada East and the profligate and somewhat Yankified English-speaking entrepreneurs of Montreal and Canada West. Yet some Maritimers were restless. Sensing the significance of certain variables in the conditions of their prosperity, they cast an anxious eye to the future. What if the Americans should close off reciprocity at the end of its first ten-year run? Upon whom could the Maritimes rely to protect their fisheries and to replace their American markets? Others, feeling that the apparent limits of Maritimes growth had been reached, were not content simply to relax in the placid contentment of an insignificant and isolated colony, however well-endowed with domestic comfort. To such – and they found their way inevitably into public life – the imperial connexion and the possibility of a union of the British American provinces appeared essential both as a guarantee against likely vagaries in American policy and as opening legitimate avenues of personal advancement. In a speech in 1860 advocating a federation of British American provinces the young Dr Charles Tupper of Nova Scotia developed these points precisely:

> The human mind naturally adapts itself to the position it occupies. The most gigantic intellect may be dwarfed by being 'Cribbed, cabined, and confined'. It requires a great country and great circumstances to develop great men.... The highest offices we have to offer, and the largest salaries we give, afford no adequate temptation, no sufficient remuneration. ... Confederation would give us nationality ...

Tupper went on to become a founder of the Canadian federal state and to earn an almost disproportionate share of national and imperial rewards. Because a majority of Maritimers continued to doubt the wisdom of a jeopardizing their regional identity and prosperity in an expansive Canadian state, the political ingenuity of Tupper and his colleagues would be sorely taxed—and many Maritimers thought of him as an Upper Canadian at heart.

Certainly the pace of change and a sense of restless urgency was most marked in the Canadas, although there too, amongst the French Canadians, there was a regional majority harbouring fears about any rapid growth of territory or economic activity. By 1861 the United Province of Canada East and Canada West had a population of 2½ million. Within the Union, the people of Canada West had begun to outnumber those of Canada East, and the disproportion became a source of irritation, since representation in the legislature remained the same for each section. Yet, while this fact bred political-racial discord, the stakes of union and expansion were high and would govern the future.

By the early sixties the pioneering stage in the Canadas was largely past. If the area was not as homogeneous as the Maritimes, its parts at least had developed a considerable integrity, and beyond regionalism there was an integrating force in the ambitions of both farmers and businessmen. With most good arable land taken up in both sections of the province, farmers were producing considerable grain surpluses for export. These, together with a thriving timber trade and the forwarding trade in imported manufactured goods, placed strains on the old canal and waggon system of transportation. Particularly after the beginning of railway building in the United States it became evident that extensive railway construction was an absolute necessity, not only for purposes of domestic distribution, but also to keep the St Lawrence trade route competitive with routes to the south of the border. And even from the point of view of survival as a 'non-American' part of North America the Canadas were forced into an intense phase of growth-investment; had the demand for such development been rejected, the mounting flow of emigration to the 'high opportunity' regions of the republic would have debilitated the Canadas and minimized their chance of independent survival. Moreover, the pace of growth which now enmeshed the St Lawrence system, together with the disappearance of a frontier of arable land, suggested that survival would depend also upon acquiring a new land frontier to sustain the expensive transportation–trading system and to provide farms for the sons of Canadian 'yeomen'. This new need led directly to a kind of Canadian 'manifest destiny'. Increasingly the thoughts of many Canadians – market-minded businessmen, land-hungry farmers, and, to some extent, French-Canadian leaders who thought to widen the base of cultural survival by sharing in possible expansion across the old fur-trading empire of the west – all these turned to the vast reaches of the prairies, mountains and the Pacific coast.

The key to this potent *mélange* of purposes and needs was found in railway-building. After tentative local starts in the late thirties a full-fledged railway boom exploded in the forties and fifties. In all the provinces short roads were built as links between trading terminals or to open up forest and farming hinterlands. The most important of these roads had the additional purpose of tapping the traffic of American railways. The Great Western, for example, was built across the south-western peninsula of Canada West between Buffalo and Detroit and thus provided a lucrative short route for American mid-western commerce across Canadian territory. A reverse aspect of this cross-border traffic rivalry was created by special American bonding laws which permitted Canadian shipments to cross American territory in bond. Thus the St Lawrence and Atlantic Railway could be built from Montreal to Portland, Maine, to provide a winter outlet for the St Lawrence which was ice-bound for five months of each year.

The rash of railway construction created as many problems as it solved. The Maritimes disliked the use of an American port as winter terminus for the St Lawrence system and began to agitate for the building of an intercolonial road to Halifax and/or Saint John. Montrealers were grieved to see interior trade in Canada West siphoned off by New York railways. Even more pervasive was the effect of the railway boom upon public finances and political life. In a pre-industrial community devoid of large private accumulations of capital and with a territorial extent that made British railway problems look puny, both the obstacles and the opportunities of the railway era came to dominate political life. Public assistance to the roads was essential and, almost to a man, the promoters went into public life. Charters had to be bargained for, routes selected, money and credit raised, and ministers of the Crown had to be persuaded to give approval. Nearly every hopeful town in the provinces pressed its case for being on a line and, in the case of the larger, nascent manufacturing centres, for having railway shops located in its centre – to the lasting aesthetic damage of many.

The men who secured government-guaranteed loans, local bond subscriptions, and heavy investment by British and local financial groups, were either members of the government or extremely close to the government. Miles O'Reilly of Hamilton, who worked in the interest of the Great Western, commented to a business friend: '. . . if it were known that members of our legislature would oppose an Act of Parliament *because* they could not effect a pecuniary arrangement with the company, it would shake the confidence of capitalists and deter them from investing their means in the great enterprises of this country.'

Sir Alan MacNab was, probably correctly, less concerned about investors' criteria, but he was equally frank when he explained to a visitor who had inquired about his politics, 'My politics are railways.' Indeed railway politics did not respect party lines. The Reform prime minister, Francis Hincks, was forced temporarily out of political life when a public investigation revealed some of his direct involvement with railway and related enterprises, while the Conservative leader of Canada East, George-Étienne Cartier, was simultaneously solicitor-general of the province and solicitor of the Grand Trunk Railway. Yet, despite these somewhat sordid ramifications, the railway question was intimately related to the growth of pressures which can only be called nationalist. And here the centre of the stage was held by a galaxy of interests surrounding the biggest project of the day, the Grand Trunk Railway.

By 1861 the Grand Trunk was completed from Sarnia to Montreal, with extensions to Quebec and Portland, Maine. It was the longest, and perhaps the costliest railway in the world. With its main line covering over 1,100 miles, and with immense public assistance, both direct and indirect, it was, by the mid sixties, almost hopelessly in debt. Vastly exaggerated estimates of traffic and revenue had induced many British investors to put up money, either through bonds or directly through the chief contracting firm of Peto, Brassey, Betts and Jackson. These, together with the financial agents of the Canadian government in London (the Barings), began to join leading Canadian businessmen-politicians in calling for heroic action to forestall total financial collapse of the Grand Trunk and of the government which had so heavily underwritten it.

Yet the high cost of the railway age, both political and financial, also bore high returns. The railways and their problems begot a dual revolution in social-economic conditions and in British-American expectations. In previously isolated farm communities the eerie shriek of wood-burning locomotives heralded a new day of social integration. In the towns, ironworks and maintenance shops rose side by side with small factories which began turning out consumer goods, from stoves and furniture to shoes and clothing. But, while new rail-connected markets could sustain the beginnings of local industrialization, they were not sufficiently lucrative to carry the indebtedness of the Grand Trunk system. It was this situation that led to a curious repetition in the tortuous development of a Canadian state. Just as the boundary settlement of 1783 (confirmed by Jay's Treaty and the Treaty of Ghent) had forced the old Montreal fur-trading empire to shift north of the Great Lakes and across the west, so the failure of the St Lawrence–Canada West railway system to garner an adequate share of the American mid-western traffic now compelled a revived 'empire of the St Lawrence' to seek salvation by extension westward across the prairies to the Pacific.

Amongst other coincident forces that were driving towards an expansive British-American confederation, perhaps none was more effective than the outbreak of the American Civil War. Tearing the States asunder, that war posed real dangers for Canada. Once again, as in 1812, many Americans were tempted to seek compensation in the north for the spurious neutrality of British policy on the high seas. And, as earlier, there was no lack of Americans to claim that such compensation would be merely the just fulfilment of the republic's manifest destiny. Special interests throughout the Union pressed the case for acquiring Canada, and in Lincoln's secretary of state, William H. Seward, they found a happy listener. There was ample cause for Canadian fears. The critically important American bonding laws were revoked, and in 1865 Washington made it known that it would terminate the Reciprocity Treaty after the required one year's notice. By 1864 the cumulative irritation of 'incidents' such as the raiding of northern commerce by the *Alabama* (which had been built in a British shipyard) and the activities of small bands of Confederates based in Canada, was a very strong temptation to punitive, acquisitive action. Although Lincoln wisely resisted the pressure for a diversionary assault on the British colonies, it was by no means certain at the time that he could continue to do so.

This ominous combination of threat and action was a potent catalyst amongst indigenous forces in the Canadas leading both to colonial federation and westward expansion. Indeed its effect was not unlike that produced in the northern States as they contemplated the possibility of western expansion of the slavocracy. And in the Canadian case, also, there were diligent proponents of urgent action.

Most outspoken of the Canadian expansionists were the Reformers of Canada West led in the late fifties and sixties by George Brown. As editor of the Toronto *Globe* Brown wielded enormous influence in the strongly Protestant farm areas of the western part of the province. He was also a keen exponent of Toronto's ambition to outbid Montreal for the commercial exploitation of the prairie west. These aspects of Brown's politics were inextricably bound up with his unbending Scottish free church position, and the mixture was further spiced by his own Gladstonian liberalism and the tendency of a more radical wing of the Reform group – the Clear Grits* – to favour such Jacksonian ideas as direct election to executive posts. All of these ambitions and principles were frustrated by the constitutional framework created in 1841 by the Act of Union, and frustration intensified the Grit demands for dramatic constitutional revision.

By 1864 a political deadlock had been reached in the United Province of Canada which involved all the issues of racial, religious and sectional friction. Almost as soon as responsible government was achieved, the Reform political alliance led by Baldwin and Lafontaine began to break up as its common objective of responsible government was replaced by more divisive issues. The most dangerous of these was the matter of sectional representation in the legislature. Reformers in Canada West began to clamour for representation according to population and the electoral cry of 'Rep. by Pop.' raised deep fears in French-Canadian breasts. Because they suspected that representation by population would produce an English-speaking legislative majority that would threaten their cultural distinctiveness (French civil law, Catholic schools, use of French in legislative proceedings, etc.) the overwhelming majority of French Canadians transferred their political allegiance from the Reformers to the Conservatives. They thus helped to form Canada's second major political party and to intensify Clear Grit

---

*The 'new reformers' were much closer to William Lyon Mackenzie than to Robert Baldwin. They were thoroughgoing democrats who wanted in their ranks only men whose grit (determination) was clear and uncompromising.

fears that Canada West would be placed permanently under 'French domination'.

The Conservative party that emerged in 1854 incorporated the older 'Compact' Tory faction and 'moderate' conservatives in both sections of the province. Led by John A. Macdonald, a young lawyer from Kingston (a town located symbolically half-way between Montreal and Toronto, where Lake Ontario empties into the St Lawrence) the Conservatives attempted to build pragmatically within the existing situation. Macdonald himself had deplored the excesses of the Tory Annexation Manifesto and now gathered around him those who believed that the union could be made to work and that nothing could be worse for the experiment than to flirt with American methods or outright continentalism. A man of great charm and political ingenuity, Macdonald understood well the basic conservatism of French-Canadian nationalism as well as the economic ambitions of English-speaking Canadian business. He was thus able to dominate Canadian politics from 1854 to his death in 1891. That a large part of his success depended upon skilful concession to major Reform criticisms does not minimize that achievement. Moreover, through his tolerant pragmatism the earlier Baldwin-Lafontaine tradition of racial cooperation was further enriched. In 1856 Macdonald wrote to the editor of the Montreal *Gazette* in words reminiscent of Bagot or Elgin:

If a Lower Canadian Britisher desires to conquer, he must 'Stoop to Conquer'. He must make friends with the French – without sacrificing the status of his race or lineage he must respect their nationality. Treat them as a nation and they will act as a free people generally do – generously ... The only danger that threatens just now is the cry of Representation by Population. ... The Peninsula [the region from Toronto to Sarnia] must not get command of the ship. It is occupied by Yankees and Covenanters, in fact the most yeasty and unsafe of populations.

In denying the principle of simple-majoritarian democracy Macdonald revealed not only his inherent conservatism but also his early understanding of the one essential element that would make the Canadian experiment in non-assimilative political nationality worthwhile.

In George-Étienne Cartier, Macdonald found a cocky, diplomatic co-leader within the Conservative alliance. Cartier believed firmly that the survival of a French-Canadian nation in North America could only be made sure if the French were prepared to run in political harness with their English-speaking compatriots. As a lawyer with a financial interest in the Grand Trunk and other business enterprises Cartier was quick to realize that the basis of such cooperation must be French-Canadian willingness to foster large commercial and transportation schemes by favourable legislation, and English-speaking acceptance of policies to support French-Canadian cultural identity. In these convictions Cartier enjoyed full support from the Roman Catholic hierarchy of Canada East.

The bishops remained persuaded that the dual cause of the church and of French-Canadian nationality found its chief threat in Americanization – whether by outright annexation, or by insidious ideological penetration. They, as well as the political Conservatives, were increasingly concerned by a growing tendency towards anti-clericalism and republicanism exhibited by the *parti-rouge*. The Rouges, led by a fiery rationalist lawyer, A. A. Dorion, were similar in their democratic views to the Clear Grits of Canada West, but they lost voting strength steadily under sustained attacks by the bishops and the Cartier Conservatives. Curiously, the vigour of the critical assault upon the Rouges was increased by the appearance, beginning in 1845, of a fine, nationalist multi-volume *Histoire du Canada*. Undertaken by François-Xavier Garneau specifically to answer Lord Durham's charge that French-Canadians lacked both a history and a literature, this colourful and careful work succeeded splendidly in both its purposes. But it was also tinted unmistakably with the hues of continental French liberalism of the thirties and forties. Conservative and clerical attacks upon the Rouges and the rationalist *Institut Canadien* were successful in political terms. They also reflected the growth of post-1848 European reaction, and later editions of Garneau's *Histoire* were innocent of the original secular-liberal connotations. The work thus became acceptable to the intensely conservative-clerical nationalism that was to sweep French Canada in the seventies and eighties.

In the meantime, Reformers in the two sections of the province found effective alliance almost impossible. Attacks by George Brown upon 'French domination' and Brown's very strong attachment to British institutions and the Empire counterbalanced both the general emphasis placed on democratic philosophy by the Reform groups, and the Rouges' distinct coolness to the British connexion. Moreover, as the Rouges declined in strength, Grit-Reformers in Canada West came to command a sectional majority, and this made it necessary to deny in practice what was frequently affirmed as the theoretical basis of union legislation – the principle of double majorities. This theory, not unlike the doctrine of concurrent majorities advanced by John C. Calhoun as a means of avoiding sectional conflict in the pre-Civil War United States, prescribed not only an overall majority for any legislation affecting specifically one of the sections but also a sub-majority of representatives from the section affected. Increasingly the Macdonald-Cartier government, which came to power in 1854, had to rely upon legislative support in which Canada East members formed a majority. While the government was able to settle the long-rankling issue of the Clergy Reserves (by securalizing them and devoting the proceeds of sales to the municipalities), and to abolish the seignorial system of land-holding in Canada East, other issues kept it in permanent jeopardy. When a basically French-Canadian majority sustained a Bill to establish state-supported separate (Catholic) schools in Canada West the appeal of Brown's charge of 'French domination' was vastly extended. Many English-speaking Protestants, deeply committed to a non-sectarian public school system which contained the promise both of excellence and enriched democracy, shifted their allegiance to the Reformers. They suspected that a revived Conservatism would use the solid *Bleu* bloc led by Cartier not only to resist democratic change but also to advance the interests of Montreal business and transportation – particularly those of the Grand Trunk.

The result of these kaleidoscopic political shifts was a degree of sectional bitterness that brought government virtually to a standstill. In 1858 the Macdonald-Cartier administration was defeated on the symbolic issue of a permanent site for the provincial capital. Since the 1849 burning of the Parliament buildings in Montreal the capital had alternated between Quebec City and Toronto. For a permanent site the French Canadians wanted Quebec or Montreal, while the Grit-Liberals of Canada West would settle only for Toronto or Kingston. In a characteristically evasive manner Macdonald and his colleagues referred the matter to Queen Victoria – a voluntary diminution of responsible government which was to have later and perhaps usefull parallels in matters affecting racial-sectional friction. The Queen compromised on the tiny lumbering village of Ottawa on the Canada West side of the river boundary between the two sections of the province. When the legislature rejected this choice, Brown and the Rouge leader, Dorion, formed an administration which survived only two days. Despite eventual acceptance of Ottawa as the capital, the following few years saw an unbroken succession of ministerial crises and short-lived governments. Perhaps the least ambiguous sign of total deadlock was the inability of any government to carry a Bill to reorganize and strengthen the militia. Since the threat of American invasion was at its peak from 1862 to 1864, and since the British government made it perfectly plain that it considered a land defence west of Montreal to be impracticable (and began withdrawing the few regular troops from Canada West), Canadian inaction on defence seemed symbolic of the total collapse of the existing constitutional structure.

While the Grit-Liberals continued to press for 'Rep. by Pop.' as a solution, such a measure would obviously have revived the old idea of 'swamping' the French in an anglicizing sea. In 1859 a Grit convention made it clear that they would accept, instead of revision of the Union, a looser federal arrangement in which local matters would be in the hands of two provincial governments while matters of common concern would fall to a central government. Closely tied to this programme was the purpose of acquiring the prairie west for both the farming and business interests of Canada West. As we have seen, the

English-speaking businessmen of Montreal, who mostly supported the Conservatives, were also anxious for westward expansion to relieve the railway debt problems and to rebuild their
old commercial empire. Indeed, A. T. Galt had only entered the
government in 1858 on condition that Cartier and Macdonald
would accept the idea of British North American federation.

Many French Canadians and Maritimers were distinctly cool
towards federation and expansion as a panacea for the troubles
of United Canada. In French Canada the charm and political
skill of Cartier persuaded his principal supporters that the dual
scheme was essential to survival and that the French might
share equally in the benefits of opening up the far west. In the
Maritimes, Tupper, as premier of Nova Scotia, persuaded many
doubters that, however golden the glow of existing prosperity,
the future was in jeopardy unless the Atlantic provinces could
secure a rail connexion through British territory to central
Canada and the assurance of a larger British North American
state, since the fisheries and communications with the St Lawrence were both imperilled by the exigencies of the American
Civil War and the likely aftermath of hostility.

With all these forces of political deadlock, economic necessity and ambition, external threats and, not least, a nascent
national feeling amongst English-speaking Canadians, the
founding of a trans-continental state required only the imagination and courage of a difficult political decision. This was displayed in June of 1864 when George Brown proposed, and both
Macdonald and Cartier accepted, a coalition whose purpose
would be to inaugurate discussions leading to a general confederation of the British American provinces. In this coalition
each of the leaders sacrificed something, yet each gained also.
For Brown and the Grits the prospect of office based upon their
steadily growing voting strength was set aside in favour of a
permanent solution of sectional strife plus opening of the west.
For Cartier and the *Bleus* of Canada East, the loss of equal
representation in a legislative union was balanced by secure
control over the cultural rights of French Canadians within a
new province plus hopes for Montreal's economic domination
of westward development and possible French-Canadian partici-

pation in that development. For Macdonald, being forced to put aside his strong belief in the virtue of legislative as opposed to federal union was more than balanced by retention of a guiding position within the coalition which would build a vast new nation within the British system. But above all, the members of the 1864 coalition held it a virtue to seek a solution beyond the obvious one of attempted coercion, beyond the simple principle of majority rule that was working itself out so tragically in the republic to the south.

It remained to be seen whether the Canadian coalition could obtain agreement from the Maritimes and from the imperial government for the daring project it had conceived.

9

'One Dominion under the name of Canada'

ONCE Macdonald had accepted the principle of confederation he allowed his mind full range to contemplate the vision of national achievement that stretched before him and before those of his colleagues who could be caught up in the excitement of the times. Showing the curious combination of romance and practical politics that marked his greatness, he seldom lost sight of the essentials of Canadian success: commitment to racial and regional tolerance coupled with a sufficiently strong material base to withstand the multiple effects of proximity to the giant American republic. In a letter of 1865 to Edward Watkin, who represented Grand Trunk interest in continental expansion, Macdonald reported that he and his colleagues would soon be in England where they could discuss the question of the west as well as other matters requiring imperial action. 'My own opinions', wrote Macdonald, 'are unchanged. If Canada is to remain a country separate from the United States, it is of great importance to her that they [the United States] should not get behind us by right or by force, and intercept the route to the Pacific.' No one was to do as much as Macdonald to guarantee that this principle would be adhered to.

But if the means to independence seemed fairly clear, there was yet an enormous amount of cajolery, reasoning and manipulating required to convince doubters in the Maritimes, amongst French Canadians, and even in London. It was also necessary to give more precision to both the nature and purpose of the proposed confederation. To these tasks Macdonald and his colleagues gave absolute priority following the formation of their 'Great Coalition' in June of 1864.

The logic of events dictated the first step. In September 1864 Maritime leaders held a conference in Charlottetown to discuss the possibilities of local union. The project of uniting the Atlantic provinces was supported by London and had considerable appeal in the provinces. The principal concern of pro-unionists was to protect Maritimes prosperity in the event of hostile action by Washington. But the very arguments advanced to support Maritimes union could be used with added force by advocates of a wider British-American federation. Macdonald seized the occasion and led a diversionary legislative delegation to Charlottetown. The Canadians aided by Tupper and other Maritimes expansionists, talked of the defence danger, the necessities of rail connexions with the St Lawrence and the destiny of a new British-American nationality. They won the day and the Maritimers agreed to postpone their own discussions in favour of attending a conference of all the provinces to be held at Quebec in October.

The Quebec Conference met for two weeks following 14 October. Behind closed doors delegates from Canada, Newfoundland, Nova Scotia, Prince Edward Island and New Brunswick debated the resolution 'that the best interests and present and future prosperity of British North America will be promoted by a federal union under the Crown of Great Britain, provided such union can be effected on principles just to the several provinces'. Each delegation had a single vote save that 'Canada' had two in recognition of her past (and anticipated) division into two provinces. Thus the unionists had to convince a majority of the members of each delegation and in this job Macdonald's diplomatic talents and careful management of detail were of first importance. It was Macdonald's private secretary, Colonel Hewitt Bernard, who became executive secretary of the conference and who later was secretary of the London conference which framed the British North America Act. Of the seventy-two Quebec Resolutions, nearly every one of importance is to be found originally in Macdonald's handwriting. Convivial and conciliatory almost to a fault, Macdonald led the unionists in persuading Maritimers that their cherished local identity would be preserved by leaving considerable powers in provincial hands while he also held out to them the hope that important central government powers in the economic field would be to their benefit in guaranteeing rail connexion with central Canada. Similar suggestions of considerable provincial autonomy were made to French Canadians and to several sceptical Grits, such as Oliver Mowat, in the Canadian delegation.

While records of the convention are sketchy, consisting mostly of Colonel Bernard's random notes of the discussions, there is no doubt that the crucial problem of central versus provincial authority was thoroughly canvassed. It is equally clear that the various delegates were persuaded that their particular interpretation of the proposed federation was the most likely to take shape. Perhaps of similar importance is the evidence that English-speaking delegates showed as much concern about maintaining provincial powers strong enough to sustain cultural differences as did the French. Indeed, largely because of fears that the proposed federal government would be too powerful and thus inimical to specifically local interests, the Prince Edward Island and Newfoundland delegations refused to endorse the resolutions. In the case of Prince Edward Island an offer of 'better terms' brought the province into the confederation in 1873. Newfoundland, with the greatest sense of separate identity, resisted union until 1949 at which time a referendum rendered a small majority in favour of becoming a Canadian province – with the heavy inducement of having existing Canadian welfare measures extended to the island.

The Quebec Resolutions spelled out the division of powers, financial arrangements and structure of government that were to become the basis of the 1867 British North America Act and thus the foundation of modern Canada. The manner of the endorsement and implementation, as well as the 'inner meaning' of the whole confederation process have long been the subject of historical debate. Competing interpretations not infrequently arouse deep racial and regional feelings and·this is particularly true in the 1960s when the very fundamentals of Canadian federalism are under sharp-eyed review. Let us, therefore, retrace briefly the steps from the Quebec Conference to the proclaiming of the Act in 1867 and then attempt a summary of the major interpretative controversies.

In February of 1865 the government of the united province of Canada moved adoption of the Quebec Resolutions in the legislature. Although Macdonald said that they must be considered as a package (he referred to the resolutions as being similar to a treaty which must be accepted or rejected *in toto*), the legislators examined the principles and the details of the scheme exhaustively. A number of Grits objected fiercely to including the Maritimes in a federation which they had envisaged as separating the local government of Canada East from that of Canada West and acquiring the west for the new Canada. They saw the resolution which pledged the new government to build an Intercolonial Railway to the Maritimes as an expensive sop to the Maritimes and also to the Grand Trunk Railway. Brown, however, had been convinced that it was necessary to include the Maritimes, partly because French Canadians saw the Atlantic provinces as a counterpoise to the political strength of Canada West and partly because an open fight with the railway interests might imperil the whole scheme. In the end, most Grits voted for the resolutions.

While Brown rallied wavering Grits, A. T. Galt assured his English-speaking business colleagues in Montreal and the Eastern Townships that jurisdiction in every important economic field would be in the hands of the central government (with an overall English-speaking majority) while the English-speaking minority in the new province on the St Lawrence would have an entrenched right to Protestant education.

The job of persuading the French Canadians was shared by several Conservative leaders but the symbol of its successful outcome was G.-E. Cartier. Arguing that French Canada had no real choice but to enter and actively participate in the proposed federation, Cartier and his Conservative compatriots foretold the doom of '*la survivance*' if any other road were followed. Absorption in conformist American democracy would certainly follow if the fabric of a new national state were not woven in the north. But if a majority of the French-Canadian legislators conceded this argument, they were only less difficult to convince than were the Maritimers. Many suspected a plot to revive the anglicizing goals of Durham under

a new disguise and many leaders of French-Canadian nationalism today still name Cartier as the original '*vendu*'. At the time,
some French-speaking Conservatives deserted Cartier, and the
bulk of the diminished Rouge group also voted against the
federal resolutions. The final count in the Canadian legislature
was 91 for, and 33 against. Amongst the representatives of
Canada East, however, the division was much closer: 27 for,
and 22 against the federal plan.

Yet, despite these signs of uneasiness, there was a clear confederate majority in each section of United Canada, and a substantial overall majority in the province. Since Newfoundland
and Prince Edward Island had rejected the federal scheme at
Quebec, it remained to secure some kind of constitutional endorsement from New Brunswick and Nova Scotia before approaching London for imperial legislation.

In Nova Scotia the Liberal-Reform leader Joseph Howe
organized a powerful anti-confederation campaign. Condemning the proposals as the Botheration Scheme, he charged that
the mature and prosperous Maritimes community would be
destroyed by union with profligate Upper Canadians whose principal purpose was to pour money into developing a vast
western preserve for themselves. The west, he argued, could be
of no interest to the Atlantic provinces which would, nevertheless, bear a disproportionate share of railway-building costs and
probably suffer from tariff increases imposed by a new federal
parliament within which Maritimes representatives would
be a small minority. So ominous was Howe's campaign that the
Conservative premier, Charles Tupper, dared not present the
federal scheme to his legislature. Instead, in close consultation
with John A. Macdonald, he delayed action while pressure was
brought to bear in London for the use of direct imperial influence.

In London, financiers with Canadian holdings spoke
emphatically to the government. Their urgent appeal for support of the federal movement was received sympathetically by
Gladstone and Bright, the real powers behind the government
of the ageing Earl Russell. Both these men flirted with theories
of imperial separatism – theories so ardently opposed by the

Colonial Reformers of Durham's day. Contemplating the triumph of Lincoln's northern democracy, many who were of John Bright's persuasion inclined to the view that political union of the whole continent was the likeliest (and not undesirable) future of North America. Recalling also the extra defence costs recently incurred as a result of unpleasant relations with the North and the continuing Fenian threats along the British North American borders, the British government decided to use its full influence in support of a federation that seemed likely to lead towards fuller autonomy for Canada, relief of the British taxpayer, and greater security for investors. When Cartier, Galt, Macdonald and Brown went to London to secure the exercise of imperial influence in their favour, Galt recorded his impression of the role played by separatist sentiment: 'I am more than ever disappointed at the tone of feeling here as to the Colonies. I cannot shut my eyes to the fact that they want to get rid of us. They have a servile fear of the United States and would rather give us up than defend us, or incur the risk of war with that country.'

Galt's assessment was exaggerated. Britain was still prepared to defend Canada, partly as a matter of prestige. But London also wanted a stronger Canada and to this end acted decisively. It recalled the governor of Nova Scotia and sent out in his place a vigorous supporter of confederation. It also ordered the governor of New Brunswick to abandon his opposition to the scheme and, indeed, to advance the federal cause 'by every means within his powers'. The means were obvious. The legislature, elected in March 1865, contained an anti-confederation majority. It was dissolved and an election called in the spring of 1866. The Reform Party of the rather conservative premier Leonard Tilley received massive aid from all interested parties including direct money contributions arranged by central Canadian Conservatives. Such help, together with the inability of the anti-confederates to propose a convincing alternative, and mounting fears generated by Fenian activities on the border, produced a fat majority for Tilley.

In Nova Scotia, Tupper now moved rapidly, fearing that imperial legislation might not be achieved before the legal expiry of his legislature. As he informed Macdonald, an election would 'be most disastrous to Confederation and would probably defeat it altogether'. Thus he obtained passage of a legislative resolution authorizing him to discuss confederation on terms more favourable to Nova Scotia than those prescribed in the Quebec Resolutions. In New Brunswick, Tilley secured a like resolution and both Maritimers ironically, if understandably, pressed Macdonald to hasten the dispatch of a Canadian delegation to London. Macdonald wisely delayed action at this point in order to gain more precise agreement on the guarantees for minority educational rights and also to enact lower Canadian tariff rates which might reduce Maritimes fears about higher taxation within the proposed federation.

Finally, amidst the Victorian dignity of the Westminster Palace Hotel in London, delegates from Canada, New Brunswick and Nova Scotia met under imperial aegis to draft an act of confederation. The resulting British North America Act did not differ basically from the Quebec Resolutions, but it did improve the financial terms for the Maritimes, tighten minority education guarantees, and provide a constitutional requirement that an Intercolonial Railway be built from the St Lawrence to the Maritimes.

In the first Canadian draft of the Bill the new nation's name was to be 'Kingdom of Canada'. The title was changed to 'Dominion' at the insistence of Lord Derby, then foreign minister, for fear that the more pretentious name might wound American sensibilities. Informed of this later by Macdonald, Lord Beaconsfield remarked 'I was not aware of the circumstances, but it is so like Derby – a very good fellow, but who lives in a region of perpetual funk.' A small matter, but it typified the unconcern about Canada's future (and indeed about that of the empire as a whole, which seemed to be in a second period of salutary neglect) which pervaded British official circles. In the Commons the B.N.A. Bill occasioned little fuss, while the governor-general's instructions to the troops underlined the perfunctory approach: '... the troops in Canada shall parade at a given hour (say eleven o'clock) on the 1st July [1867], fire royal salute, hoist royal standard, and perform such other evolutions as may best express their joy at the accomplishment of Confederation.'

Varying interpretations of the confederation years centre upon the problems of nationality, 'compact', *entente*, economic interest and political method. On the surface it seems clear enough that the process of founding a continental Canadian state differed profoundly from the American – that British, rather than American or French constitutional attitudes prevailed. No delegates were elected to a specifically constitutional convention, the basic Quebec Resolutions were approved by one of the legislatures involved, rejected in a general election in one province (New Brunswick) and never submitted to the Nova Scotia legislature. At the drafting conference in London, although Macdonald had previously suggested that the Quebec Resolutions were in the nature of a treaty to be accepted or rejected *in toto*, the ministerial delegates decided differently. After discussing the nature of their authority they decided they were not 'bound', and Macdonald himself summed up this discussion in London thus: 'The Conference can now quite understand our position, and we may now go on. We are quite free to discuss points as if they were open, although we may be bound to adhere to the Quebec scheme . . .'

This kind of logical contradiction, inherent in Macdonald's political artistry, crops up again and again in the confederation years as well as in the subsequent evolution of federal politics. It is symptomatic of the special intricacies of forming and governing a continental federation complicated by sharp racial and cultural differences. And it also leads to further difficulties of historical interpretation. In strictly formal or legal terms one cannot reasonably sustain a 'compact theory' of confederation. The provinces were not sovereign entities (such as the American revolutionary states considered themselves to be), and thus they could not legally 'delegate' some of their powers to a central authority which would then be their creature. Nor were 'the people' directly consulted. Clearly the federal Act flowed legally from London's imperial power. Yet the notion of compact has been and is still widely entertained.

The compact theory rests in part upon specific statements

made at several points in the long discussions, especially in the Canadian legislature. It depends, still more, upon the feeling that there was in the mid sixties an *entente* between the 'two founding races', an understanding about equality of status that went beyond the mere phrases on language and educational rights in the B.N.A. Act. While the concept of two equal founding partners has become prominent in recent years, it is difficult to find justification for it even in the by-ways of debate in the 1860s. Similarly, while English-speaking provincial premiers have not infrequently appealed to the 'understanding' that federal powers were to be essentially reserve powers, they have found little documentary support despite the fact that one hundred years after confederation something close to this situation seems to have matured. Ironically, too, in the case of the Maritimes, where generations of spokesmen in search of 'better terms' have argued plausibly that Nova Scotia and New Brunswick were coerced politically, one now finds widespread support for initiatives on the part of Ottawa.

In fact the terms '*entente*' and '*compact*' are largely unsatisfactory. Confederation was the product of identifiable interests, purposes and conditions which dictated specific political methods and carefully delineated agreements. Beyond doubt its central meaning was that of survival, and for each of the regions and cultures survival meant maintenance of a protective connexion with Britain. John Rose, who had just returned from settling claims arising from the Oregon Treaty, expressed this purpose in the Canadian debates. After stressing the dangerously wide support in Britain for the Manchester theory of colonial separation, Rose remarked:

... I put the case on this ground alone, that the necessity of self-preservation will for centuries – for generations at all events – prevent the possibility of these colonies asserting their independence of England, unless it were, indeed, to become a portion of the republic which adjoins us, and to which, I think, it is neither the interest nor the inclination of any member of this House to become united. (Hear hear.)

Each of the Canadian regions could and did applaud this sentiment. In the Maritimes much of the resistance to confederation found nourishment in a strong attachment to the empire and the fear that union with the Canadas would weaken both imperial ties and local autonomy. Pro-confederates in the Maritimes, conversely, saw continental union as essential to maintenance of those interests. In Canada West and amongst the English-speaking population of Canada East, continental expansion was, as we have seen, regarded as essential to the survival and prosperity of these central communities to which considerable loyalties had by now become attached. British protection and financing were as indispensable for acquiring the prairies and far west as they were for securing communications with the Maritimes. Moreover, the fears of anglicization which nagged at French-Canadian opponents of the scheme were minimized by identical considerations. Every pro-confederate French-Canadian speaker in the Canadian debate used lurid colours to depict the end of *la survivance*, of the 'French fact' in North America, if Canada were to be swallowed by the 'universal democracy' of the American republic.

While anti-Americanism as a function of survival frequently worries Canadians as being a negative basis for their nationality, it had and has distinctly positive aspects. Two, in particular, were prominent in the Confederation debate. The first was an attempt to avoid the weaknesses of American federalism revealed by the Civil War. Thus the cabinet system of responsible government was retained, 'residual powers' were given to the central, rather than to the new provincial governments, the criminal law was made a federal jurisdiction, and in other ways the central authority was stressed. The second positive aspect of this un-American survival was a good deal more subtle, and indeed potentially contradictory. This was the determination to construct a strong national state, one of whose essential purposes would be the guaranteeing of regional and minority rights. Rejecting the increasingly organic nationalism implicit in the Civil War, Canadians sought a positive, if loose-jointed definition of their own new national state. Nowhere is this goal more clearly stated than in Macdonald's contribution to the Canadian legislative debate in 1865.

Explaining the decision to abandon his earlier preference for a legislative union, and emphasizing the numerical inequality of the two language groups in British America, Macdonald remarked: 'In the first place a [legislative union] would not meet the assent of the people of Lower Canada, because they felt that in their peculiar position – being a minority, with a different language, nationality and religion from the majority – in case of a junction with the other provinces, their institutions and their laws might be assailed.'

Clearly, however, Macdonald used the word 'nationality' in two senses. In the same speech he went on to say that the new Canada would take its place amongst the nations of the world and, 'instead of looking upon us as a merely dependent colony, England will have in us a friendly nation'. He left no doubt about the full political meaning he attached to this use of 'nation' when he predicted that as Canada grew 'England will more see the advantage of maintaining the alliance between British North America and herself'. Canada was to be a federated national state: 'Thus we shall have a strong central government under which we can work out constitutional liberty as opposed to democracy, and be able to protect the minority by having a powerful central government.' These two notions of 'nationality', cultural and political, were in tension in the 1860s and are so today. The balance between them has remained uneasy yet the tension has produced a pragmatic politics receptive to change, suspicious of any form of totalitarian democracy, and deeply concerned with the multi-racial and multi-cultural problems that have come to dominate the twentieth century.

The British North America Act reflected all the considerations of environment, experience and ambition that we have mentioned. It was British in its assumptions of precedent and custom, and in the methods by which it was achieved. Relationships between the executive and the legislative branches (at both the provincial and federal levels) were not spelled out but responsible government was merely continued by the preample phrase 'a constitution similar in principle to that of the United Kingdom'. Although the sorely tested United States federal experiment was closely examined, it was used more as a warning than as a model. Thus, to avoid a 'states rights' open-

ing to the provinces, the central government was very purpose-
fully strengthened by giving to it 'all the great subjects of
legislation', and declaring that any un-named or residual powers
should reside in the central government. The provinces were
given only specific jurisdictions such as roads, direct taxation,
municipal institutions, legislation concerning 'property and
civil rights', and education. And even here, the federal government was empowered to remedy any provincial infringement
of the educational rights of minorities.

While provincial powers have been considerably enhanced by
court interpretation and political compromise in succeeding
years, such was certainly not the intention of most of the
'fathers'. Ottawa was given jurisdiction in such fields as trade
and commerce, all methods of taxation, defence, banking and
currency, and criminal law. But enumeration of these and other
federal powers was 'not so as to restrict the generality' of the
basic power 'to make Laws for the Peace, Order and good
Government of Canada, in relation to all Matters not coming
within the Classes of Subjects by this Act assigned exclusively
to the Legislature of the Provinces'. Moreover, Ottawa was to
appoint provincial lieutenant-governors who thus became in-
struments of the federal government and could reserve provincial legislation for federal approval or disallowance.

A governor-general, appointed by London, was to exercise
the chief executive powers of Canada on the advice of his
Canadian cabinet. His powers were those of 'honourable influence', the vague prerogative of refusing to grant dissolution of
parliament in extreme crises and of reserving dubious legislation for imperial consideration. Parliament itself was made
bi-cameral with an elective House of Commons and an appointive Senate. Population was the basis of representation in the
Commons, with the various provinces granted seats in proportion to the basic sixty-five prescribed for Quebec. The Senate
was at the time, and continued to be, the least satisfactory part
of the federal constitution. Designed partly to represent
regions, the new provinces of Ontario (Canada West) and
Quebec (Canada East) were each given 24 senators and the
Maritime provinces received 24 between them. But since all

the senators were to be appointed by Ottawa instead of by provincial governments or by election, their function as regional representatives was minimal. The second alleged purpose of the Senate was to act as a check against ill-considered actions by the Commons. But the confusion between the two purposes was exposed when Macdonald declared that the Senate was designed to protect minorities and 'the rich are always fewer in number than the poor'. In practice the Senate developed more as a convenient means of rewarding faithful party supporters whom it would be inconvenient or indiscreet to appoint to the bench or the cabinet. The result has been that the Senate has been even less successful than the House of Lords in opposing the full development of democratic politics centred in the Commons. It is now a distinct exception to find an important cabinet post filled by a senator.

The judicial system was a much more successful compromise between local and central powers. Administration of justice was left to the provinces, but above the county level Ottawa was to appoint the judges, provide their salaries and establish any federal courts it might deem necessary. This system left intact Quebec's civil law and also retained considerable provincial power over the definition of 'property and civil rights' elsewhere.

After spelling out the federal division of powers and providing for a small annual subsidy from the central to the local governments (based upon eighty cents per capita) the B.N.A. Act concluded with a section giving effect to two of the most central purposes of the confederation movement. The act's final clauses charged the central government with the duty of building a railway 'connecting the River St Lawrence with the City of Halifax' and empowered Ottawa (by a joint address to the Queen) to admit Newfoundland, Prince Edward Island and British Columbia into the 'Union' and similarly to admit Rupert's Land and the Northwest Territory into the federation. Although a B.N.A. Act amendment in 1871 and an imperial order-in-council in 1880 were required to tidy up some constitutional niceties in this connexion, in effect the act gave Ottawa the right, after negotiation with the curiously varied authorities of these regions, to incorporate within Canada the northern half of North America stretching to the Pole and excluding only Russian Alaska.

While the mixture of motives that produced the new national state was no purer than that which has produced other states, neither was that mixture identical with any other. If it had a strong infusion of simple economic self-interest (on both sides of the Atlantic), it had also a deep concern to avoid the Tocquevillean implications of 'majority tyranny'. Yet if there was suspicion of the direct democracy assumptions of the Americans, there was also a belief in the virtues of the parliamentary tradition and particularly in the pragmatic flexibility of that tradition. But above all there was a conviction that survival, with its connotations of regional cultural differences, could be ensured only by federation. And both risks and opportunities were embedded in this conviction.

For English-speaking central Canadians survival meant expansion and accumulating sufficient strength to resist continentalism. As the Ontario Grit-Liberal leader George Brown put it: 'The population of the Red River Settlement [in Rupert's Land] is now 12,000 and we must look forward to the day of settlement and occupation of that country. The inclusion of British Columbia and Vancouver Island is rather an extreme proposition, but it would be wrong to exclude them in the formation of the scheme. The Americans are encroaching.'

For most French Canadians survival meant guarding their language, religion and laws in the region they already occupied. With few exceptions French-Canadian emphasis was on the looseness of the new confederation. As E. P. Taché put it in his defence of the plan during the Canadian debate: 'If a federal union were obtained it would be tantamount to a separation of the provinces, and Lower Canada would thereby preserve its autonomy together with all the institutions it held so dear, and over which they could exercise the watchfulness and the surveillance necessary to preserve them unimpaired.'

The heavy shading of the meanings attached to nationalism, and to survival, was to take on sharper edges in the days of growth and frustration that lay ahead.

IO

Pragmatism and Diplomacy

CANADA'S future was no more predictable in 1867 than was that of the United States when viewed by over-sceptical European observers in the 1780s. The American Congress passed a resolution which expressed deep concern at the founding of a British monarchical state to the north; and in the same year W. H. Seward, the American secretary of state, purchased Alaska, whose probing panhandle sealed off half the coastline of British Columbia. Both Johnson and Grant gave the presidential nod to expansionist sentiment which was frequently used as a pressure in the long negotiations to settle outstanding disputes between Britain and the United States.

Perhaps it was fortunate that so much American energy was absorbed in the railway-building and other economic opportunities showered upon businessmen by the Great Barbecue in the years following the Civil War, and that the complexities of Reconstruction politics were so demanding. For, apart from sporadic propaganda in Congress and tentative diplomatic feelers, no sustained support came from Washington for those Americans who were actively penetrating the far west or who seriously sought annexation of Canada. Yet these are negative considerations. Without a positive Canadian policy of consolidation there is little doubt that most of the prairie and Pacific west would have gone to the United States by default. Such a policy was pursued with vigour and skill by Macdonald whose jaunty ways failed to conceal a deep patriotic conviction. All his conviction and wiles were required to solve the problems faced by the new state in both the east and the west – problems of provincial unrest, American penetration, foreign investment rights and even imperial diplomacy.

To no one's surprise the governor-general called upon Macdonald to form the first federal government. Nor was it unexpected that the coalition cabinet which had carried confederation in the Province of Canada should become the basis of the first federal administration. However, coalition rapidly gave way to party government which meant Conservative government. Macdonald facilitated the process by his judicious appointments, while George Brown had already left the coalition and was soon to be followed by other Grits. In this manner the Conservative Party, which had been established by the partnership of Cartier and Macdonald in 1854, became the first national party in the new Dominion and spread its organization into the Maritime provinces.

By taking care to have representatives in the cabinet from each province Macdonald also carried forward another pre-1867 practice which was to become central to the Canadian political method. The practice of regional representation in the cabinet virtually eliminated the representative function of the Senate and soon took on a still more complex quality. Not only provinces, but districts within provinces, religious and racial elements and major economic interests all came to place great store upon having 'their man' in the cabinet. The post-election correspondence of each succeeding prime minister is heavily larded with letters from bishops, Grand Masters of the Orange Lodge and other 'group spokesmen', interspersed with eloquent recommendations from railway presidents and brewers, all seeking a 'just' and 'balanced' representation in the cabinet. While the method has provided cement for the national party system it has also, on occasion, underlined the inability of a particular party to represent evenly all sections of the country. It has also meant that the cabinet-makers have frequently had to calculate the group power of a candidate rather than his inherent qualities of mind and experience.

In 1867 Macdonald moved with assurance into the stormy new region of federal politics. Overwhelming majorities against confederation had been elected to the Nova Scotia legislature and to that province's representation in the federal House of Commons. Joseph Howe once again tried to persuade London to repeal the union legislation. Yet while every opposition avenue was explored, even secession and annexation to the

United States, the repeal movement gradually weakened and Macdonald saw his opening. In 1869 a bargain was reached whereby Ottawa increased Nova Scotia's annual subsidy and Joseph Howe entered the federal cabinet – to cries of 'traitor' and to Sir John A. Macdonald's intense satisfaction. With New Brunswick's Leonard Tilley already a member of the federal government, the worst dangers of Atlantic particularian were past. By 1873 Prince Edward Island had succumbed to similar 'better terms', and by 1876 the Intercolonial Railway had been built by the federal government.

Success in this kind of inter-regional diplomacy and in attracting the active support of the most significant economic interests of central Canada made the Macdonald Conservatives the dominant national party from 1867 to 1896. During those years Conservative power was interrupted only by one Liberal interlude from 1873 to 1878. In each province the Liberals (a name gradually accepted by Grits, Rouges and Reformers) espoused provincial rights, retrenchment and less prodigal use of federal funds for expansion. This essentially negative approach on the federal political level was a serious disadvantage to the Liberals who remained much more loosely organized and a readier prey to provincialist dissension, especially since they lacked the federal largesse whose judicious disposal did much to feed Conservative loyalties.

Yet it was not 'boodling' alone that kept Sir John A. Macdonald at the helm. Intensely committed to the idea of a continent-wide national state he pursued his goal relentlessly. If he sometimes paid too little attention to detail, or assessed incorrectly concern about local autonomy or strict political probity, he more than made up for his peccadilloes by the dash and imagination which were the *sine qua non* of an improbably huge task. Nowhere were daring and free-handed determination more evident than in the acquisition of the west.

In 1869 the first big hurdle to the west was cleared. In return for a £300,000 cash payment, 45,000 acres of land adjacent to its trading posts and further land to be selected later, the Hudson's Bay Company relinquished its ancient Rupert's Land charter and its trading monopoly throughout the Northwest

Territory. Although the terms were tough and the powerful company pocketed one-twentieth of the land in the fertile belt (including some very rich mineral deposits), the deal was eased when London underwrote a loan to Canada to cover the purchase price.

But if the company appeared grasping, and if it operated under an inter-locking directorate with the Grand Trunk Railway to wring maximum profit from the Canadian west, the mixture of motives amongst those Canadians who were interested in the region was no less intricate. Ontario farmers saw the prairies as a huge patrimony for their sons and daughters and clothed this feeling in the doctrine of 'rights'. They and their commercial friends who spoke for Ontario Grit-Liberalism worked on the assumption that, west of the Ottawa River, Canada would naturally be an English-speaking culture and one for which the economic metropolis would be Toronto rather than Montreal. On the other hand, English-speaking Montrealers cherished the dream of building a successor to their old fur-trading empire in the west – a successor which would thrive on the profits of transportation, marketing, commercial investment and natural resources development. Finally, French Canadians disagreed profoundly with the English-speaking western purposes. They were prepared to resist vigorously any attempt to undermine existing cultural rights in the west or to render the region inhospitable to future French-speaking settlement.

In 1869 the Northwest Territories reverted to the Crown pending transfer to Canada whenever Ottawa should be prepared to accept the responsibility. In the whole of this western empire there was a settled population of about 7,000. And even this figure is misleading, for many of the westerners spent most of their time hunting or in services ancillary to the Hudson's Bay Company operations. Fort Garry, on the present site of Winnipeg, was the hub of settlement. Its population of slightly more than 5,000 was composed of Métis (mixed Indian and white) of both Scottish and French descent, scattered English-speaking farmers, a handful of Americans from St Paul and a small group of very active Canadians from Ontario. Many of the Red River valley Métis depended upon the highly organized buffalo hunt and some were developing agriculture beyond the subsistence point. Most had an interest in the slowly growing trade south to Minnesota.

Despite its minuscule population the Fort Garry community had developed a distinct sense of identity, almost a nascent nationality. Since 1821 these people had had few direct connexions with central Canada, while the route by boat and trail to St Paul was over 500 miles long. Few of them felt like 'Canadians', fewer felt like Americans, and even the presence of French-Canadian priests and Anglican and Methodist missionaries did little to establish ties with the east. Isolation, a mere trickle of immigration, practical bilingualism and an increasing mixture of the races all heightened the sense of differentness. As a son of the region wrote in 1861:

. . . it is an interesting fact that the half castes or mixed race, not only far outnumber all the other races in the colony put together, but engross nearly all the more important and intellectual offices – furnishing from their number the sheriff, medical officer, the postmaster, all the teachers but one, a fair proportion of the magistrates and one of the electors and proprietors of the only newspaper in the Hudson's Bay territories.

In another letter of the same period a prominent Red River inhabitant underlined the racial tolerance and near-pride of a common racial bond that provided an *entente* between French- and English-speaking compatriots: 'What if mama *were* an Indian?'

Such a community did not view dispassionately the interested fingers which were reaching towards the northern prairies from Ontario and Minnesota as the Hudson's Bay Company authority waned. Of particular concern by 1868 were the activities and loudly voiced assumptions of the 'Canadian party' of merchants, journalists and speculators. Advance agents of an English-speaking Canadian nationalism, these men laid plans for an amphibious communications route with central Canada and for the social-economic restructuring of the Red River colony. Unhappily, Macdonald ignored completely the manifold warnings of trouble. Before obtaining legal transfer of the

Northwest from British authority, Ottawa sent land-surveyors to the Red River who worked closely with the Canadian party and began a square land survey which ran athwart the slender river-front farms of the Métis. Threatened by a takeover without prior consultation on the form of government, the settlers prepared for serious resistance.

Louis Riel, a native French Métis of the Red River, quickly emerged as leader of a full-fledged rebellion. Educated at the clerical College of Montreal, Riel showed both intelligence and determination, although later events in his life were to raise questions about his stability. When Macdonald compounded his first mistake by appointing the Ontario expansionist William McDougall as governor to take over the colony (still without consulting the inhabitants or receiving the official transfer from Britain), the Métis blocked McDougall's entry to the colony. Then, after occupying strong points, Riel and his colleagues summoned a convention. Faced by continued assertion of the 'governor's' authority, many English-speaking colonists supported the rebellion and agreed to a list of rights. In order to negotiate with Canada on the basis of these rights, Riel then set up a provisional government. The position of the rebels was made clear not only in the list of rights but in a newspaper, the *New Nation*, which wrote:

... If it be said that the government [of Canada] ought not to be held responsible for the failings of individual officials, we reply that the government ought to have been more circumspect in their selection of officials, and they ought to have sent sensible men instead of snobs and shabby genteel fools.

The contemplation of the whole panorama fills us with indignation. We *may* be a small community, and a Half-breed community at that – but we are men, free and spirited men, and we will not allow even the Dominion of Canada to trample on our rights.

When the Canadian party threatened further armed resistance to the provisional government, Riel executed one of the Canadians who had been arrested earlier. Unhappily, Riel had chosen to make an example of a man who was not only arrogant and recalcitrant, but who was also an Orangeman from Ontario. The name of Thomas Scott at once became the centre of violent racial controversy in central Canada. Ontarians of both parties demanded a military expedition and Riel's head. Quebeckers saw Riel as a courageous defender of French and Catholic cultural rights and Scott as the agent of Ontario imperialism. In this dangerous political crisis Macdonald mixed conciliation with a show of force. He sent to Fort Garry an expedition of British regulars and Canadian militia which had a double utility. It showed Americans that Ottawa could still count upon some British power in asserting Canadian western claims, and it appeased Protestant suspicions in Ontario. At the same time he received a delegation from the Red River with which Ottawa negotiated the terms of entry into Confederation. Since these terms included all the essential rights demanded by Riel it is perhaps no exaggeration to say that this first Riel rebellion was in fact a successful democratic revolution. Although Riel had acted in a practical power vacuum he had in fact subverted the Canadian-ordained government of the region and replaced it with a much more representative system.

Ottawa's Manitoba Act of 1870 established the new province and gave it the same system of government as the others except that, like Quebec, there were guarantees for the equality of French and English as official languages, and for denominational schools, both Protestant and Roman Catholic. The one restriction on the powers of the Manitoba government was that ungranted lands in the province were to be 'administered by the Government of Canada for the purposes of the Dominion'. The purposes were clear enough: encouragement of immigration and subsidization of railways. And both these policies were to involve Canadian governments in immense controversy. Nevertheless, for the time being the Red River, Quebec and Ontario were all mollified. Before the military expedition from central Canada reached the scene, Riel had decided to leave for the United States and in October of 1871 the fundamental loyalty of the Métis was shown when they gathered to turn back a local Fenian raid from the south. With the prairies safely incorporated in the Dominion, Manitoba was left to work out (not very successfully) the implications of racial-religious tolerance and Macdonald turned his attention to securing the Pacific coast.

Like the prairies, the Pacific coast had been held in trust (if unwittingly) for Canada by the Hudson's Bay Company. In 1849 London created the colony of Vancouver Island to forestall loss of 'northern Oregon' by default to the settlement drive of the Americans. But the growing sway of Little Englandism meant that the Company rather than the British government would be, until 1858, the real custodian. When the mainland Cariboo gold strike of 1856 enticed prospectors north from the fading eldorado of California (as well as ever-restless settlers from Washington and Oregon territories), Governor James Douglas of Vancouver Island simply proclaimed his authority over the mainland. He wrote:

My authority for issuing that proclamation, seeing that it refers to certain districts of continental America, which are not strictly speaking, within the jurisdiction of this Government may perhaps, be called in question; but I trust that the motives which have influenced me on this occasion and the fact of my being invested with the authority over the premises of the Hudson's Bay Company, and the only authority commissioned by Her Majesty within reach, will plead my excuse. Moreover, should Her Majesty's Government not deem it advisable to enforce the rights of the Crown, as set forth in the proclamation, it may be allowed to fall to the ground and to become a mere dead letter.

Fortunately for the future Canada, London did in fact deem it advisable to enforce the rights of the Crown. In 1858 the colony of British Columbia was established ('British', as the Queen put it, because 'the citizens of the United States call their country also Columbia, at least in poetry').

This sequence of events in the far west is immensely suggestive in any interpretation of the cultural attitudes of English-speaking Canadians. For not only was the region preserved for the future Dominion, a familiar pattern was repeated. The establishment of courts and English common law, use of the army to carry out basic 'internal improvements' planned by the government, and emphasis on the continuing link with Britain all served to modify the impact of regional isolation.

That Canadians, both French- and English-speaking, have usually looked to government for the establishment of cultural patterns (and not to 'compact' or self-constituted government) has been a prominent factor amongst the many influences which make Canada different from the United States. The pervasive habits of mind which were early established are suggested by the fact that it was Canada's first Grit-Liberal prime minister, Alexander Mackenzie, who founded the Royal North-West Mounted Police in 1873 for the specific purpose of ensuring a non-American type of development in the prairie west.

In 1861 British Columbia's population was slightly more than 50,000. Of all the regions of British North America its culture was most influenced by the United States. Yet it was also, largely *because* of the threatening impact of the American mining frontier, an outstanding example of the countervailing force of a consciously imposed political-cultural pattern within a context where regional separatism was almost indigenous and the pulls of a neighbouring region were strong. In English-speaking central Canada the whole Northwest came to appear as a solution to the regional problems, both economic and ethnic, of the rest of the country. Yet there were real dangers to this aspect of expansion. While a racial *modus vivendi*, which at times went beyond the transitory, existed in central Canada, the nature and the opportunities of the Northwest were to tempt English-speaking Canadians to the unwise conclusion that English-speaking culture should become clearly dominant across the whole west of the Dominion – that somehow this was natural. It proved easy to elaborate a kind of social-Darwinist, racial-superiority doctrine to prove why the 'true north, strong and free' should be basically anglo-saxon.

Long-standing economic ambitions allied with a growing sense of English-speaking nationalism determined the future of British Columbia. In 1869, with plenty of help from central Canadians, a pro-Confederation movement in the colony swung opinion away from previous flirtation with American union. With mild approval from London, a British Columbian delegation made its way to Ottawa where, in 1871, a bargain was

struck providing for British Columbia's entrance into Confederation as a province. The inducements held out by Ottawa
were powerful. They included federal assumption of the new
province's accumulated debt and, of more lasting significance,
a promise to build a railway to the Pacific. The line was to be
started in 1873 and completed by 1883. It was a tall order but it
was also the only possible guarantee that British Columbia
would not fall into the United States orbit. In 1869 the first
United States transcontinental railway was completed and it
was not by accident that the terms of union declared that the
purpose of the promised Canadian Pacific road was 'to connect
the seaboard of British Columbia with the railway system of
Canada'. Nor was it surprising that, after this feat was accomplished, British Columbia illustrated well (as did the Maritimes)
the difficulty of a purely deterministic interpretation of history.
Political and cultural inclinations in both regions were reinforced by decisions to subsidize their relationship to the rest of
the country. While the benefits of such subsidization were very
great indeed to the capitalists of central Canada, they were by
no means insignificant to what one Liberal politician called 'the
rags and ends of Confederation'. Moreover, if each of the seaboard regions appeared physically as a northward thrust of a
contiguous American region, the fact that their economic
potentials and resources were similar seemed to breed competition and distrust more often than a desire for assimilation.

Railway planning in Canada, then, as in Bismarck's Germany,
Cavour's Italy or U. S. Grant's America, seemed essential to
nation-building. But so too were more general economic
policies. And, while Canada was a trailer in the late nineteenth-century race to match or outrun Britain's industrialism,
she shared the widely felt need both for protection and
market expansion. Thus Macdonald and his business supporters
thought naturally of a renewal of the reciprocity agreement
with the United States which had been abrogated in 1866. In
1871 an opportunity to pursue negotiations to this end presented itself. Unfortunately the opening was within the context of extremely complicated British-American diplomacy
and, before the passage was cleared, the government was

toppled in a snarl of railway corruption, diplomatic frustration and national reassessment.

In 1871 the American government invited Britain to a conference in Washington for the purpose of settling a number of outstanding issues. Some of the problems resulted from the international tensions generated by the Civil War, and particularly from claims for damage done by Confederate commerce raiders, such as the *Alabama*, which had been built in British yards. But others involved Canada very directly. Nor was there any doubt as to the expansive American hope that Canada might become the principal source of compensation. The particular issues included disagreement about the boundary line between Vancouver Island and the United States, and the rights of Americans in the inshore fisheries of the Maritimes. Because the negotiations involved Canadian interests directly, Macdonald was named as a member of the British delegation. Yet, while this action seemed to recognize an enhanced status for Canada, in fact Macdonald's experience with this form of common imperial diplomacy was bitter in the extreme and he very nearly refused to sign the final conference agreement.

In accepting the invitation Macdonald thought he had several good bargaining counters with which to pry out a new reciprocity agreement. These included Canadian claims for damage done by Fenian raids, American use of the Canadian St Lawrence and Welland canals, and relaxation of the fisheries regulations. The last point seemed particularly strong. With the lapsing of the reciprocity agreement in 1866 American inshore fishing rights reverted to the highly restrictive basis of the 1818 convention. In 1870, after abortive tariff discussions, the Canadian government rescinded its temporary licensing system, sent forth patrol vessels and impounded some 400 American fishing ships for infringement of the 1818 agreement. This action, however, merely increased American intransigence and it is more than likely that had the negotiations not been under imperial aegis (and involving British as well as Canadian interests) the outcome for Canada would have resembled that experienced by Mexico in 1848.

Macdonald raged against the attitude of his English colleagues during the negotiations in Washington. To Tupper he wrote: 'The U.S. Commissioners ... found our English friends so squeezable in nature that their audacity has grown beyond all bounds.' Yet, while the final settlement ignored most of the Canadian arguments, it was by no means totally unacceptable. The Americans gained a ten-year access to the fisheries (for which Canada was later awarded $5 million by arbitration); the western Juan de Fuca boundary was settled by arbitration as were the *Alabama* claims; Canadian fish were admitted free of duty into the United States; and an understanding was reached governing mutual carrying and navigation rights on the Great Lakes and St Lawrence. While the Americans refused to consider Canada's Fenian claims Great Britain compensated Canada directly for some of the Fenian damage. Perhaps Sir Stafford Northcote, one of the British delegates, was right when he wrote to Disraeli:

I think that the general effect of [the Treaty] is decidedly favourable to Canada, and that the only thing she loses (and that for a short term of years) is a whip which she likes to crack for the purpose of driving Americans into bargains, but which she would have been very foolish if she attempted to use. ... But beyond this, I am convinced that if it could truly be said that if any local interests had been sacrificed for the sake of a general settlement of imperial questions, it could not be said that the interests sacrificed were those of Canada, and that the party for whose benefit the sacrifice was made was England; for I believe that no part of the empire has so direct and immediate an interest in the maintenance of friendly relations between us and the Americans as Canada herself.

To Macdonald the tenor of such remarks, if not the specific words, rang true. Aware that the last British troops (save for a small garrison at the Halifax naval station) left Canada in 1871, he knew that Canada would have to accept any grinding down of her own interests that might be incident to a balanced imperial diplomacy. Nevertheless, as Macdonald also feared, the Treaty of Washington was received in Canada, especially by hypercritical Liberals, with about as much enthusiasm as that with which Americans had greeted Jay's Treaty in 1794. Across the country Liberals castigated Macdonald for his 'abject surrender'. In this nationalist issue Liberals felt they had found the necessary cement to bind together their loose alliance of disgruntled provincial organizations. And into their hopeful hands the Conservatives shoved the clinching argument of corruption.

In order to force the pace of economic and population growth as well as to fulfil the bargain made with British Columbia, the Conservatives had resorted to the old Canadian version of North American neo-mercantilism. Railway building and ancillary development were to be spurred by close (and often secret) consultation between government and business leaders. This meant, as in the day of Loyalist land grants and of pre-Confederation railway subsidization, very close ties between governments and favoured business groups. But in the 1870s a new dimension was added by the immense size of the transcontinental operation. To cope with the problem the Conservatives emulated the methods of President Grant's 'Great Barbecue'. That is, they sought to tempt capitalists into accepting the staggering responsibility of the Pacific railway by offering vast land grants in the unsettled reaches of the west in addition to cash subsidies and other privileges. The original offer involved $30 million and fifty million acres of prime western land.

To compete for this bonanza two syndicates were organized, one in Toronto and one in Montreal. Senator D. L. Macpherson's Toronto group was supported by the Grand Trunk with considerable influence in the English money market, and Sir Hugh Allan's Montreal group had heavy American support from Jay Cooke's Northern Pacific – with the clear implication of eventual American control of the Canadian road. Thus sectional competition between Montreal and Toronto for domination of the anticipated western markets was compounded by nationalist fears which were sedulously 'fanned by the Grand Trunk-Toronto group. When the government failed to induce an amalgamation Sir Hugh Allan decided he could win the contract by forcing Cartier (who was still connected with the Grand Trunk) to shift his support inside the cabinet to the Montreal group. By bribing editors and reporters and making political trouble in

Quebec, Allan forced the mortally ailing and incautious Cartier to capitulate. As Allan later wrote: 'I went to the country through which the road would pass, and called on many of the inhabitants. I visited the priests, and made friends with them, and I employed agents to go amongst the principal people and talk it up.' Furthermore, Allan made it clear that in the 1872 election he would provide enough money to enable the Conservatives to fight effectively the charges of ignoring the national interest in the Treaty of Washington and of tolerating the threat of American financial domination. While Macdonald himself made it clear that he would not promise the Pacific charter in advance of the election, there is no doubt that Allan, encouraged by Cartier, believed a Conservative victory would bring him the contract. As the perilous 1872 elections approached, Cartier wrote to Allan:

Dear Sir Hugh,
    The friends of the Government will expect to be assisted with funds in the pending elections, and any amount which you or your company shall advance for that purpose shall be recouped to you. A memorandum of immediate requirements is below ...

By the time the election was run the requirements had amounted to some $350,000 and even Macdonald had wired to Allan: 'I must have another ten thousand; will be the last time of calling; do not fail me; answer today.'

The government was returned with a reduced majority and, after Allan reorganized his company to minimize American participation, he was awarded the contract. But the price was too high. When the Liberals uncovered evidence of what George Brown's Toronto *Globe* called 'the Thermopylae of Canadian virtue', a royal commission was appointed and filled in the gaps of collusion and corruption. In November 1873, deserted by some of its own supporters and deprived of the governor-general's 'honourable influence', the Macdonald government resigned.

Writing privately to Lord Dufferin, the governor-general, Macdonald defended his own position and also summed up the philosophy and nature of contemporary Canadian politics. In the election, he noted, the government was extremely hard pressed on both diplomatic and domestic grounds. Moreover the Liberals controlled the Ontario provincial government and were using all its patronage over licensing timber limits, mining rights and other franchises to build up opposition to the Conservatives on the federal level. It was therefore not unnatural for the Conservatives to look to their supporters for funds, which, in any case, was a perfectly proper procedure, especially since Macdonald had personally assured Allan that a reorganization of his company would certainly be demanded before any contract would be given. But it was not just an ordinary political battle according to Macdonald, for,

From my point of view, I considered that on the result of the elections depended the continuance of Confederation. I may be wrong, but my opinion then was, and still is, that in the hands of the present Opposition [the Liberals], connected with and supported, as they are, by the 'alien', 'annexation', and 'independent' elements, Confederation would not last ten years.

Allan's role, according to Macdonald, was that which might be expected of any enlightened capitalist:

It was therefore of importance, to his interests and the undertaking with which he had so connected himself, that a Parliament favourable to such enterprises, and to the development of the country thereby, should be elected, and, as a man of business, he expended his money accordingly. And it suited the purposes of the Ministerial party to accept his subscriptions, as well as the subscriptions of others.

The Conservative party in England does not repudiate the action of the brewers and distillers and the Association of Licensed Victuallers in electing candidates in their interests. ... Our misfortune was that, by the base betrayal of these private communications, the names of certain members of the Government, including myself, were mixed up in the obtaining of these subscriptions. Had this betrayal not taken place, it would have been only known that Sir Hugh Allan, and the railways with which he had been connected, had taken a decided line in supporting one party in preference to another, by their influence and money.

But the base betrayal did take place and the government fell.

The Conservatives were replaced by the new country's first Liberal administration which, if it was not entirely a stranger to the ways of power, yet took a very hostile view of the *extent* of the 'pacific Scandal', and of the implications of extravagance in the Macdonald approach to nation-building.

II

The Politics of Purity

ALEXANDER MACKENZIE, who became Liberal prime minister at the end of 1873, was a contractor and editor from Sarnia at the south-western tip of the Ontario peninsula. His excessive caution, prosaic cast of mind and the fact that he began adult life as a stone mason prompted not a few quips. Goldwin Smith, England's famous intellectual expatriate, declared from his editorial chair in Toronto that Mackenzie's most distinguishing characteristic could be seen in the fact that he was 'a stone-mason still'. If so, Mackenzie certainly put together a curiously unbalanced governmental structure. Yet if Mackenzie lacked a commanding and imaginative personality it is probable that no other Liberal of the day would have been much more successful than he was in the face of a formidable set of political and economic disadvantages.

Mackenzie presided over a party and a government which expressed the least cohesive aspects of the young nation state. Mackenzie himself represented the old Grit agrarian tradition. Suspicious of prodigality, privilege, Roman Catholicism and 'big business', it was symptomatic that he gave himself the portfolio of public works and, like a junior Philip II, was perpetually bogged down in administrative detail. As finance minister Mackenzie chose Sir Richard Cartwright. A Conservative *manqué* and Kingston banker, Cartwright became chief spokesman for the doctrinaire free trade wing of the Liberal Party. While Cartwright was certainly no small businessman defender of the farmers, he nevertheless alienated most manufacturing and transportation interests by his opposition to tariff protection and a growing inclination towards commercial union with the United States.

A very different kind of Liberal opinion found its spokesman in the intellectually powerful, if mercurial, Edward Blake.

Descendant of a prosperous Anglo-Irish family, his father had been a prominent Reform leader and had risen to become chancellor of Upper Canada. Blake himself had attended the prestigious Anglican Upper Canada College and the University of Toronto. A brilliant barrister, he became premier of Ontario in 1871 and entered the Mackenzie government in 1873 as minister without portfolio. Clearly uneasy at having to work under a leader for whose policy and attitudes he had little respect, Blake resigned in 1874 in an attempt to rally a more positive nationalism, but soon returned to the cabinet as minister of justice and to a role which underlined the division of the party.

If the Liberals were divided and uncertain upon entering office, their problems were immeasurably deepened by the onset of the world-wide depression which was to undulate its crippling course right down to 1896. With sharply declining revenues and stony-faced money markets, Liberal fiscal caution became a necessity as well as a choice. Forced to adopt a policy of governmental railway construction, Mackenzie secured the laying of about 700 miles of track in Northern Ontario. Defended on the ground that railways should not outstrip the advance of settlement and that interconnecting waterways and American lines should be used at first as an economy measure, this policy produced no enthusiasm in the country. British Columbia charged that Mackenzie had broken the ten-year completion bargain, and in the political storm that resulted the British colonial secretary and the governor-general intervened in a manner which infuriated Mackenzie and raised questions about the vice-regal role in Canadian government. Moreover, when another effort to obtain a reciprocal trade agreement with the United States seemed close to success in 1874, it was rejected by the American Senate.

Balked ambitions, both regional and national, produced an ominous anti-Liberal ground swell. But even more significant than the general political problems of the federal Liberals was the varied nature of the malaise and the maturing cultural patterns it suggests.

In English-speaking central Canada, and especially in Ontario, fears that the experiment of confederation was about to founder amongst the shoals of regionalism, racial differences and lack of national conviction, led to efforts to create a more positive national spirit. In 1871 a number of young business and professional men in Toronto joined the Canada First movement which had been founded three years earlier by a group of intellectual patriots. Spurred by what they felt to be a betrayal of the national interest in the Treaty of Washington and encouraged by support from many writers and journalists, Canada First enjoyed a brief but significant life. Patriotic pieces and first-rate political comment graced the pages of its journal, the *Nation* (1874–6). Goldwin Smith lent his pen and influence while some of the more sophisticated politicians of both parties endorsed a tentative Canada First platform. Edward Blake, as leader of the urban wing of the Liberals, helped found a second nationalist paper, the *Liberal*, and in 1874, while briefly outside the Mackenzie administration, delivered a stirring address in which he seemed to accept the role of chief Canada First spokesman.

While the National Club in Toronto, the movement's principal gathering place, was certainly not socialistic in the manner of Edward Bellamy's American Nationalist Clubs of the late eighties or of the British Fabians, Canada First's principles did call for much more positive government policies than those offered by Mackenzie. 'The time will come,' declared Blake, 'when we shall realize that we are four millions of Britons who are not free.' The emphasis given to the need of Canada to have power to negotiate her own treaties led to charges by the *Globe* and more orthodox Grit-Liberals that Canada First aimed at dissolution of the empire. This was countered by arguments which were to become central to Canada's majority attitudes: 'The Empire is quite equal to the duty of self-care; its interests will be best served by our doing, or trying to do, the best possible for ourselves, and the whole be best strengthened by giving strength to its weakest part.'

As to how the 'weakest part' might best be strengthened Canada First expressed some interesting, if contradictory, views which are important because they remained the staples of political debate down to the 1930s. Prominent amongst the Canada First principles was that the revenue-raising tariff should be 'so adjusted as to afford every possible encouragement to Native Industry'. Support for higher tariff protection grew rapidly amongst the budding industrialists and growing working class of central Canada, especially after the 1874 failure to renegotiate reciprocity with the United States and with the continuance of the depression. Blake's efforts to convert the Liberals to protection during the seventies and eighties failed, but the Conservatives took heart from the evident popularity of the Canada First proposal and were to ride back to power by vigorously reasserting a protective policy.

Canada First also called for a curious combination of external policies: 'consolidation' of the empire 'and in the meantime a voice in treaties affecting Canada', and 'closer trade relations with the West Indies, with a view to ultimate political connexion'. The implications of overseas expansion proved too heady for the experimental Canadian state, and vague notions of imperial consolidation were obviously in tension with the assertive nationalism of the other planks. Yet clearly enough Canada First was deeply concerned about both the means and purposes of national survival. Continuance of close relations with the empire (however tense they might be) was essential to that survival as was also the creation of a growing population and industrial base. And to justify the claims to survival the movement demanded some basic internal reforms including an income franchise, secret ballot and compulsory voting, special representation of minorities, and reorganization of the Senate. But Canada Firsters gave heaviest emphasis to 'nationality', and in so doing reiterated the position taken by Macdonald in the Confederation Debates – that cultural nationality must be protected while a new political nationality was being developed. As W. A. Foster put it in an address to the Canadian National Association:

Our earnest desire is to do away with all invidious distinctions of nationality, creed, locality or class, and to unite the people of the Dominion, as Canadians, through affection and pride in Canada, their home. A serious impediment to our progress towards unity has been, and, unfortunately, still is, the hostility of *creed towards creed*, nationality towards nationality, class towards class, section towards section, which faction for its own selfish temporary purposes, provokes and political sharpers systematically use.

Canada First was supported by men who, like Edward Blake, realized the importance of treating French Canada as a cultural nation, and of making it possible for her leaders to associate themselves creatively with a federal party. It also contained men who took two very different views of French Canada and Canadian destiny. One view, best represented by Goldwin Smith, was that of rationalist liberalism with an intellectual legacy reaching back to the Roundheads. To Smith, French Canada was hopelessly priest-ridden, obscurantist and corrupt. It was like a drag-anchor against Canadian progress. Smith, after briefly flirting with an independent Canadian nationality, turned to a defeatist concept (which he believed to be the grand operation of history). This was the reunification of the Anglo-Saxon peoples: the undoing of the American Revolution. While he saw this as the *sine qua non* for removing from Canadian life parochial post-office politics, and even the larger corruption of railway politics, and replacing them with the civilizing purposes of Anglo-Saxondom, in more immediate terms his idea boiled down to American annexation. Despite the frustrations of the 1880s and early nineties, those who agreed with Smith declined steadily in influence. In 1891 Smith published his *Canada and the Canadian Question* in which sprightly volume he reviewed the reasons for Canadian backwardness and recommended that Canada should become the Scotland of North America. Within five years the depression which had given some colour to his arguments began to lift and 'continentalism' once again retired in disrepute.

Another wing of Canada First took a quite different view of French Canada and the Canadian future. These men, many of whom were to be prophets of Imperial Federation, saw Canada's future security and greatness as irrevocably bound up with the future of the empire. Elaborating a racial-climatic mystique of northern superiority, they obviously shared with Smith a wayward faith in racial supremacy. Unlike Smith they were basically conservative. And they tailored their doctrine to suit their purpose. Thus, wishing to avert continental union, they argued that the population of the United States was not only increasingly mongrel but was also prey to the debilitating effects of a more southerly climate. The northern races of Europe, especially the 'Anglo-Saxons', were the true custodians of constitutional liberty and martial valour. Canada, the progeny of these races, was assured of greatness as long as she kept up her association with the right people. Blessed with a northern clime, she would probably continue to attract only people from like climates. R. G. Haliburton, one of Canada First's peregrinating lecturers, put it succinctly: 'We are the Northmen of the New World' and, sealing the implications of this rhetorically, 'If climate has not had the effect of moulding races, how is it that southern nations have almost invariably been inferior to and subjugated by the men of the north?'

Curiously, down to 1896, those English-speaking Canadians who gave most vigorous voice to Anglo-Saxon superiority notions were also those who seemed best able to get along politically with French Canadians, and they provided the Conservatives with a romantic version of French Canada which enabled the Tories to sustain their optimism about conservative national purposes. According to this version the French Canadians not only measured up to the responsibilities of self-government (because, while they were not Anglo-Saxon, they *were* from the *northern* portions of France), but they also had other positive cultural virtues. They believed in a Christian society, they shared a common loyalty to the Crown, they preferred a hierarchical and agrarian society and held suspect the crasser aspects of liberalism and industrialism. In short they could be trusted as a stabilizing force in the growth of an organic Canadian society.

All of this conservative theorizing was to be flushed down the drain by the crisis of the First World War when doubts about rushing to the defence of the northern imperial capital of London severely inhibited the martial instincts of French Canadians. The imperialist, national-unity wing of Canada First had been guilty of very wishful thinking. There were plenty of straws in the wind before 1917 to denote the real direction of French-Canadian development. Indeed a careful reading of the Confederation movement itself would have helped the conservative imperialists to a more realistic assessment. In the meantime, and certainly down to the Liberal election victory of 1896, the Conservatives managed to retain federal power with the help of the *Castor* and *Bleu* sections of Quebec voters, i.e. the right-wing and middle bodies of opinion. Fearful that the Liberal government which took power under Mackenzie in 1873 would be merely a parenthesis to unbroken Conservative domination, the Liberals were furious. Inside French Canada, Liberalism (the Rouges) waged an uphill battle. Pitted against them were the *Castors*, most of the *Bleus*, the bulk of the English-speaking business community, and the Roman Catholic hierarchy. Held together by mutual benefits, this powerful alliance of interests was to be shaken only when the federal Conservative Party betrayed the hopes of French Canada – specifically in the west and generally by centralizing and anglicizing the federal system.

Continuing to view Quebec as the racial homeland of French Canadians, the political spokesmen of Quebec had to perform a delicate balancing act. While jealously guarding provincial rights they had also frequently to protest the actions of other provincial governments and to seek the use of federal powers to ensure equality of rights for those French Canadians who moved into other regions of the country. Loud protests were occasioned by New Brunswick's withdrawal of public funds from separate (Catholic) schools. Strong demands were raised for the legal use of French in the Northwest Territories. Concern was expressed for the fate of French Canadians in Ontario who, by 1880, numbered nearly 100,000. But in the Quebec homeland the leaders of the Conservative-clerical alliance developed ever more completely the potent political ideology of French and Catholic survival.

Against the claims of Liberalism the hierarchy mustered a Canadian version of European ultramontanism. To Liberals who fought against clerical intervention in politics and who argued that Conservatism bred corruption and favoured Eng-

lish-speaking big business, the Church replied that Liberalism
was irreligious. Taking his cue from Pope Pius IX, Bishop Bourget of Montreal led a fearsome crusade against the Rouges.
Mandements and pastoral letters warned against the secularizing sins of Liberalism. The *Institut Canadien*, a rationalist
literary society which boasted the membership not only of moderate Rouge lawyers like Wilfrid Laurier but also of repatriated
rebels like Louis Joseph Papineau, was pronounced anathema.
The pronouncement was endorsed by Rome, and Catholics who
continued their membership were refused the sacraments. The
war was carried to the knife. When, in 1869, one Joseph Guibord died without having renounced his membership in the
Institut, the Church refused to bury his body in a Catholic
cemetery. Friends of Guibord took the case to court. Finally,
in 1874, the Judicial Committee of the Privy Council decided on
appeal that the Church could not refuse the Guibord claims.
When a funeral procession tried to move the body to conse-
crated ground it was halted by an angry mob and turned back.
Then, under the protection of a troop detachment 1,000 strong,
Guibord was buried and the grave covered with reinforced
concrete against reprisal. But in the end Bourget won his battle.
He deconsecrated the ground.

The Bishops then went forward on all fronts. Endorsing a
Catholic programme which condemned the doctrine of separation of church and state, they asserted and exercised the right
of continuous and direct intervention in the political process.
Pastoral letters and sermons thundered against the sin of liberalism, endorsed Conservative candidates, and even threatened
loss of the sacraments to those who defected. The more moderate members of the clergy who doubted the wisdom of this
extremism were drowned out by a chorus of ultramontane
piety. The man who was to do most to reverse this unhealthy
trend was a rising Liberal politician, Wilfrid Laurier.

Laurier's methods were those of logical persuasion and careful attention to the uses of influence. He was assisted by the
accession of the relatively liberal Leo XIII to the Holy See, by
growing Quebec disappointment with the way things were
going in the west, and by the fact that after the death of G.-É.

Cartier in 1873 Macdonald failed to find an adequate replacement for his trusted Conservative co-leader in Quebec. The eventual success of Laurier in carving out a place for Liberalism in Quebec and in working with English-speaking compatriots was to earn for him in the 1960s (amongst *séparatistes*) the sobriquet of *vendu*. Whether this will be the permanent Quebec title beneath his historical niche remains to be seen; but in the late 1960s there are some signs to suggest that this may not be so.

While he insisted on the dangers of clerical intervention in politics and upon excessive emphasis on racial differences, Laurier stressed that the Church had nothing to fear from Canadian Liberalism. He had rejected the semi-republicanism of his earlier *Institut* days and replaced it with devotion to the liberal parliamentary tradition of British politics. Only by subscribing to political tolerance and avoiding the temptation of a clerical and racial party would the future either of Canada or of French Canada be safe. For this point of view Laurier secured Papal endorsement and the bishops were instructed to keep politics out of the pulpit. This formal victory, while the pontifical instructions were not infrequently winked at, was the harbinger of a fairly steady recovery of political liberalism in Quebec. The pace of that recovery was to be hastened in the late eighties and early nineties by erratic economic growth and by grave errors of judgement made by the federal Conservatives. But it was a long struggle and in the process Liberalism took on not a few conservative characteristics.

Inside the Mackenzie administration of 1873–8 the bookish and eloquent young Laurier struck a close friendship with the ponderous and stiffly aloof Edward Blake. Each recognized an aristocratic quality in the other. Each knew that he was pitted against deep biases within his own community and that one essential of Canadian statesmanship was to reduce these biases to the point where legitimate political adjustments could be made. The Blake wing of the Liberal Party was also less rigid on the matter of free trade doctrine than was the Cobdenite Mackenzie wing. Had the Blake wing been dominant it would probably have raised the tariff somewhat beyond the point of

revenue requirements and thus have eaten into the Tory support from industrialists. As it was, the Mackenzie administration was demolished by the severe depression which began in
1873 and in the midst of which the government seemed both
helpless and divided. The most it could do, beyond its somewhat hesitant railway construction, was to legislate for increased purity in election practices, endorse the use of the
Royal North-West Mounted Police to maintain order in the
federally administered territories, and create a Supreme Court
(whose jurisdiction was so limited that the most important
appeals still crossed the Atlantic to be heard before the Judicial
Committee of the British Privy Council).

The tensions in Canadian life were all acerbated by the bad
times of the seventies. So heavy was the emigration of French
Canadians to the mill towns of New England that protective
clerical nationalism saw it as the main threat to *la survivance*.
And from every other province people slipped steadily away to
the United States – frequently to be disillusioned by the onset
of a similar period of depression and industrial strife there, but
none the less damaging the young Dominion's self-confidence.
Sir Richard Cartwright, having watched the lugubrious trend
for some years, was to remark that Canadian scriptures began
with Exodus and ended in Lamentations. Yet the great nineteenth-century depression probably affected Canada no worse
than other countries. While the larger population base of the
United States, together with its vastly greater share of the temperate portions of the continent, ensured faster accumulation
of capital and more varied economic growth, nevertheless
Canada was maturing slowly in these years and laying the base
for economic 'take-off'.

Indeed for the great majority of people the shrinkage of
opportunity in the towns was less disastrous than the economic
holocaust of the 1930s. Few people did not benefit from the
essentially rural basis of society. Even for those who did not
have a family farm in their immediate background, with its
assurance of alternative subsistence, there were the choices of
work in the 'woods', as 'hired men' on the farms, as labourers
on the government railway projects and canal maintenance, or,

for the more impatient, inexpensive emigration southward. For the middle class and the élites of the provincial towns, existence on the edge of two frontiers held many advantages. If the Canadian frontiers produced their provincial vulgarities they also produced wealth which could be creamed off by merchants, bankers and railway promoters. If the sophistication of a long-established culture was tenuous in this frontier of European expansion, at least some of the delights of the mother culture could be tasted. For the more knowing and ambitious, voyages of rediscovery to Britain and Europe were not infrequent pleasures. Regular importation of the best wines and (with perhaps a year's delay) the current fashions in clothing, furniture, architecture and even literature were obvious and enjoyable features of well-to-do life in Montreal, Toronto, Halifax and Saint John. Newspapers carried serial versions of the more popular overseas fiction and conveyed a satisfying sense of involvement by long and detailed reports of the current wars and diplomacy of Europe and the multiplying crises of the new imperialism. And a feeling of immediacy was sharpened as Papal Zouaves were recruited in Quebec to save the temporal position of the Vatican, or St Lawrence raftsmen left to lend aid to General Gordon in his equally unsuccessful journey up the Nile.

Theatres in the larger towns played host to many touring companies which, with some of the outstanding names of the day, probably reached a larger percentage of the population than is the case now. And if some of the most execrable *belles lettres* ever produced appeared in newspapers and literary journals, two genuinely indigenous traditions in poetry were firmly established. In Quebec, Octave Crémazie and Louis Frechette, and in English-speaking Canada Charles G. D. Roberts and Archibald Lampman, stood out as exponents of poetry reflecting romantic, yet different aspects of the Canadian experience. Political analysis and contemporary comment, together with a long tradition of satirical humour reaching back to Thomas Chandler Haliburton in pre-Confederation Nova Scotia, maintained surprisingly high levels. The most effective pen in this field belonged to Goldwin Smith and, while it was imported from Oxford, it set a standard well emulated by Canadian practitioners.

With the highest standards set by Egerton Ryerson's Ontario public school system, education was generally both free and compulsory and universities in the four founding provinces were reaching a respectable maturity. In Quebec higher education was based largely upon the classics and scholastic philosophy and the other provinces stressed classics with a growing infusion of history, economics and political science. The differing emphases bespoke different societies. French-Canadian universities tended to produce lawyers and priests devoted to the protection of a French-Canadian nation separate from the influences both of English-speaking America and republican-rationalist France. English-speaking universities accepted much more readily modes of thought developed in Oxford and Cambridge since, whatever their nationalist feelings, they believed that Canada's destiny was to be English-oriented. And by the end of the century students from these universities were pursuing graduate studies in English and American schools.

By 1878 nearly five years of 'slow-down' and doctrinaire Liberal retrenchment had taken their political toll. All across central Canada businessmen yearned for some kind of positive government action. For merchants and grain farmers the hope lay in as close an approach to free trade as possible; but this was definitely blocked by the American Senate in 1874. Thus the cry of those who sold domestically produced goods and services grew more insistent. Whether or not their economic reasoning was sound, the small and ambitious manufacturers of central Canada clamoured loudly for protection. Support for a protective tariff came also from many bankers, insurance men, investors and promoters of a transcontinental railway, as well as from the romantic patriots of Canada First. Put crudely the demand was for the establishment of a huge system of subsidies (through higher tariffs) to manufacturers, a system which it was hoped would spread its profits beneficially throughout the rest of the country. In another light, there can be no doubt that very many Canadians believed in the political need of economic protection in order to make true the dream of 1867.

Thus, as election day 1878 drew near, Conservative drums began to beat out the rhythm of Liberal failure.

In Quebec the Tory alliance with the clergy was so close and so effective that even some Conservative politicians warned Sir John A. Macdonald that there would be a backlash. But in the business community and in most of central Canada hopes soared. It was time to take a positive forward step, to assert mastery rather than submit to stagnant drift. In the waiting west and amongst most businessmen in central Canada, the lagging pace of railway building seemed nothing less than disastrous and an invitation to the driving promoters of America's Gilded Age to take over the vast Canadian patrimony. Even to many of the slowly growing urban working class Sir John and his 'boodling' capitalists seemed preferable to the almost Spencerian Liberals. The workingmen recalled that George Brown, principal journalistic prophet of liberalism, was renowned in employers' circles for his successful stand against those of his employees who wished to unionize the Toronto *Globe*. And they remembered that the beginnings of legal recognition of trade union rights had come from the first Macdonald government.

When the Liberals decided, under particular pressure from their nervous free trade supporters in the Maritimes, not to raise the tariff in 1876 even in the face of mounting deficits, Macdonald saw that he could capture and lead what was clearly majority opinion. Thus in 1878 the Tories campaigned shrewdly for a 'National Policy'. Its basis was judicious increases in the customs tariff, full steam ahead with the western railway, a new drive for immigrants to fill up the prairie west, and a generous approach to investors of any kind. Memories of the 1873 Pacific Scandal were smothered in a round of political picnics at which Tory rhetoric proclaimed the dawn of a new day. In the 'red parlours' of a dozen hotels local manufacturers met with Conservative leaders to advance their claims for specific duties. Few left disappointed. As Sir John summarized his philosophy, 'the bigger the capitalist and the more he has invested in the country the better for the country'.

Canada's version of North America's 'Great Barbecue' was

fairly launched as the election returns revealed that Canadians had forgiven Macdonald by electing 137 Conservatives to 69 Liberals. One of Macdonald's first acts after the election showed how central to the 'National Policy' would be the western railway. Writing to London to recommend that Lord Dufferin remain for another two years as governor-general, he noted: '... Lord Dufferin has made the subject of the constitution, route and requirements of the Canadian Pacific Railway his special study. Until this great work is completed, our Dominion is little better than a "geographical expression" ...' It required no prophet to foretell that the 'politics of purity' would occupy a back seat for some time.

12

The Iron Spike and the Regina Scaffold

'LET us then, regardless of all personal consideration, still preserve the patriotic attitude we have hitherto maintained, and we will enjoy the proud satisfaction of witnessing the triumph of our principles and the prosperity of our country . . .' So wrote Sir Charles Tupper to another prominent Nova Scotian Conservative in 1869. Joseph Howe, leader of the movement to repeal Confederation, had just accepted Macdonald's invitation to join the federal cabinet after being promised slightly better financial terms for his province. The system of bribing recalcitrant provinces or regions with 'better terms' was well launched. And another somewhat ironical feature of evolving Canadian political life began to emerge at the same time – the marked tendency of leaders whose original goals had been those of provincial rights and regional advantage to slide more or less painlessly into the realm of national politics. Howe was the most dramatic example of this but there were many who followed a similar path. It may prove to be the path of future Canadian survival.

At the end of the seventies the Macdonald Conservatives felt strong enough to go ahead firmly with their National Policy. With Tupper of Nova Scotia and Tilley of New Brunswick willing to defend vigorous central government activity against Maritimes critics, the new Macdonald government moved with dispatch. The customs tariff was raised in 1879 from about $17\frac{1}{2}$ per cent to an average of 25 per cent. Countering the outraged protests of fishermen, shipbuilders, grain farmers and others who were forced to pay more for their production equipment and domestic requirements without apparent countervailing benefit, the government employed much the same arguments as those advanced by the Germans in the same year and by the Americans when the Morrill tariff was adopted during the Civil

War. Free trade, or a purely revenue tariff, they argued, was advantageous only to a country sufficiently advanced in the industrial revolution to be able to compete effectively at home and abroad with the products of other industrialized states. It was a telling argument. The businessmen of the United States, Germany and other late starters had a plausible case for protection against the immense lead enjoyed by Great Britain. And if the Americans conceded this need, how much stronger was the case for nascent Canadian industry? In the 1878 campaign hair-raising stories were circulated not only about general unfair competition from abroad but about attempts by American concerns to throttle potential Canadian competitors at birth by temporary under-pricing and 'dumping' in the Canadian market.

Whatever the theoretical merits of the case for tariff protection, once established it was there to stay. When the Liberals finally regained office in 1896 they had no plans to dismantle the system. Nor has any later government seriously assaulted the walls of tariff protection. And today the question of American ownership of a vast range of Canadian manufacturing and resource industry keeps to the fore the essential relationship between political independence and economic control. While the nature of the problem is somewhat altered, it has also been conditioned by the operation of the tariff which has made it advantageous for many American companies to establish subsidiaries inside Canada in order to avoid the operation of the tariff. Thus the attempt to assure independent Canadian economic growth (through tariff policy) was to have unsuspected long-range ironies. On the other hand, there can be little doubt that Canadian-owned industrial capacity was increased. There is little doubt, also, that Canadian beneficiaries of the tariff (including transportation and financial promoters who saw it as the guarantee of an east–west oriented economy as opposed to a north–south integration) worked actively in support of whatever party or politician would support the tariff policy.

At the outset a temporary oscillation within the long depression gave the Conservatives the break they needed. Not only did domestic business revive slightly but world money markets relented somewhat. Thus, given sufficiently attractive terms, it seemed likely that capital could be raised to build the Pacific railway at once. After protracted negotiations between the government and a syndicate of Canadian capitalists headed by George Stephen of the Bank of Montreal, a contract for the road was negotiated. Donald Smith of the Hudson's Bay Company was closely associated with the venture and helped raise English subscriptions. The syndicate was clearly under Canadian and British control. Equally clearly the terms of the contract were generous in the extreme. And before confirming the deal the government presented the contract to Parliament for ratification.

In the House, Edward Blake raked the deal fore and aft. Speaking for some seven hours he castigated the government for unmitigated profligacy. Sir Charles Tupper, charged with steering the contract through Parliament, contented himself with condemning the Liberal policy of pinch-penny caution in railway building and of throwing away golden opportunities. Given all the circumstances the conclusion was foregone and the contract was ratified in a turbulent Commons. By the agreement the Canadian Pacific Railway Company was given the 700 miles of track already completed under government contracts, a direct cash subsidy of $25 million, and twenty-five million acres of fertile or mineral-rich western land. The Company could select its land from alternate sections (a section is 640 acres) within a twenty-four mile wide belt bordering the railway line. The land subsidy idea was borrowed from the American land-grant railways but also had roots going back to the land company development policies of the early nineteenth century. It was designed not only to give profit and resources to the Company but also to encourage the C.P.R. to attract immigrants to the west and thus increase the value of their unsold lands as well as produce traffic for the road and markets for central Canadian businessmen.

This munificent endowment might have gone relatively unprotested had it been the only perquisite attached to the contract. In addition, however, the C.P.R. was relieved of taxes on its property in perpetuity, was forgiven customs duties on imported production materials, and was granted a monopoly of western traffic for twenty years. The western monopoly, to be enforced by Ottawa, committed the government to refusing a charter to any company that wished to build connecting lines south to the border and American transcontinental systems. This monopoly clause was revoked under strong political pressure in 1888 but not before it had become a major target of criticism launched by a nascent prairie populism against eastern domination and high freight rates.

As the Liberal David Mills thundered in the House, the liberality of the deal with the C.P.R. and the meagre provisions for governmental enforcement of standards threatened to make the Company the proprietor of the government of Canada. Certainly the closest links were forged between the Conservative Party and the complex of financial-commercial-industrial interests which had at its centre the Bank of Montreal and the C.P.R. For years no constituency bordering the C.P.R. main line voted anything but Tory and many friends of the government and the road benefited directly from railway sub-contracting, prior knowledge of location of track (and thus the development of town sites), and even the granting of land to in-groups for colonization purposes.

Yet, despite resentful Liberal revelations of prodigality and corruption, the C.P.R. bargain reflected accurately the impatient and opportunistic mood of the country. Moreover there is no doubt that the only reason for previous Liberal refusal to charter a private company on similar terms was the financial stringencies which persisted throughout Mackenzie's term of office. As Sir John Willison remarked when, as a later editor of the Toronto *Globe*, he looked back over the period of the 1880s, the Liberals were the party of 'voluble virtue'.

In fact the Liberals, apart from the tariff issue (on which they were themselves divided), did not entertain views of how the country should be run that were seriously different from those of the Conservatives. Thus their stock in trade was criticism of Tory mismanagement, corruption and centralization. In opposition they tended to couch such criticism in the language of principle. Thus they defended provincial rights, for example, on principle. But the principle was not unrelated to the distribution of political power, and the Liberals were much stronger in the provinces than at Ottawa. As they approached federal power in the early nineties, and certainly after they achieved it, they defended the use of Ottawa's powers with some zeal, frequently in support of the 'general interests' of the country, and sometimes in support of quite special interests. Neither party paid much attention to problems other than those of economic growth. Thus the social impact of Ottawa's western policies was largely ignored until another rebellion occurred; practically no plans were made or even advocated to assist immigrants to adjust to a new environment in the event of the expected influx; and, save for a few provincial worker's lien laws, labour and social legislation was largely distinguished by its absence. Penology was both primitive and brutal, although in Ontario some enlightened legislation governing reformation was achieved.

What public debate there was about 'the social question' in the eighties and nineties was heavily dependent upon modes of thought derived from the farming frontier and the North American vogue of social Darwinism. Some newspapers considered the shortage of domestic help to be a burning question and prodded the government towards assisting the ocean passages of such immigrants. Few people cared to engage in the kind of discussion that raged in Britain and Europe about the nature of industrial capitalism, the role of trade unions or the purposes of government intervention in economic life. For various reasons employees were slow to organize and certainly there was nothing like either the new unionism in England or the big rural unionism of Australia. The relatively small farms of central Canada and the Maritimes usually employed, at most, one 'hired man'. The work force of the towns was still small and generally accepted the conditions of the family firm or of very personal management. In some trades, unions were established and usually these were affiliated with American unions which thus came to be known as 'internationals'. The strongest of these grew naturally in the largest branch of employment, the railways, but at least until after 1900 they did not attempt anything like Eugene V. Debs's amalgamation of crafts into a single railway union. In 1885 branches of the American Knights of Labour were established but this early attempt at 'one big union' was short-lived. The Trades and Labour Congress of Canada, founded in 1886, provided the beginnings of a central organization for labour and in most industrial towns the union established local labour councils. Influenced by British working-class immigrants, tiny labour and socialist parties sprang up in central Canada and some of the small-circulation labour journals advocated socialism. But it was not until 1900 that the first specifically trade union representative, Alphonse Verville of Montreal, gained a seat in Parliament. Union growth was hobbled by the relatively small scale of Canadian industry, the staggering distances to be overcome by communications and organization and the double problem of language differences and clerical opposition in Quebec.

In these circumstances state intervention and planning continued to be neo-mercantilist. The tariff was constructed as an aid to specific businessmen and industries. Huge tracts of land, timber and mineral rights were either given or sold at bargain basement rates both by provincial and federal governments to business barons who were then further subsidized by public assistance to railway lines into their territories, navigation and port aids and other generosities. The values of a market economy went virtually unchallenged while prime urban land was deeply disfigured by railway yards, shipping facilities and the monstrosities of late Victorian industrial architecture. These and other sins such as cheap row-housing and clap-board tenements provided their unhappy evidence that new countries do not always learn the lessons provided by older lands. And the beneficiaries of the system professed the belief that their wealth came from their own unaided efforts. Most of them knew better. Many of them went into politics and all of them contributed heavily to whichever level of government and whichever party seemed most likely to take the risk out of enterprise. Certainly there was enterprise and just as clearly there were fortunes to be made, even during the continuing depression. The trick in the eighties and nineties was to keep the country going without surrendering completely to the voracious demands of special interest and without moving so cautiously that continental union could gain majority support.

The building of the C.P.R. was the outstanding example of both the costs and the achievements of this phase of Canada's neo-mercantilism. Although the terms of the 1880 contract were mouth-watering in their generosity, they seemed soon to be inadequate. No sooner was the monumental task squarely faced than the need for immense sums of immediate cash became overwhelming. The rugged challenge of the oldest and toughest rock in the world was not easily overcome. Across the bottom of the pre-Cambrian shield north of Lake Superior tons of dynamite, thousands of men, dozens of sub-contractors and a myriad of unsuspected costs had to be paid for. Then hundreds of miles of treacherous and nearly bottomless muskeg had to be beaten before the line broke on to the Manitoba prairies. Once there the line streaked across the plains, past Pile of Bones (Regina) and on to the foothills of Alberta, creating speculative land booms in its wake, making and breaking dozens of hopeful town-site promoters. To breach the forbidding mountain barrier, C.P.R. engineers chose the spectacular Kicking Horse Pass. Here again, like the sides of the pass itself, both costs and dangers soared. Construction camps perched on the edge of nothing, winter temperatures dropped to 30° and 40° below zero, snow-slides required constant vigilance, spidery trestle bridges had to be thrust up from the foaming rapids of the Columbia and other rivers, and yet more tunnels had to be blasted where there was no other recourse. Yet on 7 November 1885 Macdonald read the telegram which told him that the line was completed. Donald Smith had driven the last spike at Craigellachie where the line moving east from Port Moody (Vancouver) reached the last of the mountain camps. Unlike the golden spike which symbolized completion of the first American transcontinental line, the Canadian spike was made of iron.

The iron spike was mute testimony to the greater difficulties faced by the Canadians in their transcontinental project. Funds had been much harder to raise because the prospect of financial success was less certain. Instead of a populated and thriving middle west the C.P.R. moved first across 900 miles of uninhabited granite and muskeg – a country soon to be discovered by excited landscape painters, a land rich in mineral resources (including about 90 per cent of the world's nickel) and already penetrated along its edges by lumbering operators, but not an area to generate immediate traffic. Again, the expansive prairies held the future's hope but offered very limited traffic in the 1880s. The government's efforts through agents in Britain and Europe to attract immigrants produced meagre results, despite colourful eulogies of the Canadian West which invariably minimized the climatic hardships of pioneering on the prairies. Some communal settlement had been successful, as when groups of Icelanders and Mennonites arrived in the seventies under special government arrangements. Together with a fairly steady stream of settlers from Ontario the population of Manitoba was boosted to 150,000 and that of the remaining Northwest Territories to 50,000. But the west remained relatively empty as the brief land boom of 1882 collapsed in the following year, as European immigrants moved into the more easily available lands of the American west, and as the world depression constricted demand for the one great potential export, wheat.

Yet Macdonald had staked all on the C.P.R. When the road came again and again for further direct aid he battled the necessary measures through the House. Heeding the urgent advice of his nearly illiterate but immensely shrewd colleague, John Henry Pope, that 'the day the Canadian Pacific busts, the Conservative party busts the day after', Macdonald bought off opposition by providing comparable grants for a railway in Quebec and distributing other favours with the required abandon. When compared to the holocaust of congressional corruption symbolized by the Credit Mobilier scandal in the United States, the direct 'moral costs' of Conservative nation-building were perhaps not excessive. But there were heavy incidental costs.

If the iron spike meant a fresh chance for the old commercial empire of the St Lawrence, a chance for central Canadian businessmen to exploit the economic resources of half a continent, it meant also a sharp intensification of sectional rivalries and social discontents. Ottawa was exercising an almost overwhelming power. The lands and natural resources of the prairie west were at its disposal and the federal tariff was in many ways definitive for industrial leaders in all the provinces. Immigration, settlement patterns and even educational policy were heavily influenced by the exercise of federal powers. Naturally many interests both economic and cultural supported this trend, but many, also, bitterly opposed it. The eighties and nineties thus witnessed an almost unbroken sequence of crises in what came to be called 'dominion-provincial relations'. Behind each crisis could be found a mixture of political and commercial ambitions and concern for the cultural and regional balances within the developing state. While few people at the time put the problem in theoretical terms it is clear that metropolitan influence was far outstripping regional, frontier or provincial influence. And there were many people both on the new frontiers and in the older provinces who refused to take this lying down.

Despite many advantages enjoyed by those who controlled the Canadian policies in westward expansion, it was in the west that the biggest explosions occurred. Partly because of much slower growth, Canada did not suffer the long and bloody wars that marked American occupation of the far west. The Mounted Police maintained much tighter control of western settlements and the six-shooter never became the symbol of Canadian freedom. Ottawa negotiated treaties with the plains Indians which secured relatively peaceful opening of most fertile land and the re-location of tribes on substantial 'reserves'. By no means an ideal permanent solution to the question of Indian–White relations, this policy at least prevented large-scale illegal dispossession of the Indians. Had it been followed through with a more generous and consistent system of administration much trouble could have been avoided. But it was not. Pennypinching and indifference, not unrelated to Ottawa's absorption in C.P.R. affairs, led to mounting Indian discontent. At the same time both the white settlers and the Métis expressed with vigour their own sense of grievance with western policies.

Western farmers resented deeply the high freight rates of the C.P.R. and the high prices charged for necessary eastern-produced goods – the first sustained by the monopoly clause of the C.P.R. charter and the second by the tariff. Loudly groaning under the burden of eastern domination, and somewhat influenced by American populists who were showing no little skill in agitating similar questions south of the border, the westerners organized for action. Petitions for redress went largely ignored in Ottawa. By the end of 1884 the west from Manitoba to the British Columbia border was in a state of incipient rebellion. A petition sent to Ottawa in December 1884 by Métis and Whites sums up the points at issue: Indians, deprived of the buffalo hunt, were often near starvation; Métis in the Saskatchewan district had not received their land grants as had the Manitoba Métis, and once again the square survey threatened their riverfront lots on the Saskatchewan; early settlement land-claims of white farmers were not recognized; and, of course, the railway and tariff policies were roundly condemned. As in the Red River colony in 1869–70, self-government was seen as a necessary reform accompanying other changes in federal policy. 'Your humble petitioners', read the document, 'are of opinion that the shortest and most effectual methods of remedying these grievances would be to grant the [Northwest Territories] responsible government with control of its own resources and just representation in the Federal Parliament and Cabinet.'

Even at this late hour, with a mountain of ignored evidence in Ottawa's ministerial dockets, the government took no action. Newspapers in the Northwest Territories appealed openly to the examples of 1837 and 1870, concluding that 'If history is to be taken as a guide, what could be plainer than that without rebellion the people of the Northwest need expect nothing, while with rebellion, successful or otherwise, they may reasonably expect to get their rights.' The obvious step was to bring back the man who had led the successful Manitoba rebellion.

Louis Riel was then teaching at a school in Montana where he had emigrated with Macdonald's blessing in order to avoid the mutually unpleasant necessity of a treason trial. Friends begged him to lead their cause. 'Do not imagine', they wrote, 'that you will begin the work when you get here ... the closest union exists between the French and English and the Indians, and we have good generals to foster it. ... The whole race is calling for you!' Riel returned to Prince Albert on the Saskatchewan in the spring of 1885. Convinced that he received divine revelation, intensely proud of his 'Métis nation', and undoubtedly 'insane' by any of the accepted, if fallible, standards of medicine, Riel added the necessary final ingredient to a bubbling western brew.

In March a provisional government was set up and almost at once the second Riel movement was deserted by most of the white westerners and by the Catholic clergy who found unattractive Riel's desire to found a new church. At the same time several Indian tribes strengthened their support of Riel and, under two capable leaders, Big Bear and Poundmaker, added a frightening element which had not been present in the Red River Rebellion. At Duck Lake a clash between the Métis and Mounted Police precipitated the crisis at the end of March 1885. The police were beaten off and Poundmaker's Indians at once captured the town of Battleford. Big Bear followed this up by massacring most of the villagers of Frog Lake.

Macdonald's procrastination had failed and he quickly dispatched a force of over 7,000 men to the Northwest. Under General F. D. Middleton, who was commander of the Canadian militia and who had seen useful service in the imperial army during the Indian Mutiny, this force reached the Saskatchewan quickly. The nearly completed C.P.R. thus received vindication in the eyes of the defenders of law and order. Two battles, at Fish Creek and Batoche, dispersed the rebels and Riel surrendered on 15 May. This time a trial on the charge of high treason could not be avoided. At Regina, Riel's lawyers pleaded insanity. Riel himself refused this plea. Addressing an English-speaking and Protestant jury, the hero of the Métis was eloquent and unrepentant:

By the testimony laid before you during my trial, witnesses on both sides made it certain that petition after petition has been sent to the Federal Government, and so irresponsible is the government to the North-West, that in the course of several years beside doing nothing to satisfy the people of this great land, it has even hardly been able to answer once or to give a single response. That fact would indicate absolute lack of responsibility and therefore insanity complicated with paralysis.

The ministers of an insane and irresponsible Government and its offspring the North-West Council made up their mind to answer my petitions by surrounding me slyly and by attempting to jump upon me suddenly and upon my people in the Saskatchewan. Happily when they appeared and showed their teeth to devour, I was ready; that is what is called my crime of high treason and for which they hold me today.

The English-speaking jury was no more impressed by Riel's essentially political defence than they were by the defence lawyers' plea of insanity. In finding Riel guilty (while exonerating his English-speaking colleague, William Jackson, on the ground of insanity) the court dropped a most delicate dilemma in Sir John Macdonald's lap. Ontario Orangemen led the hue and cry for Riel's blood. Recalling the 'murder' of Thomas Scott in 1870 they pressed hard upon Macdonald to refuse commutation of the court's sentence of hanging. Quebec, conversely, and despite Riel's religious aberrations, proclaimed him the noble defender of French and Catholic minority rights. Mass meetings throughout the province proclaimed the government's guilt and the justice of Riel's cause. Yet even when Wilfrid Laurier, who was already recognized as federal Liberal leader in Quebec, declaimed on Montreal's Champs de Mars: 'Had I been born on the banks of the Saskatchewan I would myself have shouldered a musket to fight against the neglect of governments and the shameless greed of speculators', Macdonald hesitated. Finally the prime minister made his crucial and disastrous decision. Riel, he said privately, should hang 'though every dog in Quebec bark in his favour'. In fact Macdonald judged that Ontario had to be satisfied and that Quebec would stick with the Conservatives. On 16 November 1885 Riel was hanged in the Mounted Police barracks at Regina.

The Regina scaffold marked the beginning of a steady decline in Conservative fortunes. It sharpened painfully the racial and sectional frictions that required for their melioration a much clearer understanding of the 'French fact' in Canada than was shown at that time by Macdonald. To a large extent Macdonald's Regina blunder resulted from his failure to choose, and give recognized status to, a single Quebec lieutenant – a *chef* who could speak with authority inside the cabinet on matters of concern to French Canadians and who could make the wide range of political decisions (including those on patronage and organization) necessary inside the province. The point was made best by J. A. Chapleau who probably should have received the mantle of Cartier but who never quite got it. Writing to Macdonald in 1888 Chapleau reflected on the reasons for the rebellion and, by implication, for its political aftermath:

> The inner motive of the outbreak and of the subsequent agitation was the deep feeling that still exists in the minds of the minority that the political direction of the North-West affairs is entirely foreign to their aspirations and rights. Right or wrong the feeling was and still is there. The cry of the half-breed: 'Give us our rights' answered that feeling more than their claims to lands and indemnity.

On the back of this letter Macdonald scribbled the memorandum to employ more 'Franco-Canadians', especially in the Northwest. But it was too late for such a simple solution. While it took time to break the Tories' hold on federal power, the first cracks appeared quickly. Under the name *Parti National* an alliance of Quebec Liberals and dissident Conservatives ousted the Conservative provincial government in 1886. Led by an eloquent Quebec nationalist, Honoré Mercier, the new provincial government spearheaded a concerted assault upon the Conservative view of confederation. Announcing that 'the murder of Riel was a declaration of war on the influence of French Canada in Confederation, a violation of right and justice', Mercier opted for the compact theory of Confederation. Arguing that the B.N.A. Act reflected a compact amongst the provinces who merely delegated certain powers to Ottawa, he concluded that the provinces remained autonomous and equal in powers to the central government. And in this view he was supported by not a few English-speaking provincial politicians and journalists. In Ontario, Oliver Mowat's Liberal government battled Ottawa for control of the patronage-rich field of liquor licensing, for extension of the province's western boundary, and in a wide area of debatably defined jurisdictions. In Manitoba fierce resentment of the C.P.R. monopoly clause led to violent anti-Ottawa demonstrations. Most provincial governments wanted the federal power of disallowing provincial legislation removed, fearing that, in conjunction with a policy of centralizing economic controls, it could end provincial rights and unhappily diminish regional differences.

In the dangerous flood of discontent Nova Scotia made the most extreme threats against the federal power. Throughout the three Maritime provinces depression raged unchecked. The tariff operated there to great disadvantage at a time when iron and steam combined to cripple the earlier prosperity of wood, wind and sail. To Maritimers it appeared that federal fiscal and spending policies served only to tax them in the interests of central Canadian manufacturers and railway developers. Demanding a lower tariff and generally 'better terms', the Liberal premier of Nova Scotia, W. S. Fielding, obtained passage of a series of resolutions in 1886 which declared both the right and the willingness of the province to secede from Confederation if there were no redress of its grievances.

Recognizing that most of the English-speaking provinces were at least as autonomist as Quebec, Honoré Mercier played host at an Interprovincial Conference in 1887. Designed to focus attention on the need to restrain Ottawa, the 1887 Conference brought together leading provincial Liberals and set a precedent also for future federal conferences – some to be called by provincial initiative, some by Ottawa. While the resolutions of the Conference calling for higher federal subsidies to the provinces, sharp restriction of the disallowing power, unrestricted reciprocal tariff reduction with the United States, and several constitutional amendments which would enhance provincial power were not implemented specifically, they did have both a long- and a short-term impact. In the following year Ottawa began to subsidize the Nova Scotia iron and coal industry, refrained from disallowing a particularly controversial Quebec law and revoked the C.P.R.'s western monopoly rights. The programme of subsidy revision put forth by the Conference was accepted by the federal Liberal party and implemented after the Liberals returned to Ottawa. Furthermore, in the eighties and nineties several constitutional cases were decided by the Judicial Committee of the Privy Council in London which tilted the federal balance of power perceptibly away from Ottawa. By the time of the federal election of 1891 all these forces operated strongly to the Tory disadvantage.

In 1887, having led the Liberals without success in two elections, Edward Blake had secured the selection of Wilfrid Laurier as his successor. Chosen at least partly in expectation of garnering essential Quebec support for the Liberals, Laurier was beginning to find his own leadership style by 1891. He gave consistent and eloquent support to the cries for provincial rights and, over the mounting doubts of Blake, to the Liberal plank which called for 'unrestricted reciprocity' with the United States. 'U.R.' directly challenged the Conservatives' National Policy by advocating complete removal of tariffs between Canada and the United States. Not a few Liberal papers and spokesmen went so far as to endorse full commercial union as the only way to win back prosperity and cut down Tory-supporting protected monopolists.

The Old Chieftain Macdonald and his beleaguered colleagues cast caution aside in dealing with this political dynamite. Arguing that either of the Liberal versions of commercial union would lead swiftly to political union, they castigated the Liberals as the party of veiled treason – and in Quebec as Rouges anti-clericals. Campaigning for 'the old man, the old flag and the old policy', Macdonald won the last of his political wars. His sharply reduced majority was further evidence of the disastrous aftermath of Riel and of a built-in resistance in Canada to over-centralization. On the other hand his victory convinced the Liberals that unlimited continentalism was not only a loser at the polls but a policy on which the party itself could never really unite.

For all his flamboyance, fondness for the bottle, procrastination and willingness to search out and use in others the weakest side of human nature, Macdonald is yet the greatest of Canadian statesmen. While he favoured a vigorous centralization he wished only genuine partnership with French Canadians. And if in 1891 he appealed with unrivalled emotionalism to English-speaking colonialism when he cried 'a British subject I was born, a British subject I will die', no one matched him in rejecting British demands for colonial obedience. And certainly no one understood better than he the meaning and necessity of Canadian independence in North America. When he died in June of 1891, exhausted by his last campaign, his severest critics and opponents recognized his achievement. Perhaps the most hard-headed comment came from Goldwin Smith: '... who will there be to take his place? Who else is there who knows the sheep or whose voice the sheep know? Who else could make Orangemen vote for Papists, or induce half the members for Ontario to help in levying on their own province the necessary blackmail for Quebec?' Within the Tory party there was no one.

13

The Wheat Boom and Laurier Nationalism

ALREADY, before Macdonald's death, there was brewing the racial storm which would deliver the *coup de grâce* to his faltering party. Into the midst of passions still simmering in the aftermath of Riel's execution the government of Manitoba tossed a piece of legislation which brought sharply into question the very nature of Confederation.

The Manitoba School Act itself was the culmination of intense agitation of the race question. In Ontario the Orange Order and many less extreme English-speaking nationalists had taken the suppression of the Northwest Rebellion as a symbol of their conviction that Anglo-Saxon dominance in the west would be a make-weight ensuring a basically British Canada. In 1888 such opinion was shaken by the method chosen by Honoré Mercier's Quebec government to settle a major property question in his province. The property involved was known as the Jesuit Estates. This very large accumulation of land and buildings had reverted to the Crown in 1773 when the Society of Jesus was disbanded by the Papacy. When the Society regained its life in the early 1840s its Canadian province at once sought restoration of (or compensation for) its sequestered estates. The problem had baffled successive Quebec administrations until Mercier imposed a solution. Arbitrarily declaring the property to be worth $400,000 he allotted $70,000 to Quebec's Protestant schools and the remainder to the Roman Catholic Church to be divided among Jesuits and others at the discretion of the Pope. Eminently reasonable to Catholic minds, this formula was seized upon by Orangemen and their sympathizers as evidence of a deep-dyed plot to endow Papists and inject Rome into the civil affairs of Canada.

Macdonald wisely refused to disallow the Jesuit Estates Act but many of his supporters and not a few Ontario Liberals

showed infinitely less wisdom. An Ontario Tory, D'Alton Mc-
Carthy, led in forming an Equal Rights Association. This was a
serious misnomer for an increasingly powerful sentiment which
sought to halt the use of French in eastern Ontario schools where
the French-speaking population was growing, to restrict the
growth of separate (Catholic) schools in Ontario, and to revoke
Ottawa's policy of accepting French as an official language in
the Northwest Territories.

McCarthyism shattered the struggling Conservative Party.
Moderates argued that tolerance of the extension of the French
language and other minority rights was a reasonable development of the original federal *entente*. But they were badly under-
cut by fiery speeches of the McCarthyites which usually ended
by reminding audiences of the Plains of Abraham and suggestions that if the ballot box did not secure Protestant English
dominance, bayonets would. It was scarcely surprising that
more and more French Canadians began to question the old
political alliance of Quebec *Bleus* and Ontario Tories. Still further doubts arose when McCarthy's conspiracy theory captured
the minds of the government of Manitoba.

In 1890 the provincial government tore to shreds the minority guarantees of the 1870 Manitoba Act. That statute had provided for continuance of denominational school rights as they
existed prior to establishment of the province. Later, provincial
education laws established Quebec-like separate schools with
proportional state support. But by 1890 the ground was ready
for McCarthy's agitation because virtually all immigration in
the succeeding years had been English-speaking. Thus the 1890
Act abolished separate schools and forbade teaching in French
in the unified state school system. Local Catholics, strongly
supported by the Quebec episcopacy and French-Canadian opinion, at once sued in the courts to have the law declared unconstitutional. When the law was upheld the federal government
was faced with an extremely unpalatable decision. Should it
intervene in defence of minority rights or should it evade the
issue and plead provincial rights?

While a good deal of ink has been spilt debating the techni-
calities of the Manitoba Schools question there is no doubt that

both the issue and the manner of its 'solution' were essentially political, with heavy overtones of cultural conflict. During the struggle the Tories failed to unite behind any one leader with the result that a succession of four prime ministers grappled unsuccessfully with this most prickly problem. As tempers rose both in Parliament and across the country, the government sought to escape on one pretext after another. When the courts declared the Manitoba law constitutional, the government again appealed to the Supreme Court and then to the Privy Council on the ultimate question: did the federal government have the right to intervene?

Under section 93 of the British North America Act it seemed clear that if a provincial government tampered with minority educational rights which had existed at the time of Confederation, Ottawa was empowered to pass remedial legislation. Early in 1895 the Judicial Committee of the Privy Council followed up its earlier decision on constitutionality with the opinion that the federal government did, in this case, possess the right to intervene with such legislation. For months the cabinet wavered, torn by arguments for and against the dramatic step. Finally, after Manitoba had persistently refused all blandishments to enact its own remedial legislation restoring separate schools, the government at Ottawa introduced a law to force the province to restore the minority's rights.

In the early months of 1896 the fateful remedial bill was slowly strangled by debate and filibuster while the five-year legal limit of Parliament moved relentlessly closer. After a month of chaotic sittings the government gave up, dissolved the House and called an election for the spring. *In extremis* the Tories recalled the veteran Sir Charles Tupper from London for the last chance struggle. But even Tupper's fierce fighting methods could not reunite the party. With open support from the Quebec hierarchy and from many Ontario Catholics, the lines of religion and race prevented him from bringing back the McCarthyites. And on voting day his one hope was shattered when Quebec refused to follow the hierarchy.

Many things about the 1896 election seem improbable but with latter-day wisdom can be explained. Laurier was extremely fortunate in gaining the assistance of Joseph-Israel Tarte in Quebec. A disenchanted Tory, Tarte swung to the Liberals after uncovering and publicizing unsavoury corruption within the Conservative Party. His forensic skills and personal charm did much to convince many French Canadians that it would be more to their advantage to have one of their own as prime minister than it would be to obtain a coercive law against Manitoba. The latter choice would simply launch a full-scale racial struggle. Moreover, federal intervention in Manitoban affairs would violate one of French Canada's cardinal principles of provincial rights. Laurier himself moved throughout the whole crisis with extreme caution and a very sure political touch. Knowing that the principal shoal to avoid was a permanent division on racial lines, he saw also that 'rights' depended more upon mutual accommodation than upon law. Thus he wrote to W. S. Fielding, the Liberal premier of Nova Scotia, in November 1895:

It is now evident that the government are going to make a strong bid to capture the Roman Catholic vote, by introducing remedial legislation, that is to say setting aside the school law of Manitoba, and substituting a law of their own. That they will capture the Roman Catholic vote is not at all certain, for I know for a certainty that the most intelligent and far-seeing among the Roman Catholics – both clergy and laity – dread the action of the government as likely to conduce not to the re-establishment of the separate schools of Manitoba, but to an agitation for the abolition of separate schools in all the provinces.

In the bitter Commons debates and in the election campaign Laurier insisted that an approach to the government of Manitoba along the 'sunny ways' of compromise and justice would be the only successful one. His answer to the bishops who commanded their flocks to vote for the Conservatives and remedial legislation was the same as it had been in the earlier struggle over Bourget's Catholic Programme: keep politics and religion separate. In the outcome the Liberals took half of the Ontario seats, won handsomely in Quebec, and fared reasonably well in the Maritimes. The compromise that Laurier, as prime minister, worked out with Manitoba's premier Greenway provided for limited French teaching wherever there were more than ten French-speaking students, and for after-class religious instruction. Scarcely an ideal solution, it nevertheless stilled the political storm for the moment. When the Quebec bishops labelled the settlement an 'indefensible abandonment' of Catholic minority rights, Laurier's supporters secured, through a special legate, Papal instructions to moderate the clerical criticism.

The Liberal government that took office in the summer of 1896 was certainly not radical. Indeed both in its policies and its membership it strongly resembled earlier Macdonald governments. What did distinguish it was its vigour, its recognition of the strength of provincial leaders whom it incorporated in what was fondly termed a ministry of all talents, and Laurier's unquestioned devotion to a culturally tolerant Canadian nationalism. The prime minister himself seemed to incorporate most of what was best in the Canadian experiment. A distinguished and handsome orator, he was fluent in both languages and gave to his English speeches that touch of glamour inherent in a slight French accent – the counterpart of the heavy Scottish brogue which Macdonald had retained to the end. To his early classical education he had added wide reading in law and in English political-parliamentary history which made him a match for anyone in the Commons when it came to competing in precedents. If he was not very knowledgeable in financial matters and about the social-economic implications of a nascent industrial society, he was nevertheless very sure about the general meaning of Canadianism. Thus he was prepared to adopt most of the old Macdonald policies of independent national development and gave even greater weight than had Macdonald to the importance of racial accommodation within Canada.

By the time Laurier gained office he had dropped much of his earlier Rougeism. Having won his political battle against the reactionaries in the hierarchy he was anxious to make peace with them. Even more important, in the last turbulent years of the Tory dominance, the Laurier Liberals made effective understandings with a number of substantial business leaders. These contacts, most importantly with interests connected with the Toronto-based Bank of Commerce, helped offset the strong

Conservative support from the C.P.R.–Bank of Montreal grouping. Thus, despite frequent Liberal warnings about the dangers of monopoly in business growth, by 1896 the party was at least as responsive to 'big business' as was the Conservative Party. The nature of the change (a culmination, perhaps, of the practical pioneering of Edward Blake) is suggested in a letter written by Laurier in 1891 at a time when Liberal exposures of Tory corruption were having considerable impact: 'Tell me, my dear Beaugrand, whether there is not some fatality pursuing our party; it is just at the moment that we are showing up the full extent of the corruption of the Conservative Party that a similar revelation comes upon ourselves.' No longer the party of 'voluble virtue', Liberalism had persuaded much of the English-speaking business community that it intended no radical alteration in the Canadian economic system.

Laurier's finance minister symbolized the end of Liberal flirtation with free trade. W. S. Fielding, following in the footsteps of Joseph Howe, moved from Halifax to Ottawa without noticeable pain. The aged Sir Oliver Mowat, having been offered an annuity by a 'Syndicate of Toronto capitalists', left the Ontario premiership to give the new government the kudos of a long career of assiduous support of Ontario business. Joseph-Israel Tarte from Quebec (Public Works) and Clifford Sifton from Manitoba (Interior) gave promise that both patronage and western development would get careful attention.

Two great external determinants conditioned Liberal policy and also paved the way to phenomenal success. The first was American. In 1891 and again in 1896 McKinley Republicans raised the United States tariff sharply, thus weakening Canadian advocates of reciprocity. And in the same years the belief spread widely that the American frontier of good western land had closed. The fact that there was still plenty of land in the American west was less important than the curious impression (given academic endorsement by Frederick Jackson Turner) that a frontier of such land no longer existed in the United States. The second determinant was the dramatic recovery of world markets after 1896 which coincided with the discovery of substantial new gold resources in South Africa, Australia and the Canadian Yukon. For a nation heavily dependent upon exporting farm products and raw materials as well as upon capital and human imports these new conditions abroad worked wonders in the growth of an extended east–west Canadian economy. The Laurier government was quick to exploit the opportunities thus offered, and to take full credit for the results.

The Liberal Wheat Boom policies were mercantilist with a strong flavour of social Darwinism. Sifton best expressed the Darwinist theme when, commenting upon the Yukon gold rush, he declared: 'One of the principal ideas western men have is that it is right to take anything in sight provided nobody else is ahead of them.' In most respects this attitude was evident in the government's approach to social-economic affairs. But it was modified by and integrated with the *dirigisme* of tariff and immigration policies. Both were designed to direct and assist the surging streams of people and investment. And both streams, while directed towards western development were, as Sifton said, to 'send a flood of new blood from one end of this great country to the other, through every artery of commerce . . .'

Fiscal policy was quickly settled. The Fielding tariff, apart from reductions on a few western farm necessities, maintained a high level of protection. But it was protection consciously adjusted to the needs of a growing east–west economy. Thus the tariff schedules provided for reduced rates on imports from nations who reduced their charges on Canadian exports. In practice this resulted, over several years, in nearly one-third lower tariff rates on British imports, while an intermediate schedule was used to negotiate reciprocal reductions with several other countries. This root-and-branch change in traditional Liberal policy not only encouraged Canadian-British trade, it had also a marked effect upon economic relations with the United States. Speaking on the effect of the tariff in 1904, Fielding put the matter quite simply:

I think, Sir, as to whether or not it is adequate protection we have some evidence of a gratifying character that the tariff, without being excessive, is high enough to bring some American industries across the line and a tariff which is able to bring these industries into Canada looks very much like a tariff which affords adequate protection.

In fact this period did witness the beginning of American investment in Canada, the beginning of a long if erratic flow which was to create one of Canada's major political problems by the 1960s. Fostered as a means of developing Canadian industry it was to culminate in a serious threat to Canadian independence – in the American ownership of well over half of all industrial investment. In the years prior to 1922 it was the second main source of imported capital. Between 1900 and 1922 direct foreign investment in Canada rose from $1,232 million to $5,207 million. While this was less than the capital generated within Canada itself, there can be no doubt that foreign investors gave the extra push required to convert a 'normal' return to prosperity into a boom – to render certain the birth of a major industrial system. No less significant was the shifting balance between British and American investment in Canada. In 1900 Britain provided 85 per cent of foreign investment and the United States only 14 per cent. By 1922 American sources accounted for 50 per cent of such investment and British 47 per cent. One need not be a complete economic determinist to suspect an influence upon Canadian policies flowing from these developments. At the turn of the century Fielding introduced the 'British preference' tariff structure. In 1922 another Liberal government set Canada firmly in the forefront of those who would loosen the imperial tie to the point of mere symbolism. And in 1946–7, when the American share of foreign investment had reached 72 per cent, yet another Liberal government negotiated continental defence agreements which led to a further sharp increase in American ownership and control of Canadian industrial production. The effects of two world wars upon both Britain and America, as well as other factors, influenced these policy shifts. But amongst the forces at work the economic is startlingly prominent.

In the Laurier period the east–west economic system worked with astonishing success. As if to confute the dire predictions of Goldwin Smith and Sir Richard Cartwright hundreds of thousands of hopeful immigrants poured into the country, including a great many returning Canadians who had left for the United States in the preceding years of slow growth. From 16,800 arrivals in 1896 the stream swelled to flood-tide with 500,000 in 1913. With a population in 1914 of less than eight million, Canada was profoundly affected by the arrival of two and a half million people over the preceding eighteen years. While the basic structure of power was not immediately shaken, new problems of political, social and economic accommodation were sharply etched.

The most enduring of these problems was the changed ethnic balance of the country's population. Immigration in the Wheat Boom years contained virtually no people from France. Thus, despite a high birth-rate amongst French Canadians their percentage of the population declined by more than three points (to 27.9) during this period. While not disastrous, the trend disturbed Quebec leaders deeply. Moreover, a distinct new element entered Canadian demography: over half a million Europeans came from the ramshackle Austro-Hungarian empire, the Ukraine and central Europe. Romanticized by Clifford Sifton as stalwart peasants in sheepskin coats, the Europeans moved mostly through Winnipeg to settle on the frigid, awe-inspiring prairies. Often they spent their first years in sod huts while awaiting enough cash returns on their wheat crops to build a frame house. Along with even larger numbers of Americans, Ontarians and families from the British Isles, these people settled the western wheatlands, provided an enlarged domestic market for manufactured goods as well as financial and transportation services, and created real-estate booms in western towns. That they also produced a rapid increase in the total value of Canadian exports did not mean that they were easily incorporated in Canadian society. Both the Europeans and many of the English faced a strident Canadian nativism expressed principally by ex-Ontarians who occupied most western positions of influence in business, government and the churches. From newspaper, pulpit and the hustings could be heard the Canadian version of social Darwinism:

... So long as Britons and northwestern Europeans constitute the vast majority there is not so much danger of losing our national character. To healthy Britons of good behaviour our welcome is everlasting; but to make this country a dumping ground for the scum and dregs of the old world means transplanting the evils and vices that they may flourish in a new soil. ... What has happened in the United States during a century appears likely to happen in Canada in a few short years. ... The non-English-speaking immigrants are in most cases illiterate, and have minds that are unresponsive to Canadian sentiment. Their tendency is to form colonies and establish on Canadian soil their own customs, methods and traditions. ... The serious character of the problem may be stated thus: if we do not Canadianize and Christianize the newcomer, he will make us foreigners on our own soil and under our own flag. ... It seems that Canada is undertaking to solve a problem that has never successfully been worked out by any people heretofore. We must not only Canadianize the newcomer, but we must check the tide of immigration until we are better prepared to deal with it.

Both in Ontario and throughout the west the doors of shops and factories blossomed with the sign: 'No English need apply'. But the real target of English-speaking Protestant nativism was not the under-nourished refugee from Manchester, nor the supercilious remittance man with his ranch in the Alberta foothills or his ivy-covered house in Victoria, B.C. The targets were the 'hunky', the 'dago' and the 'Ruthenian'. For these were the people who were most uniformly exploited in the new environment. Sifton's immigration agents in Europe, trumpeting the opportunities and amenities of 'the last, best West', arranged for subsidized passages across the ocean, and, in Canada, by 'colonist cars' to Ontario and the prairies. In Winnipeg's barren and drafty immigration sheds the immigrants arranged with agents of the railway or of speculative land companies (and after 1908, often directly with a government agent) for farm land.

Yet many immigrants remained in the towns of Ontario or in the rapidly growing western towns such as Winnipeg, Regina, Calgary, Edmonton and Vancouver. With the most meagre assistance from church missions and lacking both language and industrial skills, thousands of the immigrants found themselves living in pestiferous urban slums. Labour unions, growing slowly against a basically hostile middle-class opinion, did something to 'Canadianize' the immigrant, while government felt its job was done with the actual transportation completed. Thus, as the inevitable social tensions and strikes increased, the 'foreigner' was most usually the scapegoat. The majority Protestant churches accepted the notion that sloth, liquor and ignorance accounted for destitution, whether amongst foreigners or native Canadians. At the same time, some ministers, of whom J. S. Woodsworth of Winnipeg was the most prominent, began the work of criticizing these aspects of the maturing Canadian capitalism. Inspired by the settlement house movement, as well as by British Fabian socialism and American social gospel spokesmen, Woodsworth and his colleagues moved towards co-operation with labour and towards social-democratic political action.

While the Laurier-Sifton immigration bonanza thus increased both productivity and social tension, it had longer range effects also. Many English-speaking Canadians used the immigrant threat as a means both of restricting labour union rights and intensifying the concept of Canada as British. This meant 'Canadianizing' the immigrant and although communities such as those of the Dukhobors and Mennonites in the west did retain strong identities, most immigrants moved fairly rapidly into at least the lower echelons of Canadian society. While they retained, often, a vigorous recollection of their origins and rejoiced in wearing European dress at various 'ethnic' celebrations, they became in fact nationalistic Canadians. Later in the twentieth century, when the European component of Canadian society was again sharply increased, it became plausible to talk not of two founding nations, but of many founding groups. Of the various sources of present French-Canadian fears about survival, this increasing multiplicity of origins, and the fact that the overwhelming majority of immigrants have assimilated to English- rather than to French-speaking culture in Canada, are amongst the most significant.

As the Wheat Boom moved towards its apex of 1913 more immediate political problems arose. Most of the wheat regions lay within the governmental unit of the Northwest Territories.

Although a form of responsible government had been created for the Territories in 1897, the new concentration of population in its southerly reaches required a provincial structure by 1905. Differences of opinion about whether there should be one or two provinces, and whether Ottawa should retain control of their natural resources 'for purposes of the Dominion' were fairly easily settled. The two provinces of Alberta and Saskatchewan were established by the Autonomy Bills in 1905, and their resources, like those of Manitoba, were reserved for central administration. But education once again caused serious trouble. The Roman Catholic and French schools, which had been permitted under the legislation which had established the Territories in 1875, had progressively lost their earlier rights. When Laurier, during the absence of Sifton, who was the chief western representative in the cabinet, inserted provisions in the draft bill to restore the earlier separate school rights, Sifton resigned. The predictable political storm that swept Ontario and the west forced Laurier to remove the school clauses and thus to aggravate Quebec fears about *la survivance*. And the aroused English-speaking Protestantism was to make ever more precarious the difficult path of racial conciliation that Laurier had chosen to follow.

In most other respects Sir Wilfrid Laurier was able to gratify the aspirations of English-speaking Canada, particularly those of the business community. Development of the west, with its huge increase in freight traffic and its burgeoning consumer market, opened golden opportunities for promoters, developers and investors. The remarkable annual increase in wheat production and the growing western demand for farm machinery and other goods from central Canadian factories made plausible the arguments for rapid expansion of transportation facilities. Thus the Laurier government subsidized the building of branch lines by the C.P.R. and deepened the canals on the Great Lakes–St Lawrence system to accommodate larger grain carriers. But the prime minister agreed readily with other promoters that this was not nearly enough to equip the country for what he said would be 'Canada's Century'.

In 1902 two business groups approached the government with

proposals to build a second transcontinental railway. The first proposal was that of the Grand Trunk which now saw the chance of successfully extending its central line east and west to reach both coasts. The second proposal came from William Mackenzie and Donald Mann, two western railway barons who had put together a prairie network (the Canadian Northern Railway) based upon local lines but which now reached the Great Lakes at Fort William. After desultory attempts to arrange an amalgamation of the two groups Laurier was carried away by his optimism about the future. Despite the resignation of A. G. Blair who, as minister of railways, was horrified by the impending expenditures, the government endorsed the construction of two more transcontinental systems. Both new roads were heavily subsidized from public revenues and both were to end in bankruptcy. Probably unaware of the extent of corrupt interest that lay behind these deals, and which flowered after their consummation, Laurier justified them by appealing to a buoyant Canadian nationalism which was perilously slanted towards English-speaking dominance. Speaking in the House in support of the new railway charters, he revealed the extent to which his shaky knowledge of finances was matched by his too rosy view of bi-racial understanding:

Why this expenditure? ... We ask parliament to assent to this policy because we believe – nay, we feel certain, and beyond a doubt – that in so doing we give voice and expression to a sentiment which is today in the mind, and still more in the heart, of every Canadian, that a railway to extend from the shores of the Pacific Ocean and to be, every inch of it, on Canadian soil, is a national as well as a commercial necessity. ... The flood tide is upon us that leads on to fortune; if we let it pass it may never recur again. ... Heaven grant that it be not already too late; heaven grant that whilst we tarry and dispute, the trade of Canada is not deviated to other channels, and that an ever vigilant competitor does not take to himself the trade that properly belongs to those who acknowledge Canada as their native or adopted land.

In the debate the ex-minister, Blair, tried to apply the brakes. 'I fail to discover,' he remarked, 'wherein we have to appeal to heaven against the possibility of a little delay in this matter. ...

I do not see why the people of this country should be saddled with an obligation of $100,000,000 and an addition to their liability ... of an amount exceeding that.' His suggestion that such public expenditures should, from the start, be based upon public ownership was ignored and the prosperity images of King Wheat carried the day.

Despite the costs in stored-up racial and social tension and over-extended public credit, the base was laid in these years for a more enduring prosperity than that which was based on a single staple export. In 1896 the discovery of gold in the Yukon produced a North American rush to the Klondike in the far north-west. Celebrated in the verses of Robert Service, the Yukon stood as a symbol for the treasure house of minerals and water-power that began to be tapped about the same time. In the mountainous Kootenay district of British Columbia more gold was found together with lead and zinc which in the long run were even more important. In northern Ontario, now penetrated by federally sponsored railways as well as by some provincial roads and railways, the pre-Cambrian Shield yielded nickel, silver, gold, copper and other metals. The massive forests of British Columbia and central Canada gave up millions of trees to make lumber for prairie homes as well as to feed a rapidly growing pulp and paper industry. At one jump whole new frontiers of almost untold wealth were opened to exploitation.

As with most frontiers those of the north and the west were controlled by metropolitan centres to which flowed the great bulk of their profits. If Ottawa endorsed the policies and raised most of the required revenues to subsidize the gigantic expansion, the real policy originators and controllers were to be found in the financial houses and the railway and industrial head-offices of Toronto and the English-speaking community of Montreal. Each of these cities, and their outpost at Winnipeg where the grain trade was controlled, experienced its own boom. Profits went into elegant houses, new-fangled luxuries such as automobiles and, even more, into industrial enterprises based upon new sources of power and raw materials. In 1906, largely to encourage industrial growth, Ontario established a

Hydroelectric Power Commission which soon produced and distributed electricity across the whole of the province – based at first upon the majestic flow of Niagara and later upon less dramatic but highly productive watercourses. Other provincial governments followed suit and in the west not only power plants but also telephone systems and even grain elevators were developed under public ownership. While there was undoubtedly some public opinion in favour of this kind of 'gas-and-water socialism', the principal explanation lies rather in the pace of growth which far outstripped the ability of private capital to provide the required services. Such precedents were later to be used to good effect both by the old-line parties and by social-democrats.

Certainly it cannot be demonstrated that experience on the various Canadian frontiers (as has been alleged about the frontier in the United States) gave to the country its basic social-political attitudes. Particularly with respect to the northern and western frontiers of mine, lumber camp and wheat belt, the high costs of transportation, communication and capital investment actually enhanced metropolitan controls. Thus, as in the days of the fur trade, Canadian economic life in the twentieth century grew along highly centralized and semi-monopolistic lines. While frontier protest against central Canadian domination and cupidity became endemic, it did not generate novel political ideas or basically different attitudes to social purpose. Rather it imported and adapted reform ideas which originated in Britain or the United States and strove to make the new growth regions as much like those from which they sprang as possible. In myth, legend and on the platform, the notion of a purifying frontier flowered, and remains a central part of Canadian folklore. Perhaps this has been all to the good for it has helped to induce Canadians to accept some policies of regional redistribution of wealth

In the years of Laurier prosperity, growing disparities, both regional and class, were veiled by the excitement of expansion. The Atlantic provinces shared scarcely at all in the period's growth. While the Cape Breton steel industry, sheltered by Ottawa's subsidy and tariff policies, profited from railway-building demands, little other industry took root and practically none of the immigrant stream tarried in the Maritimes. In the high prosperity regions of Quebec and Ontario and in some western towns a Canadian working class was steadily growing. But it was not a 'class' in the British or European sense of the word. Relatively small in numbers it was widely scattered across the country and was further deterred from collective action by differences of language and culture. In Montreal and other Quebec towns a majority of the workers were French – many but recently off the farm. Under the influence of parish clergy imbued with ideas of protective racial nationalism they resisted bi-lingual cooperation, often settling disputes on terms more satisfactory to the employers than themselves. In Ontario and the west the slow growth of unions was marked by a stronger strain of radicalism. While most workers belonged to 'international' craft unions affiliated with Samuel Gompers's cautious American Federation of Labour, not a few supported tiny local labour and socialist parties, and some national unions were founded, particularly for railway workers. Such labour radicalism as there was sprang largely from the activities of British immigrants who had worked with the New Unionism, the I.L.P. or Labour Representation Committees in Britain. In Winnipeg the Trades and Labour Council published a socialist paper and sponsored meetings such as one in 1907 which was told by Keir Hardie that it was a pleasure 'to meet again the men and women who had fought for years in the old country the battle of labour emancipation, and who now in Canada joined in rejoicing with the British labour party in their partial success in Great Britain.'

While sociologists have argued that 'upward mobility' and absence of class-consciousness were principal reasons for stunting the growth of labour radicalism in Canada, it is more likely that difficulties of communication (geographic, linguistic and cultural) were more substantial reasons. In any event British immigration and the example of British labour had as much to do with the long-run course of Canadian labour politics as the ideals of British 'Society' and imperialism had influence upon the English-speaking Canadian power-élite. And both influences helped keep Canada perceptibly different from the United States.

Yet, because socialism and organized labour were not powerful forces in Canada prior to the First World War, governments were not inclined to pay much attention to problems of reform and social welfare. While Canadians were aware of the reform purposes of the Lloyd George budget and the American progressive movement (let alone the socialist tendencies in Australia and New Zealand) there was no real counterpart to these aspects of English-speaking reformism in Canada. The provinces, led by Ontario, enacted some safety and lien laws in labour's interest, but the rights of strikers, organizers and even membership were in constant peril. In 1900 the Laurier government established a federal department of labour with the young W. L. Mackenzie King as deputy minister. King was familiar with sweatshop and other undesirable labour conditions as well as with British and American literature on industrial relations. But his humanitarian sympathy for the workers was more than matched by concern for social order and a towering political ambition. As the grandson of the 1837 rebel, William Lyon Mackenzie, King was to cherish, throughout his long and remarkable career, two closely related aims: to have the confidence of the common man (both French and English) and to obliterate his grandfather's 'failure-stigma' by becoming a successful prime minister. His achievement of both aims is undoubted, just as the assessments of his achievement are controversial in the extreme. In these early years, first as deputy – then as minister, King secured passage of an Industrial Disputes Investigation Act (1907) which prohibited strikes in industries under federal jurisdiction until an investigation had taken place. King professed confidence that widely publicized reports of impartial investigating boards would aid conciliation of disputes. In practice, however, while federal conciliators were sometimes helpful, the system was more of a hindrance to unionism than an aid, and the influence of the government appointees, including King himself, was nearly always on the side of management.

Farmers' organizations in these years were much more powerful than were those of labour. Across the west, particularly, grievances and responsibility for their redress were clearly defined and vigorously proclaimed. Ottawa responded to the farmers' demand for better and cheaper freight transport by subsidizing low rates on farm machinery and grain as well as by chartering new roads and promising to build a railway to Hudson Bay as an additional competitive outlet for the west. In 1900 a federal Grain Act attempted to regulate charges levied by storage elevator companies for handling grain. When this proved ineffectual due to collusion amongst the companies, many farmers joined a cooperative buying and selling agency, the Grain Growers' Grain Company. Initiated by E. A. Partridge, a British socialist who had himself gone through the sod-hut stage of the western frontier, the Company battled valiantly against the private companies that controlled the Winnipeg Grain Exchange. Eventually, with support from the Manitoba government, the Grain Growers' Grain Company secured a seat on the Exchange, but this still left thousands of farmers in the west without substantial protection against manipulation of storage rates and grain prices.

More and more the farmers turned towards political action. And more and more they focused their attention upon the tariff as the father of most iniquities. Drawing many of their arguments (and some of their spokesmen) from American populism, they argued that the concentration of industry, finance and trade in the hands of fewer and fewer companies and the resulting high costs of goods and services were made possible by tariff protection. In the *Grain Growers' Guide* and in meetings of United Farmers' and Grain Growers' Associations, eastern domination was loudly denounced. Speakers and editorialists used often the old Jeffersonian myths of agrarian purity, foretelling both moral and economic doom should the cities grow at the expense of honest husbandry. In the long run it would become clear that the farmers would accept *quid pro quo* policies such as government-sponsored crop insurance, marketing boards, and price stabilization – a kind of farmers' collectivism endorsed by the state at provincial and federal levels. But prior to the First World War the state, at least at the federal level, was not prepared to grant the farmers an equivalent to the manufacturers' tariff-subsidy programmes. Thus with fire in their eyes the farmers denounced the tariff and also the two major parties which they claimed were completely in the hands of eastern interests. In 1910 during his first political tour of the west, Laurier was deeply impressed by the growing clamour of criticism. Later in the year, when 800 farmers staged a 'march on Ottawa' to demand that the government lower tariffs and, if possible, secure a tariff reciprocity agreement with the United States, Laurier decided some action must be taken in order to forestall more serious political action by the farmers.

The action decided upon was perhaps Laurier's biggest political mistake, and the mistake was compounded by a fortuitous American circumstance. The American President, W. H. Taft, saw in a reciprocity agreement a means of recovering political ground he had lost to insurgents in his party when he had signed the Payne-Aldrich Tariff Bill of 1909. Thus, early in 1911, the Laurier government was able to negotiate an agreement with Washington for reciprocal lowering of tariffs on a considerable range of farm products, primary resources and some manufactured goods. The sudden reversion to the old Liberal free trade doctrine shattered Laurier's support in the business world. Clifford Sifton who, like many other westerners (and Maritimers) who moved to central Canada, had become an ardent supporter of the protected east–west economy, lined up a powerful group of Toronto businessmen in a public denunciation of reciprocity. Behind the scenes many of the biggest erstwhile contributors to the Liberal war-chest worked against Laurier throughout the summer of 1911. The defeat of the ageing Laurier government in September left little doubt that central Canadian business was more than a match for the organized farmers.

In his post-mortem on the election Laurier remarked: 'I maintain to this day, and I believe it will become more and more apparent as time goes on, that upon the 21st of September it was not the voice of reason that prevailed, but the voice of passion and prejudice . . .' The passion and the prejudice which entered the election of 1911, however, were even more evident in the disputes over issues other than American reciprocity. If Laurier was newly concerned about holding the balance between western and eastern interests, his older concern about the problems of race relations and the imperial connexion was even more significant as an explanation of his defeat. And here passion and prejudice most certainly entered the lists.

14

Empire, Race and War

In 1885, when the British government put out feelers to discover whether Canada might contribute to an expedition up the Nile for the relief of General Gordon, Sir John Macdonald shied away like a startled colt. Unlike the bishops of Quebec who in 1867 had helped organize a contingent of Papal Zouaves to join Pius IX in his fight against Garibaldi, Macdonald regarded London's predicament in the Sudan as a 'wretched business' and of no concern to Canada. 'Our men and money', he wrote to the Canadian High Commissioner in London, 'would be sacrificed to get Gladstone and Co. out of the hole they have plunged themselves into by their own imbecility.'

In public Macdonald not infrequently wrapped himself in the Union Jack to win an election. In private he spent a good deal of time restraining some of his super-British colleagues. More consistent than most when it came to Canada's imperial and other external relations, Macdonald established policy lines which were to remain dominant down to the Second World War. He recognized that Canada's political independence in North America depended ultimately upon the fact that she was British. While his own experience as one of the British team that negotiated the 1871 Treaty of Washington was somewhat bitter, he was under no illusions about the potential threats of American manifest destiny. He knew too that the general *pax britannica* was of benefit to Canadians in their limited relations with other states and particularly in their purpose of unimpeded domestic development. Yet he also realized that colonial restrictions must be gradually shorn away if Canada were to achieve the full vigour of independent growth. Pursuing this path, Macdonald sought formal diplomatic channels for communication between the British and Canadian governments, rather than the circuitous route through the Colonial Office and the governor-general. Thus in 1880 Sir A. T. Galt was designated Canadian High Commissioner in London. London refused ambassadorial rank to Galt but the office grew slowly in importance. It was one of many steps on the road to full diplomatic independence. Even before the end of the century Canada had claimed and exercised the right to negotiate, but not to sign, commercial treaties with other states.

Just at the outset of this potentially definitive trend a dramatic shift in British thinking about the empire challenged the entire direction of Canadian growth. By the mid seventies Benjamin Disraeli's 'oriental imagination' spoke for a surging new imperialism. Looking with disdain upon Little Englanders and the imperial separatism of earlier colonial reformers, the new imperialists called for a girding of the empire's loins. In the mid eighties Sir John Seeley published his ringing call to greatness, *The Expansion of England*, and supporters of a more tightly knit empire founded the Imperial Federation League. Shocked by the growth of military power on the continent and by new competition in commerce and industry, British public opinion and many political leaders turned to the empire as a desperately needed support. For a Canada moving steadily towards greater autonomy and unwilling to give automatic help in British overseas struggles, the tensions created by the new wave of European and British imperialism were grave indeed.

Two events in 1895 gave clarity and emphasis to the new directions. Lord Salisbury named as colonial secretary Joseph Chamberlain, who was perhaps the principal public spokesman of imperial federation – of the need to create a combined *Kriegsverein* and *Zollverein* in which common trade regulations and unified military planning would counterbalance Britain's relative decline in power. And in the same year the Salisbury government received a peremptory 'note' of some 10,000 words from Richard Olney, President Cleveland's secretary of state, in which Britain was informed that

Today, the United States is practically sovereign on this continent, and its fiat is law upon the subjects to which it confines its interposition. Why? It is not because of the pure friendship or goodwill felt for it. ... It is because, in addition to all other grounds, its infinite resources combined with its isolated position render it master of the situation and practically invulnerable as against any or all other powers.

The Olney note resulted from a boundary dispute between Venezuela and British Guiana which had been dragging on for eight years and which the United States insisted should go to arbitration. Salisbury rejected the demand. But the major war scare which followed was itself succeeded by a negotiated settlement in 1897 by which Britain accepted arbitration. Plainly Britain was prepared to court the newly powerful United States and this, like imperial consolidation, posed dangers for Canada. The beginnings of Britain's imperial death struggle were no pleasanter to live with than was a United States preparing to shoulder Rudyard Kipling's white man's burden.

Wilfrid Laurier, coming to office in 1896, faced the heavy Canadian backwash from these shifts in external power. Many English-speaking Canadians felt the call of the blood as Britain sought strength in the colonies. Most, while wishing to retain the imperial connexion, insisted on safeguards for Canadian autonomy. And French Canadians, to a man, held bitterly suspect any and all demands for imperial integration. Laurier had to face the issue many times and on no occasion more dramatically than at the 1897 Imperial Conference. Chamberlain seized upon the occasion of Queen Victoria's Diamond Jubilee to promote amongst the assembled colonial statesmen his programme of federation. At first Laurier seemed to waver before the flattering attentions showered upon him as the distinguished French-speaking prime minister of the senior self-governing colony. Yet, while he accepted a British knighthood, he rejected adamantly the proposal to set up a permanent Imperial Council with its implied power to regulate empire tariffs and the military-naval roles of the various colonies. 'Canada,' he declared, 'is a nation. Canada is free, and freedom is nationality.' Thus Canadian contributions to imperial strength must continue to be entirely voluntary – such as the imperial preference which the Laurier government had just written into the Canadian tariff. At later conferences in 1902 and 1907, while New Zealanders and Australians were attracted by one form or another of imperial planning, Laurier reiterated the loud Canadian 'No'.

When the Boer War broke out in 1899 Laurier faced formidable and emotional demands from English-speaking Canadians, both inside and outside his cabinet, to rally round the flag. He faced also clamorous insistence from his French-speaking compatriots that Canada's sons should not be sent to die in Britain's colonial wars – particularly in a war which did not threaten either Canadian or British security and in which a non-British racial group felt its survival to be at stake. Sir Wilfrid met the Canadian racial division with an obvious compromise. Without consulting Parliament he authorized the recruiting, equipping and transporting of 1,000 Canadian volunteers who upon arrival in South Africa would be under imperial control. Before the war was over this commitment was more than doubled when the government sent a second Canadian contingent.*

The compromise worked. But it also helped launch the twentieth-century phase of French-Canadian nationalism. In the debate over Canadian involvement passions rose rapidly. When Laurier declared that he had established no precedent and added, 'I claim for Canada this, that in future she shall be at liberty to act or not to act, to interfere or not to interfere, to do just as she pleases,' he was answered with cold Gallic logic by one of his principal Quebec supporters: 'The precedent, Mr Prime Minister, is the accomplished fact.' Laurier's tormentor was Henri Bourassa, principled and talented grandson of Louis Joseph Papineau, and one of the best speakers in the House. Much more a son of the Church than was his grandfather, Bourassa was a fierce defender of full rights for French Canadians within Confederation. Like most French-Canadian nationalists prior to the Second World War Bourassa stressed the clerical element in French-speaking culture; unlike many he was also deeply opposed to industrial capitalism and thus was to emerge in the twenties and thirties as a social reformer, bringing to his support the arguments of European liberal Catholic

---

*The number of Canadians who fought in South Africa, including those in the two contingents and those who enlisted individually in the British army, amounted to 7,300.

thought. In the racial crisis caused by Laurier's Boer War compromise, Bourassa resigned his seat and was returned by acclamation to become the rallying point of French-Canadian resistance to Canadian involvement in British wars.

For the moment, however, Laurier's position satisfied most people across the country, and he missed few opportunities to prove that Canadian national interests remained his touchstone. In 1904, in an open battle with imperial authorities, he dismissed the English commander of the Canadian armed forces and announced that henceforth the position would be filled only by Canadians. At the same time he benefited from a sharp increase in Canadian national feeling resulting from the flamboyance of President Theodore Roosevelt. Flushed from the glories of San Juan Hill and the acquisition of the Philippines in 1898, and catapulted into the White House by an assassin's bullet in 1901, Roosevelt left no doubt about his willingness to swing a big stick in the Americas. In the south he seized Panama and in the north he put aside diplomatic good faith in a bitter struggle over the Canada-Alaska boundary.

The Alaska boundary issue grew out of the Yukon gold rush. The only effective access route to the Klondike gold fields was by way of the Lynn Canal. This long arm of the Pacific cuts across the Alaska panhandle whose boundary had not been clearly determined since the Americans purchased Alaska from Russia in 1867. At stake was the lucrative supply trade funnelling through two tiny 'American' ports at the head of the canal. If the ports were judged to be in Alaska, the merchants of Seattle would continue to benefit greatly from free admission of goods, if in Canada the merchants of Vancouver would receive the customs benefits. Although the complicated treaty background of the question certainly favoured the American claim of a boundary skirting the head of the canal, the Canadian government sought British help in getting what amounted to a revision of the line. London, however, turned down the plea that British treaty concessions to the United States with respect to building a Panama canal should be used as a bargaining counter for an American concession in Alaska. Instead, Britain accepted the American proposal that the boundary question be submitted to a judicial tribunal of six impartial jurists, three to be named by each side.

The agreement to appoint a tribunal was reached in 1903 only after long and acrimonious discussions and after Roosevelt had assured the Senate and other concerned parties that he would accept only a favourable verdict. Thus the three American appointees on the tribunal were committed in advance and the British member, Lord Alverstone, voted with them against the two Canadian members for a boundary that conceded virtually all the American claims. In 1910 a Hague tribunal ruled in favour of the Canadian case in a long-standing dispute over the rights of American fishermen off Canadian Atlantic coasts, and in the same year a permanent International Joint Commission of Canadians and Americans was established to regulate traffic and water levels on the Great Lakes. Yet, while these later events took some of the sting out of the Alaska boundary débâcle, Canadian opinion remained extremely edgy – a climate of anti-Americanism which helped defeat Laurier in the reciprocity election of 1911. At the same time, however, much Canadian resentment over the 1903 award was reserved for Britain whose courting of the United States was widely interpreted as betrayal of Canadian loyalty. And this side of the coin lay exposed during a bitter debate that blew up in 1909 over the question of Canadian contributions to the naval defence of the empire.

At a special Imperial Conference in 1909 the colonial premiers were given an outline of the German naval-building threat and invited to reconsider the question of contributions to a unified imperial naval command. Laurier decided on another compromise. Canada would build her own navy and hold it, small though it would be, ready to assist in the event of any crisis which Canada considered crucial. In 1910 the Liberal government fought its Naval Bill through the House despite a dangerous storm of opposition both from Conservative members and from vocal critics outside Parliament. The Tories, now led by a vigorous lawyer from Halifax, Robert Borden, castigated the proposal as creating a 'tin-pot navy' which would do nothing for Canada's prestige, would be useless in time of war and which symbolized a deepening disunity in the empire. While much English-speaking Canadian opinion supported Laurier's Bill, Borden succeeded in tapping imperial sentiment in many parts of the country. But even more ominous was the alliance struck between Conservatives and French nationalists in Quebec. The French Canadians found their oracle in Henri Bourassa who, in the columns of his newspaper *Le Devoir*, exhorted his compatriots to resist the insistent loyalty demands of English-speaking imperialists. In 1902, even before the eruption of the naval crises, he had written:

British imperialism, as opposed to British democracy, to British traditions, to British grandeur – is a lust for land-grabbing and military dominion. ... Having undertaken more responsibilities than she is able to stand, surrounded as she is by hostile or indifferent nations, the new Britain of Mr Chamberlain is in sore need of soldiers and sailors to prop the fabric raised by her frantic ambition. Being denuded of troops at home, she turns in distress to her colonies.

And, turning to the impact of imperialism upon the relations between races inside Canada, Bourassa set the theme which has remained dominant down to the present:

From the presence of the two races in Canada, there is no reason, I believe, to dread any danger or even additional troubles, if only our politicians be willing, instead of pandering to sectional prejudices, to appeal to the best sentiments of both elements.

A mutual regard for racial sympathies on both sides, and a proper discharge of our exclusive duty to this land of ours, such is the only ground upon which it is possible for us to meet, so as to work out our national problems. ... We do not ask that our English-speaking fellow-countrymen should help us to draw closer to France; but, on the other hand, they have no right to take advantage of their overwhelming majority to infringe on the treaty of alliance, and induce us to assume, however freely and spontaneously, additional burdens in defence of Great Britain.

Ironically 'the politicians' used Bourassa's nationalism in much the way that Bourassa himself had warned against. The Quebec wing of the Conservative Party, led by F. D. Monk, expressed French-Canadian disillusionment with the long series of

Liberal compromises on racial and religious matters and was supporting plans to 'colonize' northern Quebec which amounted to recognition that French Canadians were unlikely to find guarantees for their culture elsewhere in Canada. The same Quebec Conservatives attacked the Naval Bill as a subterfuge to commit Canada in advance in any future British war. Yet, as the federal election campaign of 1911 opened, Borden managed an alliance with Monk which rode the Quebec and English-speaking Conservative horses in opposite directions to a smashing victory over the Liberals. In English-speaking Canada Laurier was effectively pilloried as the author of a reciprocity agreement which would sell the country down the river to the Yankees and a naval policy which would isolate Canada from Britain. In Quebec the Conservative-Nationaliste alliance billed him as a tool of British imperialism. In vain did Laurier point out the anomaly:

> I am branded in Quebec as a traitor to the French, and in Ontario as a traitor to the English. In Quebec I am branded as a Jingo, and in Ontario as a Separatist. ... I am neither. I am a Canadian. ... I have had before me as a pillar of fire by night and a pillar of cloud by day a policy of true Canadianism, of moderation, of conciliation.

Often called immoral, the Conservative campaign of 1911 nevertheless accurately reflected both the problems and the hopes of the country. The slogan 'No truck nor trade with the Yankees' spoke to genuine fears of continentalism, while the British loyalty cry appealed both to English-speaking emotion and the hard economic consciousness of the importance of British markets and capital. Conversely the attack on Laurier's conciliation of the 'Jingoes' was in tune with a growing Quebec emphasis on the need to protect the rural-Catholic basis of the French-Canadian nation. It remained to be seen how Robert Borden, now prime minister, would manage a country newly prosperous yet threatened by deeply divisive forces both inside and outside its borders.

Borden was a lawyer's lawyer who brought to politics a genuine Maritimer's concern for the British connexion, combined with an equally strong desire to have Canada's growth to

nationhood reflected accurately and promptly in subtle altera-
tions of the imperial relationship. A man of rigid personal propriety, he possessed little of that genial flexibility that had
permitted Macdonald and Laurier to adjust principle to expedi-
ency. Prosperous himself and well-connected in the English-
speaking business community, he found it next to impossible to
understand, let alone accommodate, the claims to recognition
advanced by French Canadians and by a working class which
objected ever more vehemently to the arrogance both of
governments and industrial management. Borden's record of
wartime leadership, while it listed considerable achievements
at the national and imperial levels, was to be lessened by its
legacy of racial and class antagonisms.

The first years of the new Conservative government were
not happy. The new-found Conservative allies in Quebec were
under-represented in the cabinet and in the first big issue faced
by the government F. D. Monk resigned from his post of Public
Works. The issue was Borden's attempt to fulfil an election
promise. It took the form of a Bill to provide a direct cash grant
of $35 million for three dreadnoughts which would join the
British fleet. Forced through the House under a new closure
rule, the Bill intensified French-Canadian fears about imperial
tribute and was killed by a Liberal majority in the Senate.
Preferring not to risk a constitutional crisis and a second
election, Borden simply shelved the whole naval issue and
took no action, either, to implement Laurier's Naval Service
Act.

Borden's problems were further complicated by the onset
of a depression which brought unemployment and declining
prices for wheat sales abroad. Thus when Britain declared war
on Germany at the beginning of August 1914, the event seemed
something like a blessing from the government's point of view.
For the first impact of the war was to give a sudden, if artificial,
stimulus to the economy and, to many people's surprise, to
slacken racial tension. In Parliament and press Canadians of
both races and both parties endorsed the British action.
Bourassa himself announced that it was Canada's duty 'to contribute within the bounds of her strength, and by means which

are proper to herself, to the triumph, and especially to the endurance, of the combined efforts of France and England'.

Unity, however, was skin-deep. Its fragile foundations rested upon several invalid assumptions. Perhaps the most important of the assumptions was that the war, like its recent predecessors in Europe, would be relatively short-lived, a matter of months. In part this incorrect analysis derived from inadequate Canadian sources of information about international relations. Only in 1909 had Ottawa established a tiny Department of External Affairs and thus had no independent sources of information on which to make judgements about either the issues involved or the likely duration of the war. Again, while no prominent Canadian in 1914 objected to the continuing diplomatic unity of the empire (which involved Canada automatically in a legal state of war when London's declaration was made), neither did Canadians expect that the nature and extent of the struggle would raise all the bitter issues of race and national autonomy that seemed at the outset to have been stilled. Had French Canadians felt for France what many of them were to feel in the days of De Gaulle, the story might well have been different. But they did not. For most, revolutionary and anticlerical France was as foreign as England.

Not surprisingly, then, Canadian involvement in World War I was as complicated as it was important. Militarily Canada contributed heavily – more heavily than was wise, in terms of threats to her existence. The Canadian army corps of four divisions eventually required more than 600,000 men. Some 8,000 men were enlisted in the navy to guard the Atlantic approaches while over 24,000 went into the British Air Services. By the end of the war more than 60,000 Canadians had been killed in action, some 12,000 more than those similarly lost by the United States. According to Lloyd George, 'The Canadians played a part of such distinction [at Courcelette on the Somme] that thenceforward they were marked out as storm troops; for the remainder of the war they were brought along to head the assault in one great battle after another.' Certainly the price paid for the Canadian reputation was heavy – in the first grisly poison gas attack at Ypres, in the *Blutbad* of the Somme, in the fierce battle for Vimy Ridge, in the penultimate tragedy of Passchendaele. Equally clearly the size of the sacrifice deepened Canada's determination to move more distinctly towards autonomy.

At the outset the first Canadian division was considered part of the Imperial Army. Borden, however, got a legal opinion from his minister of justice which justified the view that the Canadians were militiamen on active service abroad, and thus should remain under Canadian command. The government seized upon this interpretation, established its own military headquarters in London and named a Canadian, Sir Arthur Currie, to command the Canadian Corps. Borden's successful arguments for Canadian autonomy and international recognition in 1919 were substantially strengthened by his wartime attitude towards control of the armed forces.

Wartime economic growth gave further weight to autonomist logic. With demands for farm produce and raw materials almost unlimited, Canada moved dramatically away from the threatening depression of 1913–14. During the war, exports of grain and flour doubled in value. Wood, pulp, paper, lumber, meat, livestock and metals all pushed up export figures to unheard-of levels. Still more important were changing balances within the economy. By the end of the war Canada was launched as a significant industrial nation. Heavily favoured both by demand and a tax policy that virtually ignored excess profits, industrialists expanded their plants and built new ones to produce ammunition, ships, guns and then found that rising incomes gave them also expanded demand for a widening range of consumer goods. Production and trade controls were minimal although in 1917 the government set up a Board of Grain Supervisors with power to regulate the sale and price of wheat.

Money and credit for the war effort and for economic expansion came from new sources and these changes also marked the path to the future. Ottawa levied its first income tax in 1917 and was able to raise more than $2 billion by victory loans within the country. At the same time London was replaced by New York as the chief outside source of capital both for public borrowing and private investment. Provincial and city governments, as well as Ottawa, began to borrow in the United States and in the course of the war direct American investment in Canadian manufacturing and resource industries increased more than threefold. By the end of the war all levels of government had taken on heavy debt burdens which could be sustained only by steady economic growth. Moreover, the question of an expansive federal role in the directing of the economy would come under sharp review by provincial governments anxious about revenue sources and political power.

But more than purely economic balances were disturbed by the war. Most important was the imbalance of sacrifices and a complex, yet widespread, feeling that the government was unconcerned with any interest save that of a purely military victory. Farmers and urban workers felt the pinch of an uncontrolled inflation that increased the cost of living by two-thirds between 1914 and 1918. Neither wages nor the price of farm products kept pace with the spectacular profits of business, and by the end of the war a cumulative mood of disillusionment broke out in massive labour strikes and independent farmer politics. Still more dangerous, in the long run, was the crisis of conscription.

In the background of the Compulsory Service Act that was to be passed in 1917 lay a tangled mass of emotion and interest. By 1916 it was clear that Borden had blundered badly in permitting his politically incompetent minister of militia, Sir Sam Hughes, to manage anything, let alone the basic organization of the expeditionary forces and supply contracting. A succession of scandals brought the government into a disrepute which was not much relieved by Borden's decision to fire Hughes in 1916. Demands for a National or Union government were already being voiced when the question of manpower replacement took on an ominous urgency. The urgency resulted from the government's commitment to maintain four full divisions on the Western Front and from the fact that recruiting in Canada declined sharply throughout 1916. Borden moved reluctantly towards compulsion in the face of bitter opposition from organized labour, farmers and most French Canadians. But he moved also in the knowledge that much English-speaking opinion was with him. Thus, in June 1917, the government brought forward a conscription Bill and at the same time pursued negotiations with leading English-speaking Liberals for the formation of a Union government. The prime minister declared:

> I am in a position to assure the House and the country that the need of reinforcements is urgent, insistent and imperative. The effort of Russia is paralysed for the present – no one knows for how long. The effort of the United States is only beginning. It is Germany's hope to win the war before the power of the United States can become effective. ... The reinforcements now available will last for only a few months, the precise number of which, for military reasons, I am not at liberty to state ... Is there not, as I have already said in this House, an appeal from the men at the front? ...

Sir Wilfrid Laurier, who had already refused to join a Union government, led the opposition to the measure. Reasserting his support of the war, he charged the government with bad faith (Borden had said in 1916 that the commitment of 500,000 men did not mean that the government would introduce conscription), called for a referendum on the question and defended Quebec against the super-heated castigation of many English-speaking leaders:

> If the enlistment of French Canadians does not compare favourably with the enlistment of their compatriots speaking the English language, it is to be noted that the disparity between the enlistment of men who are Canadian-born and men who are British-born is also somewhat marked. ... Immigration has been constant from the British Isles, and the connexion between the British settler and his motherland has been maintained. This is not the case as between French Canadians and old France.

When the vote came more than twenty of Laurier's Liberals deserted to support conscription. For Laurier the political situation had become impossible. By this time French Canada had been almost totally alienated by a series of offensive actions and attitudes at all levels of government. At Ottawa, Sir Sam Hughes compounded his administrative ineptness by an anti-Catholic prejudice which betrayed his Ulster background. French Canadians who volunteered were seldom enrolled in French-speaking units, despite the notable military record of the Royal Twenty-Second Regiment of Quebec (the Vandoos), while in the effort to increase recruitment in 1916 several Protestant ministers were amongst the agents sent into Quebec. Still more irritating to French Canadians were the apparently deliberately provocative educational measures taken by Manitoba and Ontario during the war. In 1916 Manitoba eliminated bilingual schools entirely and in Ontario the notorious Regulation 17 sharply restricted use of French in the province's public school system. Bitterly attacking these evidences of irreconcilable English-speaking Protestant superiority, French Canadians asked why they should fight for an empire whose supporters denied them equal rights within their own country. Conscription, to Bourassa and his *nationaliste* colleagues, was the inevitable outcome of the pre-war years of concessions to imperialism. Now, he argued in *Le Devoir*, the time had come to call a halt:

... we have enlisted for the European war six per cent of our population. That is the equivalent of an army of 2,400,000 for France and 2,700,000 for the United Kingdom. Now, despite its enormous army on paper England has not yet sent to France, in the two years and ten months of the war, this number of men. ... Another question may be fairly put in respect of our principal allies: *How many French soldiers, or even British soldiers, would they send to America, if Canada was attacked by the United States?*

Logic was no match for passion – or conviction. The government made certain that it would carry the election which it called shortly after passage of the Conscription Act, and before the Act was implemented. With Laurier immobilized by Quebec sentiment, Sir Clifford Sifton completed negotiations with the Conservatives whereby N. W. Rowell, Liberal leader in Ontario, and a number of English-speaking western Liberals joined Borden in a Union government. Special electoral legislation gave the new government the advantage it needed: overseas soldiers and their women relatives in Canada were enfranchised; immigrants who had entered Canada after 1902 from enemy countries were disfranchised; the soldier vote could be, and was, distributed where most needed.

The election campaign was incendiary. While organized

labour and most farmers were hostile, the English-speaking press, pulpit and platform rang with patriotic declamation. The Rev. D. C. Chown, head of the Methodist Church, declared that conscription was 'the most moral and profoundly religious method of doing our national duty'. Adding patriotism to religion, Dr Chown continued:

> In my judgement, the elector who votes for the anti-conscription policy ... degrades the term Canadian from a synonym of glory to a by-word of reproach. 'Lo this man began to build and was not able to finish.' If I voted against a Union Government candidate I would feel that I was opposing the most patriotic movement ever known in the Dominion of Canada.

All the vote-rigging and patrioteering had been necessary. When the civilian ballots were counted the Liberals had 750,000, the Unionists 842,000. But distribution of the vote gave the Liberals all but three seats in Quebec while limiting them to a mere twenty in all the rest of Canada. The perilous divisions already evidenced in Quebec anti-conscription riots, in vigorous labour and farm protests, were now symbolized in the break-up of the traditional party system. Yet if class and regional antagonisms were sharpened in the final months of the war, those of race or culture were deepened disastrously. The price of an important Canadian role in World War I had been very high indeed.

15

Whose Empire, Whose Nation?

OUT of the war sprang a renewed Canadian nationalism. But, like most things Canadian, nationalism was to be loosely defined – if indeed it had been defined at all. To some it was reasserting Canada's right not to be American, while to others it was almost a question of Canada's right to *be* American. Sometimes the new spirit demanded firmer direction of the country by Ottawa, but just as often it demanded a flowering of provincial rights and powers. For French Canadians nationalism was French-speaking and a matter once again of survival. To the broad mass of English-speaking workers and farmers nationalism was expressed in daring demands for new modes of social justice. To federal Liberals, particularly sensitive to the political isolation of Quebec, nationalism meant a growing independence of London. To English-speaking Conservatives it meant seeking Canadian status well within the empire.

If Bourassa saw the imperial relationship in terms of tribute and blood taxes, Borden saw it as a necessary and advantageous partnership. Yet, even so, the advantages had to be fought for. In this struggle Borden carried further the trends established by Macdonald and Laurier, but with a distinctively Conservative touch. Without completely abandoning the principle of imperial diplomatic unity, he moved towards a greater dominion autonomy based on 'continuous consultation' amongst the self-governing members of the empire. And in so doing he helped lay the base of the modern Commonwealth, even though that Commonwealth was to break definitively with the unity principle.

Having won Canadian control of Canada's overseas divisions, Borden pressed hard, and even angrily, for a real share in formulating imperial policy. When the British government politely refused, on grounds of impracticability, he wrote tartly that

London could scarcely expect Canada to commit half a million men and also 'accept the position of having no more voice and receiving no more consideration than if we were toy automata'. The point was taken in London only when Lloyd George came to office and recognized the full implications of war-weariness in Britain and France. In 1917, an Imperial War Cabinet was established composed of the British War Cabinet and the prime ministers of the Dominions. The actual share in decision-making and the purpose of continuous consultation were limited, of course, by distance and the inability of the overseas ministers to be long away from their own posts. But the precedent was carried over, on the insistence of Borden and Smuts of South Africa, in organizing the imperial delegation to the Paris Peace Conference in 1919. There the Dominions participated in drawing up the Versailles settlement and each of them signed the treaty. While the subtlety of the fact that the Dominion signatures were slightly indented beneath the title of the British Empire was not easily grasped by the United States (which saw simply a ruse to obtain extra members to support Britain in the League of Nations) Borden was well satisfied. To him Canada had acquired international recognition as well as an understanding that she would be consulted in the formation of common imperial policies. Yet the bewilderment of many foreign observers was understandable and, as experience was to reveal, a common imperial foreign policy proved to be both impracticable and undesirable.

Absorbed in problems of high policy during and immediately after the war, Borden left much of the burden of domestic policy-making to his cabinet colleagues. But even had this not been the case the results would probably not have been much different. Most members of Borden's government supported an authoritarian view of society in which 'law and order' were equated with maintaining the rights of vested interests and the sanctity of contract. Conscription was one product of this view; rigged elections and support of the empire were others. And in practice investors and speculators were the principal beneficiaries. Thus at the end of the war the government moved rapidly to return the country to what Warren Gamaliel

Harding was to call 'normalcy'. Its programme of soldier re-habilitation was meagre and its desire to dismantle wartime economic controls, weak though most of those controls had been, was prominent. In 1919 Ottawa terminated the Wheat Board, the most successful of its ventures into economic plan-ning, although western farmers clamoured for the Board's con-tinuance. But the investment community was also favoured by still more drastic developments. In 1920, instead of experiment-ing with further controls, Ottawa permitted the chartered banks to impose a sudden credit halt. The move brought a brief depression in 1921–2 and thus fanned a spirit of revolt against big business and helpless government.

Perhaps the government's most startling action was also its most ambiguous one. By 1916 the transcontinental railways which had been chartered and heavily endowed by Laurier in the Wheat Boom's flush of optimism were on the edge of ruin. A combination of bad management, avarice and rising costs brought the cold realization that the country could not sustain three transcontinental systems. Borden decided to accept the majority report of an investigating commission and place all the major railways, except the Canadian Pacific which was still solvent, under public ownership. Sir Thomas White, minister of finance in 1917, put the case in the House:

> It seems to me that the continuance from year to year of the large financial assistance which we have been granting to these companies is against public opinion and public policy while the ownership of these roads remains in private hands. The true policy would seem to be that which will ensure not only the best public service but a substantial degree of public ownership in order that the benefit of the large financial assistance granted from the public exchequer during the critical period of the development of these roads shall accrue to the benefit of the public when the enterprises reach a period of fruition. If the public does the financing, the public should enjoy the ultimate reward.

While one may detect a shade of socialist reasoning in these remarks it would be unwise to suppose that Sir Thomas had become a social democrat. In fact, Ottawa's foray into public ownership, like the provincial experiments with public utilities, was clearly a matter of necessity The government's credit was bound up with that of the languishing railways – as was that of the banks who owned (together with insurance and bond houses) the bulk of the very large public debt. The initiating of public ownership, which was to develop more extensively in Canada than in the United States, resulted from the same neo-mercantilist purposes that had informed the National Policy of Sir John Macdonald. The duty of government, in the eyes of most businessmen, was to step in to provide a climate and facilities favourable to investment wherever private capital either failed or was unwilling to do the job. That the experimentation with public ownership strengthened collectivist arguments in the following years was a by-product rather than a desired end of the process.

In the case of the railways a sequence of arbitration and legislation stretching from 1917 to 1923 provided handsome compensation to the original investors (with the exception of the bitterly resentful Grand Trunk investors who were predominantly British) and created the Canadian National Railways as a publicly owned company with considerable autonomy. With 20,000 miles of track, and saddled with an inordinate book-debt owing to the salvaged original investors, the C.N.R. nevertheless made enormous strides. Under the direction of a highly talented manager, Sir Henry Thornton, the scattered components of its transcontinental network were welded into an efficient system. And to the railway base were added steamship lines, hotels, and a telegraph system. So successful did the C.N.R. become in terms of service that it came frequently under attacks which portrayed it as a huge white elephant, unable to pay its way, and a publicly endowed threat to the Canadian Pacific which remained in private hands. Its annual deficits, however, resulted from its inherited debt load and the government's requirement that it maintain essential community service even where this might be unprofitable. Much of Canada's growth in the 1920s would have been inhibited had the railway services lacked the rationalization and vigour which, in fact, they enjoyed.

Yet underlying assumptions of business and government that

the interests of the investor were of paramount importance did not go unnoticed by the common man. To thousands of wheat farmers across the prairie west, as well as to owner-operators of mixed-farms in Ontario, the hand of big business seemed to manipulate governments at Ottawa and in the provincial capitals without restraint. Tightening credit, high tariffs, and taxes for the servicing of a debt swollen by profiteering, all proved to the farmers' minds that the political system was both corrupt and undemocratic. Farmers' organizations had always opposed the high tariff and domination of political parties by big business – particularly eastern business. The defeat of reciprocity in 1911 had given a further spurt to farm protests, but wartime experiences led directly to independent political action.

A Farmers' Platform, developed by the Canadian Council of Agriculture between 1916 and 1918, was accepted by all farm organizations as the basis of political action. Heavily influenced by American populism, and especially by the Non-Partisan League of the Dakotas, the farmers' *New* National Policy called for a series of reforms ranging from drastic tariff lowering and freight-rate reductions to American-style direct democracy (initiative, referendum and recall), public ownership of utilities and natural resource development, graduated taxes on private and corporate incomes and on inherited estates, proportional representation, and the vote for women. While women's suffrage was achieved in 1919, the rest remained to be fought for.

'Ostentatious display of wealth', according to a 1919 royal commission report on industrial relations, was one of the chief causes of unrest at the end of the war. A leading example of such display was Casa Loma, a monstrous 'medieval' castle perched on a dominating cliff overlooking the city of Toronto. Its proprietor, Sir Henry Pellatt, was a stockbroker and financial speculator who had amassed a pre-war fortune sufficient to enable him to transport an entire regiment to England at his own expense to take part in the annual manoeuvres of the British army at Aldershot in 1910. His knighthood* was

---

*British titles were awarded to Canadians, largely on the recom-

awarded for services to the militia in which he rose from subaltern in 1880 to major-general in 1918. To many his career and pretension symbolized the interlocking nature of the business-political-social power élite of English-speaking Canada. While Casa Loma was the reductio ad absurdum of social contrasts, those contrasts were none the less sharp and widely recognized. In the Protestant churches a vocal minority of ministers continued the agitation for social reform which some of them had begun prior to the war. Frequently, leading spokesmen of the Social Gospel, such as Salem Bland and J. S. Woodsworth, lent open support to farmers' organizations and labour union demands. The need for basic reform of the country's socially unconcerned capitalism was dramatically articulated in the 1918 report of the Methodist Church:

The war has made clearly manifest the moral perils inherent in the system of production for profits. ... Under the shock and strain of this tremendous struggle, accepted commercial and industrial methods based on individualism and competition have gone down like mud walls in a flood. ... We do not believe this separation of labour and capital can be permanent. Its transcendence, whether through cooperation or public ownership, seems to be the only constructive and radical reform. ... This is the policy set forth by the great labour organizations and must not be rejected because it presupposes, as Jesus did, that the normal human spirit will respond more readily to the call to service than to the lure of private gain.

One year after the Methodist report was drafted, the country was swept by a wave of strikes and labour agitation. Labour union membership had doubled during the war and with peace many feared that employers would beat down long-standing labour demands for shorter hours, collective bargaining, higher wages and a system of social insurances. Encouraged by the growth of the British Labour Party and the apparent success of the Russian revolution, Canadian labour felt the need for immediate action. The resulting strikes of 1919 deprived

mendation of the Canadian cabinet, down to 1935 when the practice was discontinued by the Liberal government elected in that year. Like reform of the Senate, discontinuance of this practice was demanded in all reform platforms of the early twentieth century.

Canadian businessmen of more man-hours than were lost in any other year save 1946.

While socialism, and to some extent syndicalism, inspired many union members, there is no doubt that most, including the leaders, fought for immediate and non-revolutionary goals. They genuinely feared the effects on the labour market of returning soldiers and had no need to propagandize the suffering resulting from inflation. Business leaders conversely, and their colleagues in government, feared that unionization would get out of hand and kill the golden prospects of profit in a country newly equipped with industrial capacity. Their reaction to union demands was similar to that of government and business in the United States during the great Red Scare of 1919. Wartime censorship and repressive legislation were continued and more of the same called for. And when a general strike broke out in Winnipeg in May it was portrayed across the country as being led by Bolsheviks who aimed at nothing less than the establishment in Canada of the dictatorship of the proletariat.

The Winnipeg general strike was a social trauma for Canadians and caused political shock-waves felt down to the present. It began as a strike in the building and metal trades whose masters refused to implement industrial collective bargaining or to raise wages. Within two weeks the Winnipeg Trades and Labour Council voted overwhelmingly to strike in sympathy. Within hours the economic life of Winnipeg ground to a halt. In several other cities there was also sympathetic strike action. While one attempt at conciliation after another broke on the employers' refusal to recognize collective bargaining rights, the federal government prepared for massive intervention in support of the city and provincial governments and the businessmen's committee which was, in effect, directing anti-strike action. Although the policy of the strike leadership was firmly non-violent, the entire city police force was dismissed and replaced by 'specials', while militia and Mounted Police were assembled. When, after nearly six weeks, the strike had still not been broken, the federal government authorized the arrest of the leaders. This provoked the one major incident in which violence occurred – a peaceful march (in defiance of the mayor's ban on parades) which was broken up by Mounties and returned soldiers. In the mêlée one spectator was killed and thirty wounded. With the leaders in jail on charges of seditious conspiracy and the city patrolled by the military, the remainder of the Strike Committee called off the strike after receiving a promise from the premier that a royal commission would investigate the causes of labour's unrest and the conduct of the strike.

The report of the Robson Commission on the strike sustained the view that its goals were those of collective bargaining, higher wages and social justice, and that its methods had been non-violent. Later studies have made it clear that the principal leaders were British-born and not, as the governments and employers alleged, 'alien scum' who wished to subvert British law and order. While the immediate goals of the strike were not secured, and several of the leaders were convicted of sedition and sent to prison, the whole experience gave a distinct impetus to political action. In the Manitoba elections of 1920, four of the socialist leaders won seats in the legislature while still serving jail terms. And in the 1921 federal election J. S. Woodsworth won a Winnipeg seat for the Manitoba Independent Labour Party – to become the first socialist member of the House of Commons. Commenting on these developments, the newly established *Canadian Forum* of Toronto observed:

Never in Canada have the devotees of law and order received a ruder shock. ... The lesson is obvious yet it should be stated. Any government which attempts to throttle free men in Canada or elsewhere will fall of its own weight and be fortunate if it does not bring crashing in ruins the structure which with clumsy hands it seeks to buttress.

The events of 1919–21 brought into political focus the achievements and the frustrations of the century's first two decades. In these brief, if violent, years three men emerged who were to confront each other as national symbols of the paths open to postwar Canada: William Lyon Mackenzie King, Arthur Meighen and James Shaver Woodsworth. All three had been born in Ontario and were graduates of the University of Toronto. Meighen and Woodsworth had both spent most of their lives in Manitoba, Meighen in law and Woodsworth in various aspects of the Methodist ministry. All three were, in a sense, puritans, and all were devoted to the maintenance in Canada of British parliamentary and common law traditions. There the similarity ends.

Mackenzie King, who was to break even Walpole's record for longevity in the prime minister's role, didn't look much like a winner in 1919. In that year a national Liberal convention chose him as successor to Laurier, who had just died. His chief claim upon the delegates was that, unlike the Liberal members of the Union government, he had not deserted Laurier during the conscription crisis. He was thus *persona grata* to Quebeckers who also accepted the desirability of alternating French- and English-speaking party leadership. An unprepossessing, pudgy little man who remained a bachelor and was almost psychotically devoted to his mother's memory, King is the most enigmatic personality of Canadian political history. He professed deep concern for the social problems of industrial capitalism but in fact was about as advanced as Woodrow Wilson. While out of office from 1911 to 1922 he spent a good deal of time in the United States as industrial relations consultant for the Rockefellers, by whom he was both praised and handsomely rewarded. Although his party's 1919 platform called for old age pensions and social insurance, reform measures leading to a partial welfare state came under King only when he felt seriously threatened from the left. Yet he was a great Canadian, as one historian has observed, because 'he divided us least'. A master of compromise and cumbrously hedged prose, he would be able to transform the Commonwealth of Nations and take Canada through the Second World War without breaking it on the rocks of precise definition. At the conclusion of the 1919 convention Mackenzie King confided to his diary the reasons for his election to the leadership:

The majority was better than I had anticipated. I was too heavy of heart and soul to appreciate the tumult of applause, my thoughts were of dear mother and father and little Bell all of whom I felt to be very close to me, of grandfather and Sir Wilfrid also. I thought: it is right, it is the call of duty. I have sought nothing, it has come.

It has come from God. The dear loved ones know and are about, they are alive and with me in this great everlasting Now and Here. It is to His work I am called, and to it I dedicate my life.

For all that he was patient and even ruthless in political matters, King was essentially a timid man beset by fears which drove him eventually to spiritualism. And in Arthur Meighen he found a worthy focus for his fears. Meighen possessed a razor-sharp mind, a splendidly acid tongue and a rigid belief in the prescriptive governing rights of wealth and intelligence. His own high standards of personal integrity and duty he applied unhesitatingly to social relationships. As Borden's leading colleague in the Union government Meighen supervised the legislation that rescued the bankrupt railways and was the principal spokesman for conscription. When the Winnipeg strike broke out he depicted it unhesitatingly as a revolutionary challenge to constituted authority and utterly condemned the goal of industrial collective bargaining. Conceding that the country's employers were highly organized, he nevertheless insisted that labour must not try to duplicate such organization: 'Can anyone contemplate such an event? ... Are we to have on the one hand a concentration of employers, and on the other a concentration of all the labour interests of the Dominion, fighting it out for supremacy?' Meighen thus became the principal organizer of the force which was used to crush the strike. When the strike leaders were arrested he wired to his agent in Winnipeg: 'Notwithstanding any doubt I have as to the technical legality of the arrests and the detention at Stony Mountain [penitentiary], I feel that rapid deportation is the best course now that the arrests are made, and later we can consider ratification.' Sudden amendments to the Immigration Act to make it possible to deport British-born aliens, and an amendment to the Criminal Code (Section 98) providing twenty-year sentences for persons found guilty of a very loosely defined sedition were part of the Meighen programme of 'ratifying' the federal intervention. In external relations Meighen believed at least as strongly as did Borden in maintaining the imperial relationship and a consultative diplomatic unity. He stood even more firmly for maintaining a high tariff. In 1920 the Conservative parliamentary caucus endorsed its own record and policies by naming Meighen to succeed Borden who was retiring because of poor health.

Without anything comparable to the power bases enjoyed by King and Meighen, J. S. Woodsworth nevertheless emerged in 1921 as chief spokesman at Ottawa for the country's social conscience. Son of the pioneering superintendent of Methodist missions in the Northwest, Woodsworth had abandoned an earlier emphasis on personal salvation and immersed himself in the city mission work of the church. From this experience he concluded that the causes of urban misery lay deep in the social-economic organization of society and that the church was too enmeshed in that organization to be an effective means of reconstruction. Having visited the settlement houses and slums of London and read widely in the literature of Christian socialism, Fabianism and the American social gospel movement, Woodsworth became a social-democrat working closely with the left wing of western labour. In 1918, having lost a provincial government welfare post for openly opposing conscription, he resigned from the ministry and bitterly criticized the church for its support of the war. In 1919 he briefly edited the strikers' bulletin in Winnipeg. For this he was arrested and charged with seditious libel because, amongst other items, he had quoted an egalitarian passage from Isaiah. Although he was not convicted his reputation as a dedicated spokesman for the dispossessed spread rapidly. In 1921 he was chosen by the Independent Labour Party of Manitoba to contest a Winnipeg seat in the federal election of that year. He won the seat and held it until his death in 1942.

Woodsworth remained a pacifist to the end of his life. In 1914 he wrote:

Many are going to the front or are supporting the war in the belief that in this way they may help to bring about the triumph of right and the reign of peace. Some of us have not so learned Christ, yet we dare not dogmatize. We confess that we walk with uncertain steps. We plead that no one demand of us absolute consistency. ... More and more we must think not so much of the persons engaged in the war as of the causes that led to the war – the great social and moral wrongs that inevitably lead to disaster. These are our real foes rather than the Germans and the Austrians, and they are found not alone in the enemy's camp...

Although Woodsworth was basically concerned with urban problems and the social evils of capitalism, he knew well the grievances and isolation of prairie farmers. He and many of his colleagues in the labour movement worked closely with farmers' spokesmen – even though the farmers' organizations had opposed the general strike in Winnipeg. In 1919 hopes for a general farmer-labour alliance were raised when Ontario elected a farmers' Progressive government which depended upon the support of a handful of labour members in the legislature. The alliance did not mature, however, and one of the central political problems of the 1920s and thirties was to be that of farmer-labour cooperation. The chief beneficiary of the mutual suspicion between these two potent electoral forces was to be Mackenzie King. The stage was set by the complex federal election of December 1921.

As prime minister, Meighen fought the election on the Union government's record and stressed heavily the need to maintain a tariff for the protection of Canadian industry. The farmers, loosely organized in a Progressive party, made lower tariffs and reciprocity with the United States their main election issue – though many Progressive candidates also expounded the whole of the farmers' New National Policy. Mackenzie King led his Liberals warily through the campaign, wooing farmers and workers by vague references to the low-tariff and social welfare planks in the Liberal platform, but with insufficient precision to frighten business unduly.

The election result was a shock: Meighen's Conservatives won only 50 seats, most of them in Ontario. King captured 117 seats including all of Quebec's 65 constituencies. The Progressives emerged as the second largest group in the Commons with 41 western seats and 24 from Ontario. In one sense this was the beginning of a multi-party system in Canada even if the working out of the system was to take time and its durability remains in doubt. While King did his best to absorb the Progressives he was only partially successful. Since 1921 the two old parties have had to contend with provincial and federal parties that were either in power or in a position to threaten a government's majority.

While King failed to entice the Progressives, led by T. A. Crerar, into a coalition, he did manage to whittle away the independent spirit of a majority of the Progressive M.P.s by 1925. He granted minor tariff concessions on imported farm equipment and pointed out tirelessly that failure to support his minority government would simply return to power the implacably high-tariff Meighen. His indispensable Quebec support King ensured by finding and favouring a strong French-Canadian lieutenant, the brilliant Quebec City lawyer, Ernest Lapointe (who, at the age of forty-five had already been in Parliament seventeen years). King's choice of Lapointe as his chief colleague in the cabinet was probably his most important political decision and it is a measure of his intuitive powers that he was never in doubt about it. When he made the original appointment King recorded in his diary:

> I told him I regarded him as nearest to me & wd give him my confidence in full now & always. We would work out matters together. I regarded him as the real leader in Quebec, had sent for him first of all as promised. Asked which portfolio he wd like and said he could have it – he said Justice – that he was not good at business administr'n, that Justice gave chance to study. ... He said Justice wd give him the prestige he needed in his province. He is worthy of Justice, is just and honourable at heart – a beautiful Christian character – he shall have it.

In fact Lapointe waited until 1924 for the Justice post, for the excellent reason that he and King agreed to appease Montreal business and the conservative wing of the Quebec Liberal Party by giving the post at first to Sir Lomer Gouin, the premier of Quebec. Although Lapointe's first post was the minor one of Marine and Fisheries his advice inside the cabinet was definitive on all matters of concern to Quebec. Since these usually were also of national concern his influence is difficult to exaggerate.

Lapointe's instincts were mildly 'rouge'. During the Winnipeg strike he had sharply criticized the Borden–Meighen coercion and he was also sympathetic to many of the farmers' demands. But he also shared with King an innate caution and a deep concern for the unity of the country. Unity, as King and Lapointe defined it, was to require near paralysis on the social reform front, extreme sensitivity to provincial rights, fiscal orthodoxy and an external policy based upon total autonomy and non-commitment either to the Empire-Commonwealth or to the League of Nations. The excruciating balancing acts called for by such a strategy were, politically speaking, remarkably successful.

In the area of social justice the King government seemed little better than its predecessor. When in 1922 the giant British Empire Steel Corporation announced a wage cut of 37½ per cent for its 12,000 workers in the Nova Scotia steel and coal towns, a federal conciliation board judged that a 32½ per cent cut would be justifiable. The dispute dragged on for several years. With semi-starvation conditions in the Nova Scotia towns a delegation of mayors pleaded unsuccessfully with King to appoint a federal investigating commission. When the men struck on the job and Progressives in the House joined Woodsworth and his labour colleague from Alberta, William Irvine, in demanding federal action, King castigated them for condoning 'loafing on the job'. Ultimately the government pleaded lack of constitutional authority to intervene and the Nova Scotia government sent in special strike-breaking police. King's minister of national defence, who had been a solicitor for the Nova Scotia coal companies, ordered in the militia at the request of a judge and despite the protest of the local mayors. The Section 98 Criminal Code amendment was then used as a basis for arresting the strike leaders on charges of sedition.

In vain did Woodsworth and the more radical of the Progressives point out the anomalies in the government's position. In addition to heavy tariff protection, Ottawa had given some $19 million in subventions to the industry since the 1880s, as part of Macdonald's National Policy. If the federal government could support B.E.S.C.O. with money and troops surely it could find a way to enforce just treatment of the employees. 'Need of a serious character,' declared Woodsworth, 'knows no boundaries, provincial or even national.' Provincial rights, however, won the day. In the course of the long dispute King and Lapointe rejected proposals to establish a federal system of unemployment insurance and argued that Ottawa would have to ask for authority even to assist a province which wished to provide unemployment relief. In defence of their inaction they could point to a 1925 decision of the Judicial Committee of the Privy Council* which severely limited federal regulatory powers in the social-economic field. Yet the government seemed almost *too* happy to accept the limitation. For it obviated the problem of fighting for extended federal jurisdiction (which would entail political battles with provincial governments whose responsibilities were growing) and of persuading the party's business supporters of the need for expenditures on social security programmes. While most of the Progressives came to accept the 'necessities' of the government's position, a group of about fifteen (known as the Ginger Group) resisted the drift back into the Liberal Party. With Woodsworth as its most prominent spokesman the Ginger Group took an increasingly socialist position calling for nationalization of major tariff-supported industry, banking and other financial institutions, transportation, public utilities and natural resources.

King and Lapointe found easier Progressive support for the sharp change of direction they brought about in external relations. At the 1921 Imperial Conference, Prime Minister Meighen had succeeded in securing a common imperial policy in a matter of urgent importance to Canada. The issue was the intransigent opposition of the United States to Britain's proposal to renew the Anglo-Japanese alliance. The United Kingdom, Australia and New Zealand all saw the alliance, which had been immensely important during the war, as essential for the future – both for naval security in the Pacific and to ensure friendly relationships with an ever more potent Japan. The

---

Toronto Electric Commissioners v. Snider which invalidated the 1907 Industrial Disputes Investigation Act on the ground that it infringed upon provincial jurisdiction. The decision was part of a distinct trend whereby the Judicial Committee whittled down the federal powers of Sec. 91 of the B.N.A. Act and enlarged the provincial powers of Sec. 92.

American government feared that the alliance could only be directed against its interests in the Pacific. Meighen argued that Canada would be the principal loser if Anglo-American friendship were threatened and that Canada's voice in the matter should thus be paramount. He won his case, despite deep misgivings amongst his imperial partners. The alliance was abandoned and, instead, London accepted President Harding's invitation to a conference in Washington where multilateral treaties governing disarmament and territorial integrity around the Pacific were signed. The question remained, however, of what would happen in any case where a common policy could not be reached. Such a case arose quickly to confront the King-Lapointe team and their answer was conclusive.

In the autumn of 1922 Lloyd George asked the Dominions for help in holding a British position at Chanak against the Turks who had repudiated the Treaty of Sèvres and were advancing on the Straits. There had been no prior consultation as to whether the position should be held and, to aggravate matters, Mackenzie King read of the request in the press before he received the official telegram. King's formal reply was less forceful than were the feelings of himself and his cabinet colleagues. But he also saw clearly the opportunity of replacing the Borden-Meighen-Smuts concept of the Commonwealth with that which he and the Liberals favoured. To his diary he confided:

I confess [the official message] annoyed me. It is drafted designedly to play the imperial game, to test out centralization vs. autonomy as regards European wars. ... I have thought out my plans. ... No contingent will go without parliament being summoned in the first instance. ... I do not believe prlt. would sanction the sending of a contingent. ... The French Canadians will be opposed, I am not so sure of B.C. – I feel confident the Progressives will be opposed almost to a man. – It is the time now to bring them into the Government. ... I am sure the people of Canada are against participation in this European war.

King's analysis was correct on all counts with the single exception that he probably underestimated the number of English-speaking Conservatives who agreed with Meighen when the Tory leader declared that Canada's answer *should* have been 'Ready, Aye, Ready!' In any event the die was cast for breaking the diplomatic unity of the empire. Continuous consultation had proven impractical, and as far as King was concerned, undesirable in its implications of responsibility for accepting and implementing a common policy. At the 1923 Imperial Conference the new Canadian position was clarified and, in principle, agreed to. The Dominions in future could negotiate their own treaties and would be free to pursue their own foreign policies subject only to the courtesies of multi-lateral exchanges of information. It was in 1923 that Ernest Lapointe became the first Canadian to sign a treaty (a fisheries treaty with the United States) without the imprimatur of Great Britain. And the logic of this was followed through when, in 1927, a Canadian minister to Washington was named.

In the Imperial Conference of 1926 a formula was found in the Balfour Declaration to express the nature of the emergent Commonwealth: a group of 'autonomous communities within the British empire, equal in status, in no way subordinate one to another in any aspect of their domestic or external affairs, though united by a common allegiance to the Crown, and freely associated as members of the British Commonwealth of Nations'. The momentum of change carried over to the passage in 1931 of the British Statute of Westminster which gave complete autonomy to the Dominions. Even then, however, some ambiguities remained. At Canada's request the Judicial Committee of the Privy Council remained the final appeal court for some kinds of cases, and amendments to the British North America Act had to be made by the British Parliament (because Canadians did not reach agreement on an amending formula). Certain aspects of the monarchy and the question of whether a British declaration of war legally committed Canada, also remained to be cleared up in the future.

Restructuring of the Empire-Commonwealth, while undoubtedly endorsed by most Canadians, was viewed with dark suspicion by Meighen-style Tories. This, together with a somewhat ineffectual Liberal record in domestic policy, led to another blurred result in the federal election of 1925. The

Conservatives won 117 seats, to become the largest group in the House. The Liberals shrank to 101 and the Progressives were sliced from 65 to 24. Mackenzie King, arguing that Meighen had failed to win a clear majority, clung to office – more dependent than ever upon the unpredictable support of the Progressives. Given an issue on which the rather skittish Progressives were divided, or on which they might all oppose the government, the chances of a Tory break-through looked good. Unless, that is, King could find a magic electoral formula.

Both the issue and the magic formula lay just around the corner.

16

Prosperity and Depression

BY the mid twenties Canada was enjoying her share of a spiral-
ling North American boom. As in the United States, a good deal
of the economic recovery was markedly speculative in nature
and depended upon the willingness of governments to overlook
highly dubious methods of corporate financing and stock trading. Not surprisingly the period was scarred by several scandals
involving slack administration and corrupt influence in securing advantageous franchises – particularly for the development
of hydroelectric power. It was marked, too, by severely unequal
benefits. The Maritime provinces shared scarcely at all in the
period's business prosperity, while, despite industrial growth,
a hard core of unemployment plagued many of the cities. Most
dangerously, no government was preparing policies to counterbalance the vagaries of a market economy, and labour unions
languished in the face of heavy employer resistance to their
long-standing security demands.

Yet many Canadians prospered greatly. More and more
bought the cheap new cars mass-produced by American branch-
plant assembly points at Oshawa and Windsor in Ontario. Almost overnight provincial governments found it necessary to
improve and extend their highway systems. At the same time
the impact of urbanization* and industrialization was seen in
demands for provincial expenditures in other areas. Secondary
and technical education costs rose rapidly as did those of
administration. Most of the growth in the twenties – rapid
expansion in mining of all kinds, pulp and paper, and secondary

---

*In 1921 half the population was classed as urban. By 1931, 54 per
cent of the population was urban, and by 1968, more than 70 per
cent. Today less than a tenth of the labour force is engaged in
farming.

manufacturing – fell within areas of provincial jurisdiction. Businessmen looked to provincial governments for new services and privileges ranging from hydroelectric power to favourable tax and labour laws. At the same time, with increased responsibilities and costs, the provinces sought greater powers and revenues. Stop-gap measures, such as federal grants-in-aid for particular programmes and a growing revenue from licensing, publicly controlled liquor sales and gasoline taxes, would prove inadequate for the social-economic responsibilities taken on by the provinces in the twenties.

In much of English-speaking Canada the decade's ill-regulated prosperity seemed real enough. Radio and motion-picture entertainment boomed, while fads from America's Jazz Age (from flapper-styles to Aimey Semple McPherson and Mah Jong) held passing sway. For the middle class, auto-touring became fashionable. Many Canadian families, and a growing number of American visitors, 'took to the woods' for their summer vacations – patronizing new holiday resorts or building cottages on the endless patchwork of rocky lakes along the perimeter of the Canadian Shield. Professional ice-hockey emerged as the national sport – one of the few areas in which English- and French-speaking Canadians found themselves associated on an equal footing. Radio broadcasts of the hockey league games drew the largest listening audiences across the country while huge sports arenas were built to house the games in the major cities.

Some of these trends suggested the continued development of a Canadian way of life, but there were many cross-currents and differences of opinion about the nature and proper direction of the nearly independent nation. American movies, magazines and radio programmes penetrated Canada ever more widely. Tastes and attitudes were certainly affected. Canadians tended to be just as interested in the course of American politics, the fate of American baseball teams, the careers of American movie and gang-land heroes and heroines, as they were in their own affairs. At the same time the built-in resistance to American domination remained active. At one level the renewed search for identity (at least, English-speaking

Canadian identity) was best seen in the paintings of an immensely influential group of artists known as the Group of Seven.* Intensely nationalist, this group went straight to the land, to the brilliant colours of northern autumn, to the awful thrust of pre-cambrian rock against the purple darkness of northern lakes, and the primary patterns of winter snow. As one critic put it†:

... these canvases presented Canada in the same way that Whitman and Thoreau might have hoped to see America presented. The landscape is alive; and the painter's encounter with it is a brutal battle, rather than the polite and banal observation of a visitor from abroad. The work of this group, indeed, produced a national image that has no parallel in American paintings.

In literature Stephen Leacock's light-hearted treatment of English-speaking Canadian folkways helped to keep the country from taking itself too seriously, and occasionally rose to the level of great humour in the tradition of Thomas Chandler Haliburton. Other writers shed the romanticism of the pre-war years. F. P. Grove, W. O. Mitchell and E. J. Pratt brought to fiction and verse a new realism and intellectual content, while Morley Callaghan's novels of urban life have been compared, not inappropriately, to the work of Fitzgerald and Hemingway. In French Canada poetry of the period reflected French fashions and thus symbolized the beginnings of Quebec's rediscovery of France. But fiction was dominated by a highly *nationaliste* trend, much more didactic than its English-speaking counterpart. Here the work of Abbé Lionel Groulx was of incalculable importance. An historian by training, Groulx turned to the novel as a means of bringing to the popular level his historical thesis of the clerical-agrarian basis of French-Canadian nationality. His two best-known novels, *Chez nos gens* (1920) and *L'Appel de*

---

* The Group of Seven painters were: Tom Thomson, A. Y. Jackson, Lawren Harris, J. E. H. MacDonald, Arthur Lismer, Frank Carmichael, Franz Johnston and Frederick Varley. Thomson, the pioneer of the Group, had died in 1917, three years before the Group adopted its name.

† Hugo McPherson, in *The Canadians*, Macmillan Company of Canada, Toronto, 1967, p. 704.

la race (1922) sold widely, despite inferior literary quality, and supplemented his deep influence as an historian.

Behind all Canadian activity in the twenties, as before and since, lay a consciousness of northernness and space. If ever-growing numbers of city-dwellers seldom experienced the full rigours of life in the forests, on the northern plains or the Arctic lands of their great sprawling country, they nevertheless felt them to be part of their heritage, and for many that heritage came to life again in the twenties. Canadian 'bush pilots', many of them with wartime records in improbable wood-and-canvas airplanes, pioneered again in carrying prospectors and developers into the new frontiers of mining, pulp and paper, and hydroelectric power. In Manitoba's section of the Great Shield an old project demanded by embattled prairie wheat farmers was resumed when Mackenzie King's government authorized completion of a railway from Winnipeg to Port Churchill on Hudson Bay – a project designed to cut freight costs by an alternative competitive export route for grain, and to prove to the dwindling Progressive movement that the government had the farmers' interests at heart.

The problems of space, high transportation costs and the continuing domination of farm and frontier by the two metropolitan centres produced other effects in the twenties. In the west thousands of farmers joined Wheat Pools – huge cooperatives for the storing, transporting and selling of grain – and thus gave yet another argument for collective action by the common people. A more complicated event occurred in 1925 when a majority of the Presbyterian congregations united with the Methodist Church to form the United Church of Canada. It was a union brought about more by considerations of economy than theology. The United Church encompassed a majority of Canada's Protestants. Wealthier, per capita, than the smaller Anglican Church which remained slightly more prestigious socially, the United Church moved perceptibly away from the social reform interests of some of its social gospel ministers. To a considerable extent church union resulted from rural members' arguments about the illogicality of competition in small and isolated centres. From the same rural sources came evidence of a fundamentalism which could counter the inevitably secular influence of an increasingly urban society. The most striking and least healthy aspect of religious fundamentalism was its belief in legislated morality which resulted in the maintenance of strict sabbatarian laws and the imposition of prohibition. Bending before well-organized 'temperance' groups, all provinces except Quebec had banned consumption of alcoholic beverages by the end of the war. In the early twenties it became clear that massive evasion through forged medical prescriptions, bootlegging and home-brewing was invalidating the experiment and bringing the law itself into disrespect. One by one the provinces replaced prohibition by government liquor control boards through which alone wine and spirits could be bought. Yet the spirit of rural Protestant puritanism dominated English-speaking Canada until the years immediately following the Second World War. It was remarked by travellers from abroad that one could spend a week in Toronto on a Sunday.

In Quebec the ferment of the war period had subsided but was not followed by any complacency. For the French-Canadian home province the twenties had their own difficult cross-currents. The Anglo-Quebec business community controlled virtually all economic activity, while the rapid industrialization of the province further eroded the dubious *nationaliste* concept of an essentially rural society. Montreal's English-speaking barons of hydroelectric power, mining, pulp and paper, manufacturing, finance and transportation found little difficulty in controlling the Liberal governments of premiers Gouin and Taschereau. Nor did the Anglo-Quebeckers bother to repay their politically entrenched benefactors other than with influence and money at election time. Few of the English-speaking élite learned the French language and few French Canadians found a route to the top in the world of business. A small concession had been won in 1910 when bilingualism was made compulsory in Quebec's public service, but English remained an absolute necessity in most business operations. Changes in the educational system to produce graduates trained in mathematics, science and the social sciences came but slowly – and even such graduates met with little favour in the English-speaking business community. Frustration spread as farmers' sons flocked to menial urban employment (or unemployment) and the *nationaliste* movement remained dominated by the clergy. Labour unionism lagged far behind the growth of corporation power and was further inhibited by clerical support of reactionary labour legislation. Paths to the future were being prepared, unwittingly, by young intellectuals who went to Paris to study and who would return imbued with very secular ideas about *étatisme* and political liberalism. By the mid thirties they would be ready to take up French-Canadian nationalism where Papineau, rather than Bourget, had left off. Meanwhile the more liberal of Quebec's political spokesmen were busy inside Mackenzie King's Ottawa fold defending provincial rights, advancing Dominion autonomy, and supporting a strongly isolationist view of international relations.

Prosperity, regional and class disparities, a hesitating federalism and, above all, the drive for national autonomy lay behind the political drama that unfolded after the indecisive national elections of 1925. But King's nearly infallible political intuition was what really turned the trick for his stumbling administration.

Shortly after the 1925 election a parliamentary committee revealed evidence of massive corruption in the Customs Department. Based upon 'rum-running' to the United States, a wholesale smuggling system had developed both ways across the border and had come to include many more commodities than liquor (which was prohibited in the United States). In small seagoing vessels on both coasts and in powerful speedboats on border rivers an immense illicit trade was being conducted, as the committee reported in lurid detail, with 'not merely the tacit connivance of a multitude of Customs officials but in many cases their active cooperation in making a wholesale mockery of the Customs laws of Canada'. During the long and acrimonious debates in the House over a Conservative motion of censure it became clear that King could not rely on the twenty-four Progressives to sustain his minority government on an issue that involved corruption. Before the Tory censure motion could be brought to a vote King advised Lord Byng, the governor-general, to dissolve the House and thus permit another general election. Byng, with rigid propriety, exercised his one important prerogative and refused the dissolution. Because the previous election was less than a year past, and since the government had not demonstrated that it had the confidence of the Commons, the governor-general felt that there was a legitimate alternative to another election. King at once resigned and Byng asked Meighen to form a government.

In addition to providing King with an escape route from the Customs scandal the 'constitutional crisis' of 1926 established important precedents and directions for future Canadian politics. The central constitutional issue was the governor-general's prerogative of dissolution. King argued that Lord Byng, a British official, had subverted responsible government in Canada – that in fact the governor-general did *not* possess an absolute prerogative to refuse dissolution, and that he must invariably act on the advice of his prime minister. On this crucial point King was wrong. But Meighen, who agreed to accept responsibility for the governor-general's actions, was the one to suffer. Having assured Byng that he would have the support of the Progressives, Meighen found his government defeated within a week when the Progressives deserted him on a point of constitutional propriety. Byng then faced the embarrassing necessity of granting to Meighen the dissolution that he had refused to King – 'all reasonable expedients' having been tried. In the ensuing election the King Liberals happily ignored a mountain of precedents which supported the Byng–Meighen position. With strident claims that Lord Byng had somehow infringed 'Canadian autonomy' they managed to obliterate the Customs scandal and won the election by appeals for Canadian independence from imperial meddling. Disillusioned with political experiments, thousands of farmers had drifted back to the Liberal Party and only a handful of Progressives won seats. Within a few months, too, the austere and embittered Arthur Meighen resigned the Tory leadership to be replaced by a wealthy Calgary lawyer, Richard B. Bennett.

The indecisive elections of 1921 and 1925 also gave rise to

several other important political trends, both short- and long-term in their effects. At the outset of the ill-fated 1926 session, Mackenzie King's support depended upon twenty-four Progressive members. But this gave him a majority of only three. King quickly recognized that in practice his government's life was in the hands of the two labour members, J. S. Woodsworth and A. A. Heaps. These men at once made use of their key position. Inquiring of both King and Meighen what were the intentions of the two leaders with respect to certain reform legislation, they received from Meighen a chilly rejection and from King an invitation to talk the matter over. After the conversations King sent the two labour men a letter promising to revoke the 1919 amendments to the Criminal Code and the Immigration Act and to introduce an Old Age Pensions Act. Woodsworth read the letter into Hansard. It was greeted with howls of disapproval and charges of a 'corrupt' bargain. Meighen and Bennett, seeing their chance of defeating the government lessened, were particularly bitter, Bennett asking: 'Have parliamentary institutions fallen so low that our Criminal Code is to be amended that a government may remain in power?' Woodsworth defended his 'amendment to the Address' on the ground that there was little to choose between the two old parties in matters of corruption and that he would be delinquent did he not use his parliamentary position to the best advantage of the common people. The ploy worked. In 1927 King overrode conservative opposition within his new cabinet and an Old Age Pensions Act became law in that year. Revocation of the 1919 amendments had to wait another ten years.

Not only were old-age pensions the first serious move towards a complex system of social security. The political attitude of the Ginger Group was sharply changed. In 1922 all Progressives had believed in their doctrine of 'group government'. In essence this meant smashing the party system, electing group or class representatives (preferably on a basis of proportional representation) and re-writing the procedures of the House of Commons. The cabinet was to become, in fact, a committee of the House which could and should accept non-partisan views on legislation and should, therefore, not resign simply because a

Bill was defeated or amended, but only if it should lose a specific vote of confidence. Direct experience with the parliamentary system, and especially the success of the Woodsworth–Heaps use of that system to obtain substantive reform legislation, caused most of the radical Progressives to conclude that progress was to be found not in breaking old parties but in founding a new one.

Acceptance of the party system by an emerging socialist farmer-labour group was a major result of the constitutional crisis. Mackenzie King's experience in the period was to keep him exceptionally wary of pressure on the Left and this was to lead to further labour union and social security measures in the future. Finally, one part of the old 'group government' doctrine was to be revived in the 1960s by King's own political heirs. Because the revolt against the two old parties, intensified in the 1930s, resulted in a multi-party system in which governments frequently lack secure majorities, the Liberals themselves have employed the notion that a government need not resign merely because one of its measures is defeated or amended in the House, but only if it is defeated on a vote which is specifically understood to involve confidence. For this, as for most things, British and Commonwealth precedents are plentiful, but the evolving pattern is also peculiarly and historically Canadian. Certainly it represents a major difference in political attitudes between Canada and the United States – an un-American manner of representing minorities and of arriving at consensus.

As the federal system floundered through the political morass of the 1920s its prestige was further diminished by several other developments. On the Atlantic coast a Maritime Rights Movement gave evidence of dangerous regional discontent. In 1927 the King government, accepting some of the recommendations of a royal commission on the question, increased subsidies to the three eastern provinces in further recognition of the unequal effects of the tariff. Even so, the Maritimes remained in an economic trough and thoroughly unprepared for what was soon to come. A similar rights movement on the prairies demanded the transfer to provincial control of the region's natural resources, which had been under Ottawa's jurisdiction since the provinces were established, and the western demand was conceded at the end of the decade. On the Pacific coast, British Columbia, and especially the port of Vancouver, prospered from new growth in the mining and forest industries and from increased shipping stimulated by the Panama Canal which had opened in 1914. Yet here, too, there was an ominous note of particularism, even of independent identity. The decade's surge of provincialism was symbolized by a Dominion-Provincial Conference in 1927 at which the Tory Premier Ferguson of Ontario and the Liberal Premier Taschereau of Quebec joined in proclaiming the 'compact theory' of Confederation – a position which would give near autonomy to the provinces and which saw federal powers as being merely delegated to Ottawa by the provinces.

When the New York stock market collapsed in the autumn of 1929, and brought the western world's trading system down in ruins with it, Canada was amongst the most vulnerable victims. With a semi-developed industrial system she was heavily dependent upon foreign trade, and particularly upon the export of grain, raw materials and semi-finished products. Over the decade of the 1930s Canada's national income and gross national product actually declined. And aggravating the general impact of the depression were the facts of its unequal incidence amongst classes and regions. Many urban middle-class families suffered relatively little while a swollen working class bore the brunt of drastically lowered wages and unemployment. In the Maritimes and across the prairies economic decline was catastrophic. Hit by drought and grasshopper plagues as well as by the shrunken demand for wheat, the prairies suffered total financial collapse. Shock-waves from the western dust-bowls and from the stagnating fisheries and coal-steel industry of the Maritimes reverberated through the national economy and were not lessened by any substantial recovery of world markets. By 1933, in addition to social devastation in the Maritimes and across the prairies, some 23 per cent of the labour force was unemployed (compared to 3 per cent in 1929). Thus, besides thousands of western farm families on the verge of starvation, there were well over one and a half million Canadians with no source of earned income. The mere statistics fail to picture the wasted lives, the long lines of forlorn men waiting at city soup-kitchens or shivering against the wind on the tops of freight-trains as they rode hopelessly about the country in search of non-existent jobs, the farms lost to mortgage companies, the accumulated savings of a generation vanished in loans against a fishing schooner, the closing of a corner store, the shutting down of a small plant. In the Commons J. S. Woodsworth portrayed the country's social nadir:

In the old days we could send people from the cities to the country. If they went out today they would meet another army of unemployed coming back from the country to the city; that outlet is closed. What can these people do? They have been driven from our parks; they have been driven from our streets; they have been driven from our buildings, and in this city [Ottawa] they actually took refuge on the garbage heaps.

Mackenzie King, surrounded in his cabinet by men of basically conservative temperament, defended the barren ground of rugged individualism and, against demands for dramatic federal action, pleaded the strait-jacket of the British North America Act. In the autumn of 1930, with virtually no new programme save further tinkering with the tariff, he called a federal election. Full of false confidence, King badly underestimated the bombastic rhetorical powers of the new Tory leader, R. B. Bennett. Castigating the Liberals for 'timidity and vacillation', Bennett promised to put in hand a public works programme, assume the provinces' share of old age pensions' costs and use a heightened tariff to bargain for reciprocal concessions from other nations. Anticipating F. D. Roosevelt's 1932 assault on Herbert Hoover, Bennett thundered: 'Mackenzie King promises you conferences; I promise you action. He promises consideration of the problem of unemployment, I promise to end unemployment. Which plan do you like best?' Whether the voters really liked the Tory 'plan' or whether they simply cast their ballots in outraged frustration, they gave Bennett a majority of thirty-one seats.

Immediately following the election Bennett called a special session of Parliament. Over King's horrified cries of 'fiscal irresponsibility', the House voted $20 million for emergency relief work – without prescribing an overall plan and entrusting administration of the spending to provinces and municipalities. But the principal Conservative answer to the depression was to increase the tariff by nearly 50 per cent. In practice this over-simple, if orthodox, response had the same trade-limiting effect as did the autarchy adopted by other western nations at the same time. From a deficit of $125,332,000 in 1930 the Canadian trade balance moved to a surplus of $187,621,000 in 1935. Financiers applauded, especially since the government also refused to devalue the dollar. The Tory fiscal policy undoubtedly saved some Canadian firms from bankruptcy and protected some Canadian jobs. But if the government thus protected profits, dividends and prices, its policies seriously inhibited recovery in the base areas of the economy that depended upon exports. And by keeping the price structure artificially rigid it added appreciably to the misery of millions of people living on relief or on drastically reduced incomes.

At an Imperial Economic Conference which met amidst much fanfare in Ottawa in 1932, Canada entered preferential tariff-lowering agreements with Britain and other Commonwealth members. These agreements, however, while they slightly increased trade within the Commonwealth, were completely counterbalanced by the constriction of buying power within Canada and the high costs of Canadian production and resulting prices. As the depression steadily deepened, resentment against the government rose. Bennett reacted first by repression and, too late, by advancing a 'New Deal' programme of planning and social security. In the first four years of his administration law and order occupied a disproportionate amount of his attention. Labour spies attended most labour union meetings, unemployed marchers were dispersed by the R.C.M.P., agitators were arbitrarily arrested and deported under the Immigration Act amendments, while censorship of radical periodicals and books was extended. In the chaos of social-economic breakdown and a semi-police state atmosphere, vehement proposals for change arose on all sides.

In Alberta the curious Social Credit doctrine of a British

engineer, Major C. H. Douglas, swept the province. Led by William Aberhart, a radio evangelist, the Social Credit Party spoke directly to farmers and ranchers hard-pressed for mortgage payments. Promising to make purchasing power equal productive power (by means of paper credit), Aberhart's party won the provincial election of 1935. When the new provincial government tried to move into the fields of banking and credit its legislation was either disallowed or invalidated because it clearly invaded federal jurisdictions named in Section 91 of the B.N.A. Act. Under Aberhart and his successor, E. C. Manning, an increasingly conservative Social Credit government has been in power in Alberta ever since the 1935 upset. Based upon American-financed oil and natural gas development, Alberta governments were to show not only a growing conservatism but also a disturbing trend towards anti-semitism and restriction of civil liberty.

On the national stage a more significant political protest movement was the Cooperative Commonwealth Federation (C.C.F.). The C.C.F was founded at Regina in 1933 by representatives of farm, labour, socialist and intellectual groups. Its Regina Manifesto closed with the sentence: 'No C.C.F. government will rest content until it has eradicated capitalism and put into operation the full programme of socialized planning which will lead to the establishment in Canada of the Cooperative Commonwealth.' Most of the press was horrified and described the new party as a dangerous mixture of bolshevism and impractical idealism. In fact the C.C.F. was a natural outgrowth of the Progressive movement, particularly of the Ginger Group, and J. S. Woodsworth was elected the party's first leader almost automatically. By 1934 there were hundreds of C.C.F. clubs and locals across the country. In British Columbia and Saskatchewan the C.C.F. had become the official opposition. Clearly, socialist planning, with emphasis on Ottawa's powers and responsibility, held strong appeal. Yet in the Maritimes (apart from the coal towns) the party made little progress, and in Quebec the Roman Catholic hierarchy supported conservative *nationalistes*, condemning the C.C.F. as communistic, atheistic and English-speaking. Even so, the deep roots struck by the C.C.F. in the thirties, together with the party's allegiance to the parliamentary system and the increasing support it gained from trade unions and urban intellectuals, prevented it from meeting the fate of the American Socialist Party.

Other regional political rumblings also helped to keep the Tories on edge. In Ontario the Liberals brought to an end a twenty-nine-year Tory hegemony in 1934. Under a colourful, demagogic leader, Mitchell Hepburn, the Liberals promised action on behalf of the worker, the farmer and the unemployed. But Hepburn, despite an instinctive rapport with 'the back concessions', was no radical. By 1937 he was leading an all-out assault against industrial unionism in the province. A populist in origin, Hepburn in office became the trusted defender of American branch-plants and the provinces' mining companies.

While Hepburn was to become a major worry to Mackenzie King after King returned to federal power, a cause of still deeper concern was the rise to power in Quebec of the Union Nationale. In that province the grievances of the depression had been intensified by the fact that virtually all the major employers were English-speaking, while the majority of their employees spoke French. Charging that Premier Taschereau was hand-in-glove with the foreign capitalists, Maurice Duplessis succeeded in uniting the remnants of Quebec's Conservative Party with reformers in the provincial Liberal Party and, as Union Nationale, otherthrowing the corrupt Taschereau régime in 1936. Once in power, however, Duplessis himself made a system of corruption, and winked at the further extension of outside control of Quebec's economic life. Like Hepburn, Duplessis pointed to radicals and to arrogant federal power as the sources of provincial troubles. Like Aberhart, Duplessis aligned himself closely with his province's dominant religious orthodoxy and from it drew grateful support in his war against radical reformers. His methods included a notorious Padlock Law which permitted seizure and closing of any premises suspected of being used to propagate communism. Since this law did not define communism, its principal effect was to cripple attempts to establish the C.C.F. and to put life into Quebec's ailing trade union organizations.

Political instability and growing demands for positive government induced Bennett to take some actions that were of greater long-range than short-range importance. In 1935 the Wheat Board was re-established after half-way measures had proven ineffectual. A Bank of Canada was established in 1934 to act as financial adviser to Ottawa and to influence the volume and rates of credit. However, since private bankers controlled a majority of the stock, the new bank simply bolstered the restrictive credit policies of the chartered banks. It was not until 1938 that the Bank of Canada was fully nationalized. Deepening suspicion of uncontrolled private business led also to the establishment of the Canadian Radio Broadcasting Commission (renamed Canadian Broadcasting Corporation, 1936).* Enjoying support in both French- and English-speaking Canada, the new publicly owned radio network provided services in areas considered of no value from a profit point of view, as well as in the major centres. In addition, it provided employment for musicians and actors, an objective national news service and a heightened inter-racial communication of ideas and attitudes. The Bennett government also laid the basis of a national air transport system, partly as a relief construction project. In 1937, under the Liberals, Trans-Canada Air Lines was chartered as a crown corporation. As with the C.B.C., where private stations were not eliminated, so private airlines continued to operate, but with the T.C.A. as the dominant national line. In both cases the private sector was permitted to expand in later years and the debate about the virtues of mixing the two methods continues.

Bennett received no surge of political support as a result of his share in such measures. By 1934 he was under heavy cross-fire both inside his party and from without – to hold the line or to make a radical advance. He was also intensely irritated by personal attacks which portrayed him as a dictator, and by popular terms such as 'Bennettburgh', widely used to describe

---

*In two decisions of 1932 reversing its previous provincial rights trend, the Judicial Committee of the Privy Council gave Ottawa power to control the country's airways – both for broadcasting and transport.

the tin-and-tarpaper shanty towns which had sprung up on the outskirts of the bigger cities. Bennett decided, typically in private, to take the most dramatic political course he could think of. Having absorbed from his brother-in-law W. D. Herridge, Canadian Minister to the United States, a New Nationalist version of the New Deal, Bennett took to the airwaves in January 1935. In a series of radio broadcasts he announced a New Deal for the Canadian people. Conservative M.P.s listened in astonishment (not having been consulted) as their prime minister announced that the capitalist system lay in ruins. Bennett's hyperbole, however, eventually boiled down to this:

> In the anxious years through which you have passed, you have been the witnesses of grave defects and abuses in the capitalist system. Unemployment and waste are the proof of these. Great changes are taking place about us. New conditions prevail. These require modifications in the capitalist system to enable that system more effectively to serve the people.

The prime minister then outlined a series of reform measures which he intended to have passed by the impending pre-election parliamentary session. Despite grave misgivings amongst many of his business supporters the measures were enacted. The major Acts of the Bennett New Deal provided for unemployment and social insurance, a natural products marketing board, minimum wages and maximum hours in industry and extension of federally supported farm credit. The government further horrified many of its supporters by leaving the clear impression that it would move against price-fixing and in the direction of serious economic planning.

The handful of C.C.F. members supported the measures in general while claiming their inadequacy. But it was Mackenzie King who took greatest comfort from the new Bennett programme. At the outset of the session he carefully asked Bennett to

> tell this House whether as leader of the government, knowing that a question will come up immediately as to the jurisdiction of this Parliament, and of the provincial legislatures in matters of social legislation, he has secured an opinion from the law officers of the

Crown or from the Supreme Court of Canada which will be a sufficient guarantee to this House to proceed with these measures as
being without question within its jurisdiction.

In a further statement, no more concise, King side-stepped the
question of where the Liberals stood on the merits, as opposed
to the constitutionality, of the measures. Once again a constitutional question emerged on which King could question Tory
integrity and win an election.

17

'Parliament will decide'

THE speech from the throne has a paragraph or two respecting the Prime Minister's plans with reference to social reform and security. But what is to become of the services and security that are to be given workers in industry if the very foundations of government are being made insecure by the method that is being taken to attain these alleged ends?

So spoke Mackenzie King in the pre-election session of 1935. Bennett's New Deal legislation became a dividing wedge which King drove deep into the heart of the Tory Party. In the King version Bennett was now the complete dictator. He had insulted Parliament by giving his radical programme to the people prior to the opening of the session; he had not bothered to consult his own cabinet, let alone his back-benchers, about his sharp change of policy; and he had mischievously misled the House and the country in enacting laws which he knew would be declared unconstitutional upon the first test. In short, Bennett, like Meighen, was tearing up the delicate fabric of constitutional custom and, like his predecessor, must be stopped. And to these charges the Liberals added their indictment of high tariffs which they blamed for perpetuating the depression.

Perhaps no government which had been in power during the darkest years of the depression would have been re-elected in 1935. One which was also deeply riven by its leader's tactics and policy was certain to go down in flames. Yet the striking aspect of the election was that the Liberal victory (171 seats to 39 for the Tories) was due not to a return of voters to the Liberal banner but to the more than a million voters who showed their distrust of both the old parties and cast their ballots elsewhere. A break-away Tory, H. H. Stevens, had organized a mildly reformist Reconstruction Party which took many Conservative votes, but only elected its leader. The Social Credit Party took all the Alberta seats and two others (seventeen in all) with approximately half the vote required by the C.C.F. to elect seven M.P.s (with over 400,000 votes). The Liberal majority in the House was thus based on a minority of the popular vote while the multi-party system was further confirmed as a feature of Canadian politics. Noting the Liberal slogan: 'It's King or Chaos', one historian has written that 'Liberalism, as it emerged in Canada after 1935, was the counterpart of Baldwin conservatism in Great Britain, of *Le Front Populaire* in France, and of Rooseveltian democracy: – it represented the huddling together of frightened people uncertain of their way in a chaotic world'.*

Yet the 'huddling together' within Canadian Liberalism was something which Mackenzie King had continually to encourage. He did so by unremitting insistence on the need for caution – caution in foreign policy, caution in dominion-provincial relations, caution in governmental intervention in the social economy. His formulation of what might be called the politics of fear left a lasting impression upon Canadian attitudes and, no doubt, also expressed a deep conservatism in Canadian society – at least the Canadian society of the 1930s and 1940s. And, considering his charges against Bennett, the King formula had its own irony. Throughout his political career, King insisted upon the supremacy of Parliament. This was his touchstone when he refused to delegate any jurisdiction to an imperial council. It had been his chief point in the battles with Bennett and Meighen. It was also to be his argument for refusing prior military commitments either to the League of Nations or to the Commonwealth. Yet in practice he often contravened his frequently reiterated declaration: 'Parliament will decide'. Decision was not something that came easily to King, whether in Parliament or not. And in many ways he set far more store upon the electorate than he did upon Parliament, which he treated in a cavalier fashion. In 1926 he had saved himself by appealing beyond Parliament to the electors; in 1940 he was to treat Parliament with even greater disdain. By his policy of enhancing cabinet power and basing his mandate upon elections rather than upon debates and votes in Parliament, King

---

* A. R. M. Lower, *Colony to Nation* (Toronto, 1946), p. 519.

bequeathed to the Liberal Party a somewhat plebiscitary view of democracy that was to lead it into eventual defeat before Tory charges of arrogance. Yet, however one may delight in dissecting the past, there can be no doubt that King's mixture of caution and ruthlessness worked.

Upon resuming office King at once referred the controversial Bennett legislation to the Supreme Court.* The Court ruled in 1936 that most of the programme was unconstitutional because it infringed provincial jurisdictions, particularly the area of property and civil rights, named in Section 92 of the B.N.A. Act. The decisions were upheld in the following year by the Judicial Committee of the Privy Council. Reversing the apparent trend of the 1932 radio and aviation cases, the courts specifically denied the federal argument that the depression was a national emergency that justified wide interpretation of its Section 91 powers over trade and commerce and its responsibility for 'peace, order and good government'. The decisions seemed to confirm the King-Lapointe view of the constitutional situation. Their response, before saying anything further about social reform, was to appoint a royal commission to review the whole question of dominion-provincial relations.

The Rowell-Sirois Commission put to work a group of academic and professional specialists on an exhaustive study of the historical and contemporary federal division of responsibilities and resources. The Report, which was not issued until 1940, was a strong expression of the nationalism of the preceding decade. It left no doubt that neither the French- nor the English-speaking founders of Confederation had anticipated the halting and ineffectual role assigned to Ottawa by the courts, by ambitious provincial premiers and by investors of foreign capital. Reviewing the fiscal chaos, economic stagnation, and national frustration of the depression years, the Report recommended sweeping redistribution of responsibilities and revenue sources to restore what the commissioners believed was the balance of

---

*Unlike the American Supreme Court, the Canadian court does not confine itself to actual suits but can accept governmental requests for constitutional judgements.

powers originally conceived. They recommended that Ottawa possess key controls over the economy and accept responsibility for essential national welfare services such as unemployment insurance and relief (although local welfare services were to remain within provincial jurisdiction). A system of national adjustment grants from Ottawa to the provinces was to ensure a minimum Canadian standard of educational and social services. To enable Ottawa to shoulder a revived national planning role it was to enjoy exclusive rights to income and corporation taxes and succession duties.

To implement the Rowell-Sirois plan would have required a combination of B.N.A. Act amendments and policy agreements between Ottawa and at least a majority of the provinces. Such agreement was never reached. Throughout the Commission's period of research it was virtually boycotted by Ontario, Quebec and Alberta. When the Report was issued these provinces, supported by British Columbia, were overtly hostile. And at the 1941 Dominion-Provincial Conference called to consider the Report, Premier Hepburn of Ontario led a ferocious opposition that brought about the collapse of the conference.

In 1940, desiring industrial peace during the war and fearful of Liberal defections to the C.C.F., King obtained a B.N.A. Act amendment empowering Ottawa to establish national unemployment insurance. But, as a plan, the provincialists had killed the Report. The war and postwar periods were to see only *ad hoc* adjustments to the federal balance of powers and responsibilities. Yet, while a cohesive plan was rejected, new lines of advance were to be explored, more as a result of wartime experience, evolution of the party system, and a resurgence of French-Canadian nationalism than as an outcome of specific constitutional revision.

If Canadians found such embarrassing difficulty defining their domestic purposes and methods, their attitude to external affairs was no more precise – even if, in the long run, that attitude turned out to conform with their traditions. Here Mackenzie King's political method was seen more clearly. In imperial relations the abdication crisis was a good example of the method at work.

In 1936 Edward VIII decided that Mrs Simpson was more important to him than his throne, and the governments of the Dominions were advised of love's triumph on 9 December. This was in accordance with the Statute of Westminster which empowered Dominion Parliaments to assent to 'any alteration in the law touching the Succession to the Throne or Royal Style and Titles'. Section 4 of the Statute provided that no British law should apply to a Dominion 'unless it is expressly declared in that Act that the Dominion has requested, and consented to, the enactment thereof'. The King signed the Instrument of Abdication on 10 December, and the Westminster Parliament assembled to give effect to the abdication. In Ottawa, King seized on the ambiguity of the Statute's phrasing and had the cabinet request that the new British Act of Succession apply to Canada. There was not, said King, enough time to summon Parliament. When the Canadian Parliament did meet in January 1937, the government sought passage of an address of loyalty to George VI. For the Conservatives, C. H. Cahan, and for the C.C.F., J. S. Woodsworth condemned the whole procedure as a denigration of Parliament. The address, Woodsworth protested, should not have been passed until after the Succession Bill had been debated and passed. The oath of allegiance to George VI should certainly not have been required of the members. As it was, the King of Canada had been changed by the Liberal cabinet while Parliament was prorogued. Pursuing the logic of the situation, Woodsworth pointed out that if the prime minister could decide such important matters unilaterally he could also declare war by the same method. 'Surely,' he argued, 'if the King of the United Kingdom can be distinguished for legal purposes from the King of Canada, then the recognition of the King of the United Kingdom as King of Canada can wait until there is time to call Parliament. If the selection of the King of Canada is of such minor importance, the question arises: why a King at all?'

To this charge there was no logical answer. But there was a political answer and that answer demonstrated not only the obfuscating skills of the prime minister, but also the violent cross-currents of Canadian opinion. Time, said Mackenzie King, had been of the essence: 'If there ever was a time in British history when it was of importance that the unity of the British Empire should be demonstrated to all the world, it was when a question affecting the Crown itself was under consideration.' The constitutional unity of the British Empire was certainly not one of King's cardinal principles. From 1922 to 1930 he had been largely responsible for replacing unity by a kind of autonomy that looked more and more like independence. And in the matter of Canadian participation in collective security arrangements he had shown himself even more cautious than Sir Robert Borden, who had strongly intimated in 1919 that Canada would not feel automatically bound by Article X of the League of Nations Covenant.* In 1924, the year in which the Locarno mutual defence treaty was signed in Europe, Canada's League representative secured an Assembly resolution sharply modifying Article X – in effect, leaving the question of contributions to any League action up to each member. Senator Raoul Dandurand, who was one of King's few really close political confidants, left no doubt about how Canada interpreted the resolution when he told the League Assembly that Canadians lived 'in a fireproof house far from inflammable materials'. Another Canadian representative in Geneva, Rodolphe Lemieux, expressed the close connexion, in Canadian thinking, between empire and League commitments, when he said, 'In military matters we are governed also by and from Ottawa, and not by and from London; and we do not want to be governed by and from Geneva.'

Mackenzie King's external policies, by no accident, were a continuation of the lines laid down by Sir Wilfrid Laurier. The continual 'No' of Laurier's response to imperial federationists found its reflection in King's endlessly reiterated 'no commitments' in the face of demands from collective security advo-

---

*Article X required League members to 'respect and preserve as against external aggression the territorial integrity and existing political independence of all the members of the League'. Canada also refused to take part in the Locarno negotiations, nor did she adhere to the resulting treaty.

cates. Acutely sensitive to the divisive potential of the external relations question, King kept his thumb lightly on the country's pulse. In order to keep that pulse from over-excitement he deliberately smothered parliamentary debate, kept the cabinet post of External Affairs in his own hands, and publicly proclaimed the need of non-entanglement so that Parliament would be able to decide in the light of the circumstances surrounding any eventual crisis. To those like J. S. Woodsworth and the great newspaper editor John W. Dafoe of the *Winnipeg Free Press* who demanded clarification of the purposes for which Canada might use her new independence, King implied that his single purpose was to maintain *Canadian* unity.

There can be no doubt that in the 1930s Mackenzie King's foreign policy expressed majority feeling in Canada. Like Americans, most Canadians were isolationist. French Canada still feared her sons would be conscripted as a result of Canadian obligations to the empire. Although they turned away from Europe and its quarrels, many French Canadians, when they did consider the European situation, felt a Catholic sympathy for Italy and for the Franco cause in Spain. In English-speaking Canada the C.C.F. openly opposed Canadian participation in any foreign war (although in 1937 this was changed to any 'imperialist' war). A great many Liberals also demanded that Canada announce her intention to remain neutral in the event of a European war. Influenced by analyses of the causes and results of the First World War – ranging from J. M. Keynes and Beverley Nichols to the revelations of the American Nye Committee on the munitions lobbies – they opted for a North American future and isolation from the corrupt Old World. Yet, as the nature of Nazism became more clear, many isolationists began to hedge their position. And beyond this body of opinion was the still solid base of British loyalism that simply assumed Canadian support of Britain in any major war. This opinion was, in fact, held by King himself and it was his unvarying purpose to bring Canada united into such a war should it break out. King's course was tortuous partly because of his natural political style, partly because of the deep racial and class suspicions with which he had to deal.

In 1935 Canada's representative in Geneva, W. A. Riddell, proposed that the League add oil to the list of economic sanctions against Italy. Since Mussolini's war machine depended upon oil imports in its barbaric assault on Ethiopia, the 'Canadian' proposal might well have brought that war to a halt and might thus have redeemed the League from the impotence to which Anglo-French policy was consigning it. Certainly this was Riddell's hope. But he had misinterpreted the views of the new King government. When news of his startling initiative arrived in Ottawa he was unceremoniously repudiated. When questioned in the House about the incident, King replied: 'Do honourable members think it is Canada's role to regulate a European war?' Similarly, when in 1936 Germany violated the Versailles Treaty by formally repossessing the Rhineland, King kept Canada out of the ensuing negotiations, stating that 'the attitude of the government is to do nothing itself and if possible to prevent anything occurring which will precipitate one additional factor into the all-important dicussions which are now taking place in Europe.'

While he insisted that Canada had no commitments King nevertheless took hesitant steps towards readying the country for participation in a possible war, despite considerable opposition. When Woodsworth questioned the 1937 increase in Air Force estimates and asked against whom the government planned to use the bombing planes which were to be acquired, Ernest Lapointe replied:

Can there be anything more ludicrous than that question? ... Can [Woodsworth] cite any country in the world, any Parliament in a civilized country, where, when they organize their defence, they broadcast to the world that they are arming against this or that country? ... We have no enemies, I hope: in fact I know we have no enemies ...

The means by which enemies might be defined and by which Canada might enter the lists against them remained totally obscure. On several occasions from 1937 to September 1939 Ernest Lapointe, as minister of justice, made the legal position clear: a British declaration of war *would* involve Canada. In January 1939 King quoted with approval Laurier's statement that 'when Britain is at war, Canada is at war and liable to attack'. At the same time, the government refused to proceed to a vote on a resolution that declared Canada's right to remain neutral. King asked:

Why divide Canada to provide against a contingency that may not arise, or if it does, may not come until the situation has materially changed? The same consideration of the overwhelming importance of national unity which has led this government to decline to make premature and inappropriate statements of possible belligerency prevent it from recommending actions to declare possible neutrality.

While preparations for war production and military training were minimal, those that were made were based on the assumption that Canada would be at Britain's side. And, at least from the time of the Imperial Conference of 1937, King left Prime Minister Chamberlain in no doubt about Canada's response in the event of a major war involving Britain. At the same time King outstripped even Chamberlain in misreading the meaning of events and men in these years. In 1937 the Canadian prime minister visited Adolf Hitler. He told the Führer that Canada would undoubtedly support Britain if she were attacked. But he was also reassured by his visit. To Hitler he wrote: 'You have helped to remove much of the fear that in common with others I have, in some measure, shared. I was deeply impressed with the great constructive work you have achieved in Germany in bringing into the lives of those in humble circumstances the opportunities which each and all should possess.'

King was greatly relieved when the Munich settlement was reached and publicly congratulated Chamberlain on his work for peace. But when Hitler seized what was left of Czechoslovakia in March of 1939 and the British government abandoned appeasement in favour of guarantees to Poland and Rumania, King doubted Chamberlain's wisdom. In the House he declared that there was still no Canadian commitment and asked

what amount of knight errantry abroad do our resources permit? ... The idea that every twenty years this country should automatically and as a matter of course take part in a war overseas for democracy or self-determination of other small nations, that a country which has all it can do to run itself should feel called upon to save, periodically, a continent that cannot run itself, and to these ends risk the lives of its people, risk bankruptcy and political disunion, seems to many a nightmare and sheer madness.

In February King wrote to Hitler stating his conviction that the German leader would ignore the bad advice that must pour in upon him from other sources and expressing 'the faith I have in the purpose you have at heart, and of the friendship with yourself which you have been so kind as to permit me to share'. In July, through the German consul-general, Hitler sent an invitation to 'a number of Canadian students and officers' to visit Germany for three weeks to measure for themselves 'Greater Germany's newly-won strength and its will to peaceable constructive work'. King viewed the invitation as evidence of those 'unseen forces' (as he told an undoubtedly surprised Chamberlain) that guided his own and the world's destiny.* He accepted the invitation and told the consul-general he would himself go with the visitors. Had King gone through with the arrangements he and his co-travellers might well have spent the war in Germany. *Blitzkrieg* intervened.

Beyond doubt the King-Lapointe policy brought Canada into the Second World War without substantial overt division. With no declaration of the right of neutrality the country was, by Lapointe's precise definition, at war from the time of the British declaration on 3 September 1939. Yet the government acted as if this were not the case. In a confused special session of Parliament, where a state of war was said to exist, the government got authority to declare war, with only J. S. Woodsworth rising to establish his opposition in an unrecorded vote. Between 3 September and the Canadian declaration on 10 September the United States regarded Canada as neutral, but the legal right to neutrality was established only with the declaration of war itself.† While several French-Canadian members spoke against the

---

*The account of King's relations with Hitler is based largely on James Eayrs, *In Defence of Canada* (Toronto, 1965), pp. 53–78.

† President Roosevelt telephoned King to ask if Canada was at war or not. King said she was not at war. Thus for a full week American war material came across the border before the U.S. Neutrality Act had to be applied.

war, none forced a vote; the majority clearly accepted Lapointe's crucially important pledge that there would be no conscription.

Yet the extent of the unity can be exaggerated. Out of a
population of slightly over eleven million, some 529,000 were
still unemployed. Despite the signing of a trade agreement with
the United States in 1937, which ended the sequence of tariff
retaliation (and a further mutual reduction of tariffs in 1938),
the Canadian economy was only recovering slowly from the
depression. As a result, many of the enlistments for the first
Canadian Division were graduates of relief camps and work
projects for the unemployed who brought with them a feeling
of resignation rather than patriotic enthusiasm. Again, the
C.C.F. supported the war declaration only on the assumption
that Canada's contribution would be mostly economic, and this
was certainly true also of most French Canadians. For Quebec,
'unity' was represented by J. A. Blanchette who, for the government, seconded the address authorizing a war declaration: 'It
cannot be reasonably contended, after due reflection, that it
would not be wise to cooperate to a reasonable extent with
France and England in the present conflict, taking into account,
however, our resources, and our capacity, and without sacrificing our vital interests.'

Unity had been bought by the tactics of evasion. 'Our vital
interests' was a phrase that meant different things to different
classes and to different regions. Failure to define a specifically
Canadian relationship to the events that had led to war, let
alone to exercise any influence upon the course of those events,
meant that the country drifted into the greatest crisis of the
twentieth century by default. While the war appeared to solve
such problems as the right of neutrality, the slackness in the
economy, and even the federal distribution of powers, and
while it was to call forth extraordinary courage and organizing
abilities from the Canadian people, it also swept under the table
the unresolved questions of the thirties.

At the outset, unity depended very largely upon the government's heavily underlined promise of 'no conscription', upon
the clear impression that Canada's contribution would be prin-

cipally economic, and upon Mackenzie King's electoral tactics. In the short special session of September the government obtained a $100 million war appropriation with no strings attached. After the proroguing of Parliament an expeditionary force was organized and a host of orders-in-council issued regulating wartime economic activity and indeed the pattern of the whole war effort. In January 1940 Parliament re-assembled, expecting to debate what the government had done. However, King was anxious to get his mandate renewed before the 'phony war' gave way to more serious conflict with its inevitable increase in tension. Already the Conservatives, recalling the politics of the First World War, were pressing for a 'national Government'. In Quebec the time seemed very propitious for a federal election for, in October of 1939, Premier Duplessis had been turned out of office. His charge that federal war measures infringed provincial rights was rejected principally because Lapointe and the other Quebec ministers at Ottawa said they would resign if Duplessis was re-elected. Clearly the Quebec voters preferred King to the Conservatives, because they had faith in his position on conscription. Then, just before the session was to open in January, Premier Hepburn of Ontario made the political mistake of having a resolution passed in the provincial legislature condemning Ottawa's war effort. All but one member of King's cabinet agreed that an election was now justified and King confided to his diary his relief:

Hepburn's action has given to me and my colleagues and to the party here just what is needed to place beyond question the wisdom of an immediate election and the assurance of a victory for the Government. What really has helped to take an enormous load off my mind is that it justified an immediate appeal, avoiding thereby all the contention of a session known to be immediately preceding an election.

When the defence minister, J. L. Ralston, warned that the government would be charged with running away from parliamentary criticism, King gave to the cabinet his basic plebiscitary argument. The government, he said, would not be running away from criticism, it would be 'running into the arms of those who were our masters, not away from them. We were not asking to have our time extended, but were asking to have it ended altogether, if the people had no confidence in us and had more confidence in anyone else.'

The Throne Speech in January thus contained the bombshell news that the session was already over and Parliament would be dissolved forthwith. King recorded his impression of the occasion, noting that the speech was

certainly a real surprise to all who were present. My sight was too poor to see the expressions on the faces of many until I put on my glasses, but it was quite clear that it had taken all present as a complete surprise. I think everyone had been banking on a session in which everything would be made so difficult that we would have to dissolve and appear to be driven to the country.

The Liberals thus went to the country without having a parliamentary examination of their early war measures. The Tories won only thirty-nine seats while King took every Quebec seat and most of those in Ontario. King was able, as a result of this immensely successful tack, to face the most difficult trials of the war period with his principal provincial enemies weakened or destroyed and with an Ottawa opposition which was numerically weak and poorly led.

For the Liberal government, conscription of men for overseas service remained the greatest peril of wartime politics. Despite the raising of several regiments in Quebec early in the war, enlistment of French Canadians fell far behind that of English-speaking Canadians. With the fall of France in the summer of 1940 and the successive triumphs of Hitler's *Blitzkrieg* across western Europe, the Tories drew increasing support in Ontario, the west and the Maritimes for their demands that compulsion be applied. Yet in French Canada, despite the German conquest of its mother country, the war was still seen primarily as a British war and many of the brightest French-Canadian spokesmen saw conscription as the great symbol of English domination. The pressure for equality of sacrifice mounted however, especially when the United States was blown into the war at Pearl Harbor and immediately imposed selective compulsory service. For Mackenzie King the chief worry was how to keep his own cabinet united on the question. In the spring of 1942 the government decided on a plebiscite – not to authorize immediate conscription but, rather, to authorize it to impose conscription if, in the future, it seemed essential. Seventy-two per cent of Quebec's voters said 'no'; eighty per cent of English-speaking Canada voted 'yes' to release the government from its no-conscription pledge. While far from satisfactory, the government was technically released, but it remained King's principal concern to avoid conscription at almost any cost.

The carefully deferred political crisis arrived in the autumn of 1944. Returning from a review of Canadian forces following the invasion of Normandy, the minister of defence, J. L. Ralston, advised King that to maintain their strength voluntary enlistment would no longer suffice. King at once dismissed Ralston and replaced him with General A. G. L. McNaughton. McNaughton, who had been dismissed as Commander of the First Canadian Army in Britain a year earlier, was prepared to make a serious attempt to enlist home defence conscripts for immediate overseas service. The attempt failed badly. In November, King finally bent to the now irresistible English-speaking pressure and 16,000 conscript reinforcements were ordered overseas. One French-Canadian minister resigned, and thirty-four Quebec Liberal members opposed the government in a vote of confidence. Angry protests arose in Quebec, massive desertion and near mutiny broke out in some of the conscript camps, and the 1917 crisis seemed to loom again. King survived, however, and in a general election in June of 1945 following Germany's capitulation his government was re-elected with a reduced majority. For Quebec, King had remained the safest choice and had certainly fought to the last minute. In English-speaking Canada, while he was nowhere really popular, a grudging admiration for the efficiency of his wartime administration expressed itself in the vote. One result was that the Liberal government went on to greater political strength in the postwar years and even to an overconfidence which many came to see as arrogance.

The limited liability phase of Canadian participation in the war ended abruptly with the fall of France. Plans for major industrial expansion came to fruition and the country became a major arsenal and supply base for Britain in the gruelling months prior to full American participation. With over a million people working directly in war industry, Canada was to produce almost 800,000 motor vehicles in addition to a substantial flow of ships, aircraft, weapons, munitions and food. In the course of the war an additional million Canadians served in the armed forces. A complete army formation based upon three infantry divisions, two armoured divisions and two tank brigades went overseas. In the chaos following Dunkirk the Canadian advance guard constituted the major armed force defending Britain. Under General McNaughton the months of waiting in Britain for the invasion of Europe produced political strain and tension in morale. These months were marked also by two tragedies – one when a small contingent of inadequately trained troops was captured when Japan attacked Hong Kong in December 1941; the other when a force composed largely of Canadians conducted the bloodily unsuccessful feeler raid on Dieppe in August of 1942. In 1943, over the objections of General McNaughton (who disliked the idea of breaking up the Canadian Army), the Canadian government persuaded Winston Churchill to include a Canadian division in the invasion of Sicily. Largely because of the political tensions that developed during these arrangements, command of the Canadian Army passed to General H. D. G. Crerar who retained that post throughout the rest of the war. Canadians thus took a full role in the heavy fighting that began with the Sicilian invasion in the south and with the Normandy landing in the north. Montgomery gave a major role to the two Canadian divisions under his command in Normandy with the result that their casualty rate was higher than that of any other units in the command.

The crucial cooperation of the British Commonwealth nations in the struggle against Hitler was perhaps best displayed in the Commonwealth Air Training Plan. Preliminary discussions of such a scheme pre-dated the outbreak of war and the plan itself went into operation in 1939. Using the comparative safety of North America, the plan's directors built airfields, maintenance depots and training schools across Canada, at which thousands of air and ground crew from Britain and other Commonwealth nations received their essential training. In addition the Royal Canadian Air Force contributed trained pilots to the R.A.F., sent forty-five of its own squadrons overseas for the mounting assault on Germany, and helped patrol the North Atlantic.

While the United States, after 1941, was responsible for naval control of the western Atlantic, the Royal Canadian Navy played a very large role in that sector. During the war the strength of the R.C.N. grew from 5,000 to over 100,000. Its ships – mostly destroyers, corvettes, frigates and minesweepers – accounted for twenty-seven German submarines. The northwest Atlantic was largely a Canadian responsibility and most Allied convoys putting out from North America were escorted by Canadian ships and aircraft. Like the air force, the navy also took part in more distant operations, including the bitter convoy work on the route to Murmansk and the risky landings in Normandy.

The Canadian cost in lives – nearly 42,000 dead or missing – was slightly smaller than in the First World War largely because Canada's heaviest land battles came late in the war. But her overall contribution to the 1945 victory was immensely greater. Moreover, the impulse given by the war to Canadian economic growth carried the country definitively into the ranks of the industrialized states At home the accumulation of wealth in many forms outstripped by far what was spent on the war effort and the country thus could and did contribute substantial aid to Britain during and immediately following the conflict. National unity – that elusive and continually redefined Canadian goal – appeared to be closer by far in 1945 than it had been in 1918. Yet centralization and a host of unsettled questions of social policy hovered in the wings of the Canadian stage as the postwar drama opened.

18
Postwar Patterns

IN the spring of 1968 Pierre-Elliott Trudeau took office as the third French-speaking prime minister of the Canadian federal state. For Canadians it was an event endowed with many levels of meaning. At its most obvious level Trudeau's meteoric rise in active politics, covering the brief span of three years, reflected a widespread demand for more vigorous federal leadership. That demand was itself a result of Canada's total postwar experience – an experience which took the country from an extreme of centralization to extremes of provincialism, from apparent racial calm to intense reassertion of French-Canadian grievances and aspirations, from pride in its economic growth to nervous awareness of economic dependence upon the United States, and from confident participation in N.A.T.O. to conscious reassessment of the whole range of foreign policy. In his summons to build in Canada a 'Just Society', Prime Minister Trudeau seemed to recall the unassertive tolerance that has always lain close to the heart of the Canadian experiment. Yet Canadians learned again in the years after 1945 that tolerance has often to be fought for, that the nature of justice is not easily defined, and that even mild-mannered independence is seldom secure.

While conscription had been the most explosive issue of wartime politics, there were other matters with even longer fuses. It is now clear that conscription for service in 'British wars' is not likely again to disturb Canadian politics. But the question of Ottawa's role both domestically and in external relations (a question of which conscription was simply the ultimate illustration) remained. So too did the unfinished matters of social security and equitable distribution of wealth regionally and by class.

During the war, despite comparatively effective control of

prices and rationing through the Wartime Prices and Trade Board administered by C. D. Howe, centres of criticism remained strong. In Quebec a left-of-centre anti-war party, the Bloc Populaire, showed growing strength in by-elections. In Ontario and the west the C.C.F. was even more threatening as a popular alternative to King Liberalism. In 1943 the C.C.F. became the official opposition in Ontario and the following year, under T. C. Douglas, the socialists won power in Saskatchewan. Calling for conscription of wealth as well as of manpower, for overdue labour and welfare legislation, and for economic planning as the basis of postwar reconstruction, the C.C.F. charged that the Liberal government was overwhelmingly dominated by big business. Mackenzie King himself was disturbed by the charges. The political growth of the C.C.F., he hoped, might convince

some of our people that labour has to be dealt with in a considerate way. In my heart I am not sorry to see the mass of the people coming a little more into their own, but I do regret that it is not the Liberal Party that is winning that position for them. It should be, and it can still be that our people will learn their lesson in time. What I fear is we will begin to have a defection from our own ranks in the House to the C.C.F.

Such defection did not materialize. After its sudden surge the C.C.F. faltered and in the 1945 federal election the party won only twenty-eight seats, nearly all of them in the west. The impact of its threat, however, was seen in a reduced Liberal majority and a renewed Liberal emphasis on social reform. In 1944 a Family Allowances Act was passed by which the federal treasury paid parents up to eight dollars a month for each dependent child. The Liberal platform of 1945 promised public works and liberal financial assistance to ease the problems of employment, training and re-establishing of veterans, as well as implementation of earlier pledges such as hospital insurance. The government also promised substantial economic planning through fiscal policy, aid to housing developments, and price-maintenance for farm products. Since the Tories, with a new name (Progressive-Conservatives), and a new leader (John Bracken of Manitoba), also adopted a reform image, the centre of the political stage was crowded. In these circumstances the election of 1945 returned the Liberals largely because they were 'experienced', because the C.C.F. had been effectively smeared as communist-oriented in a well-endowed pamphlet and press campaign, and partly because Quebec, which elected only one Conservative, refused to have anything to do with the party of conscription.

Mackenzie King continued to preside over these happy Liberal fortunes until his retirement in 1948. Because he was able to hand-pick his successor, Louis St Laurent, and because a predicted postwar depression failed to develop, the 'era of Mackenzie King' lasted in practice until 1957. Like earlier phases of the King era, its last stage was marked by sharp contrasts and ironies. Economic and population growth, pride in the national war effort and the fact that Canada emerged from the war as fourth amongst the world's industrial and trading nations, combined to produce a new surge of national feeling amongst English-speaking Canadians. Yet, while federal initiative put on foot some important national policies, Ottawa found itself increasingly challenged by the provinces. And in external relations, while these seemed to be years in which independence became complete, the country drifted into a relationship with the United States that appeared to impose more commitments and inhibitions than had the British relationship at any time since 1896.

In Quebec the *nationaliste* storm that was to break at the end of the fifties and which few English-speaking Canadians anticipated in these years, was delayed by two significant events. The first was the return to office of Maurice Duplessis and the Union Nationale. Toppling the wartime Liberal government of Adélard Godbout, Duplessis also thwarted the extreme *nationalistes* of the Bloc Populaire. The result was an unbroken Union Nationale reign of sixteen years.

Duplessis was a colourful, hard-living bachelor who pursued power with single-minded devotion and infallible acumen. The power he won was retained by systematic exploitation of *nationalisme* and a method of legislative representation that favoured the rural constituencies. Playing skilfully upon the most ancient fears of anglicization, he kept, almost to the end, the support of the Roman Catholic hierarchy. But in addition to his steady resistance to 'Ottawa's encroachments' he welcomed American capital and maintained a violently anti-labour policy which left the under-represented urban workers frustrated and hostile.

As the sham nature of the Duplessis version of *nationalisme* became more and more obvious, the labour unions found themselves joined by invaluable allies. Younger liberals in the professions and in the church itself launched in the mid fifties an open and vigorous assault upon the systematic corruption and Neanderthal capitalism of the Union Nationale. Not a few of the young liberal insurgents brought to their work of demolition post-graduate training in French and American universities. Applying contemporary ideas in economics, sociology and politics to the Quebec scene, they depicted the overwhelming need of reform in church–state relations and in education, which was still heavily dominated by classical languages and medieval philosophy. They gave strong support to labour unions in a series of tough strikes and also unveiled the details of democratic corruption upon which the Duplessis system rested. At the conclusion of one sensational article by two priests of Laval university in 1956, the authors summed up the case for political reform:

... an electoral period like that through which we have just passed becomes an instrument of demoralization and dechristianization. That which makes a country Christian is not first and foremost, the number of churches, the pious declarations of politicians, the apparent temporal or political influence of the church, or the 'good relations' between Church and State. It is primarily the respect for truth, the cult of justice, integrity of consciences, the respect for liberty. The existing electoral proceedings are a frontal attack on all these values.

The central argument of the reform liberals was that the corrupt alliance of Duplessis, the hierarchy and American capital, far from securing *la survivance* of French Canada, was creating an illiberal industrial feudalism. In such a neo-colonial society neither the industrial workers nor the aspiring young professional people could hope to share in the benefits of technological growth or the exercise of real power. To safeguard provincial jurisdictions was of little use if the government at Quebec City was responsive only to conservative clerics, uneducated farmers and the demands of foreign capital. Through such papers as *Le Devoir*, edited by André Laurendau, and the union-supported *Cité Libre*, under Pierre-Elliott Trudeau and Gérard Pelletier, a secular and urban-orientated liberalism took firm root. In this new liberalism the democratic state (rid of corruption), rather than the church, was to become the agent of cultural survival and of social justice. By 1959, when Duplessis died and the Union Nationale entered a period of political disorganization, the rebels had gained control of the provincial Liberal Party and were ready to take power – as they did in the Quebec election of 1960. In the meantime, at the federal level, the second political event that had kept the lid on radical *nationalisme* was also working itself out.

In 1941, with the death of Ernest Lapointe, Mackenzie King had lost his invaluable Quebec political *chef*. Lapointe's replacement, originally thought to be for the duration of the war only, turned out to be one of King's most important political choices. Louis St Laurent was an immensely successful Quebec City lawyer. Completely self-made, St Laurent had risen through *collège classique* and the Laval law faculty from his father's country store in the Eastern Townships to the eminence of Quebec City's Grande Allée. Completely bilingual,* St Laurent enjoyed close connexions with the leading English-speaking businessmen of Montreal and Toronto by whom his law firm was often retained. His own beliefs about society were distinctly conservative and his view of Canada was essentially that of Sir Wilfrid Laurier upon whom, in many respects, he modelled himself. Convinced that the survival of French Canada was possible only within an independent Canadian federal state and also that the defeat of Hitlerite Germany was

---

*His mother was of Irish descent, his father was a French Canadian. Until he went to school he normally spoke French to his father and English to his mother.

essential, St Laurent willingly supported King's cautious conduct of Canada's wartime role. His support of the war effort, including the reluctant application of conscription, gave crucially important strength to the government in the last year of the war, despite virulent attacks upon St Laurent in Quebec as *vendu*. At the end of the war King persuaded St Laurent to stay on in the government and in 1946 moved him from Justice to External Affairs. In 1948, upon King's retirement, a Liberal convention duly transferred the mantles of party leader and prime minister to St Laurent.

From the English-speaking Canadian point of view the succession was nearly perfect. The silver-haired avuncular Quebecker was soon dubbed in the English-language press 'Uncle Louis' and quickly became the symbol of postwar stability and affluence. To some extent the very successes of the St Laurent years, since they were largely *federal* achievements, contributed to the discontents of extreme Quebec *nationalistes*. Yet, at the same time, the contrast between an old-fashioned French-Canadian reactionary in office at Quebec City and an old-fashioned French-Canadian Liberal at the head of affairs in Ottawa cooled the provincialist ardour of not a few *nationalistes*. One such, who was to become a *séparatiste* in the 1960s, wrote in 1958 that 'those who like me have experienced the bankruptcy of what is called our "national doctrine" must seek a new direction. They do not believe that the Nationalist orientation can ever produce a living culture, living politics, living men.'

Mackenzie King's last years in office, and the two St Laurent administrations (to 1957) saw the coming of age of English-speaking Canadian nationalism. In domestic affairs Ottawa presided over a sustained economic boom, rounded out the country's territorial limits, initiated further federal programmes of social insurance and regional equalization, and undertook substantial support of educational growth.

In 1949, after lengthy negotiations and an island plebiscite, Newfoundland finally entered Confederation as the tenth province. 'Britain's oldest colony' showed some reluctance to come to the altar but the outports, which stood to gain most by the arrangement, gave the necessary small majority against the St John's businessmen. During the war both Canada and the United States had spent heavily in Newfoundland on airports, naval facilities and defence installations. As part of the destroyers-for-bases deal of 1940 the United States had received a ninety-nine year lease of several points on the island, while Canada established crucially important airports at Gander and Goose Bay. The obvious importance of Newfoundland, not only for patrolling the St Lawrence approaches but also for commercial air travel, intensified Canadian concern. At the same time, while the island's fishing, mining and lumbering industries had recovered from the long and bitter depression years, the general standard of living was far below that enjoyed even by the other Canadian Atlantic provinces. The prospect of sharing in Canadian social welfare programmes, trade development and investment turned the scales in favour of Confederation. Mackenzie King, under whom the negotiations had begun, looked on their conclusion as a fitting cap to his long career, while Canadian businessmen were certainly not uninterested in the vast mineral and hydroelectric power resources in Newfoundland's continental extension in Labrador.

In these years, too, constitutional questions appeared less urgent, save for the continuing hostility of Duplessis towards Ottawa initiatives. The right of appeal from the Supreme Court to the Judicial Committee of the British Privy Council was ended and the Canadian Parliament was empowered to amend the British North America Act in matters clearly within federal jurisdiction. Small changes were made in the Royal Style and Titles Act and in the Letters Patent of the governor-general underlining Canada's constitutional independence. And in 1952 Vincent Massey became the first Canadian-born governor-general. Massey's appointment, however, while it was arranged by St Laurent, symbolized both the centralizing and 'anglophone'* character of the period's nationalism. Massey was heir

---

*The terms 'anglophone' and 'francophone' have come into fairly general use as convenient abbreviations for 'English-speaking' and 'French-speaking'. The volumes of the Royal Commission on Bi-

to a farm-machinery fortune, a former Liberal Party organizer, and a diplomat who had served in Washington and as Canadian High Commissioner in London. Noted as a patron of the arts and of higher education, Massey had family connexions and personal preferences which inclined him strongly towards the imperial connexion and acceptance of British modes in both society and government. Affecting the tweedy style of an English country gentleman, he brought to his undoubted Canadianism a very British tone – agreeable to the English-speaking élite but a matter of indifference, amusement or irritation to French Canadians and to those anglophones who felt that pseudo-aristocracy was a threat to Canadian social democracy.

Massey's appointment followed by one year the publication of the report of a Royal Commission on the Arts, Letters and Sciences of which he had been chairman. Laying heavy emphasis on the need to maintain and further develop a Canadian culture distinguishable from that of the United States, the Massey Report led directly to Ottawa's endowing a Canada Council. The Council's function is to encourage Canadian talent by means of grants and fellowships to scholars, writers, artists and a wide variety of institutions ranging from theatre and ballet companies to small magazines and, in one controversial case, a 'town fool'. Establishment of the Canada Council did much to lessen the drain of talent to the south and to enrich the country's cultural life, not least by enabling artists and scholars to study abroad at public expense. Yet, as the impact of American mass media increased in the television age, still other means of maintaining a distinctive culture were canvassed. The Canadian Broadcasting Corporation established a national television network and a private network was also built, both operating under a regulatory board which prescribes a minimum 'Canadian content' in programming. Experiments were also made with mildly discriminatory measures

---

lingualism and Biculturalism and, increasingly, the English language press, use the terms freely despite their rather exotic sound in English sentences.

against American magazines, but opposition to stricter measures made it clear that they would provoke a political storm. Even apart from the jurisdictional question (is federal 'intervention' in the field of culture an invasion of the provincial power over education?) an overtly nationalist approach to culture encountered basic difficulties. Canadians, by choice, buy more American magazines and watch more American television programmes (either on their own networks or directly from American stations) than Canadian. At the same time more and more Canadians take pride in what *is* produced in their country and have endorsed increasing public spending on cultural growth.

By and large, Canadians have opted for a competitive rather than a protective approach to cultural independence. Thus they have continued the National Film Board, begun as a wartime information agency, and it produces outstanding short-subject, documentary and experimental films. Through private investment as well as through the Film Board a beginning has been made on a feature film industry. By the end of the fifties most provinces and a number of cities had founded arts councils to supplement the work of the Canada Council. The combined effects of subsidization, prosperity and European immigration have markedly influenced the Canadian cultural climate. Private art galleries have blossomed in the larger cities, independent film-makers are beginning to supplement the efforts of the N.F.B., Canadian artists, writers and musicians do not as often as in the past seek permanent refuge abroad. While the brilliant artistic and planning success of Expo 67 is one measure of cultural development, a more enduring test is the evident willingness of Canadians to seek and accept international as well as national criteria of cultural achievement.

Despite these signs of cultural maturation, however, Canadians failed to match American expenditures on public education. Both the causes and the results of this differential are significant, if debatable. Most analysts agree that the widening education gap between the two countries helps to explain the fact that real income per head in Canada is about 20 per cent less than the comparable American figure. Thus the

Economic Council of Canada recommended that

relatively greater emphasis should be placed on facilitating expanding investment in education in relation to expanding investment in other assets ... in general accordance with the growing concern in many parts of the Canadian economy that the shortage of skilled and trained technical, professional and managerial manpower is even more critical than the problem of enlarging the physical facilities for increasing output.

In the late fifties and sixties Canadian expenditures on education rose steeply, although they still failed to overtake the American. As they rose they brought into sharper focus many related questions, not least of which was the nature of Canadian federalism. Most of the new spending on education has had to be administered by the provinces because provincial control of education is the most clearly entrenched jurisdiction in the B.N.A. Act. While Ottawa has subsidized heavily the expansion of educational facilities it is unable to give a clear national direction to the economic-social thrust of the resulting growth. One of the purposes, for example, of greater spending on education is to increase manpower productivity at all levels. But productivity is related to mobility and although Ottawa has a manpower policy it is inhibited from really active intervention in the fields of re-training and re-location by the upsurge of provincial-rights sensitivity. Thus regionalism and provincialist-federalism have a direct effect upon the inter-connected factors of education and productivity.

Still more subtle considerations obtrude to complicate the relationship between national culture and economic well-being. Because Canada lagged well behind the United States in providing not only good technical and scientific education but also in general university development, she encountered serious difficulties when she decided in the late fifties on a crash programme of education expansion. Because of previous under-development it was impossible to staff the new, and expanding older, institutions with Canadians. While few educators argued that a citizenship-test should be imposed, many were

279

nevertheless worried by the flood of Americans that poured into Canadian universities in the sixties. In Ontario, as the province founded some nine universities in a ten-year period (for a total of fifteen in 1969), it was necessary to recruit a very large proportion of new faculty from abroad. While some came from the United Kingdom, the American reservoir provided an ever larger proportion of annual faculty importation, especially for the new universities'in Ontario and the west. By 1969 some of the 'instant universities' such as Simon Fraser in British Columbia had faculties whose composition was more than two-thirds American. As with the steady importation of managerial and technical personnel there were clear advantages as well as possible risks. Without the American supply of academics the essential university expansion would have been virtually impossible. Also, the infusion of Americans gave to many Canadian universities a more international complexion than they had previously enjoyed. On the other hand, if American 'values' do differ in some respects from Canadian, a university whose faculty is two-thirds American is likely to present many subjects in an American rather than in a Canadian context. To Americanize is not necessarily to internationalize an institution – whether it be a labour union, a business firm or a university.

The reasons for Canada's tardiness in creating an educational system adequate to the demands of industrialization and cultural growth are complex. Certainly the heavy importation of skilled and professional workers after 1945 reflected the fact that (in 1951) only two-fifths of Canadians between the ages of fifteen and nineteen were still in school, while less than one in twelve of the college age group were in college. Professor John Porter argued that this situation obtained because it was agreeable to the élites of the country's two charter (founding) groups. He wrote:

The dependence on external recruitment has created the illusion of adequacy. It has also permitted the continuity of class-bound education as exemplified by the classical college system in Quebec and the academic collegiate system in Ontario. There has, too, been the upper class institution of the private school. ... When these systems are threatened by educational reforms the educational purists come strongly to their defence. Often the democratic extension of education is equated with the dilution of education.*

Beyond doubt Canadians accept egalitarian ideas less readily than do Americans. Indeed, this is one instance of a difference in values. Nevertheless, while stability, continuity and order all rank high in the consideration of both Canadian 'charter groups', the educational revolution set on foot at the end of the fifties is basic and still working itself out. Its long-range effects will include a considerable increase in social mobility as well as marked improvement in the educational level of the country's work force. Yet any simplistic comparison of Canadian and American approaches to problems such as egalitarianism in education (or to the question of social mobility) is bound to founder on the rock of historical perspective. Canadians have seldom put efficiency as high in their scale of values as have Americans nor have they often supposed that real equality and freedom are to be secured without regard to the rights of minorities and to the maintenance of order. Thus their more structured (or deferential) society has been more cautious in its advance towards a system of education geared to the needs of industry and science than has the American. In particular it has respected regional differences and resisted the potential pressures of the Canadian agents of the American industrial-military complex. One result of this real, if elusive, difference is that a very substantial proportion of the American teachers who have emigrated to Canada (particularly since 1965) have done so precisely in order to escape the increasingly totalitarian nature of American industrial society. And underlining the significant liberal rejection of an eminently efficient democratic industrial system was the massive emigration to Canada of young American draft-dodgers who refused to take part in the military manifestation of America's efficient affluence. In Canada the least friendly reception for the American

---

*The Vertical Mosaic: An Analysis of Social Class and Power in Canada, Toronto, 1965, p. 166.

immigration was from those who benefit most directly from branch-plant patronage.

In postwar external relations complex strains of nationalism also appeared. As in other aspects of Canadian policy much of what was decided reflected the proximity and enormous power of the United States. In 1940 Mackenzie King had previewed the future when he agreed with President Franklin Roosevelt at a meeting in Ogdensburg, New York, to establish a Permanent Joint Board on Defence. Signed almost casually, the Ogdensburg Agreement rested on the assumption that common planning of the defence of North America was desirable. But it also signalled a more basic shift of emphasis. One Canadian historian described it as inevitable: 'In 1940 we passed from the British century of our history to the American century. We became dependent upon the United States for our security. We have, therefore, no choice but to follow American leadership.' Whether or not that statement exaggerates the situation (and there is much reason to suppose it does) there is no doubt that liberal postwar governments have chosen to associate Canada closely with American foreign policy and, in defence arrangements, to approach an almost indissoluble integration. By a series of agreements they provided for joint construction and operation of a vast northern radar warning network and for continuous consultation on military equipment and strategy. A defence production sharing agreement provides for extensive reciprocal purchasing of defence goods which in 1968 amounted to some $400 million each way. The North American Air Defence Agreement placed the R.C.A.F. under a unified NORAD (North American Air Defence) command which controls the continental aircraft warning system and deployed both interceptor planes and nuclear-tipped missiles from bases in Canada and the United States. The NORAD commander is American, his deputy Canadian. Despite strident Tory comments on Liberal 'Americatization', both NORAD and the defence production agreement were initiated by the Diefenbaker government.

Behind the drift towards 'continentalism' lay not only the alleged necessities of the Cold War but also certain preconceptions of Liberal policy-makers. One such preconception informed Mackenzie King's attitude towards postwar international relations most markedly and was passed on to his successors (Louis St Laurent and Lester B. Pearson)* in only slightly modified form. This was a compound of suspicion of British purposes and a profound distaste for independent initiative in foreign policy. While Canada was a founding member of the United Nations, King had no more faith in the new world organization than he had shown in the old League. Nor did St Laurent declare for bold new departures. Leadership in world affairs, declared St Laurent in 1947, should be a function of power: 'There is little point in a country of our stature recommending international action, if those who must carry the burden of whatever action is taken are not in sympathy.' And if military power was to be the central criterion of this functionalism there could be little doubt about who should do the leading.

While Canada joined all the U.N. agencies, became a founding member and substantial contributor to the Columbo Plan, played a significant role in all U.N. peace-keeping operations and endorsed the principle of universal membership in the U.N., the core of her postwar collective security thinking was the American alliance system. After the communist assumption of power in Czechoslovakia in 1948 St Laurent took a prominent part in the moves to create a 'regional' military alliance. The resulting North Atlantic Treaty Organization satisfied most Canadians at the time despite the fact that it was a revolutionary departure from the traditional 'no commitments' of Mackenzie King. Sharing the fulsome, if somewhat curious, Anglo-American fear of Russia's European intentions and power, and recognizing the impossibility of a return to isolationism, the government found in N.A.T.O. a politically acceptable basis for what was presented as an essential military commitment. Both of Canada's mother countries were founding members of N.A.T.O. and thus the old political issues of imperialism were

---

*King retained the post of external affairs secretary until 1946 when he gave it to St Laurent who had until then been minister' of justice. When St Laurent became prime minister in 1948 he gave the post to L. B. Pearson who had had long experience as a diplomat in the department. In 1957 Pearson succeeded St Laurent as Liberal leader.

avoided. Furthermore, while the United States would obviously be the dominant partner in the alliance, there were soothing assurances of continuous consultation on policy. The 'inevitable' was made still more palatable when, on Canada's insistence, Article II of the Treaty declared that N.A.T.O. should pursue economic, cultural and social cooperation amongst its members. 'It must be economic,' as St Laurent put it, 'it must be moral.' Despite pressure from Lester Pearson, Article II of the Treaty remained a dead letter. On the military side Canada contributed a brigade group and twelve R.C.A.F. squadrons to N.A.T.O. in Europe and some forty ships (mostly anti-submarine) to N.A.T.O.'s naval power.

As the Cold War grew more intense the government reflected to some extent a growing body of Canadian opinion that held suspect an overtly military assessment of the problems of security and peace. In general, Ottawa took a noticeably less ideological approach to the question of coexistence than did Washington. While Canada's contribution to the U.N. action in Korea was the third largest in terms of men and money, she did not join S.E.A.T.O. and, indeed, had been on the point of recognizing the new government of China when the Korean war broke out in the spring of 1950. Nor did Ottawa see fit to join the Organization of American States despite ardent invitations from Washington and considerable sympathy amongst French Canadians towards the proposal. When the United States launched its diplomatic and economic crusade against Fidel Castro, Canada refused to break relations with Cuba and has maintained normal trade with the island.

Despite, then, the central N.A.T.O.-NORAD core of Canadian foreign and defence policy, Ottawa has tried to develop a mediating and peace-keeping role which will reflect something of the nature and purpose of the Canadian state. Lester Pearson came to symbolize that role as a skilled negotiator at the U.N. For his part in promoting peace-by-compromise in the Middle East he was awarded the Nobel Peace Prize in 1957. Pearson also developed a useful middleman function for Canada in the Commonwealth of Nations. A vigorous advocate of real equality of status amongst the white and non-white nations of the multi-racial Commonwealth that had emerged with full Canadian support at the end of the war, Canada gained the special confidence of the Afro-Asian members. Although her expenditures on aid programmes have not been large in proportion to her military expenditures, they have steadily increased. In 1956 Pearson was able to play a key role in the U.N. settlement of the Suez crisis – a situation that contained immense political perils since both Britain and France had to be balked in their anachronistic action against Egypt. Undoubtedly the 'solution' in Suez was made possible because it was one urgently desired by the United States. But since the Anglo-French action was also opposed by Afro-Asian Commonwealth members and supported by Australia and New Zealand, the Canadian role enhanced Canada's position as honest broker in the Commonwealth. In 1965 a Commonwealth meeting elected a skilled Canadian diplomat, Arnold Smith, to the new post of secretary-general of the Commonwealth. In 1966 Smith organized the Lagos Conference on the Rhodesian crisis, at which Canada's role of mediator was further developed.

While most Canadians supported the general lines of postwar foreign policy, many were uneasy and warned that the country had moved not to independence but to a new colonial relationship in which an all-powerful Washington had replaced a waning London. As it became clear that no country could hope to defend itself other than by preventing the outbreak of a nuclear war, criticism of the military alliance system gained support. The critics' case, which seemed likely to produce a considerable shift of emphasis in Canadian policy, was complex. Formal treaty membership, they urged, seriously inhibits Ottawa without in any way increasing Canadian security. Thus Canada delayed recognition of China (although selling her very large amounts of wheat) because such action would be overtly offensive to Washington. Again, while Canada became, with India and Poland, a member of the International Control Commission established in Vietnam by the 1954 Geneva Conference, her attitude on the I.C.C. was that of the 'Western member' rather than that of a neutral participant. To criticisms of such loyalty the government answered that whatever influence it had in

Washington (and elsewhere) depended upon staying inside the basic alliance structure; that it was thus enabled to exercise a quiet diplomacy which in the long run is more effective than a noisy independence. Answering a widely-supported university petition to halt the flow of Canadian war goods destined for American use in Vietnam, Prime Minister Pearson summed up the government's case: 'Confidential and quiet arguments by a responsible government are usually more effective than public ones. ... Too many public declarations and disclosures run the risk of complicating matters for those concerned. ... The more complex and dangerous the problem, the greater is the need for calm and deliberate diplomacy.'

In the same statement Mr Pearson touched upon other reasons for not rocking the North American boat, reasons which were perhaps more profound than those of diplomatic method. Pointing to the World War II origins of Canada's entanglement in continental defence, he reviewed the extent to which defence production had been integrated, the technological and mass production advantages Canada receives, and then argued that because of these advantages Canada could not, in fact, refuse to contribute to the American effort in Vietnam:

For a broad range of reasons, therefore, it is clear that the imposition of an embargo on the export of military equipment to the U.S.A., and concomitant termination of the Production Sharing Agreements, would have far-reaching consequences which no Canadian government could contemplate with equanimity. It would be interpreted as a notice of withdrawal on our part from continental defence and even from the collective defence arrangements of the Atlantic Alliance.

The far-reaching consequences include a possible deterioration of relations with the United States. Whether or not this would, in turn, lead to economic or other reprisals, that possibility bulks large in Canadian thinking. And it does so chiefly because of the extent of Canadian-American trade and the degree to which Canada's postwar prosperity has depended upon direct American investment. While official Ottawa constantly reiterates the collective security need of Canadian contributions to the American alliance system, the military case for such contributions is progressively less convincing. Canada's foremost analyst of defence-foreign policy argued that since the introduction of the Ballistic Missile Early Warning System (entirely outside Canadian territory)

for the first time in the postwar history of continental defence, Canadian cooperation was not essential. ... None of Canada's military efforts contributes significantly to the defence of North America. Neither the two squadrons of Bomarc-B interceptor guided missiles sited at North Bay, Ontario, and La Macaza, Quebec, nor the interceptor fighter aircraft assigned to the North American Air Defence Command are useful in the event of missile attack. They are meant to be useful in the event of bomber attack. Yet it is evident that any bomber attack from the Soviet Union will occur only in the wake of a missile attack which must be presumed to have destroyed the important anti-bomber defences.*

The military case for Canadian contributions to N.A.T.O. in Europe seemed equally weak. By 1963, when the CF-104 strike-reconnaissance planes were equipped with nuclear weapons, they merely added marginally to N.A.T.O.'s existing overkill capacity. Conversely, the 6,000-man brigade group constituted about one four-hundredth of N.A.T.O.'s manpower. Clearly Canada's military contributions to the alliance system were for diplomatic and prestige purposes. As a study prepared for the Commons Defence Committee in 1965 put it:

The key decisions which would determine our survival are now made outside of Canada – in centres such as Washington, Moscow, New York, Paris and Peking. We want to be able to influence those decisions, and cannot do so effectively unless we are paying, in the form of armed force, our membership fees in a number of international organizations. ... The overriding factors in determining the content of Canada's military policy can, and should, be the resolve to purchase influence.

In a section of the Conservative Party, throughout most of Quebec, and in the N.D.P., the policy of purchasing influence by military expenditures and alliance membership is rejected.

---

* James Eayrs, 'The Military Policies of Contemporary Canada', in R. H. Leach (ed.), *Contemporary Canada*, Toronto, 1968, p. 242.

As James Eayrs puts it: 'Credit may not exist, or may exist only imperfectly, in international society. The state system may not resemble a banking system. It may be impossible, or difficult, to accumulate a balance of favourable regard. Governments may have no memory or their memory may be short.'

Alternative external policies designed to aid U.N. para-military police operations, to improve the economic position of the Third World, and to end the diplomatic boycott of China, were principal subjects of a total review of Canadian foreign policy put on foot by the Trudeau government in 1969. Despite an elaborate structure for this policy review, however, many observers expected it to produce something less than a revolution in Canada's position. The new Liberal government, although seemingly more responsive to foreign policy criticism than was its predecessor, had a high regard for stability. Prime Minister Trudeau described his government's attitude succinctly when he said it was prepared to act vigorously within the 20 per cent of independence that remains to Canada in its American century. Nevertheless, that 20 per cent seems to offer some latitude. In 1969, to the disgust of the State Department and the Foreign Office, Canada decided to reduce sharply her military presence in Europe. The decision was taken despite strong objections by the Canadian External Affairs Minister and his colleague in the National Defence department. It left little doubt about the pre-eminence in the cabinet of the prime minister. At the same time negotiations were begun at the Chinese embassy in Stockholm looking to Canadian diplomatic recognition of China. While Washington frowned, Canada recognized China in 1970, and Canadians observed that this initiative was soon followed by the Nixon–Kissinger policy of détente.

19

The Mosaic and the Melting Pot

BEHIND the political upheavals that began in 1957 lay the conditioning force of the economic and population booms of the late forties and fifties. As in the days of the Laurier wheat boom, both national and international factors combined to produce explosive growth. Inside Canada pent-up wartime savings created demands for consumer goods which greatly facilitated conversion of expanded war industries to a peacetime basis. At the same time the recovery needs of Britain and western Europe opened markets for Canadian products from farm and factory. To avert what otherwise would have been shortages of capital and labour, foreign supplies of both were ready. From Britain and Europe a renewed stream of immigration poured into the country. From the United States came an immense flow of direct capital investment. All these ingredients produced the heady prosperity of the fifties with its renewed anglophone nationalism. The boom also, by quickening some basic Canadian tendencies, brought them into sharper focus and thus into heated political debate.

Immigration and concentrated urban growth wrought substantial changes. Between 1941 and 1976 Canada's population grew from eleven and a half million to over twenty-two million. Nearly two million of this remarkable increase were immigrants, of whom more than a million arrived between 1945 and 1956. From refugee camps, from Britain beset by austerity, from Hungary torn by revolt, from overpopulated Holland and Italy, the 'New Canadians' came to apply their skills and to find either security or fortune. Nearly a third of the immigrants were British and another third Italian. Unlike earlier arrivals the majority of postwar immigrants settled in cities, thus heightening the urban and industrial character of the country.

There were other significant differences from the Laurier

period. Many of the postwar immigrants brought industrial or professional skills and not a few brought small amounts of capital with them. Moreover, they arrived at a time when the children of the earlier immigration were becoming established in business, the professions and politics. By the 1950s several cities had mayors who were of non-Anglo-Saxon extraction, while European names appeared more and more frequently in the membership of local governments, provincial legislatures and the federal Parliament. While in Toronto, Montreal and several other cities some older sections were virtually taken over by particular language groups, there was much less of a nativist reaction than had been the case prior to World War I. Canadians did not press hard for immediate assimilation of immigrants and indeed seemed to welcome the infusion of European colour – the street markets, better and more varied restaurants, foreign film theatres, heavier patronage of cultural activities and greater artistic resources. After the war they liked to think of their country as a mosaic rather than a melting pot. Again, although the well-established power élites in business, politics, churches, the civil service and the professions were certainly not displaced, their ranks were more open than ever before. To some extent the sources of power began to shift from wealth and family to skill and specialized training.

Yet while English-speaking Canadians fondly talked of a mosaic, French Canada continued to see heavy immigration as the principal threat to its survival. The doors of big business and of the highest echelons of the federal civil service were not really open to francophones, and the overwhelming majority of immigrants, from whatever background, elected to become English-speaking rather than French-speaking Canadians. This fact, together with a declining French-Canadian birth-rate and a rising anglophone birth-rate, provided active catalysts in the *nationaliste* brew of the fifties and sixties.

The combination of population growth and an almost unlimited influx of foreign capital produced a postwar economic buoyancy which was interrupted only by a down-swing between 1957 and 1961. Between 1939 and 1967 the country's gross national product rocketed from six billion dollars to over sixty-two billion dollars. A sustained production boom produced many square miles of suburbs, a mushroom growth of high-rise apartment buildings, commercial skyscrapers and manufacturing facilities. And this very growth brought new and pressing construction needs. Cities, choked with their own traffic, belatedly built subways, elevated freeways and multi-lane commuter highways. Even more belatedly, provincial governments undertook hospital, school and university building programmes– programmes which required almost constant *ad hoc* adjustments of the fiscal relationships between Ottawa and the provinces.

In addition to promoting urban-industrial growth the new capital investors made deep inroads into Canada's natural resources frontiers. Canada held her position as the world's leading producer of nickel and newsprint while prospecting capital discovered and developed important new resource areas. In Labrador and the Ungava section of Quebec vast ranges of iron ore were tapped and their product fed to foreign markets and a rapidly growing Canadian steel industry. In Alberta large fields of oil and natural gas were discovered and developed, while in northern Ontario and Saskatchewan uranium discoveries made Canada a leading producer of that crucial commodity. In 1952, under the guidance of the National Research Council, Atomic Energy of Canada was established as a crown corporation to develop methods of producing atomic energy for peaceful purposes.* The CANDU power station (with 1,000 megawatt capacity per unit and unlimited extension potential) is probably the most efficient atomic generator yet developed. It was expected that by the late seventies half of all new power stations built in Canada would be run by atomic power.

Underpinning the effective use of growth capital were outsize developments in hydroelectric power and in transportation both of power and goods. In the hinterlands of the Shield and the mountains of the Pacific coast immense reserves of water power were harnessed for industrial purposes ranging from

---

*During the Second World War Canadian scientists had shared with those of the United States and the United Kingdom in the secret development of atomic energy.

mining and pulp and paper to the processing of aluminium. New rail lines and air services were inaugurated almost overnight. At the same time hundreds of miles of power transmission lines had to be built and, even more challenging, thousands of miles of pipelines for oil and gas were required. The longest of the pipelines reached 1,760 miles from Edmonton to the refineries of Sarnia in southern Ontario, while others snaked through the mountains to the Pacific and south to American markets.

The most dramatic of the transportation-power developments took place on the St Lawrence–Great Lakes. Projects for joint Canadian-American construction of a deep-water route to enable ocean-going vessels to reach ports in the continent's industrial heartland had been widely touted for fifty years and more. In 1932 an enabling treaty was signed but rejected by the American Senate which reflected opposition from railways and ocean ports in the United States. By the beginning of the 1950s, however, conditions for the success of the project were more than ripe. The huge Ungava iron range (north of Sept Isles on the lower St Lawrence) was ready to supply American and Canadian steel mills which were already threatened by depletion of the Mesabi iron range in Minnesota. In addition to mounting pressure from lake cities throughout the system for direct access to ocean shipping, the electric power demands of industry in Ontario and New York state were becoming crucial. To meet these the water power of the upper St Lawrence was the closest available source. Moreover, Canadian confidence was now running high. Thus when Canada proposed to build the entire seaway and power project on her own (using the slightly more difficult Canadian channel through the international portion of the river) pro-seaway forces in the United States, strongly backed by President Truman, prevailed upon Congress to accept a joint construction and control plan. The Treaty, ratified in 1954, provided for joint development of hydroelectric power by New York and Ontario and for the building and operation of a deep-water route throughout the entire system by the two federal governments. Officially opened in 1959 by Queen Elizabeth and President Eisenhower, traffic has grown steadily and brought with it ancillary development of port facilities.

The dramatic symbolism of the opening ceremonies at the huge locks at St Lambert, Quebec, however, had many facets. It was the last pre-1976 occasion on which the Queen could officiate on Quebec soil without the indignity of special protection against *nationaliste* demonstrations. The seaway, moreover, with its joint financing and administration, and the concomitant growth of an international electric power grid, not to mention American financing of the iron ore developments which were to provide about 40 per cent of seaway traffic, marked further giant strides towards integration of the Canadian and American economies. Finally, the high prosperity which had done much to stimulate the whole power-transportation boom, had already begun to slacken. By 1959 regional disparities, together with an ominous increase in unemployment and a precarious balance of payments situation, were aggravating serious political unrest which had first appeared in the federal elections of 1957.

Of the many painful, if predictable, readjustments of the 1950s, that which occurred in farming was perhaps the most bitter. Across the grain-growing west, as well as in the central regions of mixed farming, labour-saving machinery wrought rapid change. Thus while farm production maintained high levels, farm population actually declined. Those families that remained on relatively small farms found their operations increasingly marginal. In Ontario and Quebec substantial pockets of rural poverty appeared. In the Atlantic provinces, where farmers traditionally relied upon supplemental employment in fishing, lumbering and small industrial enterprises, the economic cushion was deflated. Few benefits from the prosperity of the fifties were felt in the Maritimes and the opening of the seaway dealt a serious blow to the ports of Saint John and Halifax. Indeed promising efforts to solve the problem of winter navigation of the seaway (it is still closed for approximately three ice-bound months each year) were inhibited by fear of still further economic repercussions on the Atlantic.

The big problems that loomed during the recession of 1957–61 were clear enough. In tune with preceding Canadian economic history, the postwar boom brought most benefits to central Canada and particularly to Montreal and Toronto. While comparatively rapid growth occurred in Winnipeg, Edmonton and Vancouver, the massive explosions of population and wealth centred in the two biggest cities. Housing and living costs in Toronto, for example, outstripped those of all but one or two American cities. And along with the new wealth came increasing variety and excitement in the largest cities. Thus regional inequality emerged as a primary political question. As in the days of the Laurier boom, the very success of the east–west Canadian economy brought regional resentments. But the biggest difference between the two boom periods was in the source of their financing.

In the Laurier period the major source of capital was Britain and the principal lines of trade were also transatlantic. In the fifties and sixties the sources of foreign financing were overwhelmingly American and the United States was the focal point for the great bulk of Canada's foreign trade. By the end of the 1950s, 70 per cent of Canadian imports came from the United States and over 75 per cent of direct foreign investment was American. 60 per cent of Canada's exports went to the United States. More than half of Canada's manufacturing industry was owned or controlled by Americans and an even larger percentage of the natural resources industry was American-owned. Continentalism, as in the 1880s and early nineties, re-emerged as the most crucial of Canadian questions – one which underlay the even more hotly debated problems of domestic federal and cultural relations. Moreover, in the mid twentieth century many new factors gave a still deeper intensity to the problem. On the one hand Canada's survival and prosperity as an independent state made debate about the future somewhat more realistic than it had seemed to many Canadians in the economically troubled post-Confederation years. On the other hand the extent of Canadian involvement with America encouraged those who echoed Goldwin Smith's argument that Canada's inevitable destiny was to become the Scotland of

North America. For, in addition to the growing Canadian-American economic integration, the United States had now clearly replaced Britain as the dominant power in the West. The impact of American 'culture patterns' through advertising, magazines, films and television, together with what seemed an almost involuntary entanglement in the American alliance system, could be seen as irreversible signposts to the future.

By the mid 1960s more and more Canadians were asking whether their country was not simply a province of the vast American 'informal empire'. The protective National Policy tariff system had served principally to inundate Canada in a wave of American investment. While this flow of capital clearly served to develop the country, the lines of that development were increasingly in American hands. In most branch firms the relationship of Canadian managers to basic industrial and commercial policy was tangential or even token. Production schedules, employment policies, marketing and disposition of profit were all matters decided either directly in American head-offices or indirectly by guidelines and periodic check-ups. While the exact extent and nature of the system are not accurately known (since, prior to 1974, there was no legislation to compel the opening of relevant records) there is little doubt about many of its main features. Canadian production and marketing are closely geared to the interests of the 'international' corporations and, not infrequently, to the dicta of the American State Department. Thus Alberta oil or gas could be sold in a particular foreign market only if the parent corporation decided that one of its other subsidiaries could not more profitably sell in that market. Canadian automobile plants will not accept orders from those communist states which appear on the State Department's blacklist. Canadian flour is sold to Cuba only by the few milling firms which are not American-owned. In multi-product corporations the decision as to which items will be manufactured in Canada and which will be imported from the corporation's factories elsewhere is made in the United States. The same is true of decisions with respect to the prospecting and developing of new resource areas, the encouragement, funding and utilization of industrial and scientific research, and the development of entirely new products.

Canadian economists differ sharply in their cost-benefit analyses of this increasingly integrated structure. Some argue that the American firms are good corporate citizens, that they serve well the general economic needs of the country and are responsive to policy suggestions from Canadian governments.* Yet a more hostile note is sounded by others.† Critics argue that ever-growing dependence upon American equity investment, with a resulting heavy outflow of profits, carries the constant threat of payments imbalance between Canada and the United States and thus makes Canada too vulnerable to changes in American fiscal policy. They charge, also, that efficiency within the system is measured by the criteria of multi-national corporations and that this militates heavily against the development and application of Canadian science, experimentation with new products, and a more even-handed regional growth.

The academic critics concede what is not always admitted at the popular level of this favourite Canadian debating topic, namely, that Canadians have only themselves to blame if the system is not to their liking. Unlike every other industrial state (and many semi-industrial nations), Canada, prior to 1974, imposed virtually no legal controls or limitations on the extent of foreign investment, the offering of shares to Canadians in the domestic market, the appointing of Canadians to directing boards or cooperation with official Canadian trade policies abroad. In proposing countervailing action most critics eschewed purely restrictive legislation. Instead they suggested greater use of tax incentives (income from investment in Canadian companies already enjoys mildly preferential tax treatment), access to corporate records, a citizenship requirement for a varying

---

*E. A. Safarian, *Foreign Ownership of Canadian Industry*, Toronto, 1966.

†M. H. Watkins, *Foreign Ownership and Structure of Canadian Industry*, Ottawa, 1968.

percentage of board members, and certain supplementary government initiatives in directing investment. One of the most common suggestions was the creation of a Canada Development Corporation under public ownership. While blueprints for the operation of such a public investment organization varied considerably (both the N.D.P. and the Liberal Party endorsed the idea), its essential role would be to funnel Canadian funds into risk areas of investment. Such areas, especially in the speculative development of natural resources, have been largely occupied by American investors who, it is argued, have access to larger capital pools than can be built up privately in Canada. While there is some truth to this it is also evident that Canadian capitalists, quite apart from the smaller investment pools which they tap, have been much less adventuresome than their American brothers. They seem to have been rather too happy to stick with safe-and-sound portfolios. Thus some economists argued that a subtle side effect of American investment was to encourage a lack of vigour in the ranks of Canadian entrepreneurs. Two possible conclusions follow from this line of analysis. One is that governments could stimulate fresh interest in purely Canadian investment by themselves taking a direct hand in the process. The other possible conclusion, or speculation, is that too many potential Canadian entrepreneurs are already entwined in the American business system to wish to move in a more independent direction. Moreover, not a few of the major party politicians have close connexions with American corporate interests, either directly or through influential constituents, and show little enthusiasm for bringing about basic changes.

Despite all the forces that seemed to be moving Canada towards continental integration, however, resistance to that outcome remained very strong, and, by the end of the 1970s, would engender a startling resurgence of economic nationalism. The old negative dislike of American 'excesses', a basically conservative strain in the Canadian make-up, led most Canadians to react strongly against the vigilante extremism of the era of Senators McCarran and McCarthy, and to eschew the ideological anti-communism of John Foster Dulles with its brinkmanship and its threat of a world divided simply between the forces of light and the forces of darkness. More positively, anglophone national sentiment was beginning to emerge from the postwar what-is-a-Canadian syndrome to a sober confidence in the Canadian future – a confidence which took pride in a foreign policy apparently based upon conciliation and peace-keeping, in a state which had managed to achieve high standards of living without imposing intolerable conformity, and which continued the search for a more just distribution of wealth both at home and abroad. As the evidence of growing American control of the economy emerged through publication of commission reports and national statistics, and as the foreign policy (and even foreign trade) inhibitions imposed by the American relationship were digested by a somewhat bemused electorate, the political system reacted violently. The first flare-up of political turbulence reflected disgust with the arrogance of a Liberal government grown over-confident and unresponsive to the mounting concern about the complex implications of American corporate influence. But just as anglophone nationalism reached full tide it was shaken by the *nationaliste* renaissance in Quebec which swept Jean Lesage into power to launch a 'quiet revolution' – a revolution not only against corruption and archaisms within Quebec but also against both American *and* English-speaking Canadian economic and cultural domination.

The federal dominance of St Laurent liberalism seemed almost beyond challenge in 1956–7. In the Commons a weak Conservative Party was led by George Drew of Ontario while the capable parliamentarians of the C.C.F. lacked the numbers to make their criticisms of an ageing and careless administration really effective. Yet there were danger signs that went largely unheeded by the Liberals – until it was too late. Amongst the provincial capitals only those in the Maritimes were in Liberal hands. The Union Nationale controlled Quebec, Ontario was firmly and prosperously Tory. Saskatchewan was in its thirteenth year of T. C. Douglas's twenty-year C.C.F. administration, Alberta was thriving on natural resources royalties under the increasingly right-wing Social Credit government of Ernest Manning, and British Columbia was under

W.A.C. Bennett's equally conservative variety of Social Credit.*
With nearly all the provincial power bases in alien hands the
Liberals should have been much more alert than they were to
signs of political disaffection on the federal level. The beginnings of an economic slow-down and the concurrent explosion
of a bitter parliamentary battle over the finances and control of
a natural-gas pipeline turned the trick – even if it took one more
hand to take the game.

At the centre of the storm was Clarence D. Howe, the economic czar of the war years. Born in the United States, Howe
would have been equally at home managing an American corporation or department of government. His principal passion
was to superintend and hasten the industrialization of his adopted country and any means that promised efficiency seemed
reasonable to him. When private capital had refused to construct a synthetic rubber industry during the war, Howe sponsored the Polymer Corporation, a crown company which was
immensely successful and which, with expansion into chemi-
cals, was permitted to continue operations in the postwar
period despite rising criticism from jealous private firms in the
field. However, when it became desirable in 1956 to build a
natural-gas pipeline from Alberta to the industrial market of
eastern Canada, Howe, who was still the most influential minister in economic matters, could see no reason why it should not
be built by capital raised by an American-controlled company.
Both Tory and C.C.F. members of the House found many contrary reasons.

The major opposition argument was that American control
of an essential east–west transportation route would be an intolerable increase of American influence on Canadian economic
policy in a period when American investment in other fields
was rising at a startling rate. In addition the parliamentary
opposition hammered home the telling point that an over-
confident government, having already committed itself to the

---

* In Manitoba an aged Liberal-Progressive government was clearly
at the end of its tether. In 1958 it was replaced by the Tories led by
Duff Roblin.

necessary legislation, had left less than three weeks to carry it before the end of the session, and would brook no delay for detailed debate of what was clearly an immensely significant undertaking. The Liberals chose the incredibly unwise course of forcing the measure through the House by imposing closure. Amidst a storm of personal taunts the Bill was rammed through, Trans-Canada Pipe Lines was incorporated with large public assistance, and the session came to a close.

The Conservatives were quick to seize their political opportunity. Taking full account of popular mistrust of a government too long in office and of an overt extension of American economic control, they became overnight a party of protest, almost a populist party. Principal symbol of this change was John Diefenbaker who had been elected as leader in 1956. A determined court-room lawyer from Prince Albert, Saskatchewan, Diefenbaker brought to politics an old-fashioned rhetorical vigour and an ability to over-simplify issues that proved to be political dynamite. He brought, too, a genuine zeal for his brand of Canadianism: unhyphenated, British in sympathy, and vociferously concerned for the common man afflicted by the operations of international corporations. In 1957 Diefenbaker forced many Tory-oriented businessmen to withdraw their earlier misgivings about him when he won a slender Conservative majority in a federal election. A year later 'Dief the Chief' led the refurbished Progressive-Conservative party to victory in Canada's biggest electoral landslide. The Liberals were cut back to 49 seats, the C.C.F. to 8, and Social Credit was wiped out. Even Quebec co-operated (61 per cent of the provincial vote there went Tory) in producing the 208 Conservative seats.

A majority of such proportions might appear to constitute a mandate. And so it did. But the mandate was, in every respect, difficult to define. It was anti-Liberal, it was anti-American, it was in favour of independent Canadian development, it was for improved welfare payments and a place in the sun for those Canadians who, like Diefenbaker himself, were not undilutedly of the 'two founding races'. It was for all these things and more – such as Diefenbaker's vision of immense developments in Canada's north. But such a mandate meant many different things to different regions and classes, and to be effectively fulfilled it required a kind of administrative talent which Diefenbaker conspicuously lacked. It required, also, favourable economic and international circumstances and a more astute approach to French–English relations than Diefenbaker was apparently able to take.

Like R. B. Bennett, Diefenbaker had to work in the unfavourable political climate produced by a painful decline in the national rate of economic growth and increasing unemployment. And since the recession was caused in part by a temporary decline in the pace of American investment, a balance of payments problem arose and caused uneasiness in the business community. Still more important, and reminiscent of the principal political error of Sir Robert Borden, Diefenbaker failed to secure a leading French-Canadian colleague who, as federal Tory *chef* in Quebec, might have shown the government how to consolidate its surprising electoral support along the St Lawrence. As it was, Quebec was won in 1960 by the Lesage Liberals, and the tentative Conservative–Union Nationale alliance at the federal level faltered. In the rest of the country the impression gained ground that Diefenbaker's flamboyant style was not being matched by deeds. Pleasantly nostalgic appeals to recover the nineteenth-century values of a small-town English-speaking Canada were inadequate substitutes for consistently decisive leadership and an understanding of what was going on in French Canada.

The most substantial success of the Diefenbaker government was in finding new markets for Canada's wheat surpluses (in China and the communist countries of Europe), and in expanding federal aid to farmers. The pattern of reviving western agriculture and lagging eastern industry, however, proved to be an indicator of a political future in which the Conservatives would find their strength in the prairie west and in the Atlantic provinces – a strange transmutation in which the Tories became a protest-populist party representing non-urban Canada, the outsiders of the country's ethnic structure, and the remnants of 'Britishism'. Diefenbaker's attitude in external relations, especially, strengthened the latter aspect. He took a leading role at the 1959 Commonwealth Conference in gaining condemnation of South Africa's apartheid policy and thus influencing South Africa's 1960 decision to leave the Commonwealth. He also fought hard against proposals for British entry into the European Common Market, showing concern for Commonwealth agricultural preferences. Yet when the British government suggested a Commonwealth free trade area Diefenbaker backed hurriedly away.

Similarly there were sharp inconsistencies in the Diefenbaker government's foreign policy. The external affairs minister, Howard Green, geared Canada's U.N. activities to advancing the cause of disarmament and to developing a position approaching that of the uncommitted nations with respect to most Cold War issues. Yet it was the Diefenbaker government that signed the 1957 NORAD agreement with Washington and thus integrated the Canadian and American components of North American air defence. Again, while the Conservative government deepened Canada's involvement in the American alliance structure, it refused to permit nuclear weapons in Canada (for Bomarc anti-aircraft missiles and aircraft rockets) or to allow Canada's ground and air forces under N.A.T.O. in Europe to be equipped with 'tactical' nuclear weapons. Reasoning that Canada's pleas to halt the spread of nuclear weapons would be seriously undermined if she herself accepted such weapons (even under American control), Green and Diefenbaker had nevertheless done nothing to lessen Canada's role within the American economic-defence orbit. Thus, when the issue of nuclear weapons for Canadian forces entered Canadian politics in the critical election of 1963, it was ill-defined and the sources of support for resistance to American pressure had been somewhat dissipated.

As Diefenbaker's credibility began to fade in the wash of economic troubles and indecision, politics again became fluid. On the left important developments of the 1950s bore fruit at the end of the decade. Following reunification of the American A.F.L.-C.I.O. (American Federation of Labor and Congress of Industrial Organizations), the Canadian counterpart organizations came together in the Canadian Labour Congress (1956).

With increasing unemployment and evidence of a toughening attitude towards labour, arguments for direct union participation in an independent political party gained wide support. Not least of the arguments was the record of the Saskatchewan C.C.F. government of 'Tommy' Douglas which capped its lengthy tenure by enacting North America's first public medical insurance plan. In 1961, following long negotiations between C.C.F. and C.L.C. leaders, the party and the union organization jointly founded the New Democratic Party.* This action, long advocated by socialists in the C.C.F. and the union movement, was directly contrary to the theory and practice of American unionism which has consistently rejected 'third party' action. While American unions have become increasingly conservative in their political attitudes, the C.L.C. has continued to endorse the N.D.P. as the political arm of labour – often in sharp resistance to clearly expressed disapproval by the international (American) headquarters of Canadian unions. Although the extent of union financial support of the N.D.P. varies it has been substantial.

In the 1960s the N.D.P. became much more of an urban party than the C.C.F. It now had firm political bases in British Columbia, Saskatchewan, Manitoba and Ontario but had so far failed to attract much support in the Atlantic provinces. In Quebec it has made gains in the Montreal region and in one or two rural ridings, while in federal politics its base was an average 18 per cent of the popular vote. The most significant role of the N.D.P. was in confirming the multi-party system within which its constant threat on the left provides a genuine electoral choice, a spur to reform, and emphatic reiteration of the interrelated importance of collective planning, social equity and Canadian independence.†

In the early sixties yet another version of Social Credit made

---

* Premier T. C. Douglas was elected leader of the N.D.P. at the party's founding convention.

† In June 1969, the N.D.P. startled many observers by winning power in Manitoba. The anti-establishment nature of the party and its significance in keeping the Canadian party system an open one were particularly evident in the Manitoba election where the leader,

its appearance in rural Quebec under the leadership of Réal Caouette. A colourful Poujadist politician, Caouette spoke for small-town and farming Quebeckers and while western-based Social Credit disappeared from federal politics the Créditistes sent fourteen M.P.s to Ottawa in the 1968 election. The growth of the N.D.P. and the rise of the Créditistes suggests that the Canadian political system will continue to reject the American two-party method of getting a federal consensus.

The Liberals in these years made a slow recovery from their traumatic defeat in the 1958 Diefenbaker landslide. In 1957 they had elected Lester B. Pearson to succeed St Laurent as leader but the federal election results of that year raised doubts in many Liberal hearts as to whether the distinguished diplomat could become the dynamic politician. In the event, he couldn't. However, the country was entering a period in which diplomatic skills might count as heavily as finger-waving rhetoric. By 1962, when the Tories asked for a renewal of their 'mandate', all three opposition parties had recovered substantially and raked Tory mismanagement fore and aft. The election left the government in a minority, with 116 seats, while the Liberals won 100, the N.D.P. 19, and Social Credit 30 (of which 26 were Quebec Créditistes). Diefenbaker retained office until defeated on a vote of confidence in February of 1963.

The 1963 general election was fought in the aftermath of direct American intervention in Canadian politics and serious revolt in the Tory party. In January, while the Diefenbaker cabinet was still heatedly debating whether or not to accept nuclear warheads, General Lauris Norstad (who had just retired as N.A.T.O. supreme commander) made a public statement in Ottawa clearly indicating Washington's view that Ottawa should at once accept the warheads. Press releases from Washington left no doubt that the Americans were furious with Canada for its shilly-shallying attitude. Since the various weapons already accepted by Canada were designed to carry nuclear tips, the argument that Canada had implicitly committed her-

---

Edward Schreyer, and a great many of the candidates were of neither English nor French extraction.

self to accepting these nuclear components was strong. At the same time, sentiment in the country against participating in the spread of nuclear weapons was rising rapidly. Both Diefenbaker and Green maintained that there was no contractual agreement to accept the nuclear warheads.

Shortly after the Norstad statement Mr Pearson withdrew his previous opposition to nuclear weapons for Canadian forces, declaring that the country must honour a commitment. In February, Douglas Harkness, minister of national defence, resigned and was shortly followed out of the cabinet by two other ministers. Thus it was a deeply divided Tory party and a confused electorate that faced the 1963 federal election. While the N.D.P. and the Créditistes agreed with the anti-nuclear wing of the Conservative Party, the election hinged more on questions of governmental bungling than on the nuclear arms debate. The Liberals promised 'sixty days of decision' in which they would re-establish the country's credit financially and in foreign affairs, and would also adopt policies to regain Canadian independence. The result of the voting was another 'house of minorities'. The Liberals won 129 seats, the Tories 95, the N.D.P. 17 and Social Credit-Créditistes 24.

The Pearson government entered not sixty days of decision but a period of false starts and devastating revelations of corruption involving several Liberal appointees and ministers. At the same time the Canadian crisis of identity was reaching another fever point. The nuclear weapons issue had illustrated deepening concern over the extent of American influence in and on Canada. When the government withdrew its first budget after provisions for preventing further American take-over of the economy had brought a storm of protest from businessmen – many of whom were executives of American branch plants – critics on the left suggested that American influence had reached a point beyond control. Yet the problem of reassessing the nature and purposes of the Canadian federal state was even more urgent in another area. The Quebec Liberal government of Jean Lesage, elected in 1960, had lost no time in launching its Quiet Revolution. Major modernizing reforms in education, limitations on the influence of the clergy, nationalization of the hydroelectric power industry and clear intimation of still wider use of state powers to achieve French-Canadian aspirations began to create uneasiness in the rest of the country.

To accommodate Quebec's claims to be *maître chez nous* Ottawa conceded an 'opting-out' formula by which any province could refuse to take part in federal-provincial shared-cost programmes such as the new Canada Pension Plan and the proposed national Medicare scheme. Under this formula a province could receive an amount of federal money equal to the sum Ottawa would have contributed had the province participated in the national programme. In practice only Quebec made use of the option. Although the province received no larger amount of money and no accretion of its admitted jurisdiction, many anglophones became worried that Quebec was steering towards a kind of autonomy that would be indistinguishable from independence, and that in the meantime it was being granted an unjustifiable special status within Confederation. In fact, *nationaliste* opinion of one kind or another was sweeping all before it in Quebec. Suddenly invigorated by the legislative potential revealed by the Lesage administration (which was re-elected in 1962), those who wished to seize the occasion to achieve much greater autonomy or even independence advanced their arguments with new assurance. Programmes for the future ranged all the way from mere augmentation of provincial powers within Confederation to 'associate states' which would be virtually sovereign cooperators within a loose federal structure – and, of course, to outright separation. Inside the provincial government *étatiste* opinion was given strong voice by René Lévesque who demanded a thorough overhaul of Confederation – an overhaul which would leave Quebec with greatly enhanced jurisdiction and revenue sources.* Outside, several or-

---

* After the defeat of the Lesage government in 1966, and having failed to persuade the provincial Liberal Party to adopt a more extreme *nationaliste* position, Lévesque left the party and formed a new movement calling for Quebec's withdrawal from Confederation and negotiation of a kind of common market between the state of Quebec and the rest of Canada. His movement adopted the name Parti Québecois.

ganizations began working for immediate, unqualified independence. The largest of the *séparatiste* groups, Rassemblement
pour l'Indépendance Nationale, led by the fiery young socialist
Pierre Bourgault, gained sufficient significance to play a role in
upsetting the Lesage government in 1966. Some of the
séparatistes resorted to violence and in February 1963 several
bombing incidents severely shook what was left of anglophone
complacency in Montreal. While no sustained terror followed,
the pot was kept boiling. In October of 1964, and despite the
obvious risks, Ottawa insisted that the Queen carry out a previously planned visit to Quebec City to commemorate the 1864
Confederation Conference. Extreme security precautions and
the accompanying rioting did nothing to conciliate *nationaliste*
sentiment nor to allay the suspicions of English-speaking Canadians.

Canada was experiencing what most other industrialized
nation-states were experiencing – the twin explosions of separatism and terrorism. Particularly in anglophone Canada the
newer forms of collective violence came as a shock. Neither
historians nor schools had prepared the people for the new
eruption (and forms) of violence in their 'peaceable kingdom'.
The little rebellions, industrial strife, religious rioting, anti-conscription protest in two wars – all seemed to have been aberrations in an essentially orderly evolution. In some respects this
legend of Canadian history was right; in others it was quite
wrong. Collective violence had always been a part of the socio-
political process and reflected, in its various forms, the fact that
Canada remained a frontier in which the social ideas and economic modes imported from Britain, Europe and the United
States were bound to reverberate. But in the 1970s (as in earlier
decades) Canada nevertheless reacted to terrorism, separatism
and the economic storms of Western industrial society in ways
which were both indigenous and distinctive.

20

Surviving Terrorism

FACED with the lively reassertion of French-Canadian aspirations, and of anglophone reluctance to contemplate substantial changes of policy, the Pearson government took several important steps. Following the advice of André Laurendau, the distinguished editor of *Le Devoir*, Ottawa appointed (July 1963) a Royal Commission on Bilingualism and Biculturalism to document the sources of the crisis and to suggest paths to a federal future of equality between 'the two founding races'. The Commission, jointly chaired by Laurendau and Davidson Dunton, President of Ottawa's Carleton University, instigated an exhaustive series of research studies and public hearings. The interim report in 1965 declared that 'Canada, without being fully conscious of the fact, is passing through the greatest crisis in its history'. While many anglophones, especially west of Ontario, were sceptical, many also took the warning at face value.

By the time the volumes of the main report began appearing in 1967, a full and genuine dialogue between anglophones and francophones was well advanced. The Commission's marshalling of facts which revealed the extent of disadvantages experienced by French-speaking Canadians who sought both to advance economically and to retain their language and culture (which were seen to be indissolubly linked) was overwhelming, especially when read in connexion with the further evidence of renewed francophone determination to achieve both goals. The thorny historical question of whether or not an original 'compact' between the 'two races' had or had not been broken took second place to that of what might be done in the present and future to reach a just accommodation. Thus the first set of Commission recommendations gained impressively broad acceptance. These recommendations called for full recognition of French and English as the official languages of Canada at the federal level (with all that such recognition implies about publications, office-holding and staffing of government offices and business management) as well as in the provinces of Ontario, Quebec and New Brunswick. The recommendations also called upon the provinces to establish special bilingual districts to provide teaching in the language of any local minority (francophone or anglophone) wherever that minority reached 10 per cent of the district's population.* In general the Report also endorsed the concept of *deux nations* (in a sociological sense) as the basis of the Canadian federal state, but stopped short of basic constitutional changes that would make Quebec *the* nation-state of the French Canadians. Rather, it underwrote the proposition that the English-speaking nation and the French-speaking nation should coexist on an equal footing everywhere in Canada, while recognizing that this ideal would be achieved much more slowly in the west than in the east.

In administrative policy the Pearson and Trudeau governments adhered to 'cooperative federalism'. In practice this has meant granting to *all* the provinces their full powers within the B.N.A. Act, including reoccupation of those fields which Ottawa tended to invade during the fifties. It has meant, also, widely expanded consultation between Ottawa and the provincial governments, both bilaterally and in full federal-provincial conferences. While this procedure of nearly continuous consultation has smoothed away some provincial irritation (and Quebec has not been alone in holding suspect Ottawa's aggrandizement) it did not eliminate the threat of *séparatiste* sentiment in Quebec.

Three elections in the late sixties served to bring the federal question into sharper focus. In 1966, to the surprise and consternation of most anglophones, the Lesage government was replaced in Quebec by a Union Nationale administration headed by Daniel Johnson. While rejuvenating his party Johnson had put anglophone nerves on edge by proclaiming that 'What we must claim and obtain for Quebec, as the main seat of a nation, is recognition as a national state'. Despite the semantic cloud

*Over considerable western opposition the federal government obtained passage of an act implementing some of these recommendations in July 1969.

surrounding such statements there was no doubt that Johnson leaned perceptibly closer to *séparatisme* than had Lesage, and as premier he continued to put forward claims to a very special status for Quebec. His extremely ambivalent position on Confederation was given dramatic prominence when it became apparent that he was not averse to playing a kind of Gallic footsie with President Charles de Gaulle. Indeed, it was a calculated performance by the French leader that brought about the most dangerous rise in anglophone fever charts to date. In 1967, during his official visit to Montreal's Expo.67, De Gaulle spoke from a balcony of the city hall and called emphatically for *'Québec Libre'*. Although Johnson issued a series of 'clarifying' statements about the incident, he also clearly consulted with the French government on various ways in which Quebec could obtain ever closer relations with France in support of an international status for the province. A slight moderation in the *séparatiste* tendencies of the Union Nationale government followed the death of Premier Johnson in 1968 and the succession of Premier Jean Bertrand.

In 1965 a federal election left very little change in the party balance at Ottawa. Yet the Liberal government, despite, or perhaps because of, its precarious position in the House, secured some important legislation and equally important shifts in policy. After a protracted and bitter debate a national flag was finally adopted on which the maple leaf, rather than a combination of the union jack and the fleur-de-lis, as proposed by some, is the only national symbol. Another measure, both practical and symbolic, was the National Medicare Act which provides for joint federal-provincial financing of publicly administered, universal medical insurance in any province that decides to participate, as all now do. Perhaps of equal importance, at least from the point of view of 'national unity', was the full support given by Ottawa to the 1967 Montreal World's Fair and to a cross-country series of centennial celebrations and projects in the same year. Expo 67 proved to be the most exciting national event ever staged in Canada and, by general consent, the most successful of all World's Fairs. For Canadians its chief significance lay in the fact that nowhere else in North America could such a truly multi-national fair have taken place, and also in the evidence of what might be achieved by full cooperation federally and culturally. At the same time, more quietly yet persistently, the government moved to secure a fairer balance between anglophones and francophones in the federal civil service and to extend both diplomatic representation and financial aid to francophone states of the Third World.

The third election was that of 1968 in which the Liberals finally got a majority of seats in the Commons at Ottawa. The electoral outcome was the result of some cooling of the cultural confrontation, some doubts in Quebec as the province looked more closely at the various versions of the *séparatiste* future, and of the impact of a personality whose force few people had suspected as little as a year before the election.

In 1965 Pierre-Elliot Trudeau and two close friends, Jean Marchand (former head of the Catholic trade union movement in Quebec) and Gérard Pelletier (editor of the large Montreal daily, *La Presse*), decided to stand for election as Liberals. Trudeau and Pelletier, as former collaborators on *Cité Libre*, had been considered social democrats and Trudeau, although not a member of the party, had spoken several times from N.D.P. platforms. Trudeau and Pelletier explained their decision on the ground that it was absolutely essential to prove to Quebec that the aspirations of French Canada could find clear and influential expression not only in Quebec City but also in Ottawa. Trudeau, especially, feared that Quebec *nationalisme* was driving in a racist direction which would not only sunder the Canadian federal state but would also lead the province into a humiliating introversion and semi-fascism. The remedy, he thought, was to reassert the tolerant Canadianism for which Laurier and Bourassa had once stood, and to do this in time to avert impending catastrophe one must work with that party which stood most chance of election. His socialist friends were livid, the Liberals were joyous, while *séparatistes* of all colours heaped scorn on him as yet another *vendu*.

All three recruits to the Liberal 'New Guard' won election in 1965 and Prime Minister Pearson appointed Marchand and Trudeau to the cabinet (the latter in 1966 as minister of justice). The widespread impression that the federal Liberals were prepared to work only with those Quebeckers who were hacks of a discredited party machine in their province was dissipated. M. Trudeau supervised the preparation of amendments to archaic portions of the criminal code dealing with divorce and sexual morality and was the principal influence behind the government's evolving position on the constitutional question. For both these reasons his name became known outside Quebec much more quickly than would have been normal for such a recent entrant to the federal arena. Early in 1968 he took a prominent (and fully televised) part in presenting Ottawa's position at a federal-provincial conference called to discuss the constitutional question. Directly refuting Daniel Johnson's argument that the B.N.A. Act needed re-writing to give Quebec the additional powers the Quebec premier believed necessary to achieve *nationaliste* purposes, Trudeau argued for a pragmatic policy of adjustment within the existing constitutional framework. He advocated, instead of the revision of the constitution, the entrenchment in the B.N.A. Act of a Bill of Rights* which would guarantee, in addition to traditional civil liberties, language and educational rights and certain protections against bureaucratic inroads on individual and collective rights. During the conference English-speaking Canadians, in particular, were impressed by the vigour of Trudeau's advocacy of the federalist position and by his willingness to confront Johnson with the specific argument that the whole of Canada, not just Quebec, must become the homeland of French Canadians.

Trudeau's remarkable rise to prominence led to his becoming a candidate for the Liberal leadership in a convention in April 1968, following Lester Pearson's decision to retire from public life. In an exciting contest Trudeau defeated several anglophone ministers who had served in previous governments and gave the impression, without being precise on policy details, that he would maintain the federal state by flexible, pragmatic adjustments, resist chauvinistic nationalism (either French- or English-speaking) and give greater prominence to youth in any government he might form.

---

* The Diefenbaker government had enacted a Bill of Rights but it was not a part of the constitution (i.e. the B.N.A. Act), and did not affect subjects within provincial jurisdiction.

After the convention M. Trudeau formed a transitional cabinet and called an election for 25 June. The campaign was dominated by the personality of the new prime minister in a manner which was both obvious and subtle: obvious in the fascinated crowds drawn by the Liberal leader, subtle in that the extent of his political impact was underestimated by observers of every stripe. There were many reasons for his success. A major factor was the extremely withdrawn and even sombre personality of the Conservative leader. Robert Stanfield, a Nova Scotia businessman, had succeeded John Diefenbaker in a bitterly contested leadership convention in the summer of 1967. Although Diefenbaker, who had fought off revolts against his leadership for several years, was beaten, he remained an active centre of division within the party – particularly of division between its western populist wing and its eastern business wing. Stanfield, who was painfully reluctant to give positive leadership, at the same time sought support in Quebec by obscure references to a 'particular status' for that province and by an even more confusing acceptance of the *deux nations* theory of Confederation. While his reluctance to declare for 'one nation' and the existing federal structure (as did Diefenbaker) brought cautious support in Quebec from the Union Nationale and *Le Devoir*,* it irritated many anglophone Tories with the curious result that they voted in considerable numbers for Trudeau's expression of 'one Canada'.

While the Conservatives were thus fatally weakened, the N.D.P. was also seriously mauled. Having accepted even more explicitly than the Tories the necessity of a special status for Quebec, the party candidates found it difficult to extricate themselves from this position which proved very unpopular in English-speaking Canada. In vain they argued that if Quebec were given new powers to regulate its own affairs then the rest of Canada could use federal powers more effectively to advance social welfare, economic development and central planning. Trying hard to concentrate on issues such as the critical housing

---

*After Laurendau's appointment to the Royal Commission on Bilingualism and Biculturalism, he was succeeded as editor of *Le Devoir* by Claude Ryan who pursued a somewhat erratic but decidedly *nationaliste* editorial policy.

shortage, inadequate manpower policy, uncontrolled foreign and domestic investment, deepening involvement in all aspects of the American empire, and planless urban growth, the party was denied its expected leap forward by the overriding sentiments surrounding the constitutional question (however vaguely formulated) and by the sheer charisma of Pierre-Elliott Trudeau. Even overt criticism of Trudeau's personal style and of the trend to 'leadership' or 'presidential' politics seemed only to damage the N.D.P.'s effort to have the election focus upon issues.

Towards the end of the campaign those Canadians who did not plan to vote Liberal were talking and writing acidly about Trudeaumania. Yet, if there were manic aspects to the teen-agers' unthinking devotion to the flower-power image they discerned in the new prime minister, there was also a perfectly sane explanation of why the Liberal Party finally got its parliamentary majority. While Trudeau was a spirited bachelor, *avant-garde* in taste and manners,* his other credentials were almost excessively solid, if less radical than most Canadians had been led to believe by their adulatory mass-media. A millionaire by inheritance, Trudeau has used his wealth to secure an enviable array of cosmopolitan experiences. These include university degrees in the social sciences and law from Canadian, American and European universities, wide and adventurous travel, active social-democratic participation in the militant trade union revival that led to the Quiet Revolution in Quebec, independent legal practice and university lecturing, and the writing of powerful analytical articles for academic journals and *Cité Libre*. To thousands of intellectuals and professional people (both anglophone and francophone) he presented an image with which they were eager to 'identify'. But, more important, Trudeau showed a formidable ability to communicate directly with all levels of Canadian society. Gracefully fluent in French and English, he was equally at home parrying the questions of curious reporters, succinctly defending his policies in the House, bandying quips with delighted youngsters, or dealing

---

*He was given to roll-neck shirts, ascot ties, noisy sports clothes, late parties and European cars. On one splendid occasion he drew outraged condemnation from Mr Diefenbaker when he appeared in the House, while minister of justice, in open-toed sandals.

with premier Johnson on the question of whether or not Quebec must go through Ottawa's External Affairs Department in its dealings with foreign states. Perhaps Trudeau's winning of a large majority of Quebec's federal ridings – a feat which seriously damaged both the *séparatistes* and the more extreme of the Union Nationale autonomists – was principally the result of his being *Québecois*. It seems probable, nevertheless, that his reassertion of the virtues of Canadian federalism, so reminiscent of his French-Canadian predecessors in Ottawa, accounts for the overall majority he secured in the country.*

The Trudeau victory was to prove that politics in a democratic society provide a framework within which one can assess the real nature of change and continuity. The man who entered the political arena primarily because he sensed a confrontation of cultures proclaimed himself an anti-nationalist. An avowed admirer of Elie Kedouri, Trudeau held suspect not only the totalitarian implications of Quebec *nationalisme* but also those of anglophone anti-Americanism. During the 1968 election campaign he expressed doubts about the widely reported recommendations of a task force (the Watkins Report) which called for stringent legislation to halt the American economic takeover and to use public authority to mobilize capital for future Canadian development. Nevertheless the continued growth of Canadian nationalist sentiment carried him a long way towards acceptance of the need for vigorous protective action. This was due to the way in which both federal and provincial politics have reflected the changing conditions and concerns of Canada, and partly to the way in which Trudeau and the Liberals reacted.

During his first parliament (1969–72) the prime minister showed the strength of his majority position. The office of the prime minister was enlarged, departmental organization streamlined, major amendments to the criminal code and divorce law passed and action taken to put into effect the 1969 Official Languages Act. Financial aid was offered to the provinces for

---

* While the Conservatives won handsomely in the Atlantic provinces, the home ground of Mr Stanfield, the Liberals regained some of the western constituencies they had lost in the Diefenbaker stampede.

this purpose and a programme of language training and job re-categorization put in hand in the federal civil service. In 1972 another recommendation of the 'Bi and Bi' Commission was acted on when the new position of minister of state responsible for multiculturalism was established. The new ministry was aided by a large advisory council and directed to fund centres and programmes in languages other than French and English, and also to develop materials for teaching other cultures. Success both of the bilingual and multicultural programmes has been mixed. Many English-speaking civil servants feared for their job security as bilingual ability was required in certain areas of the service. In the provinces west of Ontario particularly, strong opposition to speedy or too extensive re-categorization expressed itself politically and was damaging to the Liberals in the federal elections of 1972 and 1974. The 1976 report of Keith Spicer, Commissioner of Official Languages, suggested strongly that preponderant effort should be devoted to second language teaching in schools and universities rather than to crash programmes to make existing civil servants (and many people in the private sector) bilingual. Despite the show of 'French power' in Ottawa, Quebec took steps to make French the sole official language of the province (Bill 22) – reflecting *Québecois* scepticism about the efficacy of the Official Languages Act and the prime minister's hope to make all Canada the homeland of French Canadians. This Quebec policy, together with school regulations restricting for immigrants to the province the choice of language their children might be instructed in, perhaps reflected an increasing demographic disproportion which by 1971 showed about 45 per cent of Canadians to have a lineage from the British Isles and about 29 per cent from France.

All this was of concern to federalists and to *féderalistes* and the results of a Quebec provincial election in the spring of 1970 proved of crucial importance. Under a new, smooth, thirty-eight-year-old leader, Robert Bourassa, the Liberals won 72 seats with 41.8 per cent of the vote, Lévesque's *Parti Québecois* 7 seats with 23 per cent, while the *Union Nationale* dropped spectacularly to 17 seats and 17 per cent, with most of their losses being picked up by the *Créditistes* (12 seats and 11.1 per cent), a

Poujadiste party which believes firmly in cooperating with Ottawa. In English-speaking Canada these results were received with undisguised rejoicing – particularly in the Montreal business community which had given heavy support to Bourassa, as had nearly all non-French voters on election day.

The Quebec electoral battle had been fought against a background of escalating violence in strikes, protest marches and bank robberies – many of which were to raise money for extremist *nationalistes* such as those in the *Front de Libération du Québec* (F.L.Q.). Not only did both the *Parti Québecois* (*Péquistes*) and the U.N. preach separatism, but it was clear that more and more students, workers and frustrated professional people were willing to give at least tacit support to those who would 'politicize' the French Canadians through the methods of confrontation and terrorism. Widely read was a book by the leading F.L.Q. theorist Pierre Vallières, *Les Nègres Blancs de l'Amérique du Nord*, which reflected the thinking of Fanon, Sartre, the New Left and some Quebec sociologists. Yet, despite this, Bourassa, with a reduced proportion of the total vote, had won a smashing legislative victory by playing down the constitutional and language issues, promising to ease unemployment by creating 'a hundred thousand jobs' in 1971, and stressing the advantages of having the Liberals in power both at Ottawa and in Quebec.

More important were the reactions of the social-democratic *Péquistes* and of those who sympathized with the F.L.Q.–Vallières interpretation of events. 'God help us,' said one defeated *Péquiste*, 'you see it is not my defeat nor that of René Lévesque that is important ... It's the defeat of our arguments in favour of the parliamentary system.' The comparison between seats won and the percentage of the total vote gained was stunning to the *Péquistes*, who saw their defeat as the result of an inadequate representational system and a manipulated vote.* When asked if he still thought independence could be achieved 'democratically', Lévesque replied: 'I think that the last democratic chance will be in the next election ... And if

---

* A couple of years later Claude Ryan, after a visit to Western Europe, wrote in *Le Devoir* that a system of proportional representation was now essential to the maintenance of democracy in Quebec.

there is the same manipulation of elections and I'm talking more about the manipulation of the minds than of the electoral system – it's obvious that the conscious minority ... is going to have the almost irresistible temptation to blow up the institutions. But I honestly believe there is still a chance.'

Lévesque and his *Péquistes* remained democratic but extremists amongst the 'conscious minority' saw a golden opportunity in the general *nationaliste* resentment. With F.L.Q. cells taking the lead, incidents of bombing and robbery (including arms and dynamite) increased sharply throughout the summer and autumn of 1970. The first peak of this new wave of terrorism arrived when the F.L.Q. kidnapped Richard Cross, senior United Kingdom trade commissioner in Montreal, and issued a 'communiqué' addressed to 'the ruling authorities' which included the following demands as conditions for Cross's release: freeing of 'political prisoners' (i.e. about twenty-five people previously convicted or about to be tried for various acts of violence), air transport for the prisoners to Cuba or Algeria, newspaper publication of the F.L.Q. manifesto and other forms of publicity, and a 'voluntary tax' of $500,000 in gold bullion.* The federal government, after consulting premier Bourassa and the British prime minister, decided to reject the 48-hour deadline and the demands as 'wholly unreasonable' while calling upon the abductors to establish communications as a basis for negotiating acceptable terms for the return of Cross. Further communiqués followed, together with responses to them from Ottawa – all in public. While most of the anglophone and francophone press supported the position taken by the Trudeau and Bourassa governments, considerable sympathy for the F.L.Q. was also voiced by Montreal spokesmen of radical political and trade union organizations. The possible murder of Cross was seen by such people as no worse than the official violence and exploitation practised by the existing order.

Although safe conduct abroad, or 'clemency' in the courts, were jointly promised by the Quebec and Ottawa governments for the safe release of Cross, the F.L.Q. held out for its slightly

---

*The best objective account of the October crisis is J. T. Saywell, *Quebec '70* (1971).

moderated demands and proceeded to kidnap Pierre Laporte, Quebec's minister of labour and immigration – with the same threat of execution. With the federal and provincial cabinets in almost continuous crisis session, the assembling of troops near Montreal, Claude Ryan of *Le Devoir*, René Lévesque and others seeking to pressure premier Bourassa into restructuring the government, frequent but futile police raids, and the F.L.Q. lawyer, Robert Lemieux, out of jail on his own recognizance and conducting inflammatory news conferences, Montreal had become critically volatile. Further threatened by calls for mass student and worker demonstrations in the streets – to force more 'flexible' responses to F.L.Q. demands – Bourassa requested Ottawa to send in the army. Quebec opposition leaders had concurred in this request as being essential for the avoidance of anarchy and Ryan himself wrote, as the troops began their security duty, that for the government 'to do otherwise would have been to overlook its duty'.

At 4 a.m. on 16 October, Ottawa proclaimed the War Measures Act, giving virtually unlimited powers to the government in time of insurrection 'real or apprehended'. This action was requested by Bourassa, Montreal's mayor Jean Drapeau, and the director of Montreal police who remarked that 'the slowness of procedures and the restraints imposed by the legal methods and mechanisms now at our disposal do not allow us at this time to cope with the situation'. Public Order Regulations under authority of the Act gave 'peace officers' wide powers of search, seizure and detention (up to twenty-one days before being charged); the F.L.Q. was declared an unlawful association and anyone who belonged to it (or to any other organization promoting the use of force) guilty of an offence and open to jail sentences of up to five years. In the Commons and in press and television statements the government defended its actions, under the careful scrutiny of the opposition and of those who were anxious about civil liberties. The minister of justice, John Turner, specifically answered T. C. Douglas, the N.D.P. leader, who accused the government of 'using a sledge-hammer to crack a peanut' and of snatching away 'the liberties and freedom of the people of Canada'. Turner retailed the history of bombings, robbery, kidnapping and murder and contended that unrestrained terrorism in the urban-industrial milieu, together with the clearly stated ultimate purpose of the F.L.Q., justified the apprehension of insurrection. 'More disturbing,' he declared 'we have a type of erosion of the public will in the feeling among some sincere people that an exchange of prisoners for the victims of kidnapping would somehow ease the situation . . I might say, too, that the recent call for a public manifestation by men like Gagnon, Vallières and Chartrand established and escalated the whole infiltration of F.L.Q. doctrine in certain areas of society in Quebec – in the unions, among universities and in the media – and the growing feeling among the people of Quebec, particularly the citizens of Montreal, that they are living under a reign of terror.' M. Trudeau, speaking on television, added: 'These are strong powers and I find them as distasteful as I'm sure you do . . . I assure you that the government recognizes its grave responsibilities in interfering in certain cases with civil liberties, and that it remains answerable to the people of Canada for its actions. The government will revoke this proclamation as soon as possible . . . it is acting to make clear to kidnappers that in this country laws are made and changed by the elected representatives of all Canadians, not by a handful of self-styled dictators. Those who gain power through terror rule by terror.' While most of the media and public opinion* felt that the government had done the right thing, particularly in submitting its actions immediately to parliament, some suspected that Bourassa and his federalist supporters had simply handed power to Ottawa in the hope of crushing *all* their *nationaliste* and radical opponents in Quebec.

On 17 October the F.L.Q. murdered Pierre Laporte and left his bloodied body to be discovered in the trunk of an abandoned car. At once opinion hardened against those who had been demanding greater concessions in the negotiations with the F.L.Q. and, despite bitter criticism from the left, Jean Drapeau received 92 per cent of the votes and every seat in the Montreal municipal election of 25 October. Already the War Measures Act proclamation had been sustained in the Commons with

---

* As judged by public opinion polls, editorials, votes in the Commons and the Quebec assembly, Montreal elections and two federal by-elections in Quebec.

only the N.D.P. voting against the government,* while in two Quebec by-elections in November the government increased its majorities considerably. Moreover, as searches and arrests continued, as the government brought to court those who had been arrested and in December obtained passage of a bill replacing the Public Order Regulations and providing substantially more restricted powers† (all to expire in four months), and especially when James Cross was safely recovered, relative calm descended upon Montreal. Cross was freed after the R.C.M.P., following various tips and supported by other police and troops, surrounded the dingy building in which he was being held. By midnight the same day (3 December), the British diplomat was free and his kidnappers were on their way to Cuba. Three weeks later the F.L.Q. cell members who had kidnapped Laporte and brought about his assassination were located. They surrendered after the minimum concession that the government would not automatically oppose bail but would permit that matter to be settled by the courts.

The October crisis showed that Canada was not beyond the restless currents of separatist-nationalism that were sweeping across much of the world in the first half of the seventies – in the day of triumphantly expanding multi-national corporations and of ever more highly organized nation-states. The crisis also demonstrated the continuing vitality of a marked Canadian characteristic: the willingness of public authority to act quickly and decisively in the face of overt threats to constitutional government, knowing that later leniency and massive public support will legitimize its actions. In the longer run the events of that 1970 autumn reverberated distinctly. They robbed the F.L.Q. and other left-separatists of much support, both overt and merely acquiescent, while the *Parti Québecois* found its elec-

---

* Four N.D.P. members broke ranks to support the measure.

† Within two months 403 of the 465 people arrested were released without charges being laid. All charges laid under the War Measures Act were stayed in July, 1971. Eighty-six people had been charged under the Act and 62 under the criminal code. Only 5 of those charged under the Act, and who pleaded not guilty, were convicted. Those who could prove damages resulting from arrest that did not result in conviction were offered compensation.

toral strength reduced and the cause of federalism strengthened. At the same time many *Québecois* became more sensitive than ever to the problem of maintaining a genuinely francophone culture. By 1976 the resurgence of this deeply-rooted sensitivity, together with high unemployment (over seven per cent in Quebec) and an uneasy questioning of the quality of life in an increasingly corporatized society, compelled Bourassa, and Quebec Liberals in the federal parliament, to become more and more like Lévesque's *Péquistes* – while the *Parti Québecois* grew slowly more confident.

In federal-provincial conferences and ministerial meetings Bourassa grew more intransigent in defence of Quebec's special position within Confederation. He continued to insist, especially, that the Canadian 'constitution' should not be patriated* before it had been amended to include guarantees for the use of French and virtually total provincial control over social-cultural affairs. Despite the underlying importance of economic conditions the issues of language rights and of jurisdiction in social-cultural matters had re-emerged as the essence of 'the Canadian Question'. In 1976 this was heavily underlined. Alongside the toughening attitude of the *Québecois* came unmistakable signs of an anglophone backlash. Resentment over the pace and extent of the government's policy on bilingualism in the civil service forced several modifications of that policy, while rumours and revelations of widespread corruption in the preparations for the Montreal Olympic Games reinvigorated old anglophone suspicions that French Canadians were congenitally unable to adapt to the 'protestant ethic' in business and political life. Passage of Quebec's Bill 22, proposing to make French the sole official language in the province, suggested to many writers-of-letters-to-the-editor that it was finally time to let Quebec go in peace – and good riddance.

---

*The B.N.A. Act was still a British statute capable of amendment on joint address to Westminster by the Canadian Houses of Parliament. By custom such amendments were passed automatically by the British Parliament. However, the question of how many provinces should give prior assent to such amendments had not been agreed upon, let alone codified, and the whole matter remained a stumbling-block to 'patriation' of the constitution.

In the midst of this vociferous verbal battle came a nation-wide strike by Canadian airline pilots demanding an end to the use of French by either pilots or ground controllers anywhere in Canada. Prime minister Trudeau, to the sobering dismay of many federalist anglophones, depicted the 1976 air control dispute as 'the most serious since the conscription crisis of 1944'.* Anglophone leaders of the Canadian Airline Pilots Association (CALPA) maintained doggedly that their sole concern was safety; that the optional use of French in the control of Quebec air-space created serious tensions and potential confusion of instructions, and thus constituted a serious hazard in airline operations. An autonomous francophone pilots association (*les gens de l'air*), supported vehemently by francophone opinion in Quebec and Ottawa, claimed that CALPA's real aims were anglophone job-protection and destruction of the government's attempts to carry through the intentions of the Official Languages Act. A stop-gap compromise ending the strike provided for the optional use of French at a few designated airports (not internationals) and only in visual flight conditions. The compromise, which also provided for a judicial review of the alleged safety factor, satisfied no one. Each side loudly proclaimed its determination to fight again should the investigative decision go the wrong way. As tempers flared across the country the Liberal caucus in Ottawa was deeply divided, although its francophone members gave grudging support to the temporary settlement. Jean Marchand, who had come to Ottawa in 1968 with Trudeau avowedly to demonstrate the effectiveness of a strong Quebec contingent in the federal government and the worth of bilingualism, resigned from the cabinet, bitterly charging Trudeau with a sell-out to anglophone bigotry. Although he himself faced serious allegations of improperly influencing the granting of duty-free shop concessions in Canadian airports, Marchand was accorded near-hero status in Quebec. It remained to be seen whether the issue would lead Canada perceptibly toward disruption or whether the forces of tolerant accommodation would again triumph – as was predicted in both languages by

---

* During which the young Trudeau had been a demonstrative opponent of Mackenzie King's decision to send Canadian conscripted men overseas.

Trudeau and Queen Elizabeth in speeches delivered during the Twenty-first Olympiad.

Despite the confrontations of the early seventies there were clear indications that the forces of cohesion remained strong. After the trauma of the explosion of October 1970, most Canadians found themselves primarily concerned with the twin problems of inflation and unemployment. At the same time, left-of-centre anglophones were caught up in a swelling wave of nationalism. Government reports and statistics revealing the apparently inexorable growth of foreign ownership led to strident demands for positive government action to reverse the trend and restore control of economic life to Canadians. An articulate and influential Committee for an Independent Canada bombarded newspapers and governments with demands and proposals for such action. Unease in the face of economic perils – perils which were experienced unequally by class and region – was reflected in frequent strikes and in a potentially disastrous movement within the N.D.P. A left-wing caucus led by Trotskyites and academic Marxists gained sudden influence in the party. Proclaiming that national independence and socialism were inseparable goals, this 'Waffle Group' called for public ownership of natural resources and major financial and mass-production institutions as the only means to correct maldistribution of wealth and to curb foreign ownership. Despite considerable success in constituency associations and provincial conventions the Waffle failed to make an effective alliance with the *Parti Québecois* (although it went much further than the Official N.D.P. position in recognizing 'two nations') and its extreme positions on nationalism and public ownership alienated the bulk of labour union opinion – which remained sensitive to any threat to the level of investment. In 1972, following an Ontario N.D.P. convention resolution sponsored by the new young leader, Stephen Lewis, requiring the Waffle either to disband or leave the party, the group disintegrated. But the pressure from the left, gradual recovery of the *Parti Québecois*, and growing N.D.P. strength at both the provincial and federal levels created considerable concern amongst old-line political leaders.

The first Trudeau government steered a cautious course through these troubled political waters. It faced the deteriorating economic situation by emphasizing the dangers of inflation above those of unemployment, and by tight budgets in which investors were given somewhat greater benefits than individual taxpayers. The criminal code was amended further to safeguard individual rights, family allowances were mildly increased, and strong action was taken to end a Vancouver longshoremen's strike which threatened disaster to prairie wheat farmers. In asserting Canada's independence in external affairs the government was more vigorous. To the intense irritation of Washington, Canada recognized the People's Republic of China (automatically withdrawing recognition of Taiwan) and Canada's contribution to N.A.T.O. forces in Europe was cut by one half. When a federal election was called in the autumn of 1972, Robert Stanfield's Conservatives, themselves unsure of the best solution for the complex economic problems besetting the country, failed to inject the campaign with any convincing issue. David Lewis, the N.D.P. leader who had replaced T. C. Douglas, came closest to identifying an issue when he decried the injustices of the 'just society' and castigated the government for tightening up on welfare recipients and unemployment insurance 'cheaters' rather than cutting back the benefits flowing to 'corporate welfare bums'. According to Lewis, the pampering of investors and an overriding concern with inflation were the government's major sins: 'We are witnesses in Canada to a new kind of welfare rip-off ... corporations that siphon hundreds of millions of dollars each year from the public trough while they pay a declining share of the income tax needed to finance government services.' In a rather quiet election the government nevertheless suffered a serious rebuff – probably due mostly to sharply rising prices and unemployment. The Liberals won 108 seats, the Conservatives 109, the N.D.P. 30 and Social Credit 15.

The 1972 election again showed the strong roots struck by a multiparty system. While no coalition or even secret understanding between Trudeau and Lewis emerged, the N.D.P. held a balance of power and by deciding to keep the Liberals in power exercised observable influence on policy and legislation. The prime minister conceded that 'we are more forced to listen ... probably as a result of that some of our legislation will be better ... we'll have to compromise'. These compromises prompted an

N.D.P. spokesman to describe the government's 1973 programme as 'a better budget than I have seen brought before this House by any majority government'. Cuts were made in personal income taxation, old age pensions were increased substantially and there was considerable revamping of social-economic legislation. Probably the most important reflection of N.D.P. influence was a pronounced shift towards economic nationalism, long advocated by the Walter Gordon wing of the Liberal party. The first fruits of this shift were an oil-pricing policy which sheltered Canadians from OPEC price hikes, the dramatic decision to establish a national petroleum company, and the creation of a foreign investment review mechanism. Nevertheless, the N.D.P. found most of the government's new departures inadequate and finally withdrew its support – thus forcing another election in the summer of 1974. The timing of Lewis's decision proved unpopular and Trudeau's Liberals were returned to power with 140 seats compared with the Conservatives' 95, the N.D.P.'s 16 and Social Credit's 11.

While the storm clouds were to produce an ominous explosion of *nationalisme* and a startling resurgence of 'western alienation' stemming from the cornucopia of natural resources and a demographic pattern which favoured the West as much as it threatened Quebec, long-term patterns and purposes lost little of their significance.

21

The 'New' Constitution

NINETY years after Goldwin Smith published *Canada and the Canadian Question* (1891), his description of the 'natural' integrating forces of the continent was more than ever dubious. His plea that anglophone Canadians should solve the French problem by throwing themselves into the arms of the United States had been rejected decade by decade. The cumulative effect of these rejections of North American homogenization, together with the revelation of more sources of energy and minerals across the old frontiers of the Northwest, the arctic and the oceans, has been profound. They have fashioned the apparent paradox of political–social volatility on the one hand and a characteristically embarrassed nationalism on the other. The process of articulating in constitutional terms the results of this historical experience has, of recent years, been so robust as to provoke tentative thoughts of some form of external intervention – in France, the United States and Britain. By the beginning of the eighties Canadians seemed to see the complexity of their country ('nation' is used less and less frequently) as something to enjoy. Beneath the political furore, continuity absorbed change.

Cautiously controlled immigration, together with natural increase, brought Canada's population to about twenty-five million by 1986. While the number of Canadians had doubled since 1945, economic expansion came very close to counterbalancing the impact of the demographic kaleidoscope. Thus, measured in 1971 dollars, output rose from $30 billion in 1945 to over $461 billion (market price) in 1985. Unemployment, always difficult to gauge in the light of seasonal and other variants, stood at 9 per cent by 1986, yet the number of people employed had more than doubled since 1945, as had average Canadian income.

Changing population patterns, while dramatic, also contained elements of stability. Immigration accounted for an even smaller proportion of the annual population growth. In 1911, 22 per cent of the population had been born abroad; by 1986 that percentage had dropped to less than 15. The 'Canadianizing' effect of this long-term trend revealed itself in many ways: in an underlying confidence, affirmative responses to efforts to resist continentalism and a relatively quiet acceptance of a point system by which to judge immigrant applications. That system, weighted heavily in favour of skills and education, specifically excludes racial criteria. It does, however, mean an effective upper limit on annual immigration, and certainly on those of any origin who are likely to become a public burden. In a sense, the mosaic gave way to the melting-pot. Perhaps the gradualist approach to change-by-immigration helps explain Canada's relative racial tolerance and, equally, her low rates of crime and social violence. Prime minister Trudeau sought to symbolize the unity-in-diversity theme when he announced in 1979 the appointment as governor general of Edward Schreyer – ex-New Democratic premier of Manitoba, Roman Catholic, of German lineage and able to converse in Ukrainian, German, Polish, French and English.

Changes in the ethnic population mix have nevertheless interacted perceptibly with policy, economic developments and public attitudes. While proposals to move towards a republican status still founder on the rocks of continuity, the symbols of monarchy continue to dwindle: the Royal Mail is now Canada Post. In 1945 more than 50 per cent of Canadians had roots in the British Isles; by 1986 fewer than 41 per cent were of that lineage, while more than 24 per cent had other European origins – Italian, German, Ukrainian, Dutch, Greek, Portuguese. And, despite reticence in immigration policy, the 'visible minorities' have grown markedly since 1960, especially the Chinese, Japanese, Indian, Pakistani and West Indian. Enriching Canadian life, the 'new' minorities (every Canadian is now a member of a minority), without a traumatic numerical impact, have broadened Canadian perception of 'the race question'. While the venerable context of 'French–English' relations remained central, the tensions of colour and ethnicity have been added. Incidents of prejudice and individual violence, in such focal points as Toronto's 'Jane-Finch corridor', have led not only to the establishment of provincial human rights commissions but also to specific efforts to modify attitudes – such as school programmes and appointment of non-white people to police forces. In this respect, a positive attempt has been made to learn from the experiences of other countries, particularly the United States and Britain. Also following in part from experience elsewhere has been a growing attention paid to the rights of aboriginal Canadians, the Indians and the Eskimo. New concern with these groups, which together make up less than 2 per cent of the population, was also due to a refreshing self-awareness on their part. Leading to vigorous assertion of treaty and land rights, this awareness was also partly the result of a renewed growth in the numbers of the Eskimo and Indian groups, each of which has more than doubled since 1951.

Other population trends have been of equal or greater importance. As the proportion of British stock declined, so too did that of the French. In 1945 some 31 per cent of Canadians were of French descent; by 1986 the 'French fact' was no larger than 26·7 per cent. As we have seen, the *Québecois* perceived this as a much more serious threat than did their anglophone compatriots. However, by the opening of the eighties a new migratory pattern had developed which was of equal concern to anglophones and francophones everywhere east of Winnipeg. As at the end of the nineteenth century, the West beckoned insistently and effectively. Developing the resource bonanza in mine and forest has required large movements of people and capital. These have come in large measure from central and eastern Canada. From the four Maritime provinces a steady flow, particularly of young people, moved to Ontario throughout the fifties and sixties, but by the end of the seventies employment goals lay in the construction and forest industries and amongst the oil rigs of the West. The Maritimes' percentage of the Canadian population dropped from 22 in 1945 to only 9 by 1986. During the same period, Quebec's birth-rate dropped to the lowest of all the provinces, while western opportunities began to draw people from both Quebec and Ontario. By 1981 the four western provinces contained as many people as Quebec, while Alberta's population had grown to one quarter that of Ontario. These ineluctable trends in population patterns and economic strength were bound to have reverberations in politics, policies and popular attitudes.

World economic tides, as well as federal and provincial policies, played upon the shifting sands of the economy. Canada was not immune to the triumphant 'economic miracles' achieved by West German and Japanese industrial discipline, nor to the mushrooming production of industrial goods in such areas of low labour costs as Hong Kong, Taiwan and South Korea. Canadian consumer goods firms (and their employees) in textile and metal-based production clamoured insistently for increases in the tariff protection which had, since the 1870s, been the mainstay of their existence. Most of these industries were in Ontario and Quebec, while the materials of the burgeoning new western wealth, oil, gas, coal, wood products, uranium and metals, needed no such stimulus. Thus, western affluence revived old resentments and the charge that national economic policies were concocted by easterners to fatten Ontario and Quebec at the expense of western producers – especially by maintaining artificially high prices for consumer goods and imposing restrictive regulations on natural resource production and marketing.

While regional and provincial consciousness grew strident in the 1970s, the Trudeau government initiated a number of social–economic measures designed to minimize disparities both amongst regions and classes. These equalization policies met with mixed success but, taken as a package, they probably provide much of the explanation for the phoenix-like rebirths of the federal Liberal party – especially when reinforced by militant leadership in constitutional expressions of the 'Just Society'.

Prominent amongst the social justice measures was a major expansion of unemployment insurance in 1971. The new legislation, by removing the income ceiling imposed in the original 1940 act, made the system universal. With the provision of basic income support for everyone who might need it, including the self-employed and seasonal workers, some communities, especially in the Maritimes and Quebec, were sustained for months at a time by the extended system. Apoplectic businessmen charged that the new unemployment insurance simply invited urban 'drop-outs', as well as hordes of unsuccessful writers, artists, greedy fishermen and other 'part-timers', to plunder the national treasury – ignoring the ultimate business advantage of the new social 'stabilizer'. Whether or not the benefits of the total social security system (including also pensions, family allowances and health insurance), by underpinning consumer demand, outweighed governmental subsidization of the complex structure, was a hotly debated issue as annual federal deficits reached critical proportions by the end of the seventies.

Aimed more directly at reducing regional disparities were numerous programmes designed to stimulate economic growth in regions and sub-regions. In 1969 Ottawa established a Department of Regional Economic Expansion. DREE projects quickly became a symbol of the federal presence in the Maritimes and many districts of Quebec and other provinces. In cooperation with the provinces, DREE's expenditures through capital grants to selected firms and local governments were more than $500 million a year by 1981. Some economists moaned gloomily about the inefficiency of DREE, but in the port and valley towns of the Maritimes, the backwaters of the Gaspé and eastern Ontario, and in other economically sluggish districts, the people viewed Ottawa's pump-priming with no great hostility. The equalizing and stabilizing efforts of the Just Society were often compared favourably with the survival-in-the-jungle philosophy of the 1930s.

Structural changes in the economy have been startling. Between 1945 and 1986, agriculture's share of total employment dropped from 32 per cent to about 5, and its dollar share of national output from about 12 per cent to less than 3. In these same years, manufacturing and construction firms, relative to growth in other areas, also declined as employers and as contributors to economic output. The quadrupling of output and doubling of employment during this same period was the result of steady expansion in public administration and service occupations as well as more sophisticated organization in trade and finance, transportation, communications and public utilities. In other words, while farm and factory production continued to grow, the white-collar occupations and their less visible economic output grew much more rapidly – a change typical of all maturing industrial societies. Shifting economic contours meant heavier emphasis on the skills and education required by new technologies in industry, commerce and administration. They also fed the growth of towns and cities and, when acting in conjunction with a mushroom development of energy and mineral resources, complicated immensely the job of maintaining minimal economic balance across the country and amongst the three levels of government.

Apart from specific stimuli such as those of DREE, the federal government pursued more general policies which, by 1981, looked very much like economic nationalism – often with ambivalent results politically, particularly in the West. In agriculture, the Canadian Wheat Board made increasingly large sales to Russia, China and other communist states and maintained the eighty-year-old Crow's Nest Pass agreement by which prairie freight rates were kept artificially low. Beyond grain, an ever widening range of farm produce was aided by tariffs, price-support legislation, import quotas and a network of provincial marketing boards which was increasingly coordinated under a federal act passed in 1972. Despite the various forms of protection and subsidy for farmers across the country, rural Canadians sensed a growing disadvantage. Around the cities and towns speculation and developers drove up land values while increasing mechanization, and the advent of capital-intensive 'agribusiness' combined with inflation and sky-high interest rates to bankrupt many farmers and to make it difficult for their children either to maintain or acquire family farms. Some provincial governments, worried about the shrinkage of arable land and erosion of rural life, tightened their zoning laws. Saskatchewan's N.D.P. government, through judicious purchasing, assembled a large land bank from which it could provide family-size farms on a use-lease basis, thus obviating to some extent the impossibly high costs of acquiring actual ownership.

Managing the economy also grew more complex as new technologies were applied to the exploration and development of energy and other natural resources, and as the cumulative ecological effects of more mature industries became evident. Nor could economic policy avoid directly affecting the federal division of powers, ethnic and cultural relations, environmental concerns and Canadian–American relations.

Environmentalism was not just trendy; the damage was real and the threat to the future quality of life appalling. By the 1960s pollution of the Great Lakes was bad enough to pose danger to the millions who depended upon them for water supply systems and fishing. Industrial waste and drainage from fertilized farmlands had put those heartland waters in danger of ecological death. As a result of control laws passed by Ottawa, Ontario and American governments considerable rehabilitation had been achieved by the beginning of the eighties. Enforcement of disposal regulations was, however, imperfect. Raw sewage still entered the St Lawrence at Montreal, while deadly dioxin from American industrial effluence into the Niagara River and Lake Huron was discovered in fish in Lake Ontario. A yet more intractable problem was the scourge of acid rain. The result of tons of sulphur dioxide and other chemical wastes thrown into the skies by towering smokestacks in the American midwest and the nickel smelters at Sudbury, north of Lake Huron, poisonous rain clouds drifted across Ontario, Quebec and the northeastern United States. In Ontario, hundreds of lakes had 'died' by 1980 and the rest were under direct threat, as was much forest and farmland. Even the symbolic maple was vulnerable.

Other technological assaults upon the environment also caused popular concern. In the far northwest the network of oil and gas pipelines endangered animal migrations and thus the ancient cultures of Indian and Eskimo. Faced with an ominous influx of men and machines, the Dene nation (northern Indians) reasserted their treaty rights and pressed Ottawa both for compensation and local autonomy. Reporting in 1973, a Royal Commission headed by Justice Thomas Berger recommended delaying further pipeline construction in the north until native claims were settled and environmental effects fully understood. By 1981 considerable progress had been made in both directions. However, technology's outward thrusts would clearly create long-term problems of cultural adjustment, as well as jurisdictional squabbles. In the Beaufort Sea and other arctic locations, as well as on the Atlantic floors off Newfoundland and Nova Scotia, exploratory drilling in large proven fields held economic promise which began to staunch the westward seepage of people from the Maritimes. At the same time both

Atlantic and Pacific coast dwellers worried about the menace of spills from runaway wells or shipwrecked supertankers. Pollution and resource depletion were issues that bade well to equal in people's minds the agitation in the 1970s over inflation, interest rates or the constitution. Automobile emission regulations were in force by the late seventies, but, in the wake of Pennsylvania's Three Mile Island nuclear reactor burn-out, atomic jitters increased sharply. Growing reliance on the Candu reactor for generating electricity, however, was reluctantly accepted on two grounds: belief in the superior safety features of this particular Canadian product, and belief in the validity of its contribution to energy self-sufficiency.

Most of the new concerns Canada shared with other industrial countries. In some respects, however, there was a special poignancy as Canadians came to recognize ambiguities in the frontier myths of self-reliance and limitless resources. Hydroelectric potential was near its limit, fisheries and forests required ever closer regulation, much fresh water was in peril and parched Americans had tentatively proposed a large water diversion scheme. The frontiers and resources were still there, but the realities of pollution and depletion loomed large, as did the power of national and multinational corporations in resource development and land ownership – both urban and rural. Soaring world prices for oil joined with inflationary pressure from post-Vietnam America combined with a steady increase of investment from Japan, Germany, Holland and Switzerland, to produce a very complex mixture of uneven economic growth, structural unemployment and corporate mergers. Moreover, most governmental thrusts towards reform or control were seriously weakened by determined, if quiet, opposition from concentrated economic power. Within the tax structure, exemptions and concessions were the primary features for corporations, while even the tax on capital gains recommended by the Carter Commission on Taxation in 1962 was severely modified by the tax legislation of 1971. While Ottawa applauded the tariff-lowering commitments of G.A.T.T., it found ways (especially by import quotas) to keep the beleaguered factories of central Canada and the Maritimes well protected as levels of unemployment, inflation and interest all edged upwards. Again, while the Trudeau government proclaimed a need to tighten anti-combines legislation and launched devastating investigations of monopolistic practices in the press and amongst multinational oil companies, moves to curb monopoly were hesitant.

The government seemed to respond not only to direct business pressure but also to the well-established sentiment of Canadians that order, efficiency and 'development' are more desirable goals than individualism and competition – whatever rhetorical praise of free enterprise they may hear after dinner. Thus subsidies, tax concessions, controls and governmental enterprise through crown corporations or public commissions continued into the eighties to loom larger than assaults upon monopoly. In 1974, following the general reasoning of the Watkins task force (1968) and the Gray Report (1972) about the need to limit and control the operations of foreign capital, Ottawa established a Foreign Investment Review Agency. F.I.R.A. screened all new investment from abroad, including takeovers and transfers. While some F.I.R.A. decisions were contentious and even arbitrary, and although the agency approved roughly 90 per cent of the applications made to it, it influenced substantially the ownership pattern. Equally positive steps were taken when Ottawa created the Canada Development Corporation (1971), and several provincial governments followed suit with their own crown corporations for direct public investment. By 1981 the C.D.C. had acquired several large foreign-owned firms ranging in function from oil and pharmaceuticals to aircraft production. Together with a steady growth in private Canadian capital, a good deal of which accumulates from Canadian investment abroad, this growing public intervention lessened considerably the fear that Americans might obtain virtually complete 'ownership of Canada'. Indeed, by 1981, the extent of Canadian investment in the United States in such diverse enterprises as television cable systems, supermarkets and urban real-estate development had led to some anguished American cries for retaliatory restrictions.

With Ronald Reagan's accession to the American presidency many of the subtle contrasts between the United States and Canada became more visible. President Reagan's drastic reassertion of American military and economic power, his 'monetarism' which involved sharp curtailment of government spending (except on arms), his attempt to halt inflation by permitting very high interest rates, and his tough revival of anti-communism all seemed to signal the triumph of a fortress America philosophy, and thus to threaten once again the balance which Canada had traditionally sought to maintain in her relations abroad. Those Canadians who had heaped opprobrium upon their prime minister in the late seventies for his arrogance began to applaud Pierre Trudeau's use of federal authority to maintain control of the country's key economic sectors, her sovereignty in the Canadian arctic, her rights in ocean waters and offshore seabeds, and a multilateral basis of foreign trade and political relations. Sir John Macdonald would very likely approve the broadly conservative nature of the Trudeau national policies – and not least those aimed at securing 'constitutional liberty as opposed to democracy'. Certainly he would sympathize with his latter-day Liberal counterpart who faced very familiar provincial rebelliousness and recurring charges of both arrogance and procrastination.

The electoral barometer reacted violently to all these shifting patterns. Yet, while politics seemed to bring into focus profound conflict amongst the provinces and Ottawa and between anglophone and francophone conceptions of the country, by 1981 the dust was beginning to settle once again and new accommodations to come into sight.

Although the 1974 elections gave back to the Trudeau government the majority it had lost in 1972, the provinces shored up their defences against any overweening assertion of Ottawa power. Premier William Davis continued to hold Ontario for the Tories, whose 'Big Blue Machine' had survived both minority and majority situations by conceding much to the N.D.P. in labour and social policy, and had been in office nearly forty years. The Maritimes were in the Tory camp and in the west the provincial Liberal parties were virtually wiped out. Stirling Lyon's Conservatives won Manitoba from the N.D.P. in 1977, Bill Bennett's essentially conservative Social Creditors ousted the Barrett N.D.P. government in British Columbia in 1975; at the same time Peter Lougheed took Alberta for the Conservatives while Alan Blakeney's N.D.P. snatched back Saskatchewan from the Liberals. As often in the past, especially in the critical 1880s, Canadians sought to balance their regional and national interests by ensuring that provincial and federal governments were of varied political hue. While this exotic process makes for clamorous confrontations, even brinkmanship, it also ensures continuous open debate about the nature and purposes of the Canadian society. At the end of the seventies that debate reached a crescendo.

In November 1976, René Lévesque led the *Parti Québecois* to a surprise victory in which 41 per cent gave his *Péquistes* a majority of the seats in the Quebec national assembly. The popular, diminutive television commentator had managed to hold in tandem two basic francophone forces: a radical impulse towards complete political independence and the more cautious preference of the majority for compromise and a revision of the federal system which would give a still larger degree of autonomy to Quebec. In the campaign the *Parti Québecois* had played down its major plank of secession and made much of unspecified charges of corruption against Robert Bourassa's Liberal government. Victory surprised the *Péquistes* themselves and sent tremors through the rest of the country. Emigration of anglophone Quebeckers speeded up as did the movement of corporation head offices and bank accounts from Montreal to Toronto.

For the four years following 1976, Canadian political life was dominated by Trudeau and Lévesque. Some saw irony in the fact that both the federalist and provincialist causes found their most dramatic advocates in French Canada. Others charged that, as the constitution became the focal point of party division, Trudeau was hypocritically using the issue to screen his government's failure to provide effective answers to economic problems. What many missed was that ultimately the question of the constitution subsumed all other questions. Whether or not Canada would remain one country was more important than which level of government should have jurisdiction in any particular social or economic field – all the questions were unavoidably constitutional. And, following the *Péquiste* victory, Quebec necessarily held centre stage. As Trudeau had declared earlier: 'Each man has his own reasons, I suppose, as driving forces, but mine were twofold. One was to make sure that Quebec would not leave Canada through separatism and the other was to make sure that Canada wouldn't shove Quebec out through narrow-mindedness.' Both risks were real in 1976; both appeared to have been minimized by 1981.

The P.Q. government set about its tasks with despatch. Labour and electoral laws were reformed, the immense hydroelectricity project of Quebec Hydro near James Bay was pushed towards completion, legislation was enacted to put under public ownership the large asbestos mines of the American Johns Mansville company, while other crown corporations were encouraged. But if Canadian and American businessmen grew faint at the sight of this advancing *étatisme*, anglophones inside and outside the province trembled more violently before Bill 101. This language law was designed to make Quebec unilingual, proceeding from the argument that the Liberal goal of a bilingual Canada had proved unworkable. It declared French to be the province's only official language: all children, save those of parents who themselves had been educated in English in Quebec, were to be taught in French – including the children of immigrants from other provinces. All signs must be in French only and anglophone businesses must establish programmes of 'francization', while French would be the sole language of debate and record in the assembly. To enforce the law and secure, in fact, a cultural revolution, Bill 101 established an Office de la Langue Française. The work of this office, together with policies such as that requiring that construction workers must be francophone – which restricts labour mobility – moved Claude Ryan of *Le Devoir* to declare Bill 101 'rigid, dogmatic and authoritarian' and to endorse Trudeau's fears about the chauvinism of the separatists. Camille Laurin, Lévesque's minister of cultural development, summed up the global nature of the *Péquiste* programme when he declared that it was not enough to speak French, one must be French. For anglophone Quebec the racial basis of the *séparatiste* vision was underscored when Premier Lévesque dismissed a *Parti Québecois* by-election defeat in the predominantly Jewish Montreal riding of D'Arcy McGee with the comment that the constituency's voters were not 'authentically Québecois'.

Anglophone Canadians were bemused by the torrent of events,

opinion polls and editorials as Lévesque moved determinedly towards his party's major goal of secession. *Étapisme* (gradualism) was the policy forced upon *Péquiste* radicals by the passionate yet realistic premier. A referendum law gave the government the authority to frame any question put directly to the voters and to appoint two committees, one to conduct a 'yes' campaign and one for the 'no'. The government was also empowered to set the voting date, to specify the time allotted inside and outside the assembly for debate, and to authorize permissible campaign expenditures. Committed only to holding a referendum before the next provincial election, Lévesque played cat-and-mouse with his opponents, holding back until the last moment both the date of the referendum and the phrasing of the question. 'The date,' he said in 1978, 'is not for tomorrow, but it is approaching all the same with giant steps.' A year earlier he had said, 'When there is a referendum, what the question will be, will be our moral responsibility.'

Not surprisingly, tension rose steadily. Quebec Liberals selected the austere, almost priest-like, editor Claude Ryan to succeed Robert Bourassa, who resigned as party leader after losing the 1976 election. Ryan pressed daily for clarification of the 'options' which the government would pose in the referendum question. In the four years or so leading to the referendum, which was finally announced for May 1980, Lévesque and his ministers presented an increasingly ambiguous impression of the real *Péquiste* goal. On the one hand they stressed 'sovereignty-association': while Quebec would become politically independent, it would also negotiate an economic association, a kind of common market, 'with Canada'. On the other hand, the *Parti Québecois* published a formal White Paper in November 1979 in which the *séparatiste* historical litany of oppression and virtual emasculation of the *Québecois* reached the level of caricature. Moreover, according to the *Péquistes*, Ottawa continued to invade provincial jurisdictions and to operate the economy to Quebec's disadvantage. Thus Quebec must choose sovereignty, 'the only road that can open up the horizon and guarantee us a free, proud and adult national existence'. While democratic and non-violent means were to prevail, few could miss the naked appeal to race and the frightening connotations clustering around such crusades in the twentieth century.

While Lévesque was holding out for the most auspicious referendum circumstances, his opponents appeared to be in some disarray. Yet much was happening to strengthen the forces of federalism; so much, indeed, that a true perspective is very elusive. Claude Ryan, for all his gaunt and forbidding exterior, conducted a thorough-going organization of the 'non' campaign based upon relentless logic, careful analysis of the history of federalism and some specific recommendations for constitutional change. Most of anglophone Canada beyond Quebec was content (indeed, could see little alternative) simply to observe Ryan's defence of federalism. Apart from a few anglophone academics and writers who talked somewhat affectedly of 'Quebec's right of self-determination', the rest of the country confined itself largely to editorials and letters propounding the virtues of a flexible federalism.

There were two crucial exceptions to the general hands-off attitude. Each of the other provincial governments made explicit its refusal of any advance commitment to economic association with an independent Quebec, as well as its commitment to a 'renewed' federalism. More important was the cautious yet increasingly evident participation of federal Liberals in the campaign, particularly after the wording of the referendum question was announced in March 1980.* Organized by Jean Chrétien, minister of justice, the Trudeau team demonstrated two dominant facts as the speakers moved back and forth across the province. First, with French Canadians occupying key positions in Ottawa the hysterical *Péquiste* charges that 'the Conquest'

---

* The Government of Quebec has made public its proposal to negotiate a new agreement with the rest of Canada, based on the equality of nations; this agreement would enable Quebec to acquire the exclusive powers to make its laws, levy its taxes and establish relations abroad – in other words, sovereignty – and at the same time, to maintain with Canada an economic association including a common currency; no change in political status resulting from these negotiations will be effected without approval from the people through another referendum; on these terms, do you give the Government of Quebec the mandate to negotiate the proposed agreement between Quebec and Canada?'

had led to perpetual exploitation and degradation seemed dubious at best. Second, the imprecision of the referendum wording was shown to be a calculated down-playing of the undoubted goal of secession. Both the Ryan and the Chrétien organizations blended logic with emotion: while federal institutions should be further modified, Canada had achieved a constitutional flexibility which had already secured *la survivance* far more effectively than could either independence or absorption in the American union. The changes wrought in Quebec since 1960 had ensured that French would remain the dominant language in the province as francophones took over all public institutions and moved steadily into managerial positions in private enterprise. Although *Péquiste* spokesmen refused to recognize it, the traditional income and opportunity gaps between anglophone and francophone Quebeckers had been virtually closed by 1980. While speculative statistics concerning the economic prospects of an independent Quebec were summed up differently by 'oui' and 'non' speakers, it is likely that other than economic perceptions decided the outcome.

At the peak of the campaign Chrétien and Trudeau gave their most effective speeches. Arguing that Quebec had amply demonstrated by its achievements in cultural, economic and social affairs the adequacy of the existing federal structure, they underlined the threat posed by the *Péquistes*. No matter how devious the phrasing of the question, with its carrot of a second referendum, the goal was secession. Political independence under Lévesque–Laurin auspices would mean hiving off a tiny French nation in an English-speaking sea and the triumph of a self-defeating, introverted chauvinism. Far more promising would be continuance of francophone development within a federal country in which appreciation of the 'French fact' was making large strides, and where the reality of provincial powers was already more impressive than in any other federal state. Explicit in the Liberal 'non' campaign was the promise that the B.N.A. Act would be 'patriated' and the constitution so amended as to entrench francophone rights. Echoing the eloquent pleas of Cartier and Laurier the federalists called for re-commitment to Canada.

Perhaps the most characteristic aspect of the 1980 referendum debate was the almost complete absence of appeals for violence. A few anglophone fire-eaters talked of 'shouldering a musket' on the banks of the Ottawa in the event of a 'oui' majority; some radical *séparatistes* talked darkly of Papineau and the F.L.Q. Lévesque and his colleagues reiterated constantly the peaceful and democratic nature of their cause while the rest of the country appeared to assume that, in the final analysis, peaceful secession was at least possible. Such an assumption was probably not justified in view of the federal responsibilities to a million anglophone Quebeckers, the extent of federal and private property rights that would be directly affected, and the notice given by other provincial governments that they would not enter a common market with an independent Quebec. The prime minister had stated that he would use force only in the event that something 'illegal' was attempted in Quebec. Since a unilateral declaration of independence by a self-defined Quebec would, by definition, be illegal, the possibility of peaceably fragmenting Canada was, in fact, remote. There is no evidence, nevertheless, that anticipation of civil war in any way affected the outcome.

On 20 May, 59.5 per cent of Quebec's voters said 'non' to secession as defined in the softest possible terms of sovereignty-association. Of equal or greater significance, 52 per cent of the francophone vote had opposed the proposition, while only one district (north of Quebec City) showed a majority for it. Bitterly, Lévesque put secession temporarily on the shelf and prepared to join other provincial governments in an unremitting, if painfully disjointed, assault upon Ottawa's power and 'arrogance'.

The revived crusade for provincial rights was led by Premier Peter Lougheed of Alberta. Largely because of the economic and demographic shifts noted earlier, western discontent merged with a deepening concern over energy policies and the question of constitutional reform. The drama was played out against a backdrop of political pyrotechnics and personality clashes unusual in a country which could contemplate in relative calm the secession of a province whose importance to Canada was greater than that of California, Texas or even New York to the United States.

That the most serious opposition to the Trudeau government

was to be found in the provincial capitals rather than across the floor of the Commons in Ottawa was made clear in the aftermath of the 1974 general election. In that election Trudeau had returned to the sparkling whistle-stop style of 1968, and he had several distinct advantages. With him was his beautiful young wife, Margaret, with their first son – to banish the image of a 'cynical', reluctantly ageing bachelor. Also, the impression of effective leadership was strengthened by contrast with the low-key Conservative leader Robert Stanfield, and by the Tory's unpopular advocacy of wage and price controls as the essential means of curbing inflation. Further, David Lewis's N.D.P. was somewhat constrained by the fact that it had wielded obvious influence upon the Liberals' legislative policies. The decisive electoral outcome, in which the Conservatives were cut back to 36 per cent and the N.D.P. to 15.4 per cent of the vote, gave the prime minister unquestioned personal authority.

The extent to which leadership had become and would remain crucial became apparent as the government experimented its way through a series of economic and constitutional policies. In 1975, confronted by steeply escalating wage settlements and price inflation, the Liberals reversed their position on the controls issue of the 1974 election. Ottawa introduced wage and price controls in October in response to an almost universal urging by newspapers and business leaders, and despite formal opposition by the labour unions – who were uncertain about the policy and concerned that wages rather than prices would be the main target. The controls provided that wages could grow by the inflation rate plus 2 per cent and that prices could rise only when a cost rise was demonstrated. By 1978, when the controls were lifted, the wage–price rate of increase had decreased sharply, but the government had decided that continuance would be risky, especially since wages and prices were by no means the only factors in the continuing inflation.

In the midst of the struggle to maintain some sort of social–economic stability – a struggle which featured conflicting opinions in the cabinet, the resignation of finance minister John Turner, and several contradictory policy starts – Trudeau's political ratings gyrated wildly. His own philosophy of government stressed 'social engineering' to achieve broadly defined goals of justice. While he became painfully aware of the limits imposed by the power of private groupings, from business corporations to the massively growing trade unions in the public services, he continued to emphasize the need for strong government – government that could 'speak for Canada'. In so doing he sustained his love–hate relationship with the electorate, a more personal relationship, probably, than any since Macdonald. He could horrify some by calling out 'Viva Cuba, Viva Castro' during a Latin American tour in 1976; but others enjoyed such gentle twisting of the Eagle's beak. When his own marriage foundered in 1977, he became the country's leading 'single parent' and the dignity with which he endured his wife's revelations of their private life seemed to counterbalance a widely published photograph of the prime minister's insouciant pirouette behind the Queen's back. His determination, through public and private crises, to support the Canadian experiment against the threats of separatism, provincialism and corporate power probably accounts for his bizarre defeat in 1979 and startling recapturing of power in 1980.

As if to underwrite this scenario the federal Liberals made serious political mistakes both in and out of office. At a leadership convention early in 1976 the Tories replaced the stately and respected Stanfield of Nova Scotia with a nearly unknown young Albertan, Joe Clark. Mercilessly dubbed 'Joe Who?', Clark was first and foremost a politician, one who seemed more concerned with images and party machinery than with social goals. At the same time, Clark's selection as leader recognized the growing power of the West, its increasing population and its anti-Liberal stance. Under the conspicuously maladroit Clark the Conservatives expressed western provincialism as well as the interests of investors (both Canadian and American). Despite the feeling of most anglophones after Lévesque's 1976 victory that Trudeau was the one person who might avert the secession of Quebec, his public support dwindled steadily through 1978–9. To some extent this was due to Liberal preoccupation with the constitutional question and a distinctly cavalier inattention to western feelings of alienation – a conviction that western political influence at Ottawa was not commensurate with the region's importance. Equally ominous were an anti-French undercurrent and a 'neo-conservative' disapproval of 'big government'.

After much wavering, a federal election was called for May 1979. Although opinion polls showed that few Canadians thought much of Clark's leadership potential, Trudeau himself seemed weary, almost disenchanted, during the campaign – and the Liberals did almost nothing to woo back the West. A most precarious parliament was the result. While the Liberals garnered 4 per cent more of the popular vote, they carried only one constituency west of Winnipeg, lost much of urban Ontario, and found their main strength in a solid Quebec. But the West gave much of its support to the N.D.P. and thus deprived the Tories of a majority in the Commons.

Relying on Liberal reluctance to defeat the new minority government, Clark sought to establish the image of an efficient, businesslike administration and to downplay both separatism and the constitutional question. Both goals eluded him. In foreign affairs he contradicted his colleague Flora MacDonald, by announcing that Canada's Israeli embassy would be moved to Jerusalem. Immediate retaliation by Arab states frightened his business supporters and the government backed down. On his major campaign promise to 'privatize' Petrocan he was almost as indecisive; yet the threat to dismember the national oil company was politically damaging. On the constitutional issue Clark was embarrassingly eager to keep Ottawa aloof from the impending referendum and to support an overly expansive view of provincial powers with the slogan that Canada is a 'community of communities'. With only one Tory elected from Quebec the uneasy prime minister was compelled to appoint three Quebec ministers from the Senate – where they were next to invisible. More than four months' delay in convening parliament deepened public scepticism. When finance minister John Crosbie finally presented a budget early in December its principal feature was a sharp immediate increase in the price of oil and gas, with a schedule permitting Canadian prices to move rapidly to 85 per cent of a relentlessly rising world price.

Welcomed by business and the West, the budget was nevertheless contentious. Despite numerous signs of sagging confidence the Tories imagined that the Liberals were not ready to defeat the government. Thus they did nothing to ensure continuing support from the five crucal *Créditistes*, nor even to make sure that every Conservative would be present for the vote on an N.D.P. no-confidence motion. The wily Allan MacEachen of Nova Scotia, Liberal house leader, assessed the situation accurately. All his members, healthy or ill, were in place for the roll-call on December 13 and the government lost by six votes. Clark's Conservatives had held office a scant six months.

Perhaps the major reason for the Tories' calamitous over-confidence had been Trudeau's November announcement that 'it's time for a new leader' of the Liberal party. His resignation had been loudly welcomed in the Tory press and elicited some-what stilted acknowledgement from the government front bench. But with Clark's defeat the presumably leaderless Liberals ralllied with *éclat*. After some public and private agonizing, and faced with an election already set for 18 February 1980, they wisely decided against a leadership convention. Led by MacEachen, the Liberal caucus unanimously requested Trudeau to rescind his decision to resign. To the dismay of some right-wing Liberals and the ultimate joy of the party, the enigmatic Montrealer acceded.

In the ensuing election campaign surface ambiguities prolifer-ated. An apparently languid Trudeau seemed *faute de mieux* and the party failed even to produce a platform for the bemused electorate. Other than to promise that they would prevent the price of oil from rising as fast as Clark was prepared to let it, the Liberals seemed content to ride back on the dismal perform-anec of an aborted Tory regime. The tactics were sound. When the count was in the Liberals held 146 seats, the Tories 103, the N.D.P. 32, while the *Créditistes* were eliminated. Almost over-night many modern political obituaries turned rancid. Whatever doubts Trudeau may have suffered about his private or public future dissolved before the glittering chance to consummate his oft reiterated purposes.

The 1980 election was also decisive in several other respects. While the Liberals 'struck out' in the West they captured 68 per cent of the Quebec vote and 73 of the 74 seats. Endorsation of the Trudeau team by Quebec was an omen, unrecognized by many at the time, of what would happen in the long-postponed referendum later that year. A clear Liberal majority from

Ontario was also an omen: that Ontarians, like Quebeckers, perceived a need to call a halt to extreme provincialism and to reassert the original functions of the federal government. While self-interest in such matters as the price of oil and gasolene, or general economic policy, was undoubtedly a major factor, the prospect of dwindling into a mere 'community of communities' under timorous leadership was of at least equal significance. Underlining the uneasiness about the future of federal programmes was the fact that the Liberals captured 19 seats to the Tories' 13 in the four Atlantic provinces. But the core problem remained that of the West. There the Liberals won only 2 seats, both in Manitoba. However, while the Conservatives won every Alberta seat, they divided British Columbia, Saskatchewan, Manitoba and the Territories with the N.D.P. Thus, while all three parties could be called 'regional' (the N.D.P. held no seats east of Ontario), at the same time, all three retain electoral potential across the country.

For the immediate aftermath of the 1980 election, and of the referendum, the fact that the N.D.P. held 27 western seats (to the Tories' 46) was critical. Both the N.D.P. and the Conservative strength in the West resulted in part from the feeling that the West had too little influence upon federal policies – especially with respect to natural resources. However, the democratic socialists differed profoundly from the Tories when it came to a question of the purposes for which western influence should be used. The N.D.P., although with differing emphasis federally and provincially, stressed public ownership and a substantial federal role, while the Conservatives, both federally and provincially, fought for provincial dominance and minimal public intervention. In the curious political struggle over the constitution and energy policy with which the 1980s opened, these political factors were of primary significance.

'Renewed federalism' lay at the heart of the Liberal and N.D.P. positions. Trudeau especially insisted that all Canadians had made a commitment to the majority in Quebec to 'patriate' the constitution, amended by entrenching a charter of rights guaranteeing, particularly, use of the two official languages in the legislatures and courts of Quebec, Manitoba and New Brunswick and in all federal institutions and services, as well as the right in all provinces to education in either language. The chief problem lay in securing provincial agreement to an amending formula. Ever since Canada had obtained (at the urging of Quebec and Ontario) a clause in the 1931 Statute of Westminster leaving the power to amend the B.N.A. Act with the British parliament, attempts had been made to secure unanimous provincial agreement on an amending formula. All had failed. During this period a number of amendments, such as that which gave Ottawa jurisdiction over unemployment insurance (1940), had been enacted by Westminster in response to a joint address from the Canadian houses of parliament. No uniform practice of gaining provincial consent had, however, evolved. Unanimous consent of the provinces, majority consent and even no consultation at all – each procedure had been used. At Victoria, in 1971, one of the long series of federal–provincial conferences produced an agreement which included minor adjustments to the division of powers, a limited list of individual freedoms and an amending formula. But this 'Victoria Charter' foundered when Quebec Premier Bourassa encountered the charge from within his own party that Ottawa would still retain too much power in social and economic fields.

Succeeding conferences seemed to retreat steadily from the tentative agreement of Victoria, despite the continuing practical operations of many federal–provincial committees. From 1978–80, the premier of Alberta emerged as anglophone leader of a heightened assault upon Ottawa. Like a boxer, sure of a new-found strength, Peter Lougheed swung blow after blow as champion of the provincialists and guardian of Alberta's Heritage Fund. That fund, fed by provincial royalties from oil and gas production, had reached $8 billion by mid 1981. From it the Alberta government made loans to other provinces, including Quebec, reduced provincial taxation and planned a more diversified economy to offset resource depletion. Lougheed, seeking to prevent Ottawa from acquiring a greater share of the revenue bonanza or from asserting stricter marketing and corporate ownership regulations, showed his toughness in several ways. In 1978, in a statement that disconcerted Ontarians particularly, he said:

Those troops, so to speak, who are going to fight to keep Quebec within Canada in the referendum debate ... can't go in naked. They will have to go in armed with and supported by propositions, new arrangements, which will really support those people in Quebec who want to stay within Canada but do not feel the present relationship of an overly centralized direction from the federal government is adequate ... We're responding not only to the people of the west, not only to the people of the Atlantic regions, but also to the people of Quebec ... It's a strong position in terms of Canadian unity and also in terms of Quebec.

After the referendum Lougheed challenged the federal government by progressively cutting back oil production until he got an agreement which sharply modified the national energy policy.

'Alienation' and 'crisis' became the parlance of the journalists as the themes of provincial interest and constitutional change intersected throughout 1980–81. Declaring that the troops who had won the referendum and the federal election now had an obligation to patriate and amend the constitution, the Trudeau government presented to parliament motions which would become, if passed, a request for final British action on the B.N.A. Act. The prime minister was urgent: after fifty years of failing to get unanimity amongst the provinces it was time to act. Not only did the self-respect of Canadians require complete legal control of their constitution, the pledge to Quebec must be honoured. Fundamental also, in the Trudeau argument was the need to entrench in the constitution a charter of personal liberties as integral to 'renewed federalism'.

Acrid fumes from the parliamentary debate concealed an underlying momentum of change and also continuance of traditional patterns of accommodation. A politically debilitated Joe Clark led his Tories in charging that Trudeau's motions were 'illegal' because Ottawa had not secured unanimous consent from the provinces for the proposed amendments and because the government benches did not represent the west. But the accusation that Ottawa's 'unilateral' action was hasty and unconstitutional was vitiated in several ways. Important was the failure of the provincial premiers, in a last ditch conference to produce a consensus. Worse, William Davis and Richard Hatfield, Tory premiers of Ontario and New Brunswick, voiced support for the Trudeau resolutions, declaring the need to preserve sufficient federal authority to ensure economic and cultural policies of more or less equal regional advantage.

Mutual suspicion amongst Trudeau's opponents was the strongest weapon in the Ottawa armoury – but the position taken by the N.D.P. revealed two edges to that weapon. Stung by a 1977 supreme court ruling limiting provincial jurisdiction over natural resources, Premier Blakeney of Saskatchewan lined up with those provinces who thought provincial rights inadequately secured by Ottawa's constitutional 'package'. At the same time the federal N.D.P. leader, Edward Broadbent, having secured from the government an amendment which would guarantee and slightly extend those rights, aligned his party behind the constitutional resolutions. Although four Saskatchewan N.D.P. members rejected Broadbent's position, the result was that 23 western N.D.P. M.P.s endorsed it, virtually demolishing the argument that the government proposed to act on the constitution in defiance of a unanimous West.

As debate raged in the House, the Tories pressed their allegations of 'illegality' to the utmost limits of parliamentary obstruction. In concert with Premiers Lévesque, Peckford of Newfoundland and Lyon of Manitoba they also sought judicial support from provincial courts, and lobbied British M.P.s in a curiously 'colonial' attempt to persuade Westminster to reject the Canadian request – should it ever reach the British parliament. The courts in Manitoba and Quebec decided that the proposed resolutions would be neither illegal nor unconstitutional; the Newfoundland judges dissented from this view; and the British government wisely kept its own counsel.

Ultimately, in order to avoid use of closure, the Liberals agreed to submit the constitutional package to the supreme court of Canada for an opinion, with the clear understanding of speedy parliamentary approval should the verdict be favourable. However, at the very crest of the constitutional crisis there were signs that the worst of the political storm had been weathered. At the beginning of September an agreement between Ottawa and Alberta on dividing the spoils within a revised national energy policy was reached, and similar accords were quickly agreed to by British Columbia and Saskatchewan. As Lougheed joined Trudeau in rejecting the more favourable terms still demanded by the multi-nationals, the N.D.P. rapped both governments for not being tougher on the oil companies who had, according to a federal investigation, 'ripped off' Canadians monumentally over the preceding years.

Equally important, in Newfoundland and Nova Scotia agreements were near on divided federal–provincial jurisdiction and revenues in the Atlantic offshore fields, while Premier Peckford found comfort in Ottawa's support for his proposal to transmit Labrador electric power across Quebec to American markets. An indication of what would be the final outcome came in April when Premier Lévesque, having waited as long as possible after defeat in the referendum, called an election which his *Péquistes* won handily. Claude Ryan, so effective in the referendum campaign, began hastily to push his party further away from the federal Liberals, declaring at a party meeting:

Our first responsibility is to Quebec. It has always been that, perhaps just not stated as clearly in the past. At the same time we are also committed to Canadian federalism. We say the two commitments go together and it has got to be clear to everyone that first and above all we are a Quebec-based party whose first allegiance is to the people of Quebec.

Yet political–economic accomodation had done its work and Ryan was unlikely to find electoral salvation by moving further towards a fuzzy autonomism.

At the end of September the supreme court delivered a Delphic opinion, baffling yet decisive. Ottawa's constitutional resolution, said seven of the nine judges, was entirely legal. Six of the judges, however, with Chief Justice Laskin and two others dissenting, declared that legality would be vitiated by the government's failure to observe the 'federal principle' and constitutional 'convention'. Convention, according to the six judges, required 'substantial' provincial consent to any constitutional amendment affecting the provinces. The six, however, felt unable to say exactly how many provinces might add up to 'substantial'. Both 'sides' at once claimed victory. Trudeau and Chrétien invoked the springtime agreement that speedy parliamentary action would follow a favourable verdict. Clark's Tories, and the 'gang of eight' provincial premiers who had demanded the court referral, proclaimed that the judicial ruling nullified the agreement.

The court's ambivalent opinion, however, while awkward for Ottawa, proved fatal for the dissident premiers. It opened the door to unpredictable obstruction in the British parliament and thus convinced Trudeau that he must settle the issue in Canada before sending his resolution to Westminster. At the same time, with the natural resources question put to rest, seven of the eight dissidents sensed a growing public hostility to their continued obstruction. While they pursued their discussions in the additional time astutely conceded by Ottawa, Trudeau made quite clear his intention to conduct a referendum should the premiers fail to reach an acceptable agreement. All the premiers, save Lévesque, believed a referendum would (in their own province) endorse Ottawa's proposals, eliminate potential obstruction at Westminster, and wreak severe political damage on last-ditch hold-outs. In the early hours of 6 November, after intense, if circuitous, negotiations, a compromise was agreed to by Ottawa and nine of the provincial governments. Premier Hatfield commented succinctly that 'This came about because we heard the voices of Canadians', to which a morose and extremely bitter Lévesque added, 'Once again, Quebec is isolated'.

The key modification agreed to by the federal government was a slight tightening of the amending procedure to require, in most cases, majorities in the federal parliament and in the legislatures of 'at least two-thirds of the provinces that have, in the aggregate, according to the then latest general census, at least 50 per cent of the population of all the provinces'. Even so, the amending formula is less rigid than its American counterpart and contains a provincial rights guarantee requiring legislative endorsement in any province of an amendment which 'derogates from the legislative powers, the proprietary rights or any other rights or privileges' of that province. In removing the alleged requirement of unanimous provincial consent, however, no single province was left with a veto over general amendments and it was this, even more than the entrenched Charter of Rights and Freedoms, that René Lévesque felt unable to accept.

The premier of Quebec was not alone in his political discomfiture. In the House of Commons, when the slightly adjusted constitutional resolution was presented for final debate, Joe Clark's Conservatives found themselves defending positions already abandoned by nine of the ten provincial governments. Thus, in the final stages of debate, only two changes were made, reinforcing the rights of women while leaving untouched those of native peoples; and both resulted from extra-parliamentary pressure.

The constitutional resolution, more complex both in its evolution and in its final form than any previous federal legislation, was passed with the support of Liberal and N.D.P. members and on 8 December moved through the Senate with only token opposition. At the end of 1981, untidy remnants of an untidy process lay scattered about: the Quebec Court of Appeal was listening to the provincial government's argument that Quebec still possessed the right to veto the amendments, and the Court of Appeal in London was hearing the argument of the Indian Association of Alberta that the British government, despite the denials of both Ottawa and London, is still responsible for protecting Indian treaty rights. Yet first reading had been given to the Canada Act at Westminster and passage of the requested legislation was a foregone conclusion.

As with the process of confederation in the 1860s, the renewal process culminating in 1982 had clearly been dominated by one man. Macdonald had envisaged a legislative union which would become an increasingly independent 'auxiliary kingdom'. He had to make many compromises, the most important of which produced a federal rather than a legislative union. Pierre Trudeau originally envisaged a new, written constitution which would be, in the Franco–American style, the 'supreme law'. He, too, made many compromises along the way, the most important of which (like those of Macdonald) involved heavy underwriting of provincial rights. Trudeau and Chrétien, like Macdonald and Cartier, linked their successful defence of central authority to the protection of minorities as well as to national purpose. It was with restrained optimism that Trudeau remarked upon the future: 'If Canada is indeed to be a nation, there must be a national will which is something more than the lowest common denominator among the desires of provincial governments.'

Behind the symbolism of a 'new' constitution lay an even more significant continuity. Despite the penultimate threat of a referendum, the procedure had been thoroughly traditional, the work not of specially elected conventions but of political parties and legislatures. The Clark Tories, by persistent parliamentary obstruction, had induced referral of the procedural question to the supreme court, and that body's ill-defined majority opinion that proceeding with the support of only two provinces would somehow be 'unconstitutional' had led to a further brief delay. The agreement reached between Ottawa and nine provincial governments, however, not only robbed the federal Conservative opposition of its *raison d'être*, it in effect reasserted the supremacy of the political over the judicial in constitutional matters – no matter how much additional business might be added to court agendas by the Charter of Rights and Freedoms. Moreover, in law, the 'new' constitution was to be a series of amendments to the 1867 British North America Act, with *its* accumulated amendments. The heart of the Canadian constitutional process remains unwritten: the relationship, for example, of executive to legislative branches of government and retention of the Queen as the legal source of all authority. The Constitution Act 1982 was enacted in Britain under authority of the Canada Act which was itself an act of the British parliament. What makes all this legislation legally Canadian is clause 2 of the Canada Act: 'No act of the Parliament of the United Kingdom passed after the Canada Act, 1982, comes into force shall extend to Canada as part of its law.' All future constitutional legislation will thus be enacted in Canada in accordance with the new amending formulae. As with the 'divisibility of the crown', the logic of all this tends to elude republican observers, especially those who know that in theory any British parliament can repeal the legislation of its predecessors. The practicality of the process, however, was entirely consonant with an evolutionary Canadian political tradition.

The renewed federal structure, in effect, gives formal expression to existing practices and, to some extent, to political–social goals. Thus 'equalization payments' by Ottawa to guarantee 'reasonably comparable levels of public services at reasonably comparable levels of taxation' become mandatory while the division of jurisdiction over natural resources is made more specific, as is the right of provinces to enter any tax field. Least predictable is the impact of the Charter of Rights and Freedoms entrenched in the Constitution Act. Many of the rights are traditional by common law or treaty; entrenching them in codified form, often with substantial qualification such as the general provision that they are all (save the language rights) subject to 'such reasonable limits prescribed by law as can be demonstrably justified in a free and democratic society', and a provincial 'opting out' provision in certain circumstances, might not lead to the litigious extravaganza feared by critics of a written bill of rights, although by 1986 there was some cause for alarm on this count. With respect to the official languages the charter essentially entrenches existing legislation; but on minority language education rights it goes considerably further. The requirement that provinces provide primary and secondary education for either French or English linguistic minorities 'where the number of those children so warrants' will lead to a direct political confrontation between Ottawa and Quebec. Quebec law (Bill 101) denied English language education to the children of families moving to the province from other parts of Canada. The constitutional challenge to this policy, as well as Lévesque's defeat on the amending formula and on his claim that the provinces opting out of federally financed social-economic programmes should receive compensation from Ottawa, marked out the post-Constitution Act field of battle.

For René Lévesque, the immediate consequences of defeat were traumatic. He himself talked of the 'betrayal' of Quebec, but was badly shaken when a *Péquiste* convention gave a standing ovation to the convicted terrorist Jacques Rose and endorsed a policy of unvarnished secession to be implemented should the P.Q. win a simple majority of seats in the next provincial election. Claiming that the convention had been manipulated by 'agents provocateurs from God knows where', the premier set on foot a membership referendum to undo the convention's radical lurch. Whatever the outcome of that referendum, it was clear that the Parti Québecois had emerged deeply divided from the constitutional wrangle. With all of Quebec's seventy-four seats in the federal parliament held by Liberals, none of whom had voted against the constitutional resolution, the likelihood of the P.Q. being able to win a provincial election on a straight separatist platform seemed more remote than ever. Thus, too, the option of running *Péquiste* candidates in a federal election, fleetingly threatened by Lévesque, lacked credibility.

During the final months of constitutional manoeuvring the economy was sliding into serious recession and, in company with the governments of Canada's principal trading partners, Ottawa seemed to vacillate. Under heavy public pressure to reverse the threatening upward curves of inflation, interest and unemployment, the government received conflicting advice from the leading economists who disagreed, particularly, on the extent to which Canadian interest rates and other money supply policy had to keep pace with the American graphs in order to prevent a flight of investment capital. Mortgagees, small businessmen and farmers trembled before the spectre of insolvency. Similarly, in labour relations, irascibility was the order of the day. With a strike rate second to none among the industrial states Canada had evolved no system of worker participation in management, while at the same time unions were growing rapidly both in size and power – particularly in private and public service sectors.

2 2

Sacred Trust?

WHILE it would be rash to suggest that there was no relationship between general economic conditions and some startling political shifts in the years following 1982, nevertheless noneconomic forces played prominent roles. As in the past, popular perceptions of how power was used, of cultural identity and regional disparity, and not least, suspicions of political longevity toppled governments, cut down majorities and etched more deeply some familiar patterns.

Although 'the economy' slumped severely from the middle of 1981 to the end of 1982 recovery was equally marked in the following four years. The vigorous growth of those years, however, was uneven regionally, by age group and by occupation. Recovery after 1982 was very slow to affect structural unemployment. Service industries, especially in the increasingly specialized areas of business management, communications, finance, insurance and real estate, led the way; indeed, they had scarcely suffered duirng the 1982 slump. Changes in the structure of the economy, together with external influences, however, produced politically significant effects. The national rate of unemployment reached nearly 12 per cent in 1984 and by 1986 was still hovering around 9 per cent. In Newfoundland, however, unemployment in 1986 was at more than 20 per cent, in the Maritimes about 14 per cent, in Quebec 13 per cent, in British Columbia 15 per cent, in Alberta 12 per cent, while Manitoba and Saskatchewan were less than 8 per cent and Ontario edged lowest to 6 per cent. With the fall in world oil prices beginning in 1981 the Alberta energy boom ground to a near halt; unemployed people of all kinds gravitated to Ontario or British Columbia. The Lake Ontario conurbation centring on Toronto flourished almost extravagantly, receiving the lion's share of industrial investment and cementing its position as the country's financial capital.

In addition to regional anomalies other disquieting features appeared across the face of prosperity. People under twenty-five constituted a very disproportionate percentage of the unemployed. Part-time employment became more and more usual, especially for women, and wages in this category were appreciably depressed; a growing number of professional and managerial people at middle age found themselves redundant. In Vancouver, Montreal and Toronto, let alone St John's, extreme poverty rubbed shoulders with conspicuous affluence. The swollen rolls of 'beneficiaries' of unemployment insurance and other social payments began to decline after 1983 but much community damage had been suffered. Some business leaders, eyeing ever larger government deficits, pressed for cutbacks in the social security system; others proposed replacing that very complex structure with a guaranteed annual income law.

Amongst responses to the changing economic structure was a steady growth of labour unions, whose members now number 3,800,000. Not surprisingly, the three largest unions are composed of public service employees. More remarkable is a comparison with the United States. Since the mid-1950s American union strength has steadily declined and now stands at about 18 per cent of the non-agricultural labour force, while the comparable Canadian figure has reached 40 per cent. An American analyst has observed that 'the major characteristic distinguishing the two countries is that in Canada more workers are organized within virtually every industry and in particular within government, manufacturing and construction.' Moreover, unlike the American case, Canadian union leaders are taking aim at the largely unorganized groups of office, technical and professional workers in the private sector, where a crack was opened in 1984 when a small union of bank employees secured recognition after a tough fight.

While the economic nationalism of F.I.R.A. and N.E.P. would be sharply modified following the election of 1984, cumulative traditions of positive government and labour political action remained strong. As unionism deepened its roots, the Canadian Labour Congress strengthened its support of the N.D.P. Most observers concurred in viewing such 'un-Americanism' as representing a difference in values as much as a perception of economic advantage: in effect the difference between collectivist community criteria as opposed to suspicion of government *per se*. Be that as it may, the C.L.C. showed a marked concern for qualitative as well as quantitative objectives. Although many members of its constituent unions owe their jobs to industries which either pollute the environment or are involved in American-related military production, the C.L.C. is a prominent advocate of expensive pollution controls which are strenuously opposed by many American unions; it is also, along with the National Farmers' Union, on the steering committee of the Canadian Peace Alliance. The C.P.A. is the umbrella organization of anti-nuclear groups and thus supports a nuclear-weapons-free zone in Canada and 'ending all funding, research, transport, testing, production and deployment of nuclear weapons systems in Canada.'

Calling for the 'redirection of money from wasteful military spending to the funding of human needs through a program of conversion and retraining', the Peace Alliance, which is also supported by the major churches and some 250 nuclear disarmament groups, takes special aim at Canada's involvement in the development and testing of cruise missiles. Such concerns, which have considerable economic implications, together with a more vigorous assertion of women's rights to 'equal pay for work of equal value' than is made by U.S. unions, have led to a marked shift away from 'international unionism'. In 1983 such a trend seemed unlikely. In that year Lynn Williams, head of the Canadian section of the United Steel Workers, won the presidency of the international union in a sharply contested election. At almost the same time the United Automobile Workers accepted from the financially beleaguered Chrysler Corporation a pay pause for its American section while the Canadian U.A.W. director, Robert White, held out successfully for a much better deal from Chrysler

Canada. Admist mutual recriminations across the border White spearheaded a breakaway; in 1985 the tie was snapped and a national union, the Canadian Automobile Workers, was firmly established, enriched by several million dollars from U.A.W., Detroit. In 1986 the Canadian section of the International Woodworkers of America followed suit. Whether or not these moves amount to a watershed, they seem clearly to have resulted from differing views not only of immediate economic benefit but also of social-political values. Significantly, White is an outspoken supporter of the N.D.P. and his activities in this respect were not the least of the irritants in the former international union.

Other aspects of differing Canadian and American perceptions appeared from a similar mixture of causes. Perhaps the most important are attitudes towards the role of the state in economic life; and divergence here was to reach crisis proportions by 1986. Both Canada and the United States suffered mushrooming fiscal deficits in the 1980s. The American was due, principally, to heavy spending on the vast panoply of defence production, a continuing shift of consumer goods manufacturing to low-cost countries and immense private bank loans to underdeveloped nations. The resulting annual deficits, which reached $170 billion by 1986, sparked a potent demand for protection against foreign competition in American markets. Canada was not unaffected by this, especially because many American interests thought Canada 'unfairly' subsidized producers in everything from primary resources to culture. Depending on one's point of view, Canada appeared to Americans as neo-mercantilist, socialist or simply unfair competition.

There was a certain irony in the world's leading imperial power seeking protection against a junior industrialized state. Yet, despite the disparity in population-economic strength, trade between the two countries was far greater than that between any other two nations in the world. Moreover, by 1985, there was a trade surplus in Canada's favour of about $20 billion in total trade exchange of nearly $169 billion. Some of this was due to the auto pact dating from the 1960s by which American-owned auto companies must produce at least one car in Canada for every car sold in Canada. Much more of the trade surplus, however, resulted from a decline in the value of the Canadian dollar to about .71 American. Again, while Canada's fiscal deficit increased to more than $30 billion in 1986, almost 90 per cent of the federal government's borrowing was within the country. Probably because of this and of the Bank of Canada's tight restrictions on the growth of the money supply, inflation rates declined from their previous high points. On the other hand, non-governmental 'service transactions' showed a deficit of almost $20 billion, made up largely of dividend payments on foreign investment in Canada and including the $2 billion by which Canadian tourist spending abroad exceeded the spending of visitors to Canada. Again, since 1975, Canadian direct investment abroad has been greater annually than had foreign investment in Canada; Canadians began buying back some of the foreign-owned equity, partly spurred by inducements offered under the N.E.P.

Such statistics, and volumes more like them, seemed to confuse economists as much as lay people; certainly they can be juggled and 'prioritized' to produce contradictory policy prescriptions. Nevertheless, some aspects were sufficiently prominent to resist denial or obfuscation. Per capita, Canadian businessmen have more invested in the United States than do Americans in Canada: the Reichmans' group of companies, for example, show annual profits of $20 billion; builders and proprietors of the World Finance Center in New York, they are only among the most visible signs of Canadian penetration of the American economy. Yet while such operations, together with the trade surplus, contributed to American protectionist claims that Canadian governments subsidize business too heavily (through direct grants, loans and tax concessions), the total direct American investment in Canada grew steadily, mostly generated from profits accruing from prior investment in the country. While investment from West Germany, Japan, Belgium and the U.K. all grew, American investment (both direct and portfolio) remained overwhelmingly large. One clear result of the 'branch plant' aspect of many manufacturing and primary industries remained a low level of spending on research and development; at little more than 1 per cent of G.N.P. Canadian R and D was at the bottom of figures recorded by O.E.C.D. states. With all these pluses and minuses, and an economic growth rate averaging 4 per cent since 1982, one's view of 'prosperity' depended upon where one was employed — or unemployed. Canadians generally seemed less concerned about 'the economy' than about ownership, control and distribution of its product — whether goods or services. They showed, too, deepening awareness of their country's involvement in a depressingly nuclear-oriented alliance structure.

In the dying month's of Pierre Trudeau's last administration it was fashionable to proclaim that he had introduced American style leadership or presidential politics into Canadian government. Just enough political water has flowed under the Rideau bridges to justify rejecting that assessment. Trudeau was prototypical rather than atypical in this respect. His epic battles with René Lévesque recalled similar warfare between Macdonald and Mowat, King and Hepburn, as well as the historic tensions inherent in the cultural and federal structure of the country. Indeed, Canadian political life has always been as much or more leadership-oriented than has American, at least in part because the powers of prime ministers and premiers are, in practice, greater than those of presidents and governors. Again, Trudeau had more precise goals than those permitted a leader within the American party system.

By 1982 those goals, with unavoidable compromises, had largely been achieved. The passionate, cerebral Quebecker sought new paths along which to express and, perhaps, to justify the redefined Canada. Travelling abroad more frequently he gave strong support to a North–South dialogue which might address concretely the dangerous inequities between industrialized and developing nations. In particular, he offered unequivocal backing to the Contadora plan for stabilizing Central America, which further irritated Washington, whose interventions in the region were escalating insistently. When Soviet interceptors downed a Korean Airlines plane in September,

1983, Ottawa quietly suspended Russian landing rights at Gander; but Trudeau pointedly condemned 'megaphone diplomacy' and, by implication, President Reagan's bellicosity. He had similarly urged caution in responding to Poland's 'Solidarity' and was to castigate Washington's unilateral procedure in 'liberating' Grenada. Unperturbed by the frost that was gathering upon Canadian—American relations (and which was deepened by a powerful American attack upon F.I.R.A. and N.E.P.) Trudeau launched a vigorous 'peace initiative' in the autumn of 1983.

The initiative involved the prime minister visiting major world leaders to propose their meeting to discuss means of moderating the perilous levels of acerbity in East—West relations, and to agree upon formal renunciation of first use of nuclear weapons and a deeper commitment to nuclear disarmament negotiations. While some Canadians were caustic, dismissing the 'Trudeau pilgrimage' as a cynical ploy to offset Liberal party decline in opinion polls, many also expressed warm support. While Trudeau's proposals were well received in most Commonwealth countries, Washington was distinctly chilly; the Pentagon, in particular, remained adamantly opposed to renouncing the first-use option. Although Ottawa had just given permission for a lengthy programme of cruise missile testing in the Canadian north, exceedingly hostile comments became the order of the day. When the number three man in the U.S. state department blurted out that the Trudeau peace move resembled the mutterings of a misguided leftist high on marijuana, the prime minister retorted: 'The kind of third-rate, third-level pipsqueaks who say I'm not allowed to participate in the peace process because we don't contribute enough to N.A.T.O. — that's baloney'. While Trudeau received the Albert Einstein Peace Prize, that accolade came after his second retirement.

In February 1984, after a celebrated late night 'walk in the snowstorm', Trudeau announced his departure. Business leaders were edgy about mounting deficits, the West was still deeply alienated, the permanence of an economic recovery which had been underway for a bare twelve months was still in doubt and party councils were divided. An astute pollster summarized the political situation thus: 'Trudeau had really shaken the country. Every change had meant a fight and the effect was a massive culture shock.' Electoral defeat appeared more than likely; Trudeau had served longer than Laurier and his imprint upon Canada was probably deeper than that left by any previous francophone leader. The time seemed propitious for what the departing leader called a sabbatical — a parting shot which disconcerted some of his colleagues who recalled vividly the aftermath of his 1979 resignation. In the ensuing leadership convention, largely because of a party tradition of francophone-anglophone alternation, the prime ministerial mantle fell upon John Turner rather than the folksy and popular Jean Chrétien. Turner, after a brusque resignation in 1975 as Trudeau's finance minister, had spent the interval as a corporation lawyer on Toronto's Bay Street; by 1984 he seemed politically rusty and rather obviously on the party's right wing. Plainly *non grata* to Trudeau Liberals he made a calamitous error in calling an early election rather than waiting for time to smooth over the party's gaping divisions.

A period of reconciliation would have been wise, also, in the light of the drastic changes in the Tory party. With knives flashing, many of Joe Clark's *confrères* had openly challenged his ineffectual performance; in February 1983 Clark resigned. In the following June he became a candidate in a leadership convention where his critics carried a majority for their challenger, Brian Mulroney. Fluently bilingual and a native of Quebec (where Irish can often be French by adoption), the new Tory leader planned to crack traditional Liberal monopoly of his province, retain the strong western and maritime bases and make the Conservatives finally the 'government party'. Although Mulroney had never held elective position, he had many distinct advantages. From lowly beginnings in Baie-Comeau, he had risen, by 1976, to the presidency of the American-owned Iron Ore Company of Canada. He was thus well known to many corporate executives in the United States; he was, by the same token, sympathetic to the notion

of a continental economy. He was also a close friend of
Robert Bourassa, who had appointed him to a highly visible
position on the Cliche Commission, which investigated corruption in Quebec's construction industry. A diametric opposite of the issue-oriented Trudeau, Mulroney was closer to
Clark in his perception of political purpose. Eager rather than
reluctant to enter politics, he concentrated upon the mechanics
of the process : personal networking, party structure, the lubri-
cation of patronage. While at times he spoke the new right
language of a Thatcher or a Reagan, stressing the need to reduce
both inflation and deficits, to trim government, privatize many
crown corporations and liberate the job-creating private sector from 'over-regulation', he would also describe universal
social programmes as a 'sacred trust'. No ideologue, pragmatic
to a fault, Mulroney would campaign on the high ground :
the Liberal government was tired, arrogant and corrupt; it had
indulged too long in the politics of confrontation; and it had
alienated the Americans. With beguiling charm he was to
garner an unprecedented electoral majority with calls for cultural conciliation, moderation of Ottawa arrogance, restraint
in the use of patronage, more business-like management of the
economy and an open door to investment from abroad.

Well before election day in September 1984 it was clear
that Mulroney's personal advantages and careful tactics of
criticism minus precise policy statements would simply provide icing on a cake cooked by the Liberal party's warring
chefs. John Turner's campaign lacked coherence and the leader
appeared indecisive, changing aides in midstream and unsure
of his own position in the left–right party spectrum. His rather
stiff appearance and staccato speaking-manner lessened his
otherwise handsome television image and failed to mask a fatal
mistake : challenged by Mulroney to revoke a flagrant round
of midnight patronage appointments he declared that he had
'no option' but to agree to his predecessor's request that they
be made, and stood firmly by them. Mulroney made the most
of this querulous response. The election returns startled even
the Tories : 211 Conservative seats to 40 for the Liberals and
30 for the N D.P. The Liberal stranglehold on Quebec had ap-

parently been ended, their appeal in the West was nearly zero and was at best shaky in the Maritimes. Unlike the Diefenbaker sweep of 1958, however, 1984 wrought far greater damage proportionately upon the Liberals than upon the New Democrats. Ed Broadbent, indeed, continued to top opinion polls for leadership quality. He had waged effective war against both Turner and Mulroney, dubbing them the 'corporate clones'. Demanding that they come down from the '45th floor' to confront the concerns of 'ordinary Canadians', Broadbent hammered at the issues of unemployment, pollution and resource control, extra-billing by doctors within the national medical scheme and gender equality. Emerging with 19 per cent of the vote the N.D.P. preserved its established base, whereas in 1958 it had faced near annihilation. The election had confirmed a multi- rather than a two-party system. A startling dissipation of Mulroney's immense mandate in the first two years of his government, together with deep political tremors in several provinces, was to magnify the 'third party' threat. As the older parties veered toward the right the N.D.P. continued to modulate its rhetoric; by 1986 the party was viewed with alarm by 'red Tories' and 'reform Liberals' as a serious contender for that traditional route to office, the middle of the road.

Volatile provincial politics expressed an older Canadian tradition : the ensuring of counterweights against too great a power at Ottawa by ensconcing governments in the provinces of a different hue from that to which federal authority is deputed. The pattern was especially evident in Quebec and Ontario. In the fall of 1982 Claude Ryan, ruminating on his defeat by Lévesque the previous year, had resigned the Liberal leadership. Robert Bourassa, who had also been toppled by Lévesque (in 1976), had spent the intervening years preparing to resume the Liberal leadership. By 1983 he was ready to accomplish an unprecedented political rebirth. In an October leadership convention he captured 75 per cent of the votes and at once set the party's sails to catch the stiffening winds of P.Q. disillusionment.

No less *féderaliste* than before, Bourassa nevertheless understood well Lévesque's comment following Mulroney's elevation to the Tory leadership : 'Whenever a Quebecker has been elected leader of a party in Ottawa, it has cost Quebec dear; now that we have two, it will certainly cost us dear one way or the other.' The comment's characteristic ambiguity was soon dissipated; the cost would be paid by the P.Q. Already the party was slipping. Lévesque had been compelled to legislate pay cuts and tougher working conditions throughout the public services, whose employees, especially teachers, had been his foremost supporters. Moreover, the principal goals of his extended quiet revolution, other than sovereignty, had been achieved. Although the courts had ruled some clauses of Bill 101 unconstitutional, including the provision for unilingualism in the national assembly, francophone Quebeckers had clearly become 'masters in their own house'. Montreal's *Ecole des Hautes Etudes Commerciales* had turned out dozens of francophone administrators who were now in executive offices throughout both private and public sectors. Most Quebec anglophones had become, more or less, bilingual and some *émigrés* were trickling back to a Montreal they had always felt to be home. Sensing that the constitutional question (Quebec still refused to ratify the 1982 amendments) was beginning to generate *ennui* rather than *séparatiste* excitement, Lévesque tried to put sovereignty on the back burner. He succeeded only in dividing his party. In June 1985 he resigned as premier and leader. His successor, Pierre-Marc Johnson, whose father had been Union Nationale premier in 1966-8, completed the 'union nationalization' of the P.Q., making it a traditional Quebec nationalist party. Bourassa's refurbished Liberals swept back into power in December 1985 with the promise of a hydro-electric mega-project and a strongly business-oriented administration.

There were significant shadings to the political picture in Quebec. On the one hand, Bourassa had offended his federal Liberal *confrères* by giving at least tacit support to his friend Mulroney's 1984 campaign. He thus held a credit balance in Conservative Ottawa, and lost no time in demanding several constitutional amendments (to further enhance Quebec jurisdictions) as the price for Quebec acceptance of the 1982 'settlement'. Yet, while thus currying *nationaliste* favour and also moving his party towards a trendy neo-conservatism, he widened the political gap left by the apparent death tremors of the social democratic P.Q. For the first time the N.D.P. seemed poised to crack the Quebec sound barrier; by 1986 opinion polls recorded the New Democrat's federal-level support in the province at 25 per cent, fractionally ahead of the Conservatives. Political undulations elsewhere pointed in varying degree to confirmation of a multiparty system across the country.

By 1984 Ontario had been ruled by a succession of Tory governments for an astonishing forty-one years. Although three times faced with a minority government situation (1943, 1975 and 1977), they had survived by astute management, cautious budgeting and extensive patronage dispensed by their Big Blue Machine — lovingly regarded by their supporters, most daunting to their opponents. Adopting a modest range of reform policies such as legislated rent controls they had successfully pre-empted a lethargic rural Liberalism and the more strident reformism of the N.D.P. Yet, one month after Mulroney's massive federal victory, and with all signs pointing to a Bourassa triumph in Quebec, Premier William Davis announced his resignation — after nearly fourteen years of such avuncular government. While opinion polls placed the Tories well to the front, Davis's responsive political antennae may well have sensed the time-for-a-change mood that was abroad in the land. In any event, the Big Blue Machine snarled up. Tory managers underestimated the impact of an unemployment rate still running around 10 per cent and, also, of a fresh surge of egalitarian sentiment in their traditionally complacent fiefdom. Subsidization of Japanese auto assembly plants, rhetoric rather than action on environment controls, natural resource management, day-care facilties and similar matters all threatened the Tory dynasty. An equally ominous circumstance might have been identified by any budding Tory historian : substantial change in Ottawa's political colouration was likely to invite equal and opposite change at Queen's Park, Toronto. Instead of responding to strong, essentially urban, social pressures, a Conservative convention in January 1985 chose Frank Miller, a not quite couth right-winger, to succeed the smooth, pipe-smoking Davis. The more astute Tory apparatchiks had opposed Miller, who at once confirmed their judgement by calling an election for May.

Ontario's Liberals, sensing the uneasy leftward trend of opinion (and suspicion of concurrent Tory power in Ottawa, Toronto and Edmonton), borrowed reform planks from the N.D.P. Their leader, David Peterson, a young lawyer-businessman, had been nearly invisible in opposition; in manner, however, he was remarkably similar to the mild, conciliatory Davis and this proved advantageous. Most observers expected the N.D.P. to become either official opposition or government. Bob Rae, a Rhodes scholar who had become almost a media star as financial critic on the N.D.P. front bench at Ottawa, had taken over the party's Ontario leadership and had outshone Peterson in opposition. Rae eschewed overtly socialist appeals as the N.D.P. and the Liberals campaigned for the reform vote. Peterson's strong rural support and his aura of stability garnered greater gains for the Liberals than those achieved by the strongly labour-oriented N.D.P. The result left Miller's government in a minority (fifty-two seats), the Liberals as official opposition (forty-eight seats) and Rae holding the balance of power (twenty-five seats).

While the minority situation was by no means new its resolution was. In a flurry of negotiations Rae and his colleagues concluded that the electorate had determined to end the long Tory hegemony. Moreover, since the Liberals had borrowed so many N.D.P. planks (such as ending 'extra-billing' by doctors, preservation and extension of rent controls, public funding of separate Catholic high schools, women's equal pay legislation, provision of all public services in French and strengthening both environmental controls and labour legislation), it would be proper as well as expedient to support them in overthrowing the government. But, to avoid the instability inherent in a minority situation without shackling the N.D.P. in a European-style coalition, Rae and Peterson signed an accord. The precedent-setting document provided that the government would implement specified reforms, including those just mentioned, and would wait at least two years before dissolving the legislature. During that period, negative votes would not involve 'confidence' — i.e. defeat of the government. On 1 July Peterson became premier and in the following months a great deal of the 'reform agenda' was enacted.

While the substantial political turnarounds of 1984–5 at Ottawa and in the two largest provinces were not precisely mirrored elsewhere, various political indicators gave little comfort to Mulroney's federal cohorts. While Pat Carney, Mulroney's able energy minister, negotiated a shared-jurisdiction settlement of Newfoundland's claims to the resources of the continental shelf, the Tory premier Peckford faced non-stop battles with the province's unions, particularly those in the public sector. By 1986 opinion polls showed that the N.D.P., with the popular Peter Fenwick as leader, had become more worrisome than the Liberals in Britain's oldest colony. The rest of Atlantic Canada saw modified versions of the same political evolution. Traditionally suppliant at the federal throne, the Maritimes have been almost as resistant as Quebec to multipartyism. The trick had always been to guess who would form the government at Ottawa and to vote accordingly — an exception to the political counterbalancing noticeable elsewhere. There had been the occasional socialist win in the Nova Scotia coal-steel constituencies, but no reliable 'third party' base. Now an upward curve in the opinion polls, while not indicating an imminent breakthrough, recorded an average N.D.P. support of 19 per cent across the three provinces.

In the West, Howard Pauley's N.D.P. took Manitoba from the Tories in 1981. After weathering a fierce anglophone storm of protest against legislation designed to undo the unconstitutional inferiority imposed upon the French language in the 1890s and during World War I (at the cost of adulterating the long-overdue policy), the N.D.P. retained power in a 1986 spring election. In Saskatchewan, where Allan Blakeney had led the New Democrats to their biggest electoral sweep in 1978, the N.D.P. lost some cohesion as a result of differing opinions about supporting the Trudeau constitutional package in 1981-2. That, together with over-confidence, a sharp confrontation with a public service union and an attractive new Tory leader, produced a Conservative electoral victory in 1982. The new premier, Grant Devine ('the farmer who just happened to get a Ph.D.'), launched no major assault upon institutions established by previous 'socialist governments (save privatization of the land bank), but confidence in his ability to guard provincial interests (especially in resource revenue matters) waned with the advent of the Mulroney government in Ottawa. The Saskatchewan Conservatives won a 1986 election with the narrowest of margins.

With the resignation of Peter Lougheed in 1985 came another substantial rumble in provincial politics. Falling energy prices had brought widespread distress, two bank failures, considerable emigration and a steady drain on the still fat Alberta Heritage Fund. It was becoming clear also that economic diversification which was to have been financed by the province's boom-time oil and gas revenues had not occurred. Nevertheless, when Lougheed resigned, to be succeeded by the less forceful Donald Getty, most observers minimized the possibility of serious opposition appearing in the legislature. When an election was called in 1986, the Liberals took one seat while the N.D.P. moved from one to sixteen seats. For the first time since 'Bible Bill' Aberhart had electrified the foothills in the 1930s Alberta entered the multiparty system.

In British Columbia a yet more complex situation led to a surprising result. In May 1983 Premier William Bennett's Social Credit government was returned in a rowdy election featuring Social Credit warnings of a socialist dictatorship, N.D.P. counter-protestations and a lacklustre Liberal effort to re-enter the battle. Dave Barrett resigned the N.D.P. leadership and Bennett launched a full-fledged neo-conservative programme: draconian budget-paring, wholesale dismissals from the public services, all-out war against the unions and termination of seniority and tenure patterns. By playing upon particular union interests the premier warded off a serious threat from 'Solidarity', a faltering union attempt to mobilize British Columbia's traditional labour power. Completing the construction of Vancouver's Expo 86 with the help of unorganized workers,

Bennett turned the premiership over to William Vander Zalm. A self-made entrepreneur who had been born in Holland, Vander Zalm exuded boisterous confidence in west-coast private initiative. Nervous about the languishing lumber industry and above-average unemployment the new premier seized upon the middle-class euphoria of a successful world's fair to call an early election. After three years of confrontationist turmoil, Vander Zalm distanced himself from the Bennett phenomenon. Without repudiating his predecessor's policies he stressed only the need to abandon strife and concentrate on finding ways to create private-sector jobs. The election appeared not to turn on the issues of social-economic policy which the N.D.P. tried to keep in the forefront, but upon leadership imagery. Barrett's successor, Robert Skelly, was a quiet, even diffident, highschool teacher and no match for his opponent's radiant self-assurance. What had looked to be a tough battle turned suddenly into a solid Social Credit victory. Whether or not Vander Zalm's almost Reaganite political style would disillusion any substantial number of his supporters remained to be seen; shortly after his victory at the polls he called for expanded British Columbia trade with South Africa.

There was little in all the white water of provincial politics or in the jittery state of Canadian—American relations to brighten Brian Mulroney's first two years in office. It was not surprising that he should continue to stress what he had tirelessly reiterated in his campaigning : the need of civility in Ottawa's relations with provincial governments and with Washington, and avoidance of anything 'that violated the public trust or anything that displayed a degree of malice toward the Canadian people or . . . that offended the sense of propriety and dignity of our institutions.' Aware, too, that the Diefenbaker-Clark legacy (at least in the public mind) was one of maladroit bungling and of failing to accommodate Quebec's aspirations, Mulroney strove to balance images, patronage and the regional dispensing of Ottawa's largesse.

In the absence of global policy conception much depended upon specific actions and, especially, upon sound, honest administration. It was unavoidable that the credibility of the prime minister and his cabinet colleagues would become the litmus test. By the end of 1986 the government had registered some questionable results. There had been five ministerial resignations for reasons ranging from serious conflict of interest charges to biased administration and dubious morality. Any new government may expect some such difficulties, especially with a truly cumbersome parliamentary majority and the need to gratify many new and untried members. The prime minister's own credibility, however, became enmeshed when he denied knowing of an administrative decision to permit the sale of contaminated tuna, a decision about which most people believed he must at least have been advised. The brief furore over 'tunagate' added to a general impression that Mulroney attributed more importance to political personality than to policy substance or administrative integrity and that he was surprisingly indecisive. Quickly reflected in opinion polls this perception obscured the principal pluses of his first two years: moderate decline of inflation, interest rates, unemployment and the federal deficit. While none of these was spectacular they could all be applauded, except by those who saw unemployment figures (particularly their unequal regional incidence) as still unacceptable. Perhaps the most substantial change was in the atmosphere of the now regular first ministers' conferences; but this, too, was to be vitiated by transparently political criteria for distributing federal favours amongst the provinces and constituencies.

Indecision and vacillation weakened the potential of Mulroney's huge majority. Committed to budget-cutting, the government proposed to limit the 'indexing' of old age pensions; in the face of a 'grey-power', popular protest the proposal was simply withdrawn. When finance minister Michael Wilson suggested other cuts in social programmes (such as family allowances, which he thought should not be paid to the rich), the prime minister backed off, declaring that the universality of such programmes was a 'sacred trust'. Since 40 per cent of federal budgets is allocated to social spending and another 20 per cent to paying interest on the public debt, little room was left for serious deficit reduction. Those areas in which substantial cuts were made — the C.B.C., the National Research Council, the Canada Council and other cultural institutions — contained the country's most articulate people. One coincidence proved particularly embarrassing: in 1986 a Nobel Prize for chemistry was awarded to John Polanyi of the University of Toronto. Polanyi, following post-doctoral research at the N.R.C., had accurately defined the conditions necessary for a chemical laser. He commented astringently on cutbacks at the N.R.C. and also upon Star Wars, which he dubbed 'hare-brained'. Because the government had left the door wide open to Canadian corporate involvement in the Strategic Defence Initiative (which involves a central role for laser technology) and gave lip-service to the need for greater spending on research and development, policy incoherence came prominently into view.

Other Ottawa policy thrusts indicated a more surprising shortfall between an ideological stance and action to implement it: Margaret Thatcher's 'politics of conviction' seemed no part of the Mulroney formula. Despite campaign calls for privatization and deregulation, Air Canada, the C.B.C., Petro-Canada and most other large crown corporations remained in place. The prime minister seemed to be saying that most of the social-economic structure would be no more than tinkered with: 'Some people,' he remarked in 1985, 'want to buy the C.B.C. The C.B.C. is not for sale. Air Canada is not for sale. There may be some persuasive arguments in the case of Air Canada ... in regard to disposition of equity. I'll take a look at it. But Canada needs a national airline.' The tax and regulatory features of the National Energy Policy were largely removed; but the government sprang quickly to the assistance of the oil-gas industry with heavy tax relief following the near collapse of world energy prices in 1986. And the Canadian Radio-television and Telecommunications Commission retained its power to regulate all aspects of broadcasting and telecommunications. Far from 'taking government out of business', the Tories seemed to guard the ramparts of neo-mercantilism. Subsidization in many forms, together with 'political spending' across the provinces, led to mounting federal–provincial tension; the very nature of Canada's 'mixed economy' also loomed large as a roadblock in trade negotiations with the United States.

The Liberals had been adept at pork barrel politics but their successors more than matched them. The prime minister himself funnelled unusually large sums into roads and even a penitentiary (against strong departmental opinion) in his Quebec riding of Manicouagin. Equally striking was the general pattern of federal contracting and regional development expenditures. Because the Conservatives were understandably anxious to safeguard their newly acquired electoral base in Quebec, that province received a markedly disproportionate share of federal spending, at the expense of smaller provinces such as Newfoundland, whose unemployment rate was nearly twice that of Quebec. A peak of concern was reached in 1986 when Ottawa allotted a substantial contract to service newly acquired CF-18 fighter jets to the Quebec-based Canadair Ltd rather than to Manitoba's Bristol Aerospace Ltd. Debate about the relative capabilities of the two firms raged against the undoubted fact that federal Supply and Services contracts awarded to Manitoba had declined 27 per cent in the preceding year. Maintenance of a neo-mercantilist and extremely federal polity would be no advantage in forwarding the project which lay closest to the prime minister's heart.

Having called for an improved relationship with the United States and an open door to foreign investment, Mulroney moved quickly to demonstrate that both his Irish lineage and knowledge of American corporate life could be useful. On 17 March 1985 he met with President Reagan in Quebec City. The public aspect of the 'Shamrock Summit' included television coverage of the two leaders and their wives on stage singing 'When Irish Eyes are Smiling'. Savouring somewhat of Hollywood, the meeting nevertheless convinced Mulroney that he had Reagan's ear as well as his basic agreement to launch negotiations for an early dismantling of all trade barriers between the two countries. The president promised that he 'would use all his energies to pre-empt any move that would put Canada in peril from protectionism'. Two teams were assembled and began their discussions in the spring of 1986. By that time

Mulroney had nailed 'Free Trade' firmly to the masthead of Tory policy; within months this appeared to be, at best, a risky political gamble.

As debate moved from mild interest to heated controversy, public opinion polls recorded declining support for a continental common market: from a high of 78 per cent in 1984 to a dubious bare majority at the end of 1986. The free trade panacea had been decisively rejected electorally in 1891 and 1911 and reversed as secret policy by Mackenzie King in 1948, always because most Canadians doubted its economic benefits and saw it as a threat to their autonomy. Thus, while a number of leading economists argued that the country would benefit from still easier access to the American market and from a strong dose of tougher competition at home, they could not agree on which industries, regions or categories of employment would suffer in the process of adjustment — or how much. More important, the Americans insisted that *all* 'impediments' to trade, including restricted access to financial and other service sectors and 'cultural industries' must be on the negotiating table; they spoke, too, of the 'right of establishment' for multi-nationals and raised insistently the questions of Canada's industrial subsidization, regional equalization payments and even social security programmes as obstacles to creating a 'level field' of competition. Of equal delicacy was the matter of provincial participation. At the outset Mulroney assured the premiers that they would be constantly consulted during the negotiations; but this left open the question of ratification. The Americans, probably correctly, began to doubt that Ottawa could sell all the provinces on a comprehensive treaty; certainly Ontario and Quebec remained fundamentally protectionist. Indeed, the trade talks revealed to many Canadians the extent of their own interprovincial trade impediments — without producing any great demand for change.

If the drift of opinion, led by labour, nationalist groups and some spokesmen for manufacturers, seemed to duplicate that of 1911 and to be swayed by worries about conserving Canada's mixed economy and sovereignty, the Americans seemed almost to fan the flames of opposition. President Reagan, whose influence upon congressional attitudes had virtually vanished by the middle of his second term, was unable to stem the tide of protectionism in the United States. Wincing from existing levels of foreign competition and huge trade deficits, various American interests secured a series of 'countervailing duties' on items imported from Canada — ranging from groundfish and steel to cedar shakes and shingles. By the end of 1986 effective American pressure for countervailing action against 'unfairly subsidized' Canadian exports had produced what looked more like a trade war than progress towards free trade; the American negotiators had declared, too, that the right of countervail would remain even should a treaty be achieved. In these circumstances, the argument that Canada should employ the machinery of G.A.T.T. rather than bilateral negotiation with the United States gained strength. Some of those who had originally endorsed the free trade notion began to talk rather of enhanced trade and the possibility of further 'sectoral' pacts such as the Defence Production Sharing agreement or the Auto Pact of 1965. Yet even such sectoral arrangements came under fire from political economists such as Stephen Clarkson for generating 'technologically dependent, managerially backward and economically weak industries'. Fall-out from the sluggish free trade 'initiative' was potentially lethal. Originating as the centrepiece of a special relationship between a president and a prime minister, it drew with it a second credibility problem : that of a tattered White House.

Other aspects of the personal connexion also soured. Despite action by Ontario to reduce sulphur-dioxide emissions at Sudbury, and joint federal–provincial progress on industrial waste disposal methods, Reagan still dragged his feet on acid rain and environmental protection generally. The most he conceded was the appointment of two 'envoys' to 'identify efforts' to reduce acid rain. In January 1986 the envoys' tranquillizing report recommended voluntary rather than mandatory controls and that the U.S. allot $5 billion (equally apportioned between government and business) to develop the necessary technology. Reagan formally accepted the recommendations but launched no effort to extract a congressional commitment — and none came.

In the spring of 1983 the president had committed himself and some $26 billion in research funds to Star Wars — a Strategic Defence Initiative which he was convinced could provide absolute defence against intercontinental ballistic missiles and thus lead to the eventual elimination of all nuclear weapons. The Mulroney government, and especially external affairs minister Joe Clark, were 'less than enthusiastic' about this 'militarization of space'. Nevertheless, while refusing governmental support, Canadian firms were permitted to accept Star Wars contracts (very few of which were let outside the United States) and Mulroney declared that S.D.I. 'merits the approval of an ally while negotiations between the superpowers are underway'. By the time of the abortive 1986 Reykjavik summit, however, it was clear that S.D.I. was itself the major stumbling block in the path of substantial nuclear arms reduction. In addition, a growing number of Canadians were beginning to sense that various past efforts to appease Washington had jeopardized both their non-nuclear status and their Arctic sovereignty, while in no way abating the problems of pollution and protectionism.

A project director at the Institute for Policy Studies in Washington had described the Canadian-American defence entanglement thus:

Canada is integrated into virtually every aspect of U.S. military policy: some seventy treaties relating to defence; over 2,500 bilateral military policy 'agreements'; membership in N.A.T.O. and the bilateral North American Aerospace Defence Command (NORAD); membership on two permanent bilateral planning bodies; bilateral land defence plans with the U.S.; integration of early warning, testing, training and communications; and a virtual joint naval policy in the Pacific. Trying to decipher the treaties, agreements, arrangements, notes and plans is like peeling an onion. Each layer exposes new agreements and raises new questions.

Few Canadians command extensive knowledge of this defence maze; even ministers stumble over details in the House. Yet the general pattern and some obvious implications have entered political discourse. Those related to NORAD loom largest.

When the NORAD agreement was renewed in 1981 Trudeau's government permitted the word 'air' to be replaced by 'aerospace', and a sentence to be removed which had restricted Canadian participation in any ballistic missile defence system; the commander of the U.S. strategic air force would also, now, become commander of NORAD. The 1986 renewal of the agreement seemed to go further still toward integrating NORAD with American strategic nuclear planning and A.B.M. thinking: a new shared-cost North Warning System would be built for the purpose of tracking air-launched cruise missiles — missiles invisible to older radar lines as they would be also to Star Wars space installations. Questioned in Ottawa about the refurbished NORAD's possible connexion with S.D.I. planning, 'arms control ambassador' Paul Nitze replied: 'That remains to be seen. This is a research programme that hasn't yet resulted in the development of specific systems.' To critics, Canadian 'complicity' appeared to be even deeper than had been the case during the American intervention in Vietnam. The Trudeau government, under one of the myriad defence agreements, had permitted the testing of cruise missiles (part of whose guidance systems is made in Canada) in the north — where the terrain and climate resemble those of Siberia. The permission was suspended by Ottawa after two of the missiles flew out of control and crashed. When Joe Clark announced that tests would resume in 1986-7 nuclear disarmers were creating waves in all three political parties.

The linkage between the new NORAD and American strategic planning seemed irrefutable. To counter the threat of Russian air-launched cruise missiles a counter- or even pre-emptive cruise capability was required, together with a ground-based tracking and intercepting competency. Without these the anti-ballistic missile dream of S.D.I. would, indeed, be futile. A great deal of the new technology would necessitate Canadian basing. It would also require 'permission' for cruise-launching B-52s to cross Canadian airspace at will. When the 131st converted B-52 rolled on to the tarmac at the end of 1986 and Washington announced that it would no longer be bound by the (unratified) SALT II treaty, it seemed likely that 'the nuclear question' would bulk even larger in Mulroney's second election than it had in Diefenbaker's fourth. The N.D.P. had renewed its commitment to withdraw from NORAD; a Liberal convention in 1986 called for cancellation of cruise testing and enforcement of Canada's nuclear-free status. More Canadians were likely to become aware that, unlike New Zealand, Ottawa does not require the U.S. to certify that its ships are not carrying nuclear weapons before calling at Canadian ports, and that nuclear-capable weapons are regularly tested in British Columbia's coastal waters.

Related to the nuclear proliferation question, one on which Canada's voting at the United Nations seemed increasingly sanctimonious, was that of 'who owns the Arctic?' The United States has never conceded Canadian sovereignty over the Arctic archipelago (see map, p. 416), let alone the Northwest Passage and other waters separating the various northern islands. In 1969 after the American oil tanker *Manhattan*, without seeking permission, had navigated the Passage to demonstrate its feasibility as an export route from the Beaufort Sea and Alaska Slope oil-gas fields, Ottawa passed the Arctic Waters Pollution Prevention Act. In the summer of 1986, an icebreaker, *Polar Sea*, navigated the Passage from Greenland to Alaska on an unspecified research mission for the U.S. Navy. Prior notice had been given as well as agreement to comply with Canadian environmental law, but 'without prejudice' to the question of sovereignty. 'The Americans,' said Jean Chrétien, 'are using their friendship with Mulroney to take away a piece of Canada.'

Whether or not Chrétien was exaggerating, the government of which he had been a member had left Canada with little but a few small icebreakers and some long-distance surveillance planes for the job of sovereignty assertion. When three U.S. submarines surfaced at the North Pole in May 1986 many Canadians realized for the first time that beneath the ice 'their' Arctic waters were throbbing with submarines and military-scientific activity — both American and Russian. Ottawa was still at work on a defence white paper which would probably include plans for a large modern icebreaker and more effective submarine detection.* The questions of sovereignty, trade and nuclear proliferation coincided at the end of 1986 when the U.S. interior department announced that it was about to sell oil-drilling permits in an area of the Beaufort Sea lying within boundaries claimed by Canada, explaining that 'we issue permits for areas we believe are in American territory.' The issue of where Canada should spend its defence dollars, of whether it should withdraw from western Europe and band together with the other Nordic countries to maintain a nuclear-free zone throughout the Arctic had become urgent. While any comparison with 1914 Belgium might be somewhat fanciful, it had become clear that Canada, not Europe, would probably find itself the 'battleground' in any major exchange of missiles between the two superpowers.

The question of how Prime Minister Mulroney would carry out the residue of his impressive yet nebulous mandate remained. There was no doubt that his opponents had tasted a good deal of blood.

---

*When it appeared in 1987 the white paper called for the acquisition of ten nuclear submarines. Critics questioned the astronomical cost of this proposal and suggested that it had more to do with cooperation with American 'forward' defence than with protection of Canadian sovereignty in the Arctic.

23

With Malice Toward None

'I can write up anything now at a hundred yards,' wrote Stephen Leacock in his later years. The Sage of Mariposa (Orillia, Ontario, immortalized for Canadians in 1912 by Leacock's *Sunshine Sketches of a Little Town*) never took himself too seriously; and thus set an example for the writers of survey histories. In his best writing, which certainly includes *Arcadian Adventures of the Idle Rich* (1914), Leacock used a gentle irony which perfectly mirrored Canadian perceptions of themselves and of their country. While he could wax sarcastic about American foibles or the British aristocracy, he could also skewer Canadian puffery. Since he was an old-fashioned conservative in his opinions about society, politics and economics, about all of which he scribbled prolifically, he seemed the quintessential Canadian. But this means also that many of his countrymen have viewed things differently. Some attention has been given in the preceding pages to competing perceptions as expressed in the political arena. Governments and the political process, however, reflect at least as much as they create attitudes which result ultimately (with a little bit of luck) in policies — which then influence attitudes. The present chapter attempts to review the literary, academic and artistic evolution, as well as some of the social-cultural patterns, of Canada.

An eighteenth-century English historian, Lord Bolingbroke, remarked that 'history is philosophy teaching by examples.' Insofar as Bolingbroke implied a political purpose in the writing of history, his observation applies forcibly in Canada. Most Canadian historical writing in the nineteenth century was non-professional, a branch of literature ; most of it, also, had political purpose. In French Canada the first general landmark was the four-volume *istoire du Canada* (1845-52) by Francois-

382

Xavier Garneau. Garneau's history was a vigorous refutation of Lord Durham's deeply prejudiced jibe that French Canadians were a people without a history or any culture worth preserving. As we have seen, Garneau provided intellectual foundations for Quebec nationalism both in its liberal anti-clerical stage and its later ultramontanist phase. Of equal importance was Garneau's emphasis on continuity. In this respect he resembled anglophone historical writers ; although only Quebec would adopt the motto 'Je me souviens', one might say that it is simultaneously translatable across the country. What was to be remembered was not just the wars and the politics of the past; families and communities bulked large in amateur historical writing, both anglophone and francophone. The sheer extent of Canada, and even of the provinces, meant that local and genealogical history would predominate. The whole was often too difficult to capture. Much of the nineteenth-century historical writing thus anticipated an explosion of local, regional and ethnic history in the 1960s and 1970s. Reflecting and enhancing Canadian experience, the historians tended to justify the view of another eighteenth-century English Tory, Edmund Burke, who believed that patriotism begins with love of one's native valley.

At the same time, particulary in anglophone Canada, more general histories were written. Also stressing continuity, these pictured the country as an extension of Europe and as exemplifying, particularly, British political modes. The constitutional historian Alpheus Todd observed in 1867 that this was entirely natural 'in a country at a time when its institutions have to be molded, and it is necessary to collect precedents and principles from the storehouse of the past . . .' The evolution in Canada of British parliamentary government was also the theme around which J. C. Dent built two influential works, *The Last Forty Years: Canada since the Union of 1841* (1881) and *The Story of the* [1837] *Rebellion* (1885). Dent's political purpose was to celebrate compromise and moderation : both the Tory Compact and Mackenzie-Papineau republican democrats came under sharp fire while garlands were heaped upon those who developed responsible government and kept Canada British.

Anglophone Canadians, well into the twentieth century, derived their conception of the history of New France to a large extent from the elegant prose of the New Englander Francis Parkman. Parkman wrote his seven volumes from *The Conspiracy of Pontiac* (1851) to *A Half Century of Conflict* (1892) with romantic verve and the firm belief that the Anglo-French imperial struggle, while heroic and tragic, ended appropriately : French clerical autocracy was supplanted by Anglo-Saxon constitutional government. The towering figures of Pontiac, Frontenac, Montcalm and Wolfe remained in the Canadian imagination much as Parkman painted them. It was not until after World War II that Canadian historians dismantled Parkman's structure, showing, as did W. J. Eccles, that proconsuls such as La Salle and Frontenac were as much self-serving as heroic. In the later version, *The Courtier Governor* replaced *The Fighting Governor*. Even so, what many British and Europeans 'know' about the early colonial days of North America stems from Parkman laced with the equally romantic forest-life novels of James Fenimore Cooper.

In 1898 William Kingsford completed the tenth volume of his *History of Canada*. Almost too rich in detail, Kingsford's history stressed, as had Dent's, the evolutionary and, particularly, the flexible nature of Canada's political-constitutional relationships with her imperial capital. From Kingsford many writers of textbook histories drew their basic material, and not least those who saw no paradox in the relationship between a maturing Canadian nation and an all-powerful empire. As late as the 1920s authorized textbooks in Ontario bore on the frontispiece a Union Jack with the motto, 'One Flag, One Fleet, One Throne'.

The Great War for that flag and throne, however, shed light sharply on the imperial paradox. Frank Underhill, who was to become a political journalist and historian, had studied at Oxford and was wounded in France while serving as an officer in a British regiment. Later, writing some of the official history of the Canadian Corps, he declared : 'The four-years' career of her fighting troops in France forms the real testimony of Canada's entrance into nationhood, the visible demonstration that there has grown up on her soil a people not English nor

Scottish nor American but Canadian — a Canadian nation.' The nationalism stimulated by World War I was reflected in the historical writing of the inter-war years; yet the interpretative lines diverged markedly.

Now more critical of the imperial tie, yet still devoted to the idea of a nation within the British constitutional tradition, many historians concentrated upon Canada's evolution from colony to nation and strongly approved the trajectory from empire to commonwealth. Political-constitutional processes dominated the studies of scholars such as Chester Martin, R. G. Trotter, G. M. Wrong, Chester New, D. C. Harvey, J. S. Ewart, W. P. M. Kennedy, J. W. Dafoe, O. D. Skelton and R. M. Dawson. These representatives of what J. M. S. Careless has called the Political Nationhood School* were in fact documenting the achievement of Sir John A. Macdonald's dream of Canada as a progressively independent 'auxiliary kingdom' more or less within a British family alliance. Ironically, the political leader who most advanced Macdonald's conception was the Liberal Mackenzie King. Although King was, in fact, emotionally committed to the 'British connexion', he was frequently charged (not least by conservative historians such as D. G. Creighton and Roger Graham, biographers of Macdonald and Arthur Meighen respectively) with 'continentalism'. As we have seen, fear of absorption by the United States is a recurring Canadian nightmare. Most historians have striven to exorcise that particular poltergeist — without straying too far from the facts. Yet one of the branches of inter-war nationalist history sprouted some very American blossoms.

A number of scholars found sustenance for Canadianism in the writings of American 'progressive' historians such as F. J. Turner, Charles Beard and V. L. Parrington. The politically influential Americans provided an attractive schema for those Canadian historians embittered by the mud of Flanders or the stormy perils of the Dover Patrol ; who saw Canadian democracy frustrated by slavish acceptance of British aristocratic

---

*'Frontierism, Metropolitanism and Canadian History', *Canadian Historical Review*, xxxv (1), March 1954.

imperialism. The American progressives proclaimed that their democracy sprang almost exclusively from the experience of the North American frontier — 'the greatest formative influence in American history', as Turner put it. In particular, claimed the Turnerians, the frontier had made America non-Europe and progressive. Since it was the environment that had determined these things in the United States, why should not the North American environment be, similarly, the principal force in the evolution of a non-European Canadian democracy? In the 1920s and 1930s several historians developed a Canadian version of Turner's frontier thesis. W. N. Sage, A. R. M. Lower, F. Landon, A. S. Morton, A. L. Burt and F. H. Underhill found in their research a basis for defining a substantial 'American' element in the Canadian experience : a frontier environment which had rendered Canada increasingly less British or French and thus more suitably to be compared with the United States. This school of thought proclaimed that strains of individualism, agrarian 'direct' democracy, social egalitarianism and even isolationist sentiment found their roots in the early colonial frontiers and, later, in the progressivism of the prairie West. Like American frontierists, the Canadians tended to endorse the Jeffersonian arcadian myth which attributed moral superiority to rural communities and frowned upon the exploitative, corrupt role of eastern business. Thus the nineteenth-century Clear Grits and the twentieth-century western progressives were said to have sprung from the same environmental forces which in the United States had produced Jacksonian democracy and the later populist-progressive movement. As A. R. M. Lower put it, North American democracy was 'forest-born'.

In the late 1930s doubts about the frontier thesis deepened steadily; during the 1940s and 1950s frontierism was all but buried. Fresh research, together with the experience of the war and immediate post-war years, revived the perception that a frontier is not *sui generis*; it is an outreach from an older base. In the case of Canada, that very influential base was to be found in Britain and Europe. In the writing of scholars such as J. M. S. Careless and D. G. Creighton, a virtually unanswerable case was made that the principal political ideas and forces in

Canada, both of the right and of the left, originated across the Atlantic and were organized in Canada by urban- rather than rural-frontier groups. In *The Commercial Empire of the St Lawrence* (1938) Creighton extended, in political-business history, ideas propounded by the economist H. A. Innis: Canada was built by entrepreneurs using a British financial base to develop and export a series of staples to a metropolitan centre. Such entrepreneurs, with their political associates, were assisted rather than impeded by the environment of the northern half of the continent; the waterways south of the pre-Cambrian shield were a natural extension of an Atlantic trading-communications system. Creighton's Laurentian interpretation was widely accepted, but also modified by others. In *Brown of the Globe* (1959) Careless documented his argument that the Grit-Reform party of Upper Canada, while speaking for the farmers, was organized by Toronto business and professional people, urban leaders whose political notions were those of Gladstonian liberalism rather than Jacksonian democracy. Such men cherished the constitutional monarchy and saw the prairie-Pacific West as their natural patrimony. In other books and articles Careless propounded the idea that Canada has always been organized by metropolitan centres in reciprocal relationships with their own hinterlands and with larger external metropolitan centres such as London and New York. Most scholars writing after 1945 accept this, with various modifications. The work of W. L. Morton, for example, stresses the exploitation of hinterlands by metropolitan centres, as does the later writing of Lower and of scholars researching the history of the Atlantic provinces. Careless, A. F. Artibise and their 'school' of urban-metropolitan history maintain that metropolitan-hinterland relationships have been, by and large, mutually beneficial.

Historical geographers have underpinned much of the post-1945 line of intepretation. In a striking essay, R. Cole Harris has portrayed Canadian patterns of settlement and growth: 'The political map of North America sustains the illusion that Canada is a continental giant spanning 70° of longitude and some 40° of latitude; whereas on any long, clear-night flight, this Canada dissolves into an oceanic darkness spotted by occasional islands of light. These lights mark the lived-in Canada, the Canadian ecumene, an island archipelago spread over 7,200 east-west kilometres.'* Canada as an archipelago of towns, cities and regions is much closer to the reality than Canada as the northern thrust of an unbroken, westward-moving North American frontier. Corresponding to the American 'Middle West', for example, is 1,000 miles of pre-Cambrian rock north of the Great Lakes, which required that migration to the Canadian prairies should at first proceed through the United States and, later, across the Shield by rail. Again, migration out of the 'Atlantic islands' (i.e. provinces) tended to move south to the 'Boston States', being deprived of a contiguous 'west' by the northward jutting of the Appalachian highlands. One clear effect of the archipelago pattern ·Harris put thus : 'South of the border, immigrants were being absorbed into a larger America; north of it, island societies that now exported people bypassed the mixing effects of the migrations they had launched.' East-west waterways and a Laurentian interpretation remained influential, but by the 1960s and 1970s more and more historians devoted themselves to the study of regions, cities and ethnicity.

As with earlier historical writing, that of the present is not devoid of political purpose or, perhaps, interacts with political perceptions. Post-1945 immigration from Europe and the 'Third World' undoubtedly stimulated the trend just mentioned. Ironically, however, concentration upon such potentially divisive themes as ethnicity, multiculturalism and metropolitan-hinterland relationships (what the historian Ramsay Cook has called 'limited identities') usually led to emphasizing differences between Canada and the United States and thus to a newly defined sense of Canadian identity. Even a lively group of 'new social historians' centring around the journal *Labour/*

---

*'Regionalism and the Canadian Archipelago', in L. D. McCann, ed., *Heartland and Hinterland : A Geography of Canada* (Toronto, 1982), p. 459.

Le Travailleur stressed both regional and national components within Canadian class relationships.*

The pattern of historical writing in Quebec in the twentieth century showed some similarity to that in anglophone Canada. The eight-volume *Cours d'histoire du Canada* (1919-34) of Sir Thomas Chapais celebrated the safeguarding of francophone cultural identity through the political cooperation of men such as Cartier and Macdonald, Baldwin and Lafontaine and, like Kingsford, lauded the accommodating spirit of an evolving imperial relationship. Much more sceptical, and corresponding somewhat to the anglophone 'nationhood school', was the Abbé Lionel Groulx, who recorded passionately in *Notre maître le passé* (1944) the struggle of French Canada to survive as a nation; a nation guided always by the church, respectful of its heroes such as Adam Dollard and wary of a sleepless anglophone assimilative purpose. Francophone historians after World War II, perhaps responding to the second conscription crisis and certainly in support of the secularizing Quiet Revolution, attempted to reformulate Quebec's past. Michel Brunet, Guy Frégault, Maurice Séguin and others, to some extent drawing upon the economic-political analyses of Innis and Creighton, argued that a bourgeois-commercial class had evolved in New France but that it had been 'decapitated' by 'the Conquest'.† It was the departure of francophone entrepreneurs after 1759 and their replacement by the anglophone merchants who came to dominate Quebec (and then Canadian) economic life that sentenced the *Québecois* to a sluggish, church-dominated existence on the farm. Little doubt was left that the *Québecois* should now take control of their industrializing economy and

---

*Some of these trends are examined in K. McNaught, 'E. P. Thompson v. Harold Logan: Writing about Labour and the Left in the 1970s, *Canadian Historical Review*, lxii(2), June 1981.

†M. Brunet, *La Présence Anglaise et les Canadiens* (Montreal, 1946); G. Frégault, *La Civilisation de la Nouvelle France, 1713-44* (Montreal, 1944); M. Séguin, *La Nation 'Canadienne' et l'agriculture, 1760-1850* (Montreal, 1970).

reduce sharply the clerical role in educational and social institutions. The *Péquistes* took *La Conquête* as the starting point for a litany of grievances; but there was also dissent from this too-simple history. In 1966 Fernand Ouellet published *Histoire économique et sociale de Québec, 1760-1851*. Rejecting the 'decapitation' theory, Ouellet presented a more sophisticated analysis of social-economic causation. And in these same years anglophones outside Quebec were well served by a series of books and articles by a western-born historian, Ramsay Cook, who made himself sympathetically learned in the history and political present of Quebec.*

It is risky, yet interesting, to sketch some connecting lines between the trends of historical interpretation and contemporaneous endeavours by writers and artists to appropriate or express Canada. Such depiction has been facilitated by a post-World War II mushrooming of criticism and cultural analysis.† A useful starting point is the work of Canada's most widely known literary critic, Northrop Frye. From a Maritime Methodist background, Frye went to Toronto's Victoria College and then on to Oxford — the most typical pattern for Canadian scholars down to the end of the 1930s, and one which tended very strongly to engender a sense of continuity as opposed to one of North American uniqueness. Indeed, Frye's intellectual

---

*See, e.g., *Canada and the French Canadian Question* (Toronto, 1966); *Canada, Quebec and the Uses of Nationalism* (Toronto, 1986).

†e.g., C. F. Klinck, ed., *Literary History of Canada* (Toronto, 1976); R. Fulford, *An Introduction to the Arts in Canada* (Toronto, 1977); M. Ross, *The Impossible Sum of Our Traditions* (Toronto, 1986); N. Frye, *The Educated Imagination* (Toronto, 1963), *The Bush Garden* (Toronto, 1971); M. Atwood, *Survival* (Toronto, 1972); G. McGregor, *The Wacousta Syndrome* (Toronto, 1985); T. J. McGee, *The Music of Canada* (Toronto, 1985); A. Gowans, *Building Canada* (Toronto, 1966); D. Reid, *A Concise History of Canadian Painting* (Toronto, 1973); D. Burnett and M. Schiff, *Contemporary Canadian Art* (Toronto, 1983); G. Anthony, ed., *Stage Voices* (Toronto, 1978); J. C. Godin and L. Mailhot, *Le Théâtre québecois* (Montreal, 1980); P. Veronneau and P. Handling, eds., *Self-Portrait: Essays on the Canadian and Quebec Cinemas* (1980).

odyssey and professional career symbolize the several phases of Canada's colony-to-nation experience: the feeling that home-grown culture is mediocre at best, embarrassing at worst; achievement of international recognition; enjoyment of a society become cosmopolitan, so different from that in which one grew up.

Frye's fame as a literary theorist sprang from his *Fearful Symmetry* (1947), in which he demonstrated William Blake's systematic use of a symbolism derived from Milton and, ulti-mately, the Bible. In *Anatomy of Criticism* (1957) Frye de-lineated a theory of criticism based upon the assumption that all great literature is interconnected by a kind of recycling of essentially biblical archetypes and symbolism — a mosaic which he scrutinized in *The Great Code* (1982). From his premise it follows that a writer should be thoroughly at home in the archetypal structure of the West's literature; otherwise that writer would likely be at home only in the bush. And when Frye examined Canadian literature, that is about the situation he uncovered. With a few exceptions, Canadian writers pretty much down to the 1940s seemed to Frye to exhibit a 'garrison mentality'. Without the leisure to read and to appropriate the verbal-symbolic entity evolved by Shakespeare, Spenser and Mil-ton, they wrote only about what they themselves saw and felt: as it were, from the islands of Cole Harris's archipelago. When they lifted their eyes above the palisade, the town walls or the surrounding bush, it was usually to see a kind of gothic romance or, looking inward, to dredge out unmistakable trivia. Frye's sombre surveys have been replicated by one of his most distinguished protegés, Margaret Atwood. In *Survival* Atwood discerned the basic theme of Canadian literature to be victim-ization: Canadians usually see themselves as victims, she argued — victims of climate, wilderness and American power. The world of Canadian poets and novelists, she suggested, is 'a world of frozen corpses, dead gophers, dead children, and the ever-present feeling of menace, not from an enemy set over against you but from everything surrounding you'.

Such morose reconnaissance, one may imagine, reflects an environmentalism of the sort which attracted some historians in the 1920s and 1930s. As we have seen, however, attempts to apply imported American frontier interpretations foundered on the facts : Canadian frontiers were different. Literary and artistic analysts saw this from the outset; yet they could not overlook the environment. As one of them put it, in Canada the frontier is all around us. No 'myth of the garden' informs Canadian literature as it does much of American. As Gail McGregor has observed, 'Canadian writers seemingly do not even like to look upon the face of the wilderness . . . Nature seems more hostile to the Canadian because it *is* more hostile.' Margaret Atwood found a difference between Canadian and American animal stories : the American, as with Jack London, tend to depict human valour and victory; the Canadian, as with Ernest Thompson Seton (*The Biography of a Grizzly*, 1899) or Charles G. D. Roberts (*The Kindred of the Wild*, 1902) frequently attribute human feelings to animals and encourage identification with them as victims; as Roberts put it, 'death stalks joy for ever among the kindred of the wild.' Not surprisingly, more recent animal-story writers have found the habitats less formidable; but identification with the victims remains strong as in *Never Cry Wolf* (1963) and other tales by Farley Mowat.

To support this kind of analysis, in which there is considerable plausibility, various novels and memoirs have been cited, usually beginning with Major John Richardson's *Wacousta; or, The Prophecy* (1832). Richardson, who had fought alongside Tecumseh in the war of 1812, presents the wilderness as always to be feared : the enemy to be withstood and, if possible, tamed. In some respects his 'view from the fort' (which also described life *in* the garrison with some sarcasm) was echoed in other works of the nineteenth and early twentieth centuries. Yet, Susanna Moodie's *Roughing It in the Bush* (1852) and her sister Catherine Parr Traill's *The Backwoods of Canada* (1836) show differences which should warn against using either victimization or garrison mentality as infallible guideposts. While Moodie feared and rejected the surrounding bush, her sister described it, often in botanical detail, and wrote warmly of potential and improvement. Both these pioneer women anticipated what Canadian writers and artists would experience as their colonial world, pushed by technologies of transportation and communication, opened successive avenues of contact not just to the rest of the country but also to the world's metropolises and to other 'hinterlands'.

Writing in the late 1960s Frye declared that Canadian sensibility has been 'less perplexed by the question "Who am I?" than by some such riddle as "Where is here?" ' It is perhaps revealing that Canada's most original economic thinker, Harold Innis, should devote his later years to the question of communications, and especially to the manipulative-power implications of communications technology. Like many Canadian poets and novelists, Innis was deeply suspicious of centralized power. His work in *Empire and Communications* (1950), *The Bias of Communications* (1951) and *Concepts of Time* (1952) stimulated a disciple, Marshal McLuhan, to examine the significance of the electronic age in terms instantly recognizable to to Canadians — in *The Gutenberg Galaxy* (1962) and *Understanding Media* (1964). Satellite television and other instantaneous communications, McLuhan suggested in the 1960s, had made the world a 'global village' and, within that village, 'the medium is the message.' Although McLuhan's sparkling aphorisms and his light-hearted dismissal of sequential reasoning irritated many academics, his perception of the interconnectedness of time and space sprang clearly from the Canadian cultural experience. Canadian insistence upon community (or collective) values and upon the continuity of their lineage is distinctive; this is probably related, also, to a tendency in arts and letters to portray 'things' as essential to an understanding of events or people. The new electric media, facilitating ways of comprehension different from the print process, underlined the shrinkage of time and space and the significance of the medium itself.

The work of Innis and McLuhan suggests a certain fragility in the garrison—victim analogy. Canadian writers and artists have been impressed by the grandeur and terror of their environment; they have stressed the *collectivité* and the need, also, to delimit power concentrated in *any* metropolis or capital; they have also refused to indulge in sharp declarations of independence from such power. But, just as the colony-to-nation school in historical writing emphasized political evolution as opposed to American-style revolutionary independence, so literary-artistic expressions of the Canadian experience have been enlivened by a sense of participation in, rather than separation from, their Anglo-European origins. The excitement and dread of novelty have been tempered by an ever-present sense of continuity. At one level colonialism was something to be gently rolled back; at another it was a conduit for cultural as well as economic and military sustenance. The post-imperial, electronic age offers a replacement for colonialism — with both the costs and benefits somewhat enhanced. Canada's cultural expressions have reflected the altered global environment while also interacting with political life to come to terms with that environment — just as fear of an encompassing frontier was balanced by technological power to contain and exploit it.

It is in this sense that Catherine Parr Traill's somewhat Aristotelian approach of identifying and categorizing her surroundings suggests, like the work of Innis and McLuhan, that Atwood verges on hyperbole in suggesting that the role of victim in Canadian literature becomes almost a need to fail. Evidence is not hard to find that the cultural expression of Canada has always been as much outward-looking as garrison-bound; that it has reflected successively the triumphs of empire, the consciousness of nationhood and the curiously expansive opportunities of the global-village. If one sets aside the sometimes hothouse Frye–Atwood criteria, it seems evident that Canadian arts and letters came to terms with a not-so-new world; they have dealt, as have the political leaders, quite consciously, often humorously, with irreconcilable opposites. The tensions of Canadian life — ethnic, regional, economic — have led insistently to the portrayal of individual responses to the spiral of collectivities. Malcolm Ross, noting an element of tolerance in Canadian political culture, remarked that 'whereas the Fourth of July celebrated something that has already happened, July First celebrates something still happening . . . A tolerance bred in the give-and-take of the two cultures, breached ugly garrison walls and unvictimized the victim.'

From the beginning, outward-looking tendencies of the strong local, regional and provincial identities of the Canadian archipelago differentiated Canadian from American literature. The absence of a revolutionary break has perpetuated an Anglo-European context for Canadian arts and letters which is not 'American' in the usual sense of that term. Thomas Chandler Haliburton, for example, a far more 'successful' writer than Major Richardson, showed no sense of garrison confinement. Born in Nova Scotia in 1796, the Tory Anglican Haliburton suffered no identity problem: a lawyer, entrepreneur, supreme court judge, historian and humorist, his *The Clockmaker: or, Sayings and Doings of Samuel Slick of Slickville* (1836-40) won him international recognition. Using Sam Slick, a Yankee clock pedlar, to chide Nova Scotians for paucity of initiative, he also painted a warm picture of his provincial society, foreshadowing the fond satire of Leacock. A master of local idiom he also interwove Nova Scotian, American and British matter with startling facility. Forced by ill-health into early retirement, Haliburton moved to England, where, in 1859, he was elected to the House of Commons as a Tory. He was, that is, prototypical of an easy acceptance of the continuities of Canadian experience; an acceptance which, with frequent perceptions of irony, sustained the country's cultural life through the evolution from British colony to American satellite. Writing in 1976, Frye seemed to minimize the survival chances of this legacy: 'In ten years time I imagine . . . there will be very little difference in tone between Canadian and American literature.' At the end of those ten years there is little evidence to support his imagining.

Throughout the nineteenth century and down to World War I Canadian writers, especially the most popular ones, expressed an exuberant, often romantic, confidence in their society and its future — in a blend of local and aboriginal folklore, imperial 'sense of power' and incipient nationalism. The stream of novels and short fiction by authors such as William Kirby, Gilbert Parker, Agnes Laut, Ralph Connor (C. W. Gordon), Stephen Leacock and Sara J. Duncan yields scant support for 'victim' interpretation. While none (except Leacock) met the test of 'classic', all sold well abroad. Two others might well be considered children's classics: L. M. Montgomery's *Anne of Green Gables* (1908) and M. M. Saunders' *Beautiful Joe* (1894), each of which adapted English criteria to Canadian localities. Poetry in these pre-1918 years also showed an openness to both British and American influences. Duncan C. Scott, Archibald Lampman, Charles G. D. Roberts and Bliss Carman used the Canadian landscape and its imagery as a means of exploring universal themes — showing a good deal more comprehension than fear of that environment.

In the arts similar adaptation of Anglo-European forms to the land- and city-scapes of Canada reflected also continuity rather than simple emulation. A number of artists, especially francophones, studied in Europe, while most anglophone painters in the nineteenth century were either immigrants or first-generation Canadians. From the earliest *ex voto* paintings in Quebec churches, through the watercolour records of British army officers, to the adventurer-painters such as Paul Kane, Cornelius Krieghoff and Lucius O'Brien, artists conveyed in European terms the old-new land. Perhaps eclecticism is the appropriate word. Certainly an uninhibited range of styles was evident in Canadian architecture: Gothic and Romanesque cohabited with classic revival and Tudor in public buildings and farmhouses alike, while French châteaux reappeared in several large hotels which, like the Château Frontenac in Quebec City, the Château Lake Louise at Banff or the Château Laurier in Ottawa, remain to dominate their vicinities.

In 1915 the physician-poet John McCrae's poem 'In Flanders Fields' was published in *Punch*; in 1918 McCrae lay dead at Boulogne. The Canadian blood that had nourished French poppies fed also a briefly self-conscious nationalism in the arts and letters of the inter-war years. Interacting with an economic prosperity (largely vitalized by northern resource development) and the political evolution of 'nationhood', new journals such as the *Canadian Forum* (1920–), the *Dalhousie Review* (1921–) and the *University of Toronto Quarterly* (1931–), as well as existing ones such as *Queen's Quarterly* (1893–), gave wider scope to serious writing; one of them announced that 'we avow a nationalism that is not prejudice and a provincialism that is not narrowness.' Despite some excruciating chauvinism — the *Canadian Bookman* endorsed the view that 'much of our literature is superior to anything produced by any other country in any century of our era' — Canadian writers in the 1920s and 1930s benefited from two-way traffic through an open door. Mazo de la Roche repeated the earlier feats of Montgomery, Saunders, Leacock and Connor by demonstrating that popular fiction, drawing heavily upon Canadian milieux, could command a wide international following. De la Roche's *Jalna* novels, beginning in 1927, have sold more than nine million copies and provided the bases of successful stage, movie and television productions. The more elevated critics dismissed all this as trivial and much disliked her celebration of the 'imperial connexion', yet *Jalna*'s author expressed better than many a Canadian self-confidence, even righteousness, that eluded more sophisticated writers until 1945.

Poetry also profited from external influences, especially British and American, as F. R. Scott, Leo Kennedy, A. M. Klein and A. J. M. Smith (the Montreal Group) wrote modernist verse with sharply satirical barbs directed at literary nationalism. Yet they and other poets emulated the Group of Seven painters in seeking spiritual strength from the North. While the Shield, the lakes and the mountains were always treated with awe, they were also idealized; threat was modified by strength and by interaction with human beings. F. R. Scott's 'Laurentian Shield' spoke clearly of this:

Hidden in wonder and snow, or sudden with summer,
This land stares at the sun in huge silence
Endlessly repeating something we cannot hear.
Inarticulate, arctic,
Not written on by history, empty as paper,
It leans away from the world with songs in its lakes
Older than love, and lost in the miles.

This waiting is wanting.
It will choose its language
When it has chosen its technic,
A tongue to shape the vowels of its productivity.

A language of flesh and of roses.

Now there are pre-words,
Cabin syllables,
Nouns of settlement
Slowly forming, with steel syntax,
The long sentence of its exploitation.

The first cry was the hunter, hungry for fur,
And the digger for gold, nomad, no-man, a particle;
Then the bold commands of monopoly, big with machines,
Carving its kingdoms out of the public wealth;
And now the drone of the plane, scouting the ice,
Fills all the emptiness with neighbourhood
And links our future over the vanished pole.

But a deeper note is sounding, heard in the mines,
The scattered camps and the mills, a language of life,
And what will be written in the culture of occupation
Will come, presently, tomorrow,
From millions whose hands can turn this rock into children.

The narrative poetry of E. J. Pratt and Earle Birney combined heroism with the impact of technology, individual struggle with the emergent social issues of the 'dirty thirties'. Tensions between private concern, social injustice and public policy absorbed novelists such as Morley Callaghan, Anne Marriot and Irene Baird as well as poets such as Dorothy Livesay and those of the Montreal Group, as Canada moved through the Depression and towards war. Few writers or artists felt uninvolved with the deepening problems of regional and class disparities; symptomatic of the mutuality of political and cultural life was the important part played by the lawyer-poet F. R. Scott and historian-commentator F. H. Underhill in the founding both of the League for Social Reconstruction and the Co-operative Commonwealth Federation. It is also striking that most writers and artists who put their weight behind the swelling critique of unregulated capitalism veered towards the democratic socialism of the *Canadian Forum* and the C.C.F. — unlike their American cousins who moved in near unison into one or another of the Marxist sects in the United States.

For these differing tendencies there are several plausible explanations. Perhaps the most important have to do with the continuity of Canada's Anglo-European connexions. Because socialism was brought to Canada primarily by British immigrants and by Canadians who had studied at British universities, it was difficult to label it 'alien'— although some Conservatives attempted to do just that. The American tradition that the republic was non-Europe, a rejection of both monarchy and radicalism, made it difficult to weave democratic socialism into the normal fabric of American political life: since socialism was 'European' it was, by definition, unAmerican. Reinforcing this essentially cultural difference was the long-standing Canadian endorsement of positive government and its correlative notion that community values may offset individual rights. Equally influential was the constitutional context of parliamentary government. That a 'minor party' could wield effective influence upon cabinets made socialist electioneering much less difficult than in the American system where executives are not directly responsible to legislatures. Minority governments, for example, became a feature of Canadian political culture and of its present multiparty basis, which offers a wider range of democratic choice than is the case in the republic. In the 1930s the authors of biting social criticism often found hope in a believable democratic socialist politics as opposed to a cataclysmic Marxist recipe for change.

Consciousness of the crucial role played by Canada in World War II and of the country's 'middle power' status following the war was expressed by writers and artists with very little of the chauvinism that had disfigured some cultural activities in the 1920s. To match a UN-centered concern for peace-keeping and assistance to the emerging states of the post-imperial world, novelists, poets and artists (and, increasingly, dramatists) tended to use Canadian milieux unselfconsciously to explore universal themes. Novels by Hugh McLennan, Gabriel Roy, Roger Lemelin, W. O. Mitchell, Malcolm Lowry, Sinclair Ross, Ethel Wilson, Ernest Buckler and Mordecai Richler represented all the Canadian regions; they probed the psychological relationships amongst individuals, communities and 'races'. There was at the same time an explosion of poetic production. New journals such as *Tamarack Review, Fiddlehead* and *Contemporary Verse* expanded publishing opportunities for poets and also helped somewhat to decentralize publishing — although Toronto retained its dominance in the anglophone publishing field, as did Montreal in the francophone. While not eschewing social criticism, the post-1945 verse of people such as Irving Layton, P. K. Page, Louis Dudek, Raymond Souster, James Reaney, Robert Finch and Miriam Waddington was intensely experimental and open to the optimism of the period.

As suggested earlier, Canadians have opted for an active governmental role in cultural affairs as readily as in social-economic matters. Public funds channelled through the C.B.C. have nourished musicians, short-story writers, dramatists and actors; the Canada Council and provincial arts councils have subsidized (at 'arm's length' from governments) individuals and institutions in the various cultural fields; the National Film Board has achieved a fine international reputation in animated and documentary films as well as promoting fictional film; the Canada Film Development Corporation has funded many commercial films. Several aspects of this state activity in the arts and letters deserve emphasis. Perhaps most striking is the more 'European' approach adopted by Canada as opposed to the American predilection for private patronage and cultural endowments. In Canada the thrust of 'cultural nationalism' is viewed not as affording exclusionist advantages; rather, it appears essential to establish equal opportunities for Canadians in a market inundated by American television, magazines, films and their outlets, newsstands and even publishing houses. Again, the country's pervasive federalism is very evident in the subsidization of cultural life: many of the best francophone films, such as those of Claude Jutra, who directed the brilliant *Mon oncle Antoine* in 1971, were the work of N.F.B. filmmakers; in 1957 francophone and anglophone sections were administratively separated as the N.F.B. moved from Ottawa to Montreal, enabling francophone participants to live in Quebec. In much the same manner, the C.B.C. francophone networks (Radio-

Canada) are administratively separate from the anglophone; francophone sections of both the C.B.C. and the N.F.B. gave full expression to Québecois nationalism in the 1960s and 1970s — engendering some sharp anglophone comments but no serious effort to infringe their autonomy.

In film, the original proclivity to the documentary and didactic reflected a realist tradition. This tradition is rooted in a cautious approach (sometimes overemphasized, as we have seen) to an environment which is not easily apprehended or possessed; it also incorporates the vigilant attitude of Canadians towards the absorptive capacity of their giant republican neighbour. Yet, as the post-1945 cultural subsidy policies bore fruit in the 1960s and 1970s there was evidence of that sense of confidence which has always been contrapuntal to the undertones of fearfulness and national fragility. The vigilance, the subdued confidence and an irrepressible satirical tradition all glitter in Margaret Atwood's poem 'Backdrop addresses cowboy':

Starspangled cowboy
sauntering out of the almost
silly West, on your face
a porcelain grin,
tugging a papier-mâché cactus
on wheels behind you with a string.

you are innocent as a bathtub
full of bullets.

Your righteous eyes, your laconic
trigger-fingers
people the streets with villains:
as you move, the air in front of you
blossoms with targets

and you leave behind you a heroic
trail of desolation:
beer bottles
slaughtered by the side
of the road, bird-
skulls bleaching in the sunset.

I ought to be watching
from behind a cliff or a cardboard storefront
when the shooting starts, hands clasped
in admiration,
but I am elsewhere.

Then what about me

what about the I
confronting you on that border
you are always trying to cross?

I am the horizon
you ride towards, the thing you can never lasso

I am also what surrounds you:
my brain
scattered with your
tincans, bones, empty shells,
The litter of your invasions.

I am the space you desecrate
as you pass through.

The years which saw a prolonged American invasion of
Vietnam, the credibility problems of Watergate and then
President Reagan's cripplingly heavy expenditures in defence
of the American empire saw also the Quiet Revolution and the
séparatiste crises in Canada. Yet, this latest period, perhaps
surprisingly, exhibited more of a sense of continuity and
'legitimacy' than of insecurity. Indeed, questions of security
and even of identity seemed to absorb Americans rather more
than they did Canadians. In the fields of music, theatre and
the graphic arts, as well as in those of leisure, good food and
folk festivals, the impact of post-1945 immigration was very
noticeable. European as well as West Indian and Asian infusions
underlined earlier acceptance of cultural linkages beyond the
the irresistible American ones. Journals such as George Wood-
cock's *Canadian Literature* and *Canadian Fiction Magazine*
applied a high standard of practical criticism and began re-

assessment of earlier Canadian authors — some of whom, such as Sara Jeannette Duncan and Mazo de la Roche in her earlier work, had been unjustly underrated. The fiction of Margaret Laurence, Alice Munro, Timothy Findley, Adele Wiseman, Thomas Raddall, Rudy Wiebe, Hugh Hood, Joy Kogawa, Mavis Gallant, Antoinine Maillet, Hubert Aquin, Marie-Claire Blais, Roch Carrier drew upon a wide range of regional milieux and ethnic backgrounds; the period was in a sense capped in 1986 when Margaret Atwood's *The Handmaid's Tale* and Robertson Davies' *What's Bred in the Bone* were short-listed for the Booker Prize.

Contemporary poetry and art are markedly experimental while continuing the traditions of irony and satire. The work of poets such as Atwood, Dennis Lee, bp Nichol, Michael Ondatje, J. R. Columbo, Leonard Cohen, Robert Kroetsch, Jay Macpherson, Eli Mandel, Margaret Avison and D. G. Jones has built upon the work of the 1950s and 1960s; Canadians are now amongst the world's heaviest 'consumers' of poetry. In art some distinctive characteristics have been noticed. While refusing to cut themselves off from their European roots, according to the Quebec art-historian François-Marc Gagnon, Canadian artists, 'freed from a heavy weight of traditions, display a certain inventiveness, imposed by isolation, by adaptation to difficult physical conditions . . . the French influence, completely lacking in the United States, is too overwhelming in Canadian art not to maintain an essential distinction between the art forms of the two countries.' More arresting is Gagnon's judgement that the French influence in art 'is true not only for Quebec and French Canadian artists, but for all Canadian artists. Moreover, federal institutions like the Canada Council, the Art Bank and the National Gallery have succeeded in creating among contemporary Canadian artists a sense of community that goes beyond the language barrier and seeks a specific Canadian answer to the problems of art in our day.' The work and interaction of painters such as Paul-Emile Borduas, Jean-Paul Riopelle, Fernand Leduc, Jack Bush, Harold Town, Aba Bayevsky and the photographer Yousuf Karsh offer evidence in support of Gagnon's view.

A similar interpretation may well apply to contemporary architecture, drama, film and music. Architects such as Arthur Erikson, E. H. Zeidler and John Andrews have adapted international styles to produce a discernibly Canadian feeling as, for example, in subterranean urban complexes, specific relationships to topogaphy and a growing attention to elegance. Since 1945 dramatists have written almost explosively and have been widely staged in a proliferation of legitimate theatres and on the C.B.C. The work of anglophones such as James Reaney, Lister Sinclair, George Ryga, W. O. Mitchell, Rick Salutin, Erika Ritter, David Fennario (a successfully bilingual writer), Allen Stratton and John Gray develops Canadian themes from hockey and World War I to aboriginal tragedy, urban workers and nineteenth-century bigotry. The tradition of amused, satirical self-depreciation also found full expression in the very popular genre of musical reviews, from Gratien Gélinas's *Frindolinades* to Mavor Moore's *Spring Thaw*, McGill University's *My Fur Lady*, Clémence Desrocher's *La Grosse Tête*, Mark Shekter's *Toronto, Toronto* and a host of counterparts across the country. Francophone plays and films have been remarkably successful when presented in anglophone centres either in French or in translation. In the work of Gratien Gélinas, Michael Tremblay or Denys Arcand (in the sharply cynical film *The Decline of the American Empire*), as in other francophone arts and letters, the Canadian proclivity to satire and irony is intensified by a fascination with death — sometimes thought by analysts to symbolize the sinuosities of *la survivance*.

In music, while experimentation was long in coming, and performers in particular had to look abroad for recognition, the inter-war years saw a steady growth of symphony orchestras, string groups, music schools and festivals. The earlier work of conductors such as Sir Ernest Macmillan and Jean-Marie Beaudet, and some accomplished singers, composers and instrumentalists was largely in one or another Anglo-European mode. After 1945 came a burst of self-confidence in good part due to arts subsidization and supportive facilities ranging from recording studios, auditoriums and some thirty faculties of music to professional associations and journals. In no field was the multi-ethnic fact felt more profoundly, while, at the same time, experimentation and the use of indigenous folk music and subject-matter blended with adaptation of international trends. Ranging from classical to popular forms, notable singers such as Lois Marshal, Maureen Forrester, Jon Vickers, Teresa Stratas, Monique Léyrac, Anne Murray, Gordon Lightfoot and Joni Mitchell gained international reputations, as did instrumentalists such as Anton Kuerti, Glenn Gould, Zara Nelsova and Liona Boyd, and composers Gabriel Charpentier, Oskar Morawetz, Murray Adaskin, Harry Freedman, Godfrey Ridout and Harry Somers.

Much of what has been ruthlessly compressed above seems to support a recent comment made by Malcolm Ross, himself one of the most assiduous expediters in the 'recovery' of Canadian literature and the expansion of 'Canadian studies':

A. M. Klein was the first to 'naturalize' for all of us the rich idiom of the Talmud, Torah and the Chassidic mysteries. Into the mainstream of our literature came other Jewish writers like Irving Layton, Leonard Cohen, Adele Wiseman and Mordecai Richler; first-and second-generation writers of Polish, Hungarian, Icelandic, Mennonite and Japanese origin like Louis Dudek, John Marlyn, Laura Salverson, Rudy Wiebe and Roy Kiyooka. This phenomenon meant not only the enrichment of the artist's palette; it also meant an incredible extension of the sense we have of our position in time . . . We are not really a young people, even if we are a rather young nation; we are as old as the British, the Poles, the Hungarians, the children of Israel. As John Moss put it in *Patterns of Isolation*, 'Unlike immigrants to the United States . . . the newcomers to Canada are neither absolved nor relieved of their participation in the world they left behind.'

Ross stresses not only the regional and continuing European-Asian cultural continuities but also the cumulative effect of heavy public funding of cultural activity. Such subsidization, initiated federally and expanded provincially, is a counterpart to Ottawa's equalization payments to the less wealthy provinces, an advanced social security system and the expansive array of crown corporations. The interlocking structure — political-economic-social-cultural — is clearly protective; it is also the positive expression of a deep-rooted sense of identity which feels little need to articulate itself as a 'doctrine' or 'ideology'. Americans, especially investors, publishers and the media, find this somewhat alien and, heedless of the huge differentials in demographic-economic strength, talk of unfair competition, even neo-mercantilism. Ross's rejoinder that the whole public enterprise has been developed 'with malice toward none' seems not unreasonable.

An ambivalent conclusion to this scattergun review stems from a remark of the British author Anthony Burgess: 'John Kenneth Galbraith and Marshal McLuhan are the two greatest modern Canadians the United States has produced.' Galbraith and McLuhan here stand for two sides of a popular legend: there is greater professional opportunity in the United States and, if a Canadian wishes recognition he/she must first gain fame south of the border. Like most legends this originated in truth; its relationship to fact has steadily diminished. More and more Canadians appreciate that they may have their cake and eat it too. They can exploit the expanded home-base of cultural activity with confidence that recognition there will often bring recognition abroad, and especially in the United States; they may also move, almost invisibly, into the belly of the republican whale and do anything except become president. A growing number, having done just this, opt for a return to where 'small is beautiful'. Dave Broadfoot and Mordecai Richler illustrate the trend. Richler, a Montrealer, went abroad early and from 1954 to 1972 lived in England, where he wrote *The Apprenticeship of Duddy Kravitz* (1959) and also some articles and *The Incomparable Atuk*, commenting on Canadian nationalism with sizzling sarcasm. Returning to Montreal he could continue his fiction and also broach the American market for scriptwriting, winning a Screen Writers' Guild of America award in 1974. Broadfoot, a brilliant comedian who has performed widely in the United States, settled for a primary base in Canada, where he finds sufficient satisfaction, especially as a key person in the C.B.C.'s mordant *Royal Canadian Air Farce*.

Yet few Canadians realize how many of their compatriot 'snowbirds' have become American household names. Unlike the recent invasion by Canadian investor-developers the migratory pattern is largely unknown also to Americans. A very selective listing includes: Mary Pickford, Joseph Medill (founder of the *Chicago Tribune*), Guy Lombardo, Hume and Jessica Cronyn, Walter Pidgeon, Lorne Green, Jack Warner, Louis B. Meyer, Robert MacNeil, Peter Kent, Rich Little, Saul Bellow, Arthur Hailey, Ross Macdonald and a surprising array of academics including more than a handful of university presidents. Today, what was previously a near-haemorrage has been considerably staunched — except, perhaps, in the category of science-technology where the funding ancillary to the American defence budget is a substantial inducement.

Whatever the ebb and flow of nationalist fevers in Canada, or in Quebec, it seems clear that in their cultural, as in their political affairs, Canadians settle for the *via media*. While eschewing extremes they have nevertheless accumulated their own distinctiveness. They do not always, however, escape the ironies which, as a rule, they are quick to perceive. Writing in 1927, F. B. Houser declared that:

Our British and European connexion in fact, so far as creative expression in Canada is concerned, has been a millstone about our neck ... For Canada to find a complete racial expression of herself through art, a complete break with European traditions was necessary ... The message that the Group of Seven art movement gives to this age is that here in the North has arisen a young nation with faith in its own creative genius.

In 1984 Roald Nasgaard produced a book, supported by an exhibition at the Art Gallery of Ontario, in which he demonstrated the very strong, direct influence exercised upon the Canadian group by Scandinavian painting. Nasgaard quotes the remark made by J. E. H. MacDonald after MacDonald and Lawren Harris had visited a 1913 exhibition of Scandinavian art in Buffalo: 'Except in minor points, the pictures might all have been Canadian and we felt "This is what we want to do with Canada."' It was, in fact, what they *did* do, and thus what made them not just Canadian but also part of the European symbolist movement.

Canada, then, is still a frontier; but it is a frontier that has decided to accept its roots, not declare that they have been severed.

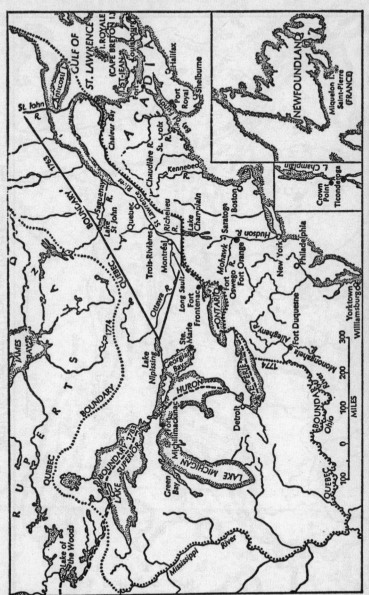

French Canada and the Old Province of Quebec, 1608–1783

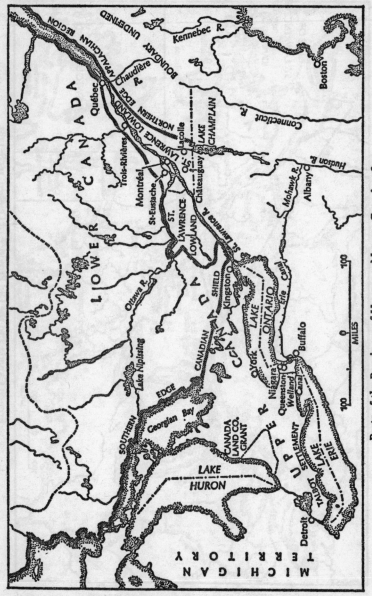

Parts of the Provinces of Upper and Lower Canada, 1830

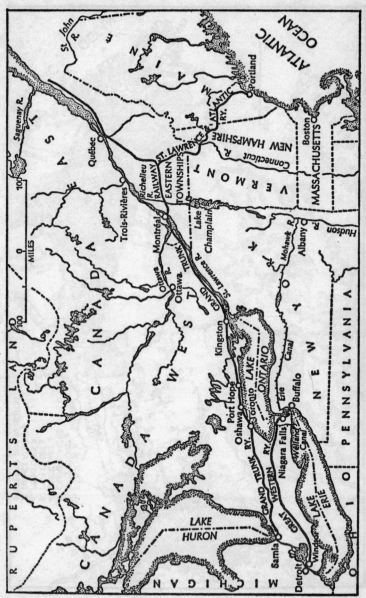

The Province of Canada, 1860, showing major railways

Canada, 1898

1. BATOCHE ■
2. BATTLEFORD ■
3. CRAIGELLACHIE
4. DUCK LAKE ■
5. FISH CREEK ■
6. FROG LAKE ■
7. PRINCE ALBERT ■
■ SITES OF 1885 REBELLION

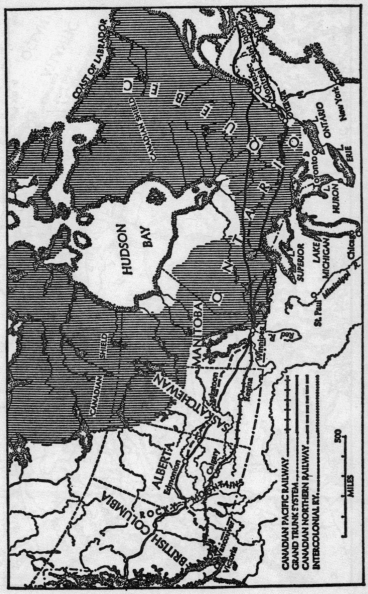

Canada, 1916, showing major transcontinental railways. The Canadian Shield shown shaded.

Canada, 1969

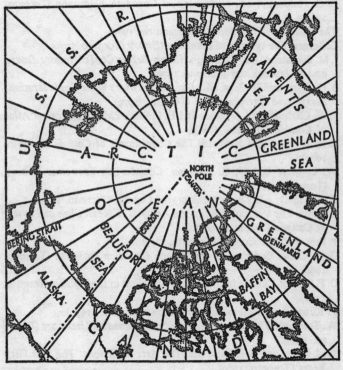

Canada's northern frontiers in the air age, showing Canada's claim –
based on the sector principle and first made publicly in 1925 – to the
extension of her boundaries to the North Pole.

Maps drawn by Mr C. C. J. Bond of the Map Division of the Public
Archives of Canada.

Suggestions for further reading

I. THEMES, INTERPRETATIONS AND REFERENCE WORKS

F. G. Halpenny, ed., *Dictionary of Canadian Biography* (Toronto, 1966—).

The Canadian Encyclopedia (Edmonton, 1985).

C. Berger, *The Writing of Canadian History* (Toronto, 1976).

J. M. Bumstead, ed., *Canadian History Before Confederation: Essays and Interpretations* (Toronto, 1979).

B. Hodgins and R. Page, eds., *Canadian History Since Confederation: Essays and Interpretations* (Toronto, 1979).

J. W. Chalmers, W. J. Eccles and H. Fullard, *Philips' Historical Atlas of Canada* (Toronto, 1966).

R. M. Dawson and N. Ward, *The Government of Canada* (Toronto, 1970).

W. L. Marr and D. G. Paterson, *Canada: An Economic History* (Toronto, 1980).

C. F. Klinck, ed., *Literary History of Canada* (Toronto, 1976).

J. Porter, *The Vertical Mosaic: An Analysis of Social Class and Power in Canada* (Toronto, 1965).

P. Fox, *Politics: Canada* (Toronto, 1979).

G. R. Cook, *Canada and the French Canadian Question* (Toronto, 1966).

D. F. Smiley, *Canada in Question: Federalism in the Eighties* (Toronto, 1980).

P. Russell, ed., *Nationalism in Canada* (Toronto, 1979).

W. Toye, ed., *The Oxford Companion to Canadian Literature* (Toronto, 1983).

W. J. Keith and B. Z. Shek, eds., *The Arts in Canada: The Last Fifty Years* (Toronto, 1980).

M. Wade, *The French Canadians* (Toronto, 1968).

L. D. McCann, ed., *Heartland and Hinterland: A Geography of Canada* (Toronto, 1982).

Suggestions for further reading

2. EXPLORATION AND SETTLEMENT TO 1763

J. B. Brebner, *The Explorers of North America* (London, 1933).
G. Frégault, *La Civilisation de la Nouvelle France* (Montreal, 1944).
O. Filteau, *La Naissance d'une Nation* (Montreal, 1937).
W. J. Eccles, *Canada under Louis XIV, 1663–1701* (Toronto, 1964).
—, *France in America* (New York, 1972).
C. P. Stacey, *Quebec, 1759* (Toronto, 1959).

3. THE BRITISH COLONIES, 1763–1867

A. L. Burt, *The Old Province of Quebec* (Minneapolis, 1933).
D. G. Creighton, *John A. Macdonald*, vol. I (Toronto, 1952).
—, *Empire of the St Lawrence* (Toronto, 1956).
J. M. S. Careless, *The Union of the Canadas, 1841–1867* (Toronto, 1967).
—, *Brown of the Globe* (Toronto, 1959).
H. Neatby, *The Revolutionary Age, 1760–1791* (Toronto, 1966).
H. T. Manning, *The Revolt of French Canada* (New York, 1962).
F. Ouellet, *Histoire Economique et Sociale du Québec, 1760–1851* Montreal, 1966).
W. S. McNutt, *The Atlantic Provinces, 1712–1857* (Toronto, 1965).
P. B. Waite, *Life and Times of Confederation* (Toronto, 1962).
W. L. Morton, *The Critical Years, 1857–1873* (Toronto, 1965).

4. THE YOUNG DOMINION, 1867–1918

C. Berger, *The Sense of Power* (Toronto, 1969).
D. G. Creighton, *John A. Macdonald*, vol. II (Toronto, 1955).
G. F. G. Stanley, *The Birth of Western Canada* (Toronto, 1960).
O. D. Skelton, *The Life and Letters of Sir Wilfrid Laurier* (Toronto, 1965).
J. T. Saywell, ed., *The Canadian Journal of Lady Aberdeen* (Toronto, 1960).
W. L. Morton, *Manitoba: A History* (Toronto, 1957).
E. Armstrong, *The Crisis of Quebec* (New York, 1937).
R. Graham, *Arthur Meighen* (Toronto, 1963).
R. M. Dawson, *William Lyon Mackenzie King* (Toronto, 1958).
R. Rumilly, *Henri Bourassa* (Montreal, 1940).
C. P. Stacey, *Canada and the Age of Conflict*, vol. I (Toronto, 1977).
R. C. Brown and R. Cook, *A Nation Transformed* (Toronto, 1971).
P. B. Waite, *Arduous Destiny: Canada, 1874–1896* (Toronto, 1971).
R. C. Brown, *Robert Laird Borden* (Toronto, 1975).

Suggestions for further reading

A. R. McCormack, *Reformer, Rebels and Revolutionaries* (Toronto, 1979).

G. Kealey, *Toronto Workers Respond to Industrial Capitalism, 1867–1892* (Toronto, 1980).

R. Allen, *The Social Passion* (Toronto, 1971).

V. Nelles, *The Politics of Development* (Toronto, 1974).

M. Robin, *Radical Politics and Canadian Labour* (Kingston, 1968).

T. E. Flanagan, *Riel and the Rebellion: 1885 Reconsidered* (Toronto, 1983).

5. CANADA SINCE 1918

B. Neatby, *William Lyon Mackenzie King*, 2 vols. (Toronto, 1976).

W. L. Morton, *The Progressive Party in Canada* (Toronto, 1950).

K. McNaught, *A Prophet in Politics* (Toronto, 1959).

A. Laurendeau, *La Crise de la Conscription* (Montreal, 1962).

M. Rioux and Y. Martin, *French Canadian Society* (Toronto, 1964).

D. Thompson, *Louis St Laurent* (Toronto, 1967).

P. Newman, *Renegade in Power* (Toronto, 1962).

C. B. Macpherson, *Democracy in Alberta* (Toronto, 1956).

P. E. Trudeau, *Federalism and the French Canadians* (New York, 1968).

G. Horowitz, *Canadian Labour and Politics* (Toronto, 1967).

J. Eayrs, *In Defence of Canada* (Toronto, 1964–).

C. P. Stacey, *Canada and the Age Conflict*, vol. II (Toronto, 1981).

R. Whitaker, *The Government Party* (Toronto, 1977).

J. Granatstein, *Canada: 1957–1967* (Toronto, 1986).

D. Bercuson, J. Granatstein and W. Young, *Sacred Trust?* (Toronto, 1986).

W. Young, *The Anatomy of a Party: The National CCF* (Toronto, 1969).

J. T. Saywell, *The Rise of the Parti Québecois* (Toronto, 1977).

J. H. Thompson and A. Seager, *Canada: 1922–1939* (Toronto, 1985).

C. McCall-Newman, *Grits: An Intimate Portrait of the Liberal Party* (Toronto, 1982).

D. Morton, *The New Democrats, 1961–1986* (Toronto, 1986).

G. Fraser, *René Lévesque and the Parti Québecois in Power* (Toronto, 1984).

R. Cook, *Canada, Quebec and the Uses of Nationalism* (Toronto, 1986).

R. Bothwell, I. Drummond and J. English, *Canada since 1945* (Toronto, 1981).

Index

419

Index

FOR THE BEST IN PAPERBACKS, LOOK FOR THE

In every corner of the world, on every subject under the sun, Penguin represents quality and variety – the very best in publishing today.

For complete information about books available from Penguin – including Puffins, Penguin Classics and Arkana – and how to order them, write to us at the appropriate address below. Please note that for copyright reasons the selection of books varies from country to country.

In the United Kingdom: Please write to *Dept E.P., Penguin Books Ltd, Harmondsworth, Middlesex, UB7 0DA.*

If you have any difficulty in obtaining a title, please send your order with the correct money, plus ten per cent for postage and packaging, to *PO Box No 11, West Drayton, Middlesex*

In the United States: Please write to *Dept BA, Penguin, 299 Murray Hill Parkway, East Rutherford, New Jersey 07073*

In Canada: Please write to *Penguin Books Canada Ltd, 2801 John Street, Markham, Ontario L3R 1B4*

In Australia: Please write to the *Marketing Department, Penguin Books Australia Ltd, P.O. Box 257, Ringwood, Victoria 3134*

In New Zealand: Please write to the *Marketing Department, Penguin Books (NZ) Ltd, Private Bag, Takapuna, Auckland 9*

In India: Please write to *Penguin Overseas Ltd, 706 Eros Apartments, 56 Nehru Place, New Delhi, 110019*

In the Netherlands: Please write to *Penguin Books Netherlands B.V., Postbus 195, NL–1380AD Weesp*

In West Germany: Please write to *Penguin Books Ltd, Friedrichstrasse 10–12, D–6000 Frankfurt/Main 1*

In Spain: Please write to *Longman Penguin España, Calle San Nicolas 15, E–28013 Madrid*

In Italy: Please write to *Penguin Italia s.r.l., Via Como 4, I-20096 Pioltello (Milano)*

In France: Please write to *Penguin Books Ltd, 39 Rue de Montmorency, F-75003 Paris*

In Japan: Please write to *Longman Penguin Japan Co Ltd, Yamaguchi Building, 2–12–9 Kanda Jimbocho, Chiyoda-Ku, Tokyo 101*

PENGUIN HISTORY ·

The Germans   Gordon A. Craig

An intimate study of a complex and fascinating nation by 'one of the ablest and most distinguished American historians of modern Germany' – Hugh Trevor-Roper

Imperial Spain 1469–1716   J. H. Elliot

A brilliant modern study of the sudden rise of a barren and isolated country to the greatest power on earth, and of its equally sudden decline. 'Outstandingly good' – *Daily Telegraph*

British Society 1914–1945   John Stevenson

A major contribution to the *Penguin Social History of Britain*, which 'will undoubtedly be the standard work for students of modern Britain for many years to come' – *The Times Educational Supplement*

A History of Christianity   Paul Johnson

'Masterly … It is a huge and crowded canvas – a tremendous theme running through twenty centuries of history – a cosmic soap opera involving kings and beggars, philosophers and crackpots, scholars and illiterate *exaltés*, popes and pilgrims and wild anchorites in the wilderness' – Malcolm Muggeridge

The Penguin History of Greece   A. R. Burn

Readable, erudite, enthusiastic and balanced, this one-volume history of Hellas sweeps the reader along from the days of Mycenae and the splendours of Athens to the conquests of Alexander and the final dark decades.

A History of Latin America   George Pendle

'Ought to be compulsory reading in every sixth form … this book is right on target' – *Sunday Times*. 'A beginner's guide to the continent … lively, and full of anecdote' – *Financial Times*

FOR THE BEST IN PAPERBACKS, LOOK FOR THE 🐧

PENGUIN HISTORY

The Penguin History of the United States Hugh Brogan

'An extraordinarily engaging book' – *The Times Literary Supplement*. 'Compelling reading ... Hugh Brogan's book will delight the general reader as much as the student' – *The Times Educational Supplement*. 'He will be welcomed by American readers no less than those in his own country' – J. K. Galbraith

The Making of the English Working Class E. P. Thompson

Probably the most imaginative – and the most famous – post-war work of English social history.

The Waning of the Middle Ages Johan Huizinga

A magnificent study of life, thought and art in 14th- and 15th-century France and the Netherlands, long established as a classic.

The City in History Lewis Mumford

Often prophetic in tone and containing a wealth of photographs, *The City in History* is among the most deeply learned and warmly human studies of man as a social creature.

The Habsburg Monarchy 1809–1918 A. J. P. Taylor

Dissolved in 1918, the Habsburg Empire 'had a unique character, out of time and out of place'. Scholarly and vividly accessible, this 'very good book indeed' (*Spectator*) elucidates the problems always inherent in the attempt to give peace, stability and a common loyalty to a heterogeneous population.

Inside Nazi Germany Conformity, Opposition and Racism in Everyday Life
Detlev J. K. Peukert

An authoritative study – and a challenging and original analysis – of the realities of daily existence under the Third Reich. 'A fascinating study ... captures the whole range of popular attitudes and the complexity of their relationship with the Nazi state' – Richard Geary

PENGUIN HISTORY

The Victorian Underworld   Kellow Chesney

A superbly evocative survey of the vast substratum of vice that lay below the respectable surface of Victorian England – the showmen, religious fakes, pickpockets and prostitutes – and of the penal methods of that 'most enlightened age'. 'Charged with nightmare detail' – *Sunday Times*

A History of Modern France   Alfred Cobban

Professor Cobban's renowned three-volume history, skilfully steering the reader through France's political and social problems from 1715 to the Third Republic, remains essential reading for anyone wishing to understand the development of a great European nation.

Stalin   Isaac Deutscher

'The Greatest Genius in History' and the 'Life-Giving Force of Socialism'? Or a tyrant more ruthless than Ivan the Terrible whose policies facilitated the rise of Nazism? An outstanding biographical study of a revolutionary despot by a great historian.

Montaillou   Cathars and Catholics in a French Village 1294–1324
Emmanuel Le Roy Ladurie

'A classic adventure in eavesdropping across time' – Michael Ratcliffe in *The Times*

The Second World War   A. J. P. Taylor

A brilliant and detailed illustrated history, enlivened by all Professor Taylor's customary iconaclasm and wit.

Industry and Empire   E. J. Hobsbawm

Volume 3 of the *Penguin Economic History of Britain* covers the period of the Industrial Revolution: 'the most fundamental transformation in the history of the world recorded in written documents.' 'A book that attracts and deserves attention … by far the most gifted historian now writing' – John Vaizey in the *Listener*

PENGUIN ARCHAEOLOGY

The Dead Sea Scrolls in English   G. Vermes

This established and authoritative English translation of the non-biblical Qumran scrolls – offering a revolutionary insight into Palestinian Jewish life and ideology at a crucial period in the development of Jewish and Christian religious thought – now includes the Temple Scroll, the most voluminous scroll of them all.

Hadrian's Wall   David J. Breeze and Brian Dobson

A penetrating history of the best-known, best-preserved and most spectacular monument to the Roman Empire in Britain. 'A masterpiece of the controlled use of archaeological and epigraphical evidence in a fluent narrative that will satisfy any level of interest' – *The Times Educational Supplement*

Before Civilization   The Radiocarbon Revolution and Prehistoric Europe Colin Renfrew

'I have little doubt that this is one of the most important archaeological books for a very long time' – Barry Cunliffe in the *New Scientist*. 'Pure stimulation from beginning to end ... a book which provokes thought, aids understanding, and above all is immensely enjoyable' – *Scotsman*

The Ancient Civilizations of Peru   J. Alden Mason

The archaeological, historical, artistic, geographical and ethnographical discoveries that have resurrected the rich variety of Inca and pre-Inca culture and civilization – wiped out by the Spanish Conquest – are surveyed in this now classic work.

PENGUIN RELIGION

Islam in the World Malise Ruthven

This informed and informative book places the contemporary Islamic revival in context, providing a fascinating introduction – the first of its kind – to Islamic origins, beliefs, history, geography, politics and society.

The Orthodox Church Timothy Ware

In response to increasing interest among western Christians, and believing that a thorough understanding of Orthodoxy is necessary if the Roman Catholic and Protestant Churches are to be reunited, Timothy Ware explains Orthodox views on a vast range of matters from Free Will to the Papacy.

Judaism Isidore Epstein

The comprehensive account of Judaism as a religion and as a distinctive way of life, presented against a background of 4,000 years of Jewish history.

Mysticism F. C. Happold

What is mysticism? This simple and illuminating book combines a study of mysticism – as experience, as spiritual knowledge and as a way of life – with an illustrative anthology of mystical writings, ranging from Plato and Plotinus to Dante.

The Penguin History of the Church: 4 Gerald R. Cragg
The Church and the Age of Reason

Gerald Cragg's elegant and stimulating assessment of the era from the Peace of Westphalia to the French Revolution – a formative period in the Church's history – ranges from the Church life of France under Louis XIV to the high noon of rationalism and beyond.

The Gnostic Gospels Elaine Pagels

Written over 2,000 years ago and discovered in 1945 buried in the Upper Egyptian desert, the so-called gnostic gospels – revealing unprecedented information about the early Christian Church – are examined in this 'fascinating' (*The Times*) book.

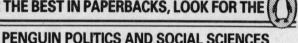

FOR THE BEST IN PAPERBACKS, LOOK FOR THE 🐧

PENGUIN POLITICS AND SOCIAL SCIENCES

Political Ideas David Thomson (ed.)

From Machiavelli to Marx – a stimulating and informative introduction to the last 500 years of European political thinkers and political thought.

On Revolution Hannah Arendt

Arendt's classic analysis of a relatively recent political phenomenon examines the underlying principles common to all revolutions, and the evolution of revolutionary theory and practice. 'Never dull, enormously erudite, always imaginative' – *Sunday Times*

The Apartheid Handbook Roger Omond

The facts behind the headlines: the essential hard information about how apartheid actually works from day to day.

The Social Construction of Reality Peter Berger and Thomas Luckmann

Concerned with the sociology of 'everything that passes for knowledge in society' and particularly with that which passes for common sense, this is 'a serious, open-minded book, upon a serious subject' – *Listener*

The Care of the Self Michel Foucault
The History of Sexuality Vol 3

Foucault examines the transformation of sexual discourse from the Hellenistic to the Roman world in an inquiry which 'bristles with provocative insights into the tangled liaison of sex and self' – *The Times Higher Educational Supplement*

A Fate Worse than Debt Susan George

How did Third World countries accumulate a staggering trillion dollars' worth of debt? Who really shoulders the burden of reimbursement? How should we deal with the debt crisis? Susan George answers these questions with the solid evidence and verve familiar to readers of *How the Other Half Dies*.

PENGUIN POLITICS AND SOCIAL SCIENCES

Comparative Government S. E. Finer

'A considerable *tour de force* ... few teachers of politics in Britain would fail to learn a great deal from it ... Above all, it is the work of a great teacher who breathes into every page his own enthusiasm for the discipline' – Anthony King in *New Society*

Karl Marx: Selected Writings in Sociology and Social Philosophy
T. B. Bottomore and Maximilien Rubel (eds.)

'It makes available, in coherent form and lucid English, some of Marx's most important ideas. As an introduction to Marx's thought, it has very few rivals indeed' – *British Journal of Sociology*

Post-War Britain A Political History Alan Sked and Chris Cook

Major political figures from Attlee to Thatcher, the aims and achievements of governments and the changing fortunes of Britain in the period since 1945 are thoroughly scrutinized in this readable history.

Inside the Third World Paul Harrison

From climate and colonialism to land hunger, exploding cities and illiteracy, this comprehensive book brings home a wealth of facts and analysis on the often tragic realities of life for the poor people and communities of Asia, Africa and Latin America.

Housewife Ann Oakley

'A fresh and challenging account' – *Economist*. 'Informative and rational enough to deserve a serious place in any discussion on the position of women in modern society' – *The Times Educational Supplement*

The Raw and the Cooked Claude Lévi-Strauss

Deliberately, brilliantly and inimitably challenging, Lévi-Strauss's seminal work of structural anthropology cuts wide and deep into the mind of mankind, as he finds in the myths of the South American Indians a comprehensible psychological pattern.

I: The Philosophy and Psychology of Personal Identity Jonathan Glover

From cases of split brains and multiple personalities to the importance of memory and recognition by others, the author of *Causing Death and Saving Lives* tackles the vexed questions of personal identity. 'Fascinating ... the ideas which Glover pours forth in profusion deserve more detailed consideration' – Anthony Storr

Minds, Brains and Science John Searle

Based on Professor Searle's acclaimed series of Reith Lectures, *Minds, Brains and Science* is 'punchy and engaging ... a timely exposé of those woolly-minded computer-lovers who believe that computers can think, and indeed that the human mind is just a biological computer' – *The Times Literary Supplement*

Ethics Inventing Right and Wrong J. L. Mackie

Widely used as a text, Mackie's complete and clear treatise on moral theory deals with the status and content of ethics, sketches a practical moral system and examines the frontiers at which ethics touches psychology, theology, law and politics.

The Penguin History of Western Philosophy D. W. Hamlyn

'Well-crafted and readable ... neither laden with footnotes nor weighed down with technical language ... a general guide to three millennia of philosophizing in the West' – *The Times Literary Supplement*

Science and Philosophy: Past and Present Derek Gjertsen

Philosophy and science, once intimately connected, are today often seen as widely different disciplines. Ranging from Aristotle to Einstein, from quantum theory to renaissance magic, Confucius and parapsychology, this penetrating and original study shows such a view to be both naive and ill-informed.

The Problem of Knowledge A. J. Ayer

How do you *know* that this is a book? How do you *know* that you know? In *The Problem of Knowledge* A. J. Ayer presented the sceptic's arguments as forcefully as possible, investigating the extent to which they can be met. 'Thorough ... penetrating, vigorous ... readable and manageable' – *Spectator*

FOR THE BEST IN PAPERBACKS, LOOK FOR THE 🐧

PENGUIN LITERARY CRITICISM

The English Novel Walter Allen

In this 'refreshingly alert' (*The Times Literary Supplement*) landmark panorama of English fiction, the development of the novel is traced from *Pilgrim's Progress* to Joyce and Lawrence.

Film as Film V. F. Perkins

Acknowledging the unique qualities of cinema as essentially a bastard medium – neither purely a visual nor a dramatic art – this pioneering text remains 'one of the most sophisticated and commendable works of film criticism' – *Tribune*

A Short History of English Literature Ifor Evans

'He relates the arts to society instead of penning them in his study … He is fair to all and gushes over none … a mastery of phrase which makes the writing lively without being exhaustingly exhibitionistic' – Ivor Brown in the *Observer*

The Modern World Ten Great Writers Malcolm Bradbury

From Conrad to Kafka, from Proust to Pirandello, Professor Bradbury provides a fresh introduction to ten influential writers of the modern age and the Modernist movement. Each, in their individual way, followed Ezra Pound's famous dictum – 'Make it new'.

Art and Literature Sigmund Freud

Volume 14 of the *Penguin Freud Library* contains Freud's major essays on Leonardo, Dostoyevsky and Michelangelo, plus shorter pieces on Shakespeare, the nature of creativity and much more.

The Literature of the United States Marcus Cunliffe

'Still the best short history [of American literature] … written with notable critical tact' – Warner Berthoff. 'Cunliffe retains the happy faculty (which he shares with Edmund Wilson) of reading familiar books with fresh eyes and of writing in an engaging style' – Howard Mumford Jones

FOR THE BEST IN PAPERBACKS, LOOK FOR THE 🐧

PENGUIN REFERENCE BOOKS

The New Penguin English Dictionary

Over 1,000 pages long and with over 68,000 definitions, this cheap, compact and totally up-to-date book is ideal for today's needs. It includes many technical and colloquial terms, guides to pronunciation and common abbreviations.

The Penguin Spelling Dictionary

What are the plurals of *octopus* and *rhinoceros*? What is the difference between *stationary* and *stationery*? And how about *annex* and *annexe*, *agape* and *Agape*? This comprehensive new book, the fullest spelling dictionary now available, provides the answers.

Roget's Thesaurus of English Words and Phrases   Betty Kirkpatrick (ed.)

This new edition of Roget's classic work, now brought up to date for the nineties, will increase anyone's command of the English language. Fully cross-referenced, it includes synonyms of every kind (formal or colloquial, idiomatic and figurative) for almost 900 headings. It is a must for writers and utterly fascinating for any English speaker.

The Penguin Dictionary of Quotations

A treasure-trove of over 12,000 new gems and old favourites, from Aesop and Matthew Arnold to Xenophon and Zola.

The Penguin Wordmaster Dictionary
Martin H. Manser and Nigel D. Turton

This dictionary puts the pleasure back into word-seeking. Every time you look at a page you get a bonus – a panel telling you everything about a particular word or expression. It is, therefore, a dictionary to be read as well as used for its concise and up-to-date definitions.